WHO IS

DISCOVERING OUR TRUE IDENTITY IN JESUS CHRIST AND WHY IT MATTERS!

BOOK II

THE ROOT

Donna M. Rogers

Published by:
Angel of Love & Light Ministries
Tampa, Florida, U.S.A.
www.angeloffaith777.com
Printed in the U.S.A.

Cover design by James Nesbit

Edited by Mary Post

Illustrations by Kristen Schipfer-Barrett

TABLE OF CONTENTS

TABLE OF CONTENTS

TABLE OF CONTENTS

INTRODUCTION

Y
ou have purchased Book 2, in this series of four books, which is "one" message to the body of Christ the Lord has placed upon my heart to proclaim to His people for a time such as this.

I have broken down this comprehensive, in-depth teaching into four different books based on the content of what I am conveying. They *must* be read in sequence as indicated below and on the following page because they build upon each other.

And, it is for this very reason; Book #2 will start at Chapter 19, rather than Chapter 1; Book #3 (Volume I) will start at Chapter 37, rather than Chapter 1, and Book #3 (Volume II) will start at Chapter 57, rather than Chapter 1 as indicated below and on the following page.

BOOK #1

Title: *Who is Israel? Discovering Our True Identity in Jesus Christ and Why it Matters!*

Subtitle: *The Foundation*

Scope of Book #1: Foreword; Acknowledgements; Preface; Introduction; Chapters 1 through 18; Epilogue; References; Connect with the Author; and About the Author.

1

Who is Israel? Discovering our True Identity in Jesus Christ and Why it Matters! The Root

BOOK #2

Title: *Who is Israel? Discovering Our True Identity in Jesus Christ and Why it Matters!*

Subtitle: *The Root*

Scope of Book #2: Introduction; Chapters 19 through 36; Epilogue; References; Connect with the Author; and About the Author.

BOOK #3 (Volume I)

Title: *Who is Israel? Discovering Our True Identity in Jesus Christ and Why it Matters!*

Subtitle: *The Branches and the Fruit*

Scope of Book #3 (Volume I): Introduction; Chapters 37 through 56; References; Connect with the Author; and About the Author.

BOOK #3 (Volume II)

Title: *Who is Israel? Discovering Our True Identity in Jesus Christ and Why it Matters!*

Subtitle: *The Branches and the Fruit*

Scope of Book #3 (Volume II): Introduction; Chapters 57 through 70; Epilogue; References; Connect with the Author; and About the Author.

Again, it is of utmost importance that you read all four books of this three-part series in sequence. God's people *must* understand the "big" picture to fully comprehend what the entire Bible is about and what His Spirit is saying to His Church for a time such as this. We are fast approaching the "midnight" hour ushering in the second coming of Jesus Christ.

One of the reasons for breaking down this critical message to the body of Christ into four separate books is because this message would have been too large to have published as one book. The Lord insisted I use Scripture in context based on the *whole* counsel of His Word to back up everything I am proclaiming and teaching. Hence, because I use entire passages of Scripture to substantiate what I am saying, this book is significantly larger as a result.

If you have not read Book 1, subtitled, *The Foundation,* it is imperative you do so *before* you read this book which builds on the foundation of understanding "who" Israel is first and foremost.

Book 1 not only answers the question of "who" Israel is, but it also unveils our true identity in Christ, and what our main mandate is as God's sons and daughters.

Furthermore, since we are heirs according to the covenants of promise because we are from Abraham's seed, then we as believers in Jesus Christ must know what the promises are that God gave to Abraham when He established the *everlasting* covenant with him. Also, we must know what Abraham and his descendants had to do to receive these covenant promises from God, based on their faith in God which was evidenced by their obedience.

Therefore, in this book, I will fully convey what the *Abrahamic* Covenant is and how it is still applicable to New Covenant believers. Many of God's people are *unknowingly* breaking this *everlasting* covenant that our heavenly Father *Yehóvah* established with Abraham.

This is due to our ignorance of the *whole* counsel of God's Word, and a lack of understanding concerning our "Hebraic" roots in Christianity. Notice, that I did not say our "Jewish" roots in Christianity. Abraham was not Jewish; he was Hebrew. I covered this fact in Chapter 5 of Book 1.

Once we know "who" Israel is, and we understand the *Abrahamic* Covenant and its relevance to New Covenant believers, then we must answer the question, "Why does it matter?"

I respond to this question and so much more in Book 3 subtitled, *The Branches and the Fruit.*

It is imperative that I first lay the foundation for the reader in Book 1 and Book 2 *before* I will convey the "meat" of this entire message in Book 3 and Book 4. In Book 3 (Volume I and II), I will expose many of the false teachings in the body of Christ, so we can repent and make a course correction before it is too late for all eternity. God is in the process of ushering in the greatest and final "reformation" the body of Christ has ever experienced throughout the *synergy of the ages.*

The Lord is orchestrating in this, the "midnight" hour, the total "restoration" and "reconciliation" of all things, especially concerning all Israel.

It begins with His people understanding the *everlasting* covenant God established with Abraham and his descendants. Especially, since we are "heirs" of the promises God gave to Abraham when He established this *everlasting* covenant with him.

The covenant vows God gave to Abraham are based on this *everlasting* covenant that Jesus Christ fulfilled (consummated, executed, ratified [confirmed]) with His precious blood when He became the "mediator" of the New Covenant.

So let's begin our journey in Chapter 19, to understand "when," "why," and for "what" reasons, God was willing to establish this *everlasting* covenant with Abraham, the "Father of Many Nations," who is the father of our faith.

This knowledge is necessary, so we will fully comprehend why this is relevant to New Covenant believers.

CHAPTER 19

WHAT IS THE ABRAHAMIC COVENANT?

Befo**B**re God establishes a covenant with anyone; you first need to be called by God. Therefore, I will systematically walk you through the sequence of events with the corresponding Scriptures for you to fully understand what transpired and why we are to honor and not break the *Abrahamic* Covenant.

This covenant God established with Abraham is an *everlasting* covenant God swore by Himself to defend and uphold forever!

In other words, God pledged His throne never to break this *everlasting* covenant with Abraham and his descendants.

THE CALL OF ABRAM

> *"Now the LORD had said to Abram: 'GET OUT of your COUNTRY, From your FAMILY And from your FATHER'S HOUSE, To a LAND that I will SHOW you.'"* (Gen. 12:1, NKJV) (emphasis added).

Therefore, based on Genesis 12:1 above, *before* God would do anything for Abram, he was faced with a choice to answer the call of God on his life. And, to birth the call God put on his life, Abram had to choose whether or not he would be

7

obedient and "do" what God told him to do. In other words, God required Abram to take action!

The Lord commanded and required Abram to walk out by faith, not by sight or based on his own understanding. As such, Abram had to do the following:

1. Leave his country.
2. Leave his family behind.
3. Leave his father's house.
4. Go to a land the Lord would show him.

It is important to take note that God did not tell Abram where He was taking him in advance.

Therefore, Abram had to put his faith and trust in *Yehôvah* not knowing *where* he was going or *why* he was going.

In return for Abram's obedience to "do" what God had commanded him, God promised Abram the following in Genesis 12:2–3 below:

> *"I will make you* [Abram] *a GREAT NATION; I will BLESS you And make YOUR NAME great; And you shall be a BLESSING. I will BLESS those who BLESS you, And I will CURSE him who CURSES you; And in you* [Abram] *all the FAMILIES of the EARTH shall be BLESSED."* (Gen. 12:2–3, NKJV) (emphasis added).

This Scripture in Genesis 12:2–3, is the "essence" of what Christendom calls the *Abrahamic* Covenant. However, this covenant is not in the Bible under this name.

Rather, this covenant that God established with Abram is the "Covenant of Circumcision," which is the "sign" of this covenant that *Yehóvah* entered into with Abram and his descendants.

Wow! What a promise *Yehóvah* made to Abram *if* he would have faith, trust, and obey Him.

Therefore, *if* Abram responded to the call on his life with total allegiance to *Yehóvah,* God would do the following:

1.   Make Abram into a great nation.

2.   Bless Abram.

3.   Make Abram's name great (talk about fame!).

4.   Abram would be a blessing.

5.   Bless those who blessed Abram.

6.   Curse those who cursed Abram.

7.   In Abram, all the families of the earth shall be blessed.

So let's see *if* Abram stepped out in faith and he was willing to go into unfamiliar territory, leaving behind everything that he knew, based on his faith, trust, and obedience to *Yehôvâh* his God.

We are told in Genesis 12:4–10, that Abram was seventy-five years old when he departed from Haran. And, Abram took Sarai his wife, and Lot his nephew, who was his brother's son, as they set off to go to the land of Canaan with the people whom they had acquired in Haran.

Also, do not dismiss the significance that the Lord "appeared" to Abram in Canaan and said, *"To your descendants, I will give this land."*

The land of Canaan was one of the promises God gave to Abraham.

This is substantiated in Genesis 12:4–10, which says the following:

> *"So Abram DEPARTED as the LORD had SPOKEN to HIM, and LOT went with HIM. And ABRAM was SEVENTY-FIVE YEARS OLD when he DEPARTED from Haran. Then ABRAM took SARAI HIS WIFE and LOT HIS BROTHER'S SON, and all their POSSESSIONS that they had GATHERED, and the PEOPLE whom they had ACQUIRED in HARAN, and they DEPARTED to go to the LAND of*

CANAAN. So they CAME to the LAND of CANAAN. Abram PASSED through the LAND to the PLACE of SHECHEM [a place in Palestine], as FAR as the TEREBINTH TREE of MOREH. And the CANAANITES were THEN in the LAND." (Gen. 12:4–6, NKJV) (emphasis added).

"Then the LORD APPEARED to Abram and said, 'To YOUR DESCENDANTS I will GIVE this LAND.' And there he [Abram] BUILT an ALTAR to the LORD, who had APPEARED to him [Abram]. And he MOVED from there to the MOUNTAIN east of BETHEL, and he PITCHED his TENT with BETHEL on the west and AI on the east; there he [Abram] BUILT an ALTAR to the LORD and CALLED on the NAME of the LORD. So Abram JOURNEYED, GOING on still TOWARD the South. Now there was a FAMINE in the LAND, and Abram went DOWN to EGYPT to DWELL there, for the FAMINE was SEVERE in the LAND." (Gen. 12:7–10, NKJV) (emphasis added).

Notice that based on Genesis 12:7–10, this was a time of severe famine in the land, so Abram was forced to go down to Egypt to dwell there for a little while. Abram going to Egypt was a prophetic shadow picture of how Joseph and Mary would later travel to Egypt with Jesus when He was a young

Child, remaining there until the death of King Herod came to pass, based on Matthew 2:13–15. Also, do not dismiss the significance in Genesis 12:7–10, the Lord adds a new promise to encourage Abram in his obedience thus far. The Lord said He would give this land to Abram's descendants, even though Abram had no descendants at this point.

Also worth mentioning, not once, but twice, Abram sets up altars to worship the Lord and to get in His presence so Abram can receive further instructions from Him.

When Abram sought God's presence, this is what we would call in today's vernacular establishing a prayer altar in our hearts and our homes. We do this to bring God's manifest presence and His divine providence in our lives.

Abram took the time to seek God's will before he would do anything. This indicates Abram was very dependent on the Lord and wanted to rely on Him every step of the way.

Therefore, if we want to see our heavenly Father intervene in our lives and bless us, then we need to follow in Abram's footsteps and seek the Lord's face and not His hand, as we enter into His gates with thanksgiving and into His courts with worship and praise—hallowing His holy name.

When we praise the Lord and "hallow" His holy name, this will get God to answer our prayers as we draw His manifest presence. Like Abram, we must step out in faith, not by sight, and "do" *only* what God tells us to do through His Holy Spirit.

Yehôvãh used the unfortunate circumstances of a severe famine in the land to force Abram to go into Egypt so *Yehôvãh* could give Abram great wealth and riches.

Therefore, there are two critical things we need to glean from this example:

1. Abram had to step out in faith *first* before *Yehôvãh* would bless him with the resources he needed to do what *Yehôvãh* wanted him to do.

2. *Yehôvãh* gave Abram great wealth and riches because Abram was more interested in seeking after the *Lord of the harvest*, rather than receiving the blessings that *Yehôvãh* could offer him.

In Chapter 33 of this book, I will convey in detail "how" *Yehôvãh* did indeed bless Abram with great wealth and riches. This is substantiated in the following Scriptures:

> *"The LORD has BLESSED my MASTER greatly, and he* [Abram] *has become great; and He* [*Yehôvãh*] *has given him* [Abram] *FLOCKS and HERDS, SILVER and GOLD, male and female SERVANTS, and CAMELS and DONKEYS."* (Gen. 24:35, NKJV) (emphasis added).

> *"Abram was very RICH in LIVESTOCK, in SILVER, and in GOLD."* (Gen. 13:2, NKJV) (emphasis added).

13

In the next chapter, I will cover in detail exactly *what* God promised to Abram when He established His *everlasting* covenant with Abram and his descendants.

CHAPTER 20

WHAT DID GOD PROMISE TO ABRAM WHEN HE ESTABLISHED THE EVERLASTING COVENANT WITH HIM?

S ince God swore by Himself to keep His end of this *everlasting* covenant He established with Abram and his descendants; then I would hope that disciples of Jesus Christ would want to know everything about the *Abrahamic* Covenant to ensure that we do not break it.

As such, we must take a closer look at exactly *what* God promised to Abram when He established this *everlasting* covenant with him.

Especially, since we are heirs of the *covenant* blessings God promised to Abram and his descendants long ago because of our faith and trust in Jesus Christ—*if* we do not "break" covenant with God by being "disobedient" to His Voice and His Word.

Now we will take a look at what the Lord said to Abram based on Genesis 15:1–11.

As you read this Scripture, do not dismiss the fact that in Genesis 15:6, we learn Abram "believed" what *Yehovah* had told him and God credited Abram's faith in Him as being *righteous.*

Hence, Abram "believed" in the Lord long before *the Word*

15

would come to the earth as the Son of Man in the Person of Jesus Christ.

Genesis 15:1–11, says the following:

> *"After these things the WORD of the LORD came to Abram in a VISION, saying, 'Do not be afraid, Abram. I am your SHIELD, your exceedingly GREAT REWARD.'"* (Gen. 15:1, NKJV) (emphasis added).

> *"But Abram said, 'Lord GOD, what will You give me, seeing I go CHILDLESS, and the HEIR of my HOUSE is ELIEZER of DAMASCUS?' Then Abram said, 'Look, You have given me NO OFFSPRING; indeed one BORN in my HOUSE is my HEIR!'"* (Gen. 15:2–3, NKJV) (emphasis added).

> *"And behold, the WORD of the LORD came to him* [Abram]*, saying, 'This ONE shall not be your HEIR, but one who will come from your OWN BODY shall be your HEIR* [Isaac]*.' Then He* [Yehôvah] *brought him* [Abram] *outside and said, 'Look now toward heaven, and count the stars if you are able to number them.' And He* [Yehôvah] *said to him* [Abram]*, 'So shall your descendants be.'"* (Gen. 15:4–5, NKJV) (emphasis added).

"And he [Abram] *BELIEVED in the LORD, and He* [*Yehôvăh*] *ACCOUNTED it to him* [Abram] *for RIGHTEOUSNESS."* (Gen. 15:6, NKJV) (emphasis added).

"Then He [*Yehôvăh*] *said to him* [Abram], *'I am the* LORD, *who brought you out of Ur of the Chaldeans, to GIVE you this LAND to INHERIT it.' And he said, 'Lord* GOD, *how shall I know that I will INHERIT it?'"* (Gen. 15:7–8, NKJV) (emphasis added).

"So He [*Yehôvăh*] *said to him* [Abram], *'Bring Me a three-year-old heifer, a three-year-old female goat, a three-year-old ram, a turtledove, and a young pigeon.' Then he* [Abram] *brought all these to Him* [*Yehôvăh*] *and cut them in two, down the middle, and placed each piece opposite the other; but he did not cut the birds in two. And when the vultures came down on the carcasses, Abram drove them away."* (Gen. 15:9–11, NKJV) (emphasis added).

Therefore, this *everlasting* covenant, referred to as the *Abrahamic* Covenant, was not based on the behavior and obedience of the Israelites (the Hebrew people).

Rather, this *everlasting* covenant God established with Abram was due to Abram's faith, trust, devotion, and obedience to *Yehôvăh*—period! Also, notice that *the Word* of the Lord came to Abram not once, but twice. Who is *the Word* that

17

became flesh as the Son of Man? Jesus Christ. Next in Genesis 15:12, something peculiar happens to Abram as the Lord caused a deep sleep to "fall upon" Abram and he experienced horror when great darkness "fell upon" him. Genesis 15:12, says the following:

> *"Now when the SUN WAS GOING DOWN, a DEEP SLEEP fell UPON Abram; and behold, HORROR and GREAT DARKNESS fell UPON him."* (Gen. 15:12, NKJV) (emphasis added).

This *deep* sleep that "fell upon" Abram *when* he experienced *horror* and *great* "darkness" means that Abram fell into a trance.

The word "sleep" as used in this passage of Scripture is based on *Strong's Hebrew Lexicon* #H8639 and is the Hebrew word "tardêmah" (pronounced "tar-day-maw'"), which means: Lethargy or (by implication) *trance*; *or* deep sleep.

The following passages of Scripture refer to God causing someone to go into a *deep* sleep: Genesis 2:21; First Samuel 26:12; Job 4:13; Isaiah 29:10; Daniel 10:9, and Acts 20:9.

And, Job 4:13, alludes to "disquieting" thoughts from the "visions of the night," that happens when *deep* sleep "falls upon" men.

Moreover, Isaiah 29:10 says that the Lord causes the "spirit" of *deep* sleep to "fall upon" the prophets, namely the seers, which the prophet Daniel says happened to him in Daniel 8:18.

Why is this relevant? I believe it was at this point the *gospel of the kingdom* was preached to Abram *before the Word* came to the earth as the Son of Man in the Person of Jesus Christ to fulfill (consummate, execute, and ratify [confirm]) the *first* covenant with His precious blood.

Again, the *first* covenant God established with all the children of Israel through His servant Moses was because of this *everlasting* covenant God was now establishing with Abram. We are specifically told this truth: Since God would "justify" the Gentiles by faith, the *gospel of the kingdom* was preached to Abraham who believed. This truth is substantiated in Galatians 3:5–9, which says the following:

> *"Therefore He who SUPPLIES the SPIRIT to you and works MIRACLES among you, does He do it by the WORKS of the LAW, or by the HEARING of FAITH?—just as Abraham 'BELIEVED God, and it* [Abraham's faith] *was ACCOUNTED to him* [Abraham] *for RIGHTEOUSNESS.' Therefore know that only those who are of FAITH are SONS of ABRAHAM. And the Scripture, foreseeing that God would JUSTIFY the GENTILES by FAITH, preached the GOSPEL to Abraham BEFOREHAND, saying, 'In you* [Abraham] *all the NATIONS shall be BLESSED. So then those*

who are of FAITH are BLESSED with BELIEVING Abraham.'" (Gal. 3:5–9, NKJV) (emphasis added).

In other words, the Lord caused Abram to receive a *prophetic* revelation of what would happen *when* Jesus Christ died, went into Sheol (hell) in the heart of the earth for three days and three nights just like Jonah the prophet was three days and three nights in the belly of the great fish.

It would come to pass after Jesus was in the heart of the earth for three days and three nights, He would be resurrected on the *third* day. And, I will prove this is what happened based on God's Word *when* God asked Abram to sacrifice his son Isaac later on in Chapter 25 of this book.

Moreover, as Abram modeled for us all, we are made "righteous" by our faith in Jesus Christ. However, the evidence that we have faith in God will be determined by our trust and obedience in Him alone!

Only then will it come to pass, that Jesus Christ Himself through His Holy Spirit will *sanctify* us completely so that our spirit, soul, and body will be preserved blameless at His coming.

However, this does not happen automatically. We play an integral role in our *sanctification* process as we submit to God's Holy Spirit that lives in us, who will convict us to be "obedient" to God's Voice and His Word. Therefore, contrary to what is taught—salvation is a lifelong process and is why the apostle Paul tells us in Philippians 2:12, we must *work out* our *own* salvation with fear and trembling!

And, this is also why it is impossible to be saved and to please God *without* "faith." This truth is substantiated in Hebrews 11:6, which says the following:

> *"But without FAITH it is IMPOSSIBLE to PLEASE Him, for he who comes to God must BELIEVE that He is* [who He says that He is which includes Him doing *what* He says that He will *do* according to His *eternal* Word] *and that He is a REWARDER of those who DILIGENTLY SEEK Him."* (Heb. 11:6, NKJV) (emphasis added).

Many people are trying to be saved by "doing" good works and please God by keeping the *letter of the law*, as is often the case with our Jewish sisters and brothers from the House of Judah. However, it is by our "faith" in God's only *begotten* Son, Jesus Christ, we "become" saved.

Nevertheless, once we "become" saved, then we will want to please God by keeping His commandments because we believe *the Word* who became flesh as the Son of Man in the Person of Jesus Christ is the *only* absolute truth that exists. He is the *only* One we can trust with our very lives and our eternal salvation! And, indeed this is true because it is only by the Word of God that all creation is sustained, including us, His created.

21

Moreover, as disciples of Jesus Christ, we *should* believe God will "do" what He says He shall "do" according to His *eternal* Word which goes forth from His mouth for it shall not return to Him void. Rather, it shall accomplish what He pleases, and it shall prosper in the thing for which He sent it. Otherwise, what do we have to stand on and *who* can we trust? Especially, based on the fact that we are counting on having "eternal" life based on our faith and trust in Jesus who is *the Word* that became flesh!

Now let's refocus our attention on what transpired when God established this *everlasting* covenant with Abram. We will learn in Genesis 15:12–16, God has given Abram more promises associated with this *everlasting* covenant along with a bit of "bad news" that would surely come to pass, but end well. Genesis 15:12–16, says the following:

> *"Now when the SUN WAS GOING DOWN, a deep SLEEP fell upon Abram; and behold, HORROR and great DARKNESS fell upon him. Then He [Yehovah] said to Abram: 'Know certainly that YOUR DESCENDANTS will be STRANGERS in a LAND that is not theirs, and will serve them, and they will AFFLICT them FOUR HUNDRED YEARS. And also the NATION whom they serve I will JUDGE; afterward, they shall COME OUT with great POSSESSIONS. Now as for you [Abraham], you shall go to YOUR FATHERS in PEACE; you*

shall be BURIED at a GOOD OLD AGE. But in the FOURTH GENERATION they [Abraham's descendants] *shall RETURN HERE, for the INIQUITY of the **AMORITES*** [H567: *'ĕmôrî: publicity,* that is, prominence; thus a *mountaineer,* an *Emorite,* one of the Canaanitish tribes who practiced following and *worshiping* false idols or gods based on 1 Kings 21:26] *is not yet COMPLETE.' "* (Gen. 15:12–16, NKJV) (emphasis added).

In Genesis 15:12–16 above, God shares with Abram that his *spiritual* descendants would be strangers in a foreign land where they would be "afflicted" for four hundred years. However, God reassures Abram that He would judge this nation and his descendants would come out from their enslavement with great possessions.

Also, God tells Abram that he will live to be an old man, but he will not be alive to see his descendants, in the fourth generation, possess the land God promised to give to his descendants.

It is at this point *after* God had revealed to Abram some of the things which would come to pass, that the Lord made a "covenant" with Abram *when* a burning torch passed between the pieces of the sacrificed animals.

It was at this point God promised Abram his descendants would inherit the land of the Canaanites based on Genesis 15:17–21, which says the following:

23

"*And it came to pass, when the SUN WENT DOWN and it was DARK, that behold, there APPEARED a SMOKING OVEN and a BURNING TORCH that PASSED between those PIECES. On the SAME DAY the LORD made a COVENANT* (2) [H1285: *b'rîyth*: in the sense of cutting; a *compact* (made by passing between *pieces* of flesh); confederacy, league] *with Abram, saying: 'To YOUR DESCENDANTS I have GIVEN this LAND, from the river of Egypt to the great river, the River Euphrates— the Kenites, the Kenezzites, the Kadmonites, the Hittites, the Perizzites, the Rephaim, the Amorites, the Canaanites, the Girgashites, and the Jebusites.'*" (Gen. 15:17–21, NKJV) (emphasis added).

Also, notice that in Genesis 15:17–21 above, it specifically says that *when* the sun went down and it was dark, there appeared a smoking oven and a burning torch that passed between those pieces and on that *same* day the LORD made a covenant with Abram.

Concerning the darkness which ensued when God established the covenant with Abram, this is similar to what happened when *Yehóváh* established the New Covenant with Jesus Christ's precious blood. There was darkness over all the land from the sixth hour until the ninth hour based on Matthew 27:45. Also, Luke 23:45, proclaims, *"Then the SUN*

24

was *DARKENED, and the VEIL of the TEMPLE was TORN in TWO."* (NKJV) (emphasis added).

Moreover, worth mentioning at this time is this fact: On the very day that God made this *everlasting* covenant with Abram, the Lord specifically said to Abram, *"To your DESCENDANTS I have GIVEN this LAND..."* (NKJV) (emphasis added).

The Lord did not say to Abram that He will give this land to his descendants.

Rather, the Lord stated that He has given this land to Abram's descendants. Therefore, when the Lord "spoke" forth His *eternal* Word to Abram, it was already done—even though Abram's descendants would not inherit or take possession of the land for at least four hundred years.

In summary, based on Genesis 15:1–21, which details God's *everlasting* covenant with Abram and his descendants, we are told the following:

1. God came to Abram in a vision and said to Abram, *"Do not be afraid, Abram. I am your SHIELD, your exceedingly great REWARD."* (NKJV) (emphasis added).

2. God told Abram that *Eliezer of Damascus* would not be his heir. Rather, Abram's heir would come from his own body.

3. God told Abram to look toward heaven and count the stars if he can number them and then the Lord said to

Abram, *"So shall your DESCENDANTS be."* (NKJV) (emphasis added).

4. Abram "believed" what God had said to him. And, as a result, God accounted Abram's faith in Him for *righteousness.*

5. The Lord then told Abram He is the one who brought Abram out of *Ur of the Chaldeans* to give Abram this land of Canaan as an inheritance.

6. Abram asked the Lord how he would know he would "inherit" the land.

To which the Lord responded *when* He caused a *deep* sleep to "fall upon" Abram. As the sun went down and it was dark, there "appeared" a smoking oven and a burning torch which passed between the sacrifice the Lord had instructed Abram to offer Him. This sacrifice consisted of the following: A three-year-old heifer, a three-year-old female goat, a three-year-old ram, a turtledove, and a young pigeon that Abram had brought to the Lord. Except for the birds, Abram had cut them in two, down the middle, and he placed each piece opposite the other.

7. On this *same* day, the Lord made an *everlasting* covenant with Abram and his descendants. And, the Lord told Abram the following five things:

1. The Lord gave Abram His Word, saying Abram would know with certainty that his descendants would be strangers in a land that was not theirs. They would serve the people of that nation, and they would suffer affliction for four hundred years.

2. However, the Lord told Abram in the fourth generation his descendants would return to the land of Canaan because the "iniquity" of the *Amorites* was not yet complete.

3. Also, the Lord told Abram that He would judge the nation Abram's descendants served and afterward they would come out of Egypt with great possessions.

4. And, the Lord told Abram he would go to his fathers in peace, and he would die at a good old age. In other words, Abram would not be alive when his descendants inherited the promises God gave him, especially concerning the land.

5. The Lord told Abram He has given *this* land— the land of Canaan, to Abram's descendants.

The Lord specifically said to Abram, *"To your DESCENDANTS I have GIVEN this LAND."* (NKJV) (emphasis added).

Based on Genesis 15:18–21, this land's boundaries are from the river of Egypt to the great river—the River Euphrates. At the time God gave the land of Canaan to Abram and his descendants, this land was occupied by the Kenites, the Kenezzites, the Kadmonites, the Hittites, the Perizzites, the Rephaim, the Amorites, the Canaanites, the Girgashites, and the Jebusites.

In the next chapter, we will continue to learn more about this *everlasting* covenant that God made with Abram and his descendants and what the "sign" of this covenant would be.

CHAPTER 21

THE DEAL IS "SEALED" BY THE COVENANT OF CIRCUMCISION

T he willingness of God to establish this *everlasting* covenant with Abram in the first place was because of Abram's faith, trust, and devotion to *Yehôvăh* period. Therefore, it was not based on the "collective" behavior of the Israelites.

Also, God always keeps His end of the covenants (plural) that He establishes with mankind and creation throughout the *synergy of the ages.* Some of the covenants God established with mankind throughout the *synergy of the ages* are contingent upon our "obedience" and us <u>not</u> breaking "covenant" with God once we become saved.

Again, the *first* covenant God established with all twelve tribes of the children of Israel through His servant Moses was the result of this *everlasting* covenant God established with Abraham and his descendants.

As I have already conveyed in the Introduction section of Book 1, a covenant is a "legally" binding written agreement between two parties, which is usually confirmed by blood.

God does not lie, and God is faithful! Therefore, God *always* keeps His end of His covenants (plural) that He establishes with His people and all creation, but do we? All the covenants (plural) God establishes with His people, and all creation requires blood to be shed. Hence, this is one of the reasons *why* circumcision is the "sign" of *this* particular covenant God established with Abram and his descendants. For with every male child who was circumcised in the flesh of their foreskins, blood is shed.

Shortly we will carefully examine what the terms and conditions of this covenant God established with Abram in which the "sign" of this particular covenant is detailed in Genesis 17:1–14.

Also, worth mentioning at this time is this fact: The terms and conditions of this covenant are given to Abram by God twenty-four years after Abram left his country, his family, and his father's house to go to a land the Lord would show him.

When Abram was first called by the Lord, he was seventy-five years old based on Genesis 12:4–6. We are told in Genesis 17:1–8, that Abram is now ninety-nine years old.

Therefore, as you read Genesis 17:1–8, know that *some* of the things God says concerning Abram apply to New Covenant believers because of our faith in Jesus Christ. For all true disciples of Jesus Christ are from the *spiritual* "seed" of Abraham.

Moreover, we are "heirs" of these covenant promises as well *if* we "do" what God requires for us to walk in a covenant relationship with Him after we become saved by grace through faith in Jesus Christ. In addition, take note of the

Hebrew meaning of the words "kings" and "descendants" as used in Genesis 17:1–8, which says the following:

"When Abram was NINETY-NINE YEARS OLD, the LORD APPEARED to Abram and said to him, 'I am Almighty God; WALK before Me and be BLAMELESS. And I will make My **COVENANT** (1) [H1285: *bᵉriyth*: in the sense of cutting; a *compact* (made by passing between *pieces* of flesh); confederacy, league] *between Me and you, and will MULTIPLY you exceedingly.' Then Abram fell on his face, and God talked with him, saying: 'As for Me, behold, My* **COVENANT** (1) *is with you, and you shall be a FATHER of many* **NATIONS** (2) [H1471: *gôy*: a foreign nation; hence a Gentile, heathen people]. *NO LONGER shall your NAME be called ABRAM, but your NAME shall be* **ABRAHAM** (3) [H85: *'Abrâhâm*: to *be populous; father of a multitude*]; *for I have made you a FATHER of many* **NATIONS**. (2) *I will make you exceedingly* **FRUITFUL** (4) [H6509: *pârâh*: to *bear fruit;* bear, bring forth (fruit), (be, cause to be, make) fruitful, grow, increase]; *and I will make* **NATIONS** (2) *of you, and* **KINGS** (5) (6) [H4428: *melek*: a *royal* king; H4427: *mâlak*: to *reign*; inceptively to *ascend the throne*; causatively to *induct* into royalty; hence (by implication) to *take counsel*; consult;*

rule and reign as a king or queen] *shall come from you. And I will* **ESTABLISH** [7] [H6965: *qûm*: to *rise*; confirm, strengthen, ordain, continue; get up; perform, accomplish, stand by and make sure] *My* **COVENANT** [1] *between Me and you and your* **DESCENDANTS** [8] [9] [H2233: *zera*: *seed*; figuratively *fruit, plant, sowing time, posterity;* child; H2232: *zâra*: to *sow*; figuratively to *disseminate, plant, fructify;* bear, conceive seed, set with, sow (-er), yield] *after you in their GENERATIONS, for an* **EVERLASTING** [10] [H5769: *ôlâm*: properly *concealed*, that is, the *vanishing* point; generally time *out of mind* (past or future), that is, (practically) *eternity* from the beginning of the world and is without end] *COVENANT,* [1] *to be GOD to YOU and your* **DESCENDANTS** [8] [9] *after YOU. Also I GIVE to YOU and YOUR* **DESCENDANTS** [8] [9] *after YOU the LAND in which you are a stranger, all the LAND of CANAAN, as an* **EVERLASTING** [10] **POSSESSION** [11] [H272: *'achuzzâh*: something which is *seized*, that is, a possession (especially of land)]*; and I will be their God.'"* (Gen. 17:1–8, NKJV) (emphasis added).

Before we continue to see what else God says about this

everlasting covenant He established with Abraham and his descendants, I want to point out a few things we must glean from Genesis 17:1–8.

First, based on the Hebrew meaning of the word "kings" as used in this passage of Scripture, this is talking about disciples of Jesus Christ who are a *royal* priesthood from the *order of Melchizedek* because our Great High Priest, Jesus Christ, is Melchizedek, *king of Salem.*

Long before *the Word* was sent to the earth as the Son of Man in the Person Jesus Christ, He appeared to Abraham as Melchizedek, *king of Salem.*

I will cover in-depth in Chapter 43 of Book 3, that *the Word* before He became the Son of Man in the flesh as the Person of Jesus Christ is Melchizedek, *king of Salem.*

And, He would "confirm" this *everlasting* covenant with Abram that God established with him in the beginning, and *the Word* would use "bread" and "wine" to do so.

This is substantiated in Genesis 14:18, which says, *"Then Melchizedek king of Salem brought out bread and wine; he was the priest of God Most High."* (NKJV)

In addition, this is a prophetic enactment of what Jesus would later do with His disciples at Passover just before He became "the" perfect Passover Lamb.

Furthermore, the apostle Paul tells us in Hebrews 5:9–10, Jesus Christ having been perfected, He became the author of eternal salvation to all who "obey" Him, called by God as High Priest according to the *order of Melchizedek*.

And, it is for this very reason, why *the Word* would indeed "confirm" all of God's *everlasting* covenants (plural) He has made with mankind and creation throughout the *synergy of the ages*.

Also, based on the Hebrew meaning of the word "establish" Jesus would "confirm" or "strengthen" *this* particular *everlasting* covenant God is establishing with Abraham and his descendants, which is based on Genesis 17:1–8.

In addition, do not dismiss this fact: God has promised Abraham He will "confirm" (strengthen) this *everlasting* covenant God made with Abraham and his descendants who come *after* him in all their generations throughout the *synergy of the ages*.

This is long before *the Word* would come to the earth as the Son of Man in the Person of Jesus Christ to "confirm" the *first* covenant God established with all the children of Israel when the law was given at the base of Mount Sinai through His servant Moses.

Again, this *first* covenant was the result of this *everlasting* covenant God is now establishing with Abraham—the "Father of Many Nations" and his descendants who will come *after* him in all their generations throughout the *synergy of the ages*.

JESUS CHRIST "CONFIRMED" THE FIRST COVENANT, WHICH WAS THE RESULT OF THE ABRAHAMIC COVENANT, ON THE CROSS AT CALVARY

When did *the Word* come to the earth to "confirm" the *first* covenant God established with all the children of Israel when the law was given at the base of Mount Sinai through His servant Moses? It was on the cross at Calvary it would come to pass that *the Word* would once again "confirm" this *everlasting* covenant.

Our heavenly *Father* sent *the Word* to the earth as the Son of Man in the Person of Jesus Christ to become "the" mediator of the New Covenant which was "confirmed" (strengthened) with His precious blood.

And, it will come to pass once again, before all things are fulfilled, which God has spoken from the mouths of the "Prophets of Old" throughout the *synergy of the ages* is accomplished, *the Word* will once again "confirm" (strengthen) this *everlasting* covenant.

This is based on Revelation 11:19, which says the following:

> *"Then the TEMPLE of GOD was OPENED in HEAVEN, and the ARK of His COVENANT [Jesus is the "ark" of the New Covenant] was SEEN in His TEMPLE. And there were lightnings, noises, thunderings, an earthquake, and great hail."* (Rev. 11:19, NKJV)

35

As such, the "He" in Daniel 9:27, is our Messiah Jesus Christ, who will "confirm" this *everlasting* covenant at the end of all the *synergy of the ages.* It is not the Antichrist who will "establish" a peace treaty.

In fact, the word "covenant" as used in Daniel 9:27, has the same exact meaning as the word "covenant" in Genesis 15:17–21, when God established this *everlasting* covenant with Abraham and his descendants.

The word "covenant" as used in Daniel 9:27 according to *Strong's Hebrew Lexicon* #H1285, is the Hebrew word "bᵉrîyth" (pronounced "ber-eeth'"), and is from H1262 which means: In the sense of *cutting* (like H1254); a *compact* (made by passing between *pieces* of flesh): confederacy, [con-]feder[-ate], covenant, league.

Therefore, the covenant which shall be "confirmed" in Daniel 9:27, is not a peace treaty. I will cover this fact in detail in Chapter 67 of Book 3.

Now let's refocus our attention on the "land" God promised to give to Abraham's descendants. It is critical we take notice of the fact the Lord says to Abraham He will give to him and his descendants *after* him all the land of Canaan as an *everlasting* possession. The word "possession" means: *to be seized.* Remember this Hebrew meaning of the word "possession" as used in this passage of Scripture. It will play an instrumental role in what will happen in the final "Year of

Jubilee" when the apostle Paul talks about us being "caught up" (raptured) at the end of all the ages. I will cover this subject in-depth in Chapter 67 of Book 3.

The Lord also tells Abraham He will be our God and we will be His people. The word "everlasting" as used in all these promises that God gave to Abraham in the Hebrew means from the beginning of the world and is without end—for all eternity. This is why in Christ, we are the "seed" of Abraham and "heirs" according to the promises God gave to Abraham and his descendants under the New Covenant.

Therefore, God still requires His people to be "circumcised" in the foreskins of our flesh because this is the "sign" of this *everlasting* covenant God established with Abraham and his descendants.

"CIRCUMCISION" IS THE "SIGN" OF THE ABRAHAMIC COVENANT

Now let's continue our journey to discover what else the Lord says to Abraham concerning what the terms and conditions of this *everlasting* covenant are based on Genesis 17:9–14, which says the following:

> *"And God said to Abraham: 'As for you, YOU shall KEEP My* **COVENANT** [1] [H1285: *b'rîyth*: in the sense of cutting; a *compact* (made by passing between *pieces* of flesh); confederacy,

37

league], *YOU and YOUR **DESCENDANTS*** [8] [9] [H2233: *zera*: *seed*; figuratively *fruit, plant, sowing time, posterity*; child; H2232: *zâra*: to *sow*; figuratively to *disseminate, plant, fructify*; bear, conceive seed, set with, sow (-er), yield] *after YOU throughout their GENERATIONS. This is My **COVENANT*** [1] *which YOU shall KEEP, between Me and YOU and YOUR **DESCENDANTS*** [8] [9] *after you: Every MALE CHILD among you shall be **CIRCUMCISED*** [12] [H4135: *mûl*: to *cut* short, that is, *curtail* (specifically the prepuce, that is, to *circumcise*); by implication to *blunt*; figuratively to *destroy*]; *and YOU shall be **CIRCUMCISED*** [12] *in the FLESH of your FORESKINS, and it* [circumcision] *shall be a **SIGN*** [13] [H226: *ôth*: a *signal* (literally or figuratively), evidence or mark] *of the **COVENANT*** [1] *between Me and you. He who is EIGHT DAYS OLD among you shall be **CIRCUMCISED***, [12] *every MALE CHILD in YOUR GENERATIONS, he who is BORN IN YOUR HOUSE or BOUGHT WITH MONEY from any FOREIGNER who is not YOUR **DESCENDANT***. [8] [9] *He who is BORN IN YOUR HOUSE and he who is BOUGHT WITH YOUR MONEY must be **CIRCUMCISED***, [12] *and My **COVENANT*** [1] *shall be in YOUR FLESH for an **EVERLASTING*** [10] [H5769:

ōlâm: properly *concealed*, that is, the *vanishing* point; generally time *out of mind* (past or future), that is, (practically) *eternity* from the beginning of the world and is without end] *COVENANT*. [1] *And the UNCIRCUMCISED MALE CHILD, who is not CIRCUMCISED* [12] *in the flesh of his foreskin, THAT PERSON shall be CUT OFF* [14] [**H3772**: *kârath*: which means by implication to *destroy* or *consume*; specifically to covenant] *from HIS PEOPLE; he has BROKEN* [15] [**H6565**: *pârar*: cause to cease, disannul, dissolve, to make of non-effect or to make void] *My COVENANT*.'" [1] (Gen. 17:9–14, NKJV) (emphasis added).

WHAT ARE THE TERMS AND CONDITIONS THAT GOD REQUIRES FROM HIS PEOPLE IN ORDER TO KEEP THE ABRAHAMIC COVENANT?

Below and on the next page is a synopsis of the terms and conditions of this "Covenant of Circumcision" God established with Abraham and his descendants when Abraham was ninety-nine years old.

God required the following from Abraham and his descendants who come *after* him in all their generations throughout the *synergy of the ages*:

1. Abraham must "walk" before God in faith by placing

his trust in God's ability rather than his own and be *blameless* in his "walk" before God—above reproach in all his ways and in every area of his life.

2. The "Covenant of Circumcision" God made with Abraham was made through his flesh by the "act" of circumcision and would be a "sign" of this *everlasting* covenant with Abraham and all his descendants who would come *after* him throughout the *synergy of the ages.*

This is reiterated and substantiated in Acts 7:8, which says the following:

"Then He gave him [Abraham] *the* **COVENANT** (16) [**G1242:** *diathēkē:* a disposition, that is (specifically) a contract, covenant, testament (especially a devisory will)] *of* **CIRCUMCISION** (17) [**G4061:** *peritomē:* circumcision (the rite, the condition or the people, literally or figuratively); circumcised]*; and so Abraham begot Isaac and CIRCUMCISED him* [Isaac] *on the EIGHTH day; and Isaac begot Jacob, and Jacob begot the twelve patriarchs."* (Acts 7:8, NKJV) (emphasis added).

How long is this "Covenant of Circumcision" in force? Forever! Also, worth mentioning is this fact: Ishmael was thirteen years old when he was circumcised in his foreskin. This is based on Genesis 17:25, which says, *"And Ishmael his son* [Abraham's son with Hagar] *was THIRTEEN YEARS OLD when he was CIRCUMCISED* (12) [H4135: *mûl* to *cut short, that is, curtail* (specifically the prepuce, that is, to *circumcise*); by implication to *blunt*] *in the FLESH of his FORESKIN."* (NKJV) (emphasis added).

Up until this time God did not tell Abraham what the "sign" of this *everlasting* covenant would be. Otherwise, Ishmael would have become the *Son of the Promise* instead of Isaac.

Therefore, all male children eight days old *must* be circumcised, and this includes those who are born in Abraham's household or bought with money from a foreigner (those who are not Abraham's offspring). God's "Covenant of Circumcision" with Abraham was made through his flesh by the "act" of circumcision, so this covenant was sealed with his blood.

This "act" of circumcision which was acted upon by Abraham is a prophetic enactment of what Jesus Christ would later do with His body as He shed His precious blood. Jesus did this to "confirm" all of God's *everlasting* covenants (plural), including this *everlasting* covenant God established with Abraham and his descendants who came *after* him in all their generations throughout the *synergy of the ages.*

Also, Abraham's descendants must keep God's covenant with

41

the "sign" of circumcision which shall be in our flesh for an *everlasting* covenant.

Hence, circumcision was required of *every* boy who was eight days old to be circumcised in the flesh of their foreskins. This is based on Genesis 17:10, which says the following:

> *"This is My COVENANT* [(1)] [H1285: *b'rîyth*: in the sense of cutting; a *compact* (made by passing between *pieces* of flesh); confederacy, league] *which you shall KEEP, between Me and YOU and YOUR DESCENDANTS after YOU: Every MALE CHILD among you shall be CIRCUMCISED* [(12)] [H4135: *mûl*: to *cut* short, that is, *curtail* (specifically the prepuce, that is, to *circumcise*); by implication to *blunt*]..."* (Gen. 17:10, NKJV) (emphasis added).

Therefore, when God says to us that you "shall be" or you "shall keep" what He has said according to His *eternal* Word, then this is a commandment from Him, it is not a suggestion.

As such, since Jesus Christ is our Lord, our Master, and the author of His eternal Word, He expects His people to "consent" to or to "agree" with what He has established and decreed since the beginning of the world for all *eternity*.

And, His people are to "obey" His Voice and His Word without grumbling or complaining as well.

Donna M. Rogers

GOD'S PEOPLE MUST BE "CIRCUMCISED" IN THEIR FLESH BECAUSE IT IS AN EVERLASTING COVENANT

This "Covenant of Circumcision" *Yehóváh* established as an *everlasting* covenant with Abraham and his descendants *after* him requires God's people to be circumcised in the flesh of our foreskins based on the following Scriptures:

> "*...and you shall be CIRCUMCISED* [12] [H4135: *múl*: to *cut* short, that is, *curtail* (specifically the prepuce, that is, to *circumcise*); by implication to *blunt*] in the FLESH of your FORESKINS, and it shall be a *SIGN* [13] [H226: *óth*: evidence or mark] of the *COVENANT* [1] [H1285: *b'ríyth*: in the sense of cutting; a *compact* (made by passing between *pieces* of flesh); confederacy, league] between Me and you.*" (Gen. 17:11, NKJV) (emphasis added).

> "*He who is BORN IN YOUR HOUSE and he who is BOUGHT WITH YOUR MONEY must be CIRCUMCISED* [12] [H4135: *múl*: to *cut* short, that is, *curtail* (specifically the prepuce, that is, to *circumcise*); by implication to *blunt*], and My *COVENANT* [1] [H1285: *b'ríyth*: in the sense of cutting; a *compact* (made by passing between *pieces* of flesh); confederacy, league] shall be in YOUR FLESH for an *EVERLASTING*

43

(10) [H5769: *ôlâm*: properly *concealed*, that is, the *vanishing* point; generally time *out of mind* (past or future), that is, (practically) *eternity* from the beginning of the world and is without end] *COVENANT*." (1) (Gen. 17:13, NKJV) (emphasis added).

Also, what is interesting is this fact: God commanded all male children to be circumcised on the eighth day after a child is born.

This is based on Genesis 17:12, which says, *"He who is EIGHT DAYS OLD among you shall be CIRCUMCISED* (12) [H4135: *mûl*: to *cut* short, that is, *curtail* (specifically the prepuce, that is, to *circumcise*); by implication to *blunt*], *every MALE CHILD in YOUR GENERATIONS, he who is BORN IN YOUR HOUSE or BOUGHT WITH MONEY from any FOREIGNER who is not YOUR DESCENDANT."* (Gen. 17:12, NKJV) (emphasis added).

Why must the child be eight days old when he is circumcised and why is the number eight significant? The number eight means "new beginnings" when this number is used in the Bible.

And, it is for this very reason, why Isaac, the *Son of the Promise*, was a prophetic shadow picture of Jesus Christ, "the" *Son of the Promise* because God started a "new" beginning with them. In fact, they were both "circumcised" when they were exactly eight days old to "confirm" the "Covenant of Circumcision" God established with Abraham and his descendants.

ISAAC AND JESUS CHRIST WERE "CIRCUMCISED" WHEN THEY WERE EIGHT DAYS OLD

We are told in Genesis 21:4, Abraham circumcised his son Isaac, the *Son of the Promise*, when he was eight days old which fulfilled God's requirement as detailed in Genesis 17:12.

Then it would come to pass "the" *Son of the Promise—the Word* who became flesh as the Son of Man in the Person of Jesus Christ—would also be circumcised when He was only eight days old.

As I have said many times before, but it bears repeating, Jesus *never* did anything contrary to *Yehovah's* commandments found in the Torah, even when He was a baby. Jesus' earthly father Joseph, and His mother Mary, carefully followed *Yehovah's* instructions in the Torah.

This is why when Jesus was born He *physically* tabernacled in a "sukkot" which is more commonly referred to as a manger.

Sukkot is a Hebrew word meaning "booths" or "huts" that God's people in the land of Israel must *temporarily* dwell in during the Feast of Tabernacles (*Feast of Booths* or *Feast of the Ingathering*). This feast is also referred to as "Sukkot" in the Hebrew. In other words, Jesus was lying in a manger in this *temporary* dwelling place, otherwise referred to as a "sukkot" because Jesus was born during the Feast of Tabernacles.

And, this is why we are commanded by *Yehovâh* to celebrate His Feast of Tabernacles with great joy because this was when the earth received her King as a baby born in a manger—named Immanuel, which in the Hebrew means: "God is with us."

For it is believed that it was during *Yehovâh's* fall feast—the Feast of Tabernacles—our heavenly Father's seventh holy convocation based on Leviticus 23, our Jewish Messiah, Jesus Christ, was born and is when He first *physically* tabernacled amongst men as a baby in a body of flesh and blood.

The Word would be sent to the earth as the Son of Man in the Person of Jesus Christ as a baby born to a virgin, named Mary, for this purpose: To testify to the truth of His Father's instructions written in the Torah and to fulfill His divine destiny in order to die for the salvation of the world, including its inhabitants.

Jesus came to "bear witness" to His heavenly Father's instructions written in the Torah. This is substantiated in John 7:16 in which Jesus answered them and said, *"My doctrine is not Mine, but His* [*Yehovâh,* His heavenly

Father] *who sent Me."* And, in John 18:37, Jesus answered Pilate and said to him, *"You say rightly that I am a king. For this cause I was born, and for this cause I have come into the world, that I should BEAR WITNESS to the TRUTH. Everyone who is of the truth hears My voice."* (NKJV) (emphasis added).

In other words, the doctrine of Christ is based on His heavenly Father's instructions written in the Torah which is the truth.

As such, the "eternal" Word of God became the Son of Man in the Person of Jesus Christ and was and is the living Torah who became flesh.

JESUS CHRIST "CONFIRMED" THIS EVERLASTING COVENANT GOD ESTABLISHED WITH ABRAHAM LONG BEFORE HE WOULD "CONFIRM" IT ONCE AGAIN ON THE CROSS AT CALVARY

Jesus was circumcised eight days after He was born to be compliant with His heavenly Father's commandments based on Genesis 17:12–13.

It was during the Jewish circumcision ceremony called the *B'rit Milah,* Jesus was circumcised to fulfill the "sign" of the "Covenant of Circumcision" His heavenly Father *Yehôvâh* established with Abraham and his descendants.

This is substantiated in Luke 2:21, which says the following:

> *"And when EIGHT DAYS were COMPLETED for the* **CIRCUMCISION** [18] *[G4059: peritemnō: to cut around, that is, (specifically) to circumcise] of the Child, His NAME was called **JESUS*** [19] [20] *[G2424: Iēsous: which is of Hebrew origin [H3091]; Jesus (that is, Jehoshua), the name of our Lord; H3091: Yhôshûâ': Jehovah-saved; Jehoshua (that is, Joshua), the Jewish leader], the NAME given by the ANGEL before He was CONCEIVED in the WOMB."* (Luke 2:21, NKJV) (emphasis added).

Thus Jesus' earthly father Joseph, and His mother Mary, kept this *everlasting* "Covenant of Circumcision."

They made sure that Jesus was compliant with God's law requiring *every* male child *must be* circumcised to fulfill the "sign" of the *Abrahamic* Covenant or the "Covenant of Circumcision" His heavenly Father, *Yehôvâh*, established with Abraham and his descendants.

As such, Jesus "confirmed" this *everlasting* covenant God established with Abraham with the shedding of His blood as He was circumcised, long before He would "confirm" (strengthen) it once again on the cross at Calvary when He became "the" final sacrifice and atonement for our sins forevermore.

And, at the end of all the *synergy of the ages*, at His second appearing, Jesus Christ will once again "confirm" this *everlasting* covenant God established with Abraham and his descendants.

Again, this is substantiated in Revelation 11:19, which says the following:

> *"Then the TEMPLE of GOD was OPENED in HEAVEN, and the ARK of His COVENANT* [Jesus is the "ark" of the New Covenant] *was SEEN in His TEMPLE. And there were lightnings, noises, thunderings, an earthquake, and great hail."* (Rev. 11:19, NKJV) (emphasis added).

Therefore, the "He" in Daniel 9:27, is Jesus Christ who will "confirm" this *everlasting* covenant God established with Abraham and his descendants because this "covenant" already exists.

GOD'S PROMISES TO ABRAHAM BASED ON GENESIS 15:1–21 AND GENESIS 17:1–14

Based on God's *everlasting* covenant He made with Abraham and his descendants; let's review what we have learned so far based on Genesis 15:1–21 and Genesis 17:1–14.

This summary does not include the portion of the covenant promises God gave to Abraham concerning his wife, Sarah. She would bear Abraham a son named Isaac according to God's "spoken" Word.

I will cover this in-depth in Chapter 24 of this book, which will convey why Isaac is the *Son of the Promise* rather than Ishmael, Abraham's *firstborn* son, who was born through Sarah's handmaiden, Hagar.

Therefore, based on Genesis 15:1–21 and Genesis 17:1–14, God told Abraham that He would do the following:

1.   Multiply Abraham exceedingly.

2.   Change Abram's name to Abraham which means the "Father of Many Nations."

3.   Make Abraham exceedingly "fruitful."

4.   Make nations (plural) from Abraham.

5.   Make kings from Abraham.

> Again, based on the Hebrew meaning of the word "kings" this is talking about disciples of Jesus Christ who are a *royal* priesthood from the *order of Melchizedek* because our Great High Priest Jesus Christ is Melchizedek, *king of Salem.*

He brought out "bread" and "wine" to "confirm" this *everlasting* covenant with Abraham. This is a prophetic enactment of what Jesus Christ would later do with His disciples at Passover just before He became "the" perfect Passover Lamb.

6.   Establish this covenant with Abraham's descendants after Abraham's death in all their generations as an *everlasting* covenant. *Yehôvah*, Abraham's God, would be the God of Abraham's *spiritual* descendants as well.

7.   The Lord is Abraham's shield and his very *great* reward. And, as disciples of Jesus Christ, the Lord is our shield too.

Moreover, like Abraham, as long as we "obey" God's Voice and "keep" His testimony—great will be our reward!

Our heavenly Father's "testimony" is based on His *laws*, His *statutes*, His *commandments*, and His *judgments,* which we shall "keep" *if* we have the reverential fear of the Lord.

This is based on Psalm 19:7–11, which says the following:

"The LAW [21] [H8451: *tôrah*: a *precept* or *statute*, especially the *Decalogue* or *Pentateuch*: direction or instruction based on the *Mosaic* or *Deuteronomic* Law] *of the* LORD *is PERFECT* [22] [H8549: *tâmîym*: *entire* (literally, figuratively or morally); also (as noun) *integrity, truth;*

51

without blemish, complete, full, perfect, sincerely (-ity), sound, without spot, undefiled, upright (-ly), whole], **CONVERTING** (23) [H7725: *shûb*: to *turn* back; *repent* by turning away] *the SOUL; The* **TESTIMONY** (24) (25) (26) [H5715: *'êdûth*: *witness;* H5707: *êd*: specifically a recorder, that is, Prince as a witness; H5749: *ûd*: *duplicate* or *repeat,* by implication to *protest, testify;* admonish, charge, lift up, call to record, testify, give warning or to bear witness] *of the LORD is SURE, making wise the simple; The* **STATUTES** (27) [H6490: *piqqûd*: *appointed,* that is, a *mandate* (of God; plural only, collectively for the Law); commandment, precept] *of the LORD are RIGHT, rejoicing the heart; The* **COMMANDMENT** (28) [H4687: *mitsvâh*: a *command,* whether human or divine (collectively the Law); (which was) commanded (-ment), law, ordinance, precept] *of the LORD is PURE, enlightening the eyes; The* **FEAR** (29) [H3374: *yir'âh*: morally *reverence*] *of the LORD is CLEAN, enduring FOREVER; The* **JUDGMENTS** (30) [H4941: *mishpât*: *verdict* (favorable or unfavorable) pronounced judicially, especially a *sentence* or formal decree of divine *law;* including a particular *right,* or *privilege* (statutory or customary), or even a *style:* based on a ceremony or custom, manner of law, ordinance, or sentence] *of the LORD are TRUE and RIGHTEOUS altogether. More to be DESIRED are they than GOLD, Yea, than much fine gold; sweeter also than honey and the honeycomb. Moreover by THEM your SERVANT is WARNED, And in KEEPING THEM there is GREAT REWARD."* (Psalm 19:7–11, NKJV) (emphasis added).

As God was to Abraham, as his descendants, based on our faith in Jesus Christ, God is our:

- ❖ Deliverer
- ❖ Fortress
- ❖ Glory
- ❖ Great Reward
- ❖ Help
- ❖ Hiding Place
- ❖ High Tower
- ❖ Horn of our Salvation
- ❖ Lifter of our Head
- ❖ Place of Refuge
- ❖ Rock
- ❖ Strength
- ❖ Stronghold
- ❖ Sun and Shield

The Lord will bless the "righteous" and be all these things for those who trust in Him, fear Him, and "walk" uprightly.

This truth is substantiated in the following Scriptures:

"But You, O Lord, are a SHIELD for me, My GLORY and the One who LIFTS UP my HEAD." (Psalm 3:3, NKJV) (emphasis added).

"For You, O Lord, will BLESS the RIGHTEOUS; With FAVOR You will SURROUND HIM as with a SHIELD." (Psalm 5:12, NKJV) (emphasis added).

"The Lord is my ROCK and my FORTRESS and my DELIVERER; My God, my STRENGTH, in whom I will TRUST; My SHIELD and the HORN of my SALVATION, my STRONGHOLD." (Psalm 18:2, NKJV) (emphasis added).

"As for God, His WAY is PERFECT; The WORD of the LORD is PROVEN; He is a SHIELD to all who TRUST in Him." (Psalm 18:30, NKJV) (emphasis added).

"You have also GIVEN me the SHIELD of Your SALVATION; Your RIGHT HAND has HELD ME UP, Your GENTLENESS has made me GREAT." (Psalm 18:35, NKJV) (emphasis added).

"The Lord is my STRENGTH and my SHIELD; My heart TRUSTED in Him, and I am HELPED; Therefore my HEART greatly REJOICES, And with MY SONG I will PRAISE Him." (Psalm 28:7, NKJV) (emphasis added).

Donna M. Rogers

"Our SOUL waits for the Lord; He is our HELP and our SHIELD." (Psalm 33:20, NKJV)

"The PRINCES of the PEOPLE have GATHERED TOGETHER, The PEOPLE of the GOD of ABRAHAM. For the SHIELDS of the EARTH belong to God; He is greatly EXALTED." (Psalm 47:9, NKJV) (emphasis added).

"For the Lord God is a SUN and SHIELD; The Lord will give GRACE and GLORY; No GOOD THING will He WITHHOLD From THOSE who WALK UPRIGHTLY." (Psalm 84:11, NKJV) (emphasis added).

"For our SHIELD belongs to the Lord, And our KING to the HOLY ONE of ISRAEL." (Psalm 89:18, NKJV) (emphasis added).

"He shall COVER you with His FEATHERS, And under His WINGS you shall take REFUGE; His TRUTH shall be your SHIELD and BUCKLER." (Psalm 91:4, NKJV)

"O Israel, TRUST in the Lord; He is their HELP and their SHIELD." (Psalm 115:9, NKJV) (emphasis added).

"You who FEAR the Lord, TRUST in the Lord;

55

He is their HELP and their SHIELD." (Psalm 115:11, NKJV) (emphasis added).

"You are my HIDING PLACE and my SHIELD; I hope in Your WORD." (Psalm 119:114, NKJV) (emphasis added).

"My LOVINGKINDNESS and my FORTRESS, My HIGH TOWER and my DELIVERER, My SHIELD and the ONE IN WHOM I TAKE REFUGE, Who SUBDUES MY PEOPLE UNDER ME." (Psalm 144:2, NKJV) (emphasis added).

"He stores up SOUND WISDOM for the UPRIGHT; He is a SHIELD to those who WALK UPRIGHTLY..." (Prov. 2:7, NKJV) (emphasis added).

"Every WORD of GOD is PURE; He is a SHIELD to those who put their TRUST in HIM." (Prov. 30:5, NKJV) (emphasis added).

"REJOICE and be exceedingly GLAD, for great is your REWARD in HEAVEN, for so they persecuted the prophets who were before you." (Matt. 5:12, NKJV) (emphasis added).

"REJOICE in that DAY and LEAP for JOY! For

*indeed your REWARD is GREAT in HEAVEN,
For in like manner their fathers did to the
prophets."* (Luke 6:23, NKJV) (emphasis
added).

*"But LOVE your ENEMIES, do GOOD, and
LEND, hoping for NOTHING IN RETURN;
and YOUR REWARD will be GREAT, and YOU
will be SONS of the MOST HIGH. For He is
KIND to the UNTHANKFUL and EVIL."* (Luke
6:35, NKJV) (emphasis added).

*"Therefore DO not CAST AWAY your
CONFIDENCE, which has GREAT REWARD."*
(Hebrews 10:35, NKJV) (emphasis added).

All these Scriptures are for disciples of Jesus Christ because we
are the spiritual "seed" of Abraham and we are "heirs" of
these promises based on the *everlasting* covenant God
established with him and his descendants.

8.   Abraham would have a son from his flesh and blood to
be his heir from his body. This son is Isaac, not
Ishmael because the *son of the promise* was to be from
the firstfruits of Sarah's womb.

9.   Because Abraham "believed" in the Lord, it was
evidenced by Abraham's "obedience" to His Voice and
His Word. Therefore, the Lord credited Abraham's
"faith" in Him as *righteousness.*

10. Based on Exodus 12:40, for four hundred and thirty years Abraham's descendants would be afflicted in Egypt.

The children of Israel—God's Hebrew people, the Israelites, would be strangers in a country not their own, and they would be enslaved under the rule of Pharaoh, *king of Egypt*, who knew not Joseph. But it would come to pass that God would punish the nation that they served as slaves, and afterward, they would come out with great possessions during their exodus under the leadership of Moses. Exodus 12:40, says the following:

> *"Now the SOJOURN of the CHILDREN of ISRAEL who lived in EGYPT was FOUR HUNDRED and THIRTY[430] YEARS."* (Exod. 12:40, NKJV) (emphasis added).

Then we are told that *Yehovah* heard their groaning because of their bondage and He heard their cry and *Yehovah* "remembered" His covenant with Abraham, Isaac, and Jacob (Israel).

This is based on Exodus 2:23–25, which says the following:

> *"Now it happened in the PROCESS of TIME that the king of Egypt died. Then the CHILDREN of ISRAEL groaned because of the BONDAGE, and they CRIED OUT; and their*

CRY CAME UP to GOD because of the
BONDAGE. So God HEARD their GROANING,
and God REMEMBERED His COVENANT with
ABRAHAM, with ISAAC, and with JACOB. And
God LOOKED upon the CHILDREN of
ISRAEL, and God ACKNOWLEDGED them."
(Exod. 2:23–25, NKJV) (emphasis added).

11. In the fourth generation, Abraham's descendants
     would come back to their land. And, this happened
     under the leadership of Joshua as the children of Israel
     crossed the Jordan River and took possession of the
     Promised Land which God promised to Abraham and
     his descendants based on Genesis 15:17–21.

12. The Lord would give to Abraham and his descendants,
     except the Levites, the land which Abraham was a
     stranger in—the land of Canaan, which is an
     everlasting possession.

Abraham and his descendants would be given the *whole* land
of Canaan by God.

Again, the *whole* land of Canaan would be an *everlasting*
possession to Abraham and his descendants because it was a
gift from God and the gifts from God are irrevocable.

In other words, God does not take back the gifts He freely
gives to His children. However, this does not mean that His
children will not walk away from His gifts and not use the gifts

that they were freely given by God for His Kingdom purposes and His glory to prevail rather than our selfish ambitions.

Therefore, the land God promised Israel through the *everlasting* covenant He established with Abraham and his descendants is part of a "legally" binding covenant—ratified first by the blood of animals, then "confirmed" (ratified) by the blood of Jesus Christ.

As such, anyone or any nation forcing Israel to divide Jerusalem or give away any of Israel's land will be "cursed" by God Himself because they are violating and breaking God's *everlasting* covenant He made with Abraham and his descendants. This covenant God swore by Himself to keep for all *eternity*!

The Promised Land God promised to Abraham's descendants, which is based on Genesis 15:18–21, would be as follows: The land from the Wadi of Egypt to the great river, the Euphrates—the land of the Kenites, Kenizzites, Kadmonites, Hittites, Perizzites, Rephaites, Amorites, Canaanites, Girgashites, and Jebusites.

Moreover, Israel is the only *physical* nation defined by the "land" God promised to give to Abraham and his descendants.

Israel is the only *physical* nation in the entire world God established as a *literal* nation on the earth which would bring

60

forth the *firstfruits* of His increase based on the *Abrahamic* Covenant God made a vow by Himself never to break.

In other words, God pledged His throne and existence as the terms and conditions of keeping His end of this *everlasting* covenant.

Hence, the land of Israel is God's land. This is based on Joel 3:2, which says the following:

> *"I will also GATHER all NATIONS, And BRING them DOWN to the VALLEY of JEHOSHAPHAT; And I will ENTER into JUDGMENT with them THERE On ACCOUNT of My PEOPLE, My HERITAGE ISRAEL, Whom they have SCATTERED AMONG THE NATIONS; They have also DIVIDED UP My LAND."* (Joel 3:2, NKJV) (emphasis added).

Notice in Joel 3:2, God uses the following phrases: "My people," "My heritage Israel," and "My land."

Therefore, any individual, or nation, which goes against God's people—the children of Israel, or divides up God's land, is going against God Almighty Himself and will reap His judgment!

And, as the apostle Paul exhorts in Hebrews 10:31, *"It is a FEARFUL thing to FALL into the HANDS of the LIVING GOD."* (NKJV) (emphasis added).

61

THE "COVENANT OF CIRCUMCISION" IS THE "SIGN" OF WALKING IN A COVENANT RELATIONSHIP WITH THE GOD OF ABRAHAM, ISAAC, AND JACOB (ISRAEL)

God required Abraham and his male descendants to be "circumcised" in the flesh of their foreskin which is the "sign" of this *everlasting* covenant, referred to as the "Covenant of Circumcision."

Therefore, since we are Abraham's *spiritual* descendants by our faith in Jesus Christ and "heirs" according to this *everlasting* covenant God established with Abraham and his descendants, God requires the following from His people:

We must be "circumcised" in the flesh of our foreskin which is still the "sign" of "walking" in a covenant relationship with *Yehóvâh*—God the Father, who is also *El Elyon* (the *Most High God*).

And, He is the God of Abraham, Isaac, and Jacob (Israel) who is the Holy One of Israel.

However, I want to be clear that Abraham was "justified" in God's sight by his faith and trust in God *before* he was circumcised. In fact, the "sign" of circumcision is a "seal" of the "righteousness of the faith" which Abraham had while he was still uncircumcised, so he might be the father of all those who believes in Abraham's God and will "walk" in the steps of the faith like Abraham did.

This truth is substantiated in Romans 4:9–12, which says the following:

"Does this BLESSEDNESS then COME UPON the CIRCUMCISED ONLY, or UPON the UNCIRCUMCISED ALSO? For we say that FAITH was COUNTED to ABRAHAM for RIGHTEOUSNESS." (Rom. 4:9, NKJV) (emphasis added).

"How then was it ACCOUNTED? While he was CIRCUMCISED, or UNCIRCUMCISED? Not while CIRCUMCISED, but while UNCIRCUMCISED." (Rom. 4:10, NKJV) (emphasis added)

"And he [Abraham] RECEIVED the SIGN of CIRCUMCISION, a SEAL of the RIGHTEOUSNESS of the FAITH which he had while still UNCIRCUMCISED, that he might be the FATHER of all those who BELIEVE, though they are UNCIRCUMCISED, that RIGHTEOUSNESS might be IMPUTED TO THEM ALSO, and the FATHER of CIRCUMCISION to those WHO NOT ONLY ARE OF THE CIRCUMCISION, but who also WALK IN THE STEPS of the FAITH WHICH OUR FATHER ABRAHAM HAD WHILE STILL UNCIRCUMCISED." (Rom. 4:11–12, NKJV) (emphasis added).

63

The "seal" of the "righteousness of the faith" as used in Romans 4:9–12, according to *Strong's Greek Lexicon* #G4973, is the Greek word "sphragis" (pronounced "sfragece"), which means: A "mark" from God as in a signet (His signet ring), or His stamp of approval, signifying "genuineness" in His people from God's perspective.

UNDER THE NEW COVENANT WE MUST "CIRCUMCISE" THE FORESKIN OF OUR HEART

Since *now* in Christ there is no longer any difference between Jew or Gentile, slave or free, male or female under the New Covenant, the "sign" of us "walking" in a covenant relationship with *Yehôvâh* our heavenly Father, is based on us allowing God to "circumcise" the foreskin of our hearts.

Our hearts will become "circumcised" *after* we have placed our faith and our trust in His only *begotten* Son—Jesus Christ. This circumcision of our hearts will occur *if* we submit ourselves to the *sanctification* process of the Holy Spirit and we "obey" and "keep" God's Voice and His *eternal* Word.

And, for those who follow in the footsteps of Abraham by "obeying" God's Voice and "keeping" His covenant, then we shall receive God's "seal" of the "righteousness of the faith" like Abraham did. This "seal" which shall be placed on the foreheads of God's faithful remnant during the tribulation period will be a "sign" of our "genuineness" from God's perspective that we are indeed His "covenant" people. This is despite the fact that Jesus Christ shed His precious blood on the cross at Calvary for the forgiveness of our sins.

Again, Jesus did this so we *may* be "restored" and "reconciled" back into "walking" in a covenant relationship with our heavenly Father that both the House of Judah and the House of Israel broke due to their *spiritual* harlotry.

Also, Jesus Christ's blood is the "sign" of the New Covenant which was shed for many for the remission of our sins.

However, God first established "the blood" as a "sign" in the Old Testament in Exodus 12:13. We are specifically told that when God saw "the blood" from the lamb slain during the very first Passover while His people were in the land of Goshen, and they did what Moses instructed them to do, then God would "pass over" them so the plagues would not destroy them when He struck the land of Egypt with His judgments.

The Hebrew people "applied" the blood of the lamb they ate during the very first Passover to the two doorposts and onto the lintel of their houses, obediently "doing" as Moses had instructed.

A point worth mentioning at this time is this: Do we think God would have "passed over" His people as He released His judgments upon Egypt and the Egyptian people *if* they did not heed and "do" what Moses had instructed them to do according to His Word? No!

God kept His Hebrew people in the land of Goshen safe because they "acted" on what they heard Moses instruct them to do, which was evidenced when they actually "applied" the blood of the Passover lamb onto the doorpost of their houses!

And, so it is with us. We must "apply" the blood of our Passover Lamb who is Word of God that shed His precious blood for us by "acting" and "living" according to our heavenly Father's instructions written by His servant Moses.

This substantiates this fact: Our "obedience" to God's Voice and His Word is better than sacrifice from God's perspective, and our "obedience" will result in us having "circumcised" hearts only *if* we submit to His Lordship in every area of our lives.

As it was in the beginning, so it shall be in the end. When God releases His judgments upon all the nations of the world during the tribulation period, His people will be supernaturally protected only if we "apply" the blood of our Passover Lamb by being "obedient" to His Voice and His Word.

The death angel will "pass over" God's Hebrew people—the children of Israel in this generation who are obedient to "do" the will of our heavenly Father based on His instructions given to us by His servant Moses which is reiterated and demonstrated by Jesus in the gospels.

Long after the very first Passover took place in the Book of

Exodus, it would come to pass before Jesus became "the" Passover Lamb on *that* particular Passover over two thousand years ago, Jesus would once again "confirm" this *everlasting* covenant that God established with Abraham with His disciples.

This is substantiated in Matthew 26:27–28, when Jesus took the "cup" which symbolized His *lot* or *fate* He was about to suffer; He gave thanks and gave it (the cup) to His disciples and said, *"Drink from it, all of you. For this is My BLOOD of the NEW COVENANT, which is SHED for MANY for the REMISSION of SINS."* (NKJV) (emphasis added).

As such, Jesus' blood "confirmed" (ratified) the New Covenant as well as all of God's *everlasting* covenants (plural) God established with mankind and creation throughout the *synergy of the ages,* including this *everlasting* "Covenant of Circumcision" God made with Abraham and his descendants.

Therefore, in the next chapter, we will learn that this "Covenant of Circumcision" is still in effect for New Covenant believers. Because, after all, it is a "sign" of this *everlasting* covenant God made with Abraham and his descendants who would come *after* him in all their generations throughout the *synergy of the ages.*

CHAPTER 22

HOW IS THE "SIGN" OF THE COVENANT OF CIRCUMCISION STILL APPLICABLE TO NEW COVENANT BELIEVERS?

I n Genesis 17:13, God says to us, His people, that he who is born in Abraham's house, including those who were purchased with his money, must be circumcised.

Then the Lord specifically says, this is His covenant which shall be in our flesh for an *everlasting* covenant. Genesis 17:13, says the following:

> *"He who is BORN IN YOUR HOUSE and he who is BOUGHT WITH YOUR MONEY must be CIRCUMCISED* [1] [H4135: *mul*: to *cut short*, that is, *curtail* (specifically the prepuce, that is, to *circumcise*); by implication to *blunt*], *and My COVENANT* [2] [H1285: *bĕrîyth*: in the sense of cutting; a *compact* (made by passing between *pieces* of flesh); confederacy, league] *shall be in YOUR FLESH for an EVERLASTING* [3] [H5769: *ôlâm*: properly *concealed*, that is, the *vanishing* point; generally time *out of mind* (past or future), that is, (practically) *eternity* from the beginning of the world and is without end] *COVENANT."* [2] (Gen. 17:13, NKJV) (emphasis added).

69

Therefore, since we have been grafted into the commonwealth of Israel by receiving Jesus Christ as our Lord and Savior, we have also been bought for an extremely high price because Jesus Christ purchased us with the shedding of His precious blood and we are not our own. Hence, this commandment God gave to all His people based on Genesis 17:13, is still applicable to New Covenant believers.

As such, as disciples of Jesus Christ, "how" do we circumcise the flesh of our foreskins? The answer is this: We will allow God to circumcise the foreskin of our hearts, which shall only be accomplished by us circumcising our minds and our hearts by crucifying our flesh and picking up our cross on a daily basis! In addition, this is one of the many reasons why we must "walk" *through* various trials and tribulations while we are still living on the earth.

God requires His people to die to ourselves and follow in the footsteps of Jesus Christ. Therefore, we must *learn* to be "obedient" by the things which we suffer as we "walk" through the various trials and tribulations we are promised that we will have in this world, just as Jesus did. The apostle Paul substantiates this truth in Hebrews 5:7–9, which says the following:

> *"...Who, in the days of His flesh, when He [Jesus] had offered up prayers and supplications, with vehement cries and tears to*

Him who was able to save Him from death, and was heard because of His godly fear, THOUGH HE WAS A SON, YET HE LEARNED OBEDIENCE BY THE THINGS WHICH HE SUFFERED. And having been perfected, He became the author of eternal salvation to all who obey Him..." (Heb. 5:7–9, NKJV) (emphasis added).

Jesus became the author of eternal salvation to all who "obey" Him. Therefore, like Jesus, we will "learn" obedience by the things which we suffer as God refines us to be more Christ-like by His refining fire and the trials and tribulations we must "walk" through to lay hold of "our" Promised Land.

In fact, God promises us He will be with us "when," not "if," we go through the fiery furnace of trials and tribulations while we are still living on the earth. However, the "good news" is that the *same* God who supernaturally spared Shadrach, Meshach, and Abed-Nego from the fiery furnace can and will do the same for those who believe no matter what may come.

He is our *refuge* and our *fortress* when we place our trust in Him, no matter what the outcome may be. As I will shortly convey in the next chapter, Abraham had to be willing to sacrifice Isaac, his beloved son. God tested Abraham with the one thing which was most dear to him!

And, the same applies to us as well before we will cross over to possess "our" Promised Land and inherit the "covenant" promises thereof.

Also, according to God's Word both the Jews from the House of Judah and those of us who were formerly Gentiles from the House of Israel, have now been grafted into the commonwealth of Israel and are "justified" by our faith in Jesus Christ. Thus, we will inherit the same "covenant" blessings promised to Abraham, the father of our faith, by us practicing "righteousness" which is a by-product of us having faith and placing our trust in Jesus Christ alone!

Again, Jesus Christ has already paid the high cost required for the forgiveness of our sins by His precious blood, and we are to glorify God in our body and our spirit. This is based on First Corinthians 6:20, which proclaims, *"For you were BOUGHT at a PRICE; therefore GLORIFY God in your BODY and in your SPIRIT, which are GOD'S."* (NKJV) (emphasis added).

Therefore, like Abraham, all believers who receive Jesus Christ as their Lord and Savior are "justified" by our faith in Jesus *before* we become "circumcised" in our hearts. However, *after* we "become" saved by grace through faith in Jesus Christ, then we are to become "circumcised" in our hearts as we submit ourselves to the *sanctification* process of the Holy Spirit.

To reiterate, how do believers become "circumcised" in our hearts, which is one of the "signs" of "walking" in a covenant relationship with our heavenly Father? We do so by crucifying our flesh; we must stop sinning. God's grace empowers us to "do" everything He requires of us, so we will be "obedient" to His Voice and His Word.

When God tells us to "circumcise" the foreskin of our heart, He is telling us we must crucify our flesh, "cutting away" all impurities and filth from our heart, mind, spirit, and lives.

If we choose not to crucify our flesh and "circumcise" the foreskin of our hearts, then we shall be "cut off" from being His covenant people despite the fact Jesus Christ ratified (confirmed) all of God's *everlasting* covenants (plural) with His precious blood.

He became "the" mediator of the New Covenant where God has now put His laws in our minds and written them on our hearts instead of on two tablets of stone.

In Deuteronomy 30:6, it specifically says God will "circumcise" our hearts.

However, this is contingent upon us submitting to the *sanctification* process of the Holy Spirit as we meditate on God's Word so that our mind and heart can be "cleansed" and "renewed" by the washing of the Word of God. Yet we must "obey" His commandments by "applying" them to the way we live our lives, so we will "walk" in a covenant relationship with our heavenly Father and our Lord and Savior Jesus Christ. God's Word commands us to "circumcise" the foreskin of our heart based on the following Scriptures:

> *"Therefore CIRCUMCISE the FORESKIN of your HEART, and be STIFF-NECKED no longer."* (Deut. 10:16, NKJV) (emphasis added).

> *"And the LORD your God will CIRCUMCISE your HEART and the HEART of your DESCENDANTS, to LOVE the LORD your God with all your HEART and with all your SOUL, that you may LIVE."* (Deut. 30:6, NKJV) (emphasis added).

> *"In HIM you were also CIRCUMCISED with the CIRCUMCISION made without HANDS, by PUTTING OFF the BODY of the SINS of the FLESH, by the CIRCUMCISION of CHRIST, buried with Him in BAPTISM, in which you also were RAISED with Him through FAITH in the WORKING of GOD, who RAISED Him from the DEAD."* (Col. 2:11–12, NKJV) (emphasis added).

This Scripture in Colossians 2:11–12, has so many substantial truths we must examine it more closely. In Colossians 2:11, the apostle Paul says to us, *"In Him [Jesus Christ] you were also CIRCUMCISED with the CIRCUMCISION made without HANDS, by PUTTING OFF the BODY of the SINS of the FLESH, by the CIRCUMCISION of CHRIST..."* (NKJV) (emphasis added).

Therefore, what the apostle Paul is saying to us, Jesus' disciples, is as follows:

We must **cast off** the *works of darkness*, and **put on** the *armor of light* based on Romans 13:12.

We must **put off** our *former conduct*, which is our old man that grows *corrupt* according to *deceitful lusts* based on Ephesians 4:22.

We must **put off** *anger, wrath, malice, blasphemy,* and *filthy language* out of our mouths based on Colossians 3:8.

We must **put off** *lying* to one another, so we do **not** *grieve* the Spirit based on Ephesians 4:25.

We must **put away** the *foreign gods* that are among us, *purify* ourselves, and *change* our garments based on Genesis 35:2.

We must **put away** the *evil* from our midst based on Deuteronomy 13:5.

We must **put away** the *Baals* and the *Ashtoreths* and *serve* the LORD *only* based on First Samuel 7:4.

We must **put away** far from us a *deceitful* mouth and *perverse* lips based on Proverbs 4:24.

We must **remove** *sorrow* from our heart and **put away** *evil* from our flesh based on Ecclesiastes 11:10.

We must **wash** and **make** ourselves *clean* by **putting away** the *evil* of our doings and *cease to do evil* before the eyes of God based on Isaiah 1:16.

We must **put away** *childish* things we *spoke, understood,* and *thought* **before** we became a "new" man based on First Corinthians 13:11.

And last, but certainly not least, the Lord says *if* we will return to Him and **put away** our *abominations* out of His sight, then we shall not be moved based on Jeremiah 4:1.

Do not dismiss this fact: All these Scriptures I have listed require God's people to take "action."

This is why the apostle Paul tells us to *work out* (another "action" word) our *own* salvation with fear and trembling!

It is only by us being "crucified" in Christ and allowing the Holy Spirit to "circumcise" our hearts; we will be empowered to "do" the following:

We will **put on** our *robe of righteousness* based on Job 29:14.

We will **put on** our *armor of light* to **cast off** the *works of darkness* based on Romans 13:12.

We will **put on** the Lord Jesus Christ and make **no** *provision* for the *flesh* to fulfill its lusts based on Romans 13:14.

We will **put on** our "new" man that was created according to God in **true** *righteousness* and *holiness* based on Ephesians 4:24.

We will **put on** the *whole* armor of God, so we will be able to "stand" against the *wiles of the devil.*

This is based on Ephesians 6:13–17, which includes the following seven things which require our action:

1. **Gird** our waist with truth.

2. **Put on** the breastplate of *righteousness.*

3. **Shod** our feet with the preparation of the *gospel of peace.*

4. **Hold up** the *shield of faith.*

5. **Wear** the *helmet of our salvation.*

6. **Fight** with the *Sword of the Spirit* which is the Word of God.

7. **Put on** the *bond of perfection* which is "love" based on Colossians 3:14.

Therefore, as we *work out* our *own* salvation with fear and trembling, let us always remember what the Lord says to us in Genesis 17:14, concerning this *everlasting* "Covenant of Circumcision," which is a "sign" that Abraham's God is our God and we are His people. Genesis 17:14, says the following:

> *"And the UNCIRCUMCISED MALE CHILD, who is not **CIRCUMCISED*** [1] [H4135: *mûl*: to cut short, that is, *curtail* (specifically the prepuce, that is, to *circumcise*); by implication

77

to *blunt,* figuratively to *destroy]* in the *FLESH of his FORESKIN, THAT PERSON shall be CUT OFF* [4] [H3772: *kârath:* which means by implication to *destroy* or *consume;* specifically to covenant] *from HIS PEOPLE; he has BROKEN* [5] [H6565: *pârar:* cause to cease, disannul, dissolve, to make of non-effect or to make void] *My COVENANT* [2] [H1285: *b'rîyth:* in the sense of cutting; a *compact* (made by passing between *pieces* of flesh); confederacy, league]." (Gen. 17:14, NKJV) (emphasis added).

Do not dismiss the significance of this truth: The phrase "cut off" as used in Genesis 17:14, is *Strong's Hebrew Lexicon* #H3772, and is the Hebrew word "kârath" (pronounced "kawrath"), which means: To "destroy" or "consume," specifically related to covenant. I will cover this critical subject in-depth in Book 3.

However, for the subject at hand, what this means is this: Come Judgment Day, at the brightness of Jesus Christ's appearing, God will "destroy" or "consume" those who have broken [to make of no effect or to make void] the *everlasting* covenant He established with Abraham and his descendants.

From God's perspective, they have rejected His *eternal* Word who became the Son of Man in the Person of Jesus Christ in the flesh because they practice "lawlessness." Jesus will say to those who practice "lawlessness" come Judgment Day to depart from Him because He never knew them. This is based on Matthew 7:23, which says, *"...I never KNEW you; DEPART from Me, you who practice LAWLESSNESS!"* (NKJV) (emphasis added).

This indicates how serious God is when it comes to those who "break" His *everlasting* covenant He made with Abraham and his descendants.

This is emphasized by the fact we are told by the apostle Paul in Galatians 3:26–29, we were baptized into Christ. And, because we have "put on" Christ, there is now no distinction, *spiritually* speaking, of either Jew or Greek [Gentile], slave or free, male or female—for we are all "one" in Christ Jesus. We are Abraham's "seed" and "heirs" according to the promise.

Therefore, this "warning" God gives us in Genesis 17:14, is relevant for all of God's people under the New Covenant. God requires each of us to be "circumcised" in our hearts before we will *fully* receive the blessings of His "covenant" promises God promised to Abraham and his descendants in all their generations.

Moreover, just as the Israelites who were led by Joshua had to be "circumcised" *before* they were allowed to enter and take possession of the Promised Land the same requirement applies to New Covenant believers.

We will be allowed to enter and take possession of "our" Promised Land when we "activate" our faith. However, for us to "inherit" these promises, we must be "obedient" to God's Voice and His Word.

In the next chapter, we will take a closer look at the fact that God called Abraham His friend. Abraham cultivated such a personal and intimate relationship with *Yehováh*; God came down to the earth to speak to Abraham face-to-face about the impending destruction of Sodom and Gomorrah.

Also, God came to announce to Sarah, Abraham's wife, that she would conceive Isaac, the *Son of the Promise.* This was one of the many promises God gave to Abraham because he "believed" God, which was evidenced by Abraham's "obedience" to His Voice.

CHAPTER 23

ABRAHAM WAS CALLED GOD'S FRIEND BECAUSE OF THE PERSONAL, INTIMATE RELATIONSHIP HE CULTIVATED WITH *YEHOVAH*

Abraham inherited the promises of God based on a personal, intimate relationship he cultivated with *Yehovah*. In fact, Abraham's devotion and obedience to God were so great God called Abraham His friend.

This truth is proclaimed in James 2:23, which says, *"And the Scripture was fulfilled which says, 'Abraham BELIEVED God, and it was ACCOUNTED to him* [Abraham] *for RIGHTEOUSNESS.' And he* [Abraham] *was called the FRIEND of GOD."* (NKJV) (emphasis added).

As a matter of fact, Abraham had such as a close relationship with *Yehovah*, the Lord came down from heaven to the earth, to speak to Abraham face-to-face for two reasons.

First, it was to announce Sarah would conceive and give birth to Isaac, the son of God's promise to Abraham.

This is based on Genesis 18:1–15, which says the following:

"Then the LORD APPEARED to him [Abraham] *by the terebinth trees of Mamre, as he was sitting in the tent door in the heat of the day.*

81

So he [Abraham] LIFTED his EYES and LOOKED, and behold, THREE MEN were STANDING by him; and when he saw them, he ran from the tent door to meet them, and bowed himself to the ground, and said, 'My Lord, if I have now FOUND FAVOR IN YOUR SIGHT, do not PASS ON BY YOUR SERVANT. Please let a little water be brought, and wash your feet, and rest yourselves under the tree. And I will bring a morsel of bread, that you may refresh your hearts. After that you may pass by, inasmuch as you have come to your servant.' They said, 'Do as you have said.'" (Gen. 18:1–5, NKJV) (emphasis added).

"So Abraham hurried into the tent to Sarah and said, 'Quickly, make ready three measures of fine meal; knead it and make cakes.' And Abraham ran to the herd, took a tender and good calf, gave it to a young man, and he hastened to prepare it. So he took butter and milk and the calf which he had prepared, and SET IT BEFORE THEM; and HE STOOD BY THEM UNDER THE TREE AS THEY ATE. Then they said to him, 'WHERE IS SARAH YOUR WIFE?' So he said, 'Here, in the tent.'" (Gen. 18:6–9, NKJV) (emphasis added).

"And He [Yehóvah] said, 'I will certainly
RETURN TO YOU according to the TIME of
LIFE, and behold, SARAH YOUR WIFE shall
have a SON.' (Sarah was listening in the tent
door which was behind him.) Now Abraham
and Sarah were old, WELL ADVANCED IN
AGE; and Sarah had PASSED the AGE of
CHILDBEARING. Therefore SARAH
LAUGHED within HERSELF, saying, 'AFTER I
HAVE GROWN OLD, SHALL I HAVE
PLEASURE, MY LORD BEING OLD ALSO?'
And the LORD said to Abraham, 'WHY DID
SARAH LAUGH, SAYING, 'SHALL I SURELY
BEAR A CHILD, SINCE I AM OLD?' IS
ANYTHING TOO HARD FOR THE LORD? At
the APPOINTED TIME I will RETURN to YOU,
according to the TIME of LIFE, and SARAH
shall have a SON.' But Sarah denied it, saying, 'I
did not LAUGH,' for she was AFRAID. And He
[Yehóvah] said, 'No, but you did laugh!'" (Gen.
18:10–15, NKJV) (emphasis added).

The second reason God came down to the earth at this time
was to consult Abraham face-to-face about the impending
destruction of Sodom and Gomorrah.

In fact, this is where God and His two angels went directly
following God's discussion with Abraham *after* they had
shared a meal. This account is detailed in Genesis 18:16–33,
which says the following:

"Then the MEN ROSE FROM THERE and
LOOKED TOWARD SODOM, and ABRAHAM
WENT WITH THEM to send them on the way.
And the LORD said, 'Shall I HIDE from
Abraham WHAT I am DOING, since Abraham
shall surely become a great and mighty
NATION, and all the NATIONS of the EARTH
shall be BLESSED in him? For I have **KNOWN**
[1] [H3045: *yâda*: to *know* (properly to ascertain
by *seeing*); be aware of, observe, care for,
recognize, instruct, acknowledge, answer,
appoint, comprehend, familiar friend, kinsman,
cause to let make known or given privy to
knowledge or to be or make self-known] *HIM,
in order that he* [Abraham] *may COMMAND
his CHILDREN and his HOUSEHOLD after
him, that they KEEP the WAY of the LORD, to
do RIGHTEOUSNESS and JUSTICE, that the
LORD may BRING to Abraham what he has
SPOKEN to him.' And the LORD said, 'Because
the OUTCRY AGAINST Sodom and Gomorrah
is great, and because THEIR SIN is very
GRAVE, I will GO DOWN NOW and SEE
whether they have DONE altogether
ACCORDING TO THE OUTCRY AGAINST IT
THAT HAS COME TO ME; and if not, I will
KNOW.'"* (Gen. 18:16–21, NKJV) (emphasis
added).

"Then the MEN TURNED AWAY FROM THERE and WENT TOWARD SODOM, but ABRAHAM STILL STOOD before the LORD. And Abraham came near and said, 'Would You also DESTROY the RIGHTEOUS with the WICKED? Suppose there were FIFTY RIGHTEOUS within the CITY; would You also DESTROY the PLACE and not SPARE it for the FIFTY RIGHTEOUS that were in it? FAR BE IT FROM YOU TO DO SUCH A THING AS THIS, to SLAY the RIGHTEOUS with the WICKED, so that the RIGHTEOUS should be as the WICKED; far be it from You! Shall not the JUDGE of all the EARTH do RIGHT?' So the LORD said, 'If I find in Sodom FIFTY RIGHTEOUS within the CITY, then I will SPARE all the PLACE for their SAKES.'" (Gen. 18:22–26, NKJV) (emphasis added).

"Then Abraham answered and said, 'Indeed now, I who am but dust and ashes have taken it upon myself to speak to the Lord: Suppose there were FIVE LESS than the FIFTY RIGHTEOUS; would You DESTROY all of the CITY for LACK of FIVE?' So He said, 'If I find there FORTY-FIVE, I will not DESTROY it.' And he spoke to Him yet again and said, 'Suppose there should be FORTY found there?' So He said, 'I will not do it for the SAKE of FORTY.'

Then he said, 'Let not the Lord be angry, and I will speak: Suppose THIRTY should be found there?' So He said, 'I will not do it if I find THIRTY there.' And he said, 'Indeed now, I have taken it upon myself to speak to the LORD: Suppose TWENTY should be found there?' So He said, 'I will not DESTROY it for the SAKE of TWENTY.'" (Gen. 18:27–31, NKJV) (emphasis added).

"Then he said, 'Let not the Lord be angry, and I will speak but once more: Suppose TEN should be found there?' And He said, 'I will not DESTROY it for the SAKE of TEN.' So the LORD went his way as soon as he had finished speaking with Abraham; and Abraham returned to his place." (Gen. 18:32–33, NKJV) (emphasis added).

Yet we all know God did indeed destroy Sodom and Gomorrah because evidently there were not even ten righteous people who lived there!

The chain of events which led up to the destruction of Sodom and Gomorrah is detailed in the very next chapter of God's Word beginning in Genesis 19.

However, God is always faithful to His *righteous* people. Just before God destroyed Sodom and Gomorrah, the angels of the Lord removed Lot and his family for the following three reasons:

1. Because of Abraham's intercession and righteousness.

2. Because Lot was "righteous" and he was "oppressed" by the filthy conduct of the wicked based on Second Peter 2:7.

3. So God could bring the promises to pass He made to Abraham so that his children and his household after him *might* keep "the way" of the Lord and establish His "righteousness" and His "justice" throughout the land.

Furthermore, do not dismiss the significance that these are very same reasons why God spared Noah's family when He wiped out all the *unrepentant* wicked inhabitants who lived on the earth at the time of the flood! It was due to Noah's *righteousness* that his family was spared and the only ones who were "left behind" were those who practiced "righteousness." Out of all the inhabitants of the entire world, only a *faithful* "remnant" of eight people were spared when God rendered His judgment.

In addition, based on Genesis 18:16–21, God expected Abraham to command his children and his household after him to keep "the way" of the Lord and to practice "righteousness" and to enact "justice" so God could bring to Abraham and his descendants the promises God had spoken to him. This is God's will for all fathers to keep "the way" of

87

the Lord and teach it to their children and to "walk" according to "the way" of the Lord for the benefit of their households.

This is based on the following Scriptures:

> *"And what great NATION is there that has such* **STATUTES** [2] *[H2706:* **chôq:** an enactment; hence an appointment at a set time; law or ordinance] *and RIGHTEOUS JUDGMENTS* [3] *[H4941:* **mishpât:** verdict (favorable or unfavorable pronounced judicially, especially a *sentence* or formal decree of divine law; justice] *as are in all this LAW* [4] *[H8451:* **tôrâh:** a *precept* or *statute,* especially the *Decalogue* or *Pentateuch:* direction or instruction based on the *Mosaic* or *Deuteronomic* Law] *which I SET before you this DAY? Only take HEED to YOURSELF, and diligently KEEP YOURSELF, lest you FORGET the THINGS your EYES have SEEN, and lest they DEPART from your HEART all the DAYS of your LIFE. And TEACH THEM to your CHILDREN and your GRANDCHILDREN, especially CONCERNING the DAY you stood before the LORD your God in Horeb, when the LORD said to me, 'gather the people to Me, and I will let them HEAR My WORDS, that they may LEARN to FEAR Me all*

the DAYS they LIVE on the EARTH, and that they may TEACH their CHILDREN.'" (Deut. 4:8–10, NKJV) (emphasis added).

"And these WORDS which I COMMAND you TODAY shall be in YOUR HEART. You shall TEACH them diligently to YOUR CHILDREN, and shall TALK OF THEM when you SIT in your HOUSE, when you WALK by THE WAY, when you LIE DOWN, and when you RISE UP. You shall BIND THEM as a SIGN [5] [H226: ôth: evidence or mark] on YOUR HAND, and they shall be as FRONTLETS BETWEEN YOUR EYES [our mind is located behind our forehead that is between our eyes]. You shall WRITE [6] [H3789: kâthab: to grave; by implication to write] them on the DOORPOSTS OF YOUR HOUSE [under the New Covenant the "doorpost of our house" is in our heart] and on YOUR GATES [under the New Covenant our "gates" are our eyes, ears, and mind]." (Deut. 6:6–9, NKJV) (emphasis added).

"And you, FATHERS, do not PROVOKE your children to WRATH, but BRING THEM UP in the TRAINING [7] [G3809: paideia: tutorage, that is, education or training; by implication disciplinary correction; chastening, chastisement, instruction, nurture] and

ADMONITION [8] [G3559: *nouthesia*: calling attention to, that is, mild *rebuke* or *warning*] of *the LORD.*" (Eph. 6:4, NKJV) (emphasis added).

Therefore, men, keep at the forefront of your mind that God has commanded you to command your children and your household to keep "the way" of the Lord. It is your responsibility to "raise up" your children in the training and admonition of the Lord!

Equally important, you must be determined no matter what the cost involved, to "know" on a personal, intimate basis, the God of the Bible.

No matter what happens, continue to show your wife, your children, and your entire household, what it means to take a stand for God's "righteousness" and "justice" despite what everyone else deems acceptable and right in their own eyes.

And ladies, if your father or your husband has not and will not step up to the plate to be the *spiritual* leader in your house, then for your sake, and the sake of your children, and your grandchildren, you must do so.

Furthermore, as was the case concerning both Noah and Abraham, God is looking for those few who are willing to "raise up" the foundations of many generations and become the *Repairers of the Breach* that Isaiah 58:12 talks about for their children and their entire household.

In this, the "midnight" hour, it is God's desire to bring the total "restoration" and "reconciliation" to all things, especially concerning our families! Therefore, never stop interceding for your family members, and people in your circles of influence, who are not walking with the Lord as they should be.

Also worth mentioning at this time, based on Deuteronomy 6:6–9 is this fact: One of the "signs" (mark or evidence) that God will mark His people's foreheads with during the tribulation period is the "seal of the living God" the apostle Paul talks about in Romans 4:9–12.

This "seal" of the "righteousness of the faith" as used in Romans 4:9–12, is a "mark" from God as in a signet (His signet ring), or His stamp of approval, signifying "genuineness" in His people from God's perspective.

Again, this "seal" of the "righteousness of the faith" will be placed on the foreheads of God's "covenant" people instead of the *spiritual* "mark of the beast." It will distinguish the difference between those who are "walking" in a covenant relationship with the God of Abraham versus those who are not.

Notice in Deuteronomy 6:6–9, God specifically tells us that all these words He is commanding us *today* shall be in our heart.

He also admonishes us to bind them as a "sign" on our "hand" and as frontlets between our eyes, on our "forehead" where our mind is. Furthermore, under the New Covenant

God says that He will put His laws in our mind and write them on our hearts instead of on two tablets of stone by His Holy Spirit.

Therefore, this "sign" will also distinguish the difference between those who will receive the *spiritual* "mark of God" versus those who will receive the *spiritual* "mark of the beast" which will be received either on our "right hand" or on our "forehead."

The *spiritual* "mark of God" versus the *spiritual* "mark of the beast" has to do with "which" God we are truly worshiping. I will cover this fact in-depth in Chapter 66 of Book 3.

Again, this is just how serious God is concerning His *everlasting* covenant He made with Abraham and his descendants.

Now let's refocus our attention on Isaac, the *Son of the Promise* that God told Sarah she would conceive and give birth to as the *firstfruits* of her womb, despite her "unbelief" because she was well past her childbearing years.

And, so it would indeed come to pass that God's promise to Abraham for an heir from his loins and the *firstfruits* of Sarah's womb was fulfilled through Isaac. Isaac's name means "laughter" because Sarah mocked God with her laughter because of her old age. Yet despite Sarah's "unbelief," God would honor His promise to Abraham based on the following Scriptures:

"Then God said: 'No, SARAH your WIFE shall BEAR you a SON, and you shall call his NAME ISAAC (9) [H3327: *Yitscháq*: *laughter* (that is, *mockery*) *Jitschak* (or Isaac), son of Abraham]; I will ESTABLISH (10) [H6965: *qûm*: to *rise* (in various applications, literally, figuratively, intensively and causatively); accomplish, confirm, ordain, strengthen, continue; get up; perform; stand up and make sure] My COVENANT (11) [H1285: *b'rîyth*: a *compact* (made by passing between *pieces* of flesh)] with him for an EVERLASTING (12) [H5769: *ôlâm*: properly *concealed*, that is, the *vanishing* point; generally time *out of mind* (past or future), that is, (practically) *eternity*] COVENANT, (11) and with his DESCENDANTS *after* him.'" (Gen. 17:19, NKJV) (emphasis added).

"But My COVENANT (11) I will ESTABLISH (10) with ISAAC, (9) whom Sarah shall BEAR to you [Abraham] at this SET TIME (13) [H4150: *mô'êd*: an *appointment*, that is, a *fixed* time or season; specifically a *festival*; conventionally a *year*; by implication, an *assembly* (as convened for a definite purpose); appointed (sign, time); appointed feast; place of solemn assembly] next YEAR." (Gen. 17:21, NKJV) (emphasis added).

"And the Lord VISITED (14) [H6485: *pâqad*: to

visit (with friendly or hostile intent); appointed, bestowed, committed, counted, delivered to keep, enjoin, (call to) remember (-brance)] *Sarah as He had said, and the Lord DID for Sarah as He had SPOKEN."* (Gen. 21:1, NKJV) (emphasis added).

"And Abraham called the NAME of his son who was BORN to him—whom Sarah BORE to him—ISAAC." [(9)] (Gen. 21:3, NKJV) (emphasis added).

"Then Abraham CIRCUMCISED [(15)] [H4135: *mûl*: to *cut* short, that is, *curtail* (specifically the prepuce, that is, to *circumcise*); by implication to *blunt*, figuratively to *destroy*] *his son ISAAC* [(9)] *WHEN he was EIGHT DAYS OLD, as God had COMMANDED him."* (Gen. 21:4, NKJV) (emphasis added).

"Now Abraham was ONE HUNDRED YEARS OLD when his son ISAAC [(9)] *was BORN to him."* (Gen. 21:5, NKJV) (emphasis added).

It took a total of twenty-five years for God's promise to Abraham that he would have a son and an heir from his flesh and blood to be fulfilled.

This son would come forth from Sarah's womb and in Isaac;

his seed shall be called because Isaac is the *Son of the Promise*. And, it is for this reason, Isaac was circumcised when he was eight days old because this is the "sign" of the "Covenant of Circumcision" for those *spiritual* descendants of Abraham whose God is the God of Abraham—the "Father of Many Nations."

Twenty-five long years of "hope deferred" had passed since the time God called Abram to leave his country, his family, and his father's house and go to a land the Lord would show him. For when Abram was first called by the Lord he was seventy-five years old based on Genesis 12:4–6.

God's "spoken" Word did not return to Him void for God did indeed bless Abraham with his beloved son Isaac, at one hundred years old.

God had followed through on His "spoken" promise that He would return to Abraham and Sarah the "time of life" to their mortal bodies.

This truth attests to the fact that nothing is impossible with God, despite our unbelief!

So if you are waiting on God to bring to pass a promise He has given you, don't despair. For at the "appointed" time God shall bring it to pass because He is faithful and a covenant-keeping God!

In the next few chapters, we must take some time to understand how *Yehóvâh* would bring to pass the promises

He gave to Abraham by His "oath" He swore to Isaac, the *Son of the Promise.* Then in the next generation, God would "confirm" it to Jacob for a "statute" to Israel as an *everlasting* covenant.

And, it is for this very reason, in the next chapter, we will take a look at why Isaac, not Ishmael, is the son with whom the promises God gave to Abraham would come to pass. God "remembered" Abraham His friend and the *everlasting* covenant He established with him and his descendants.

CHAPTER 24

WHY IS ISAAC THE "SON OF THE PROMISE" THAT GOD PROMISED TO ABRAHAM?

L et's take a look at the fact that God's "eternal" plan to have sons and daughters on the earth who will "love" Him, "walk" with Him, "serve" Him, and "worship" Him will not be thwarted by the enemy.

As such, God determined He would bring forth His *spiritual* sons and daughters through the progeny of His friend Abraham.

First, Abraham begot two sons named Ishmael and Isaac. Abraham's *firstborn* son, Ishmael, was brought forth when Abram and Sarai became impatient to wait for God's promise to come to pass and took matters into their own hands.

Therefore, Ishmael was born from the "seed" (egg) of Sarah's Egyptian maidservant, Hagar, when Abram was eighty-six years old. This is based on Genesis 16:16, which says, *"Abram was EIGHTY-SIX YEARS OLD when Hagar bore Ishmael to Abram."* (NKJV) (emphasis added).

Abraham was one hundred years old when Isaac was born.

This is based on Genesis 21:5, which says, *"Now Abraham was ONE HUNDRED YEARS OLD when his son Isaac was born to him."* (NKJV) (emphasis added).

97

Also, notice based on these passages of Scripture, God changed Abram's name to Abraham, which means the "Father of Many Nations," *after* Ishmael was born, but *before* Isaac was born.

Therefore, it would be through Isaac that the promises God gave to Abraham would begin to come to pass based on the *everlasting* covenant God established with Abraham and his descendants.

Second, Ishmael was born *before* God told Abram that "circumcision" would be the "sign" of the "Covenant of Circumcision."

Therefore, Ishmael was born *before* Abram was circumcised. Again, Ishmael, Abram's *firstborn* son, was not circumcised in the flesh until he was thirteen years old.

This is based on Genesis 17:25, which says, *"And ISHMAEL his son was THIRTEEN YEARS OLD when he was CIRCUMCISED in the FLESH of his FORESKIN."* (NKJV) (emphasis added).

Third, it was only *after* Abram was circumcised, which was the "sign" of the covenant that sealed (ratified) the *Abrahamic* Covenant, that God's Word refers to as the "Covenant of Circumcision" then it would come to pass that God changed Abram's name to Abraham. Again, this was *after* Ishmael was conceived and born and *before* Isaac, the *Son of the Promise* would be conceived by Abraham's *physical* "seed" (sperm) from his loins as it fertilized the "seed" (egg) of his wife, Sarah.

This would be the beginning of the fulfillment of Genesis 3:15, which says, *"And I will put ENMITY Between YOU and the WOMAN, And between YOUR SEED and HER SEED; He shall BRUISE your HEAD, And you shall BRUISE His HEEL."* (NKJV) (emphasis added).

Accordingly, Abraham's *second* born son, Isaac, would begin the *spiritual* "lineage" or be the *spiritual* "seed" of the *spiritual* "descendants" who would also become heirs according to all the promises God gave to Abraham and his descendants.

And, it would be for this very reason, that through Abraham's *spiritual* "seed" Abraham would become the "Father of Many Nations" of people that would serve God and be called according to His purpose for His glory to prevail while they still lived on the earth.

Fourth, Abram's wife Sarai's name would be changed to Sarah because she would become the *spiritual* "mother" of nations, kings, and peoples.

Therefore, all of God's promises to Abraham would begin to come to fruition from her *physical* "seed" (egg) which was from her body and be brought forth from the *firstfruits* of her womb. Due to all the reasons I have cited in this chapter, this is *why* Ishmael was not the "seed" or the "son" according to

God's promises to Abraham, despite what the Islam religion professes.

In summary, it was Isaac, Abraham's *second* born son, not Ishmael his *firstborn* son, who would come from Sarah's "seed" (egg) and be the *Son of the Promise* because Isaac was the *firstfruits* from Sarah's womb to which the promises of God that He gave to Abraham were based on.

For God's promise to Abraham was based on Sarah's "seed" (egg) conceiving and bearing him a son; it was not based on Hagar's "seed" (egg) bearing Abraham, a son.

Again, this is substantiated in Genesis 17:19, in which God said, *"No, SARAH your WIFE shall BEAR you a SON, and you shall call his name ISAAC; I will establish My COVENANT with him for an everlasting COVENANT, and with his DESCENDANTS after him."* (NKJV) (emphasis added).

However, for Abraham's sake in answer to his prayer to *Yehóvah*, God did not forget about Abraham's *firstborn* son Ishmael.

Even though *Yehóvah* would establish the twelve tribes of Israel through Abraham's second born son Isaac—the *Son of the Promise*, listen to what God tells Abraham concerning his *firstborn* son, Ishmael in Genesis 17:20, which says the following:

*"And as for **ISHMAEL** [1] [H3458: Yíshmá'e'l*

God will hear; Jishmael, the name of Abraham's oldest son], *I have heard you. Behold, I have BLESSED him, and will make him FRUITFUL, and will MULTIPLY him exceedingly. He shall beget TWELVE PRINCES* (2) [**H5387: nâsîy:** an *exalted* one, that is, a *king* or *sheik;* captain, governor, ruler], *and I will make him a great NATION."* (Gen. 17:20, NKJV) (emphasis added).

Therefore, *Yehóvǎh* would bless Ishmael, make him fruitful, multiply him exceedingly, and would also establish twelve princes through him and make him a great nation as well. Accordingly, both Isaac and Ishmael were prophesied to be *great* nations.

What is very interesting to take notice of is this fact: It would come to pass that through Abraham's "seed," his *firstborn* son Ishmael would beget twelve princes who would become "kings" or "sheiks." Whereas, it would also come to pass that through Abraham's second born son Isaac—the *Son of the Promise*—he would beget the twelve tribes of Israel.

According to *Strong's Hebrew Lexicon* #H7626, the word "tribes" as used in the phrase the "twelve tribes of Israel" is the Hebrew word "shēbeṭ" (pronounced "shay'-bet"), which means: To *branch* off; a *scion,* that is, (literally) a *stick* (for punishing, writing, fighting, ruling, walking, etc.); rod, scepter, staff or tribe.

Now fast forward to the twenty-first century, and we now know that Isaac is the *Son of the Promise* for the children of Israel.

Again, the children of Israel is comprised of both Jews from the House of Judah, and those of us who were formerly Gentiles from the House of Israel (Jacob/Joseph/Ephraim), who have put their faith and trust in Jesus Christ.

In addition, the twelve tribes of Israel have been scattered all over the world based on James 1:1, which says, *"James, a bondservant of God and of the Lord Jesus Christ, To the TWELVE TRIBES which are SCATTERED ABROAD: Greetings."* (NKJV) (emphasis added).

However, Ishmael is the "Father of the Arab People" whose descendants originated from the Arabian Peninsula in Saudi Arabia. Ishmael's descendants have, for the most part, continued to reside in the Middle East throughout the *synergy of the ages.*

For God did hear Abraham and answered his prayer concerning his *firstborn* son Ishmael, who did indeed bring forth twelve princes (*kings* or *sheiks*) according to their nations as the Lord had spoken to Abraham. These nations are listed in Genesis 25:12–18, which says the following:

> *"Now this is the GENEALOGY of ISHMAEL, Abraham's son, whom Hagar the Egyptian, Sarah's maidservant, bore to Abraham. And these were the names of the SONS of ISHMAEL, by their NAMES, according to their*

GENERATIONS: The firstborn of Ishmael, Nebajoth; then Kedar, Adbeel, Mibsam, Mishma, Dumah, Massa, Hadar, Tema, Jetur, Naphish, and Kedemah. These were the SONS of ISHMAEL and these were their NAMES, by their TOWNS and their SETTLEMENTS, twelve PRINCES ACCORDING to their NATIONS. These were the YEARS of the LIFE of Ishmael: ONE HUNDRED AND THIRTY-SEVEN years; and HE BREATHED HIS LAST and DIED, and was GATHERED to his PEOPLE. (They dwelt from Havilah as far as Shur, which is EAST of EGYPT as you go toward Assyria.) He DIED in the PRESENCE of all his BRETHREN." (Gen. 25:12–18, NKJV) (emphasis added).

Again, we know that the majority of the Arab or Muslim people who practice the Islam religion still reside in the Middle East to this *very* day. Whereas, for the most part, the twelve tribes of Israel are still scattered abroad into all the nations of the world as it is to this *very* day.

Therefore, this "ancient" battle has always been about establishing the "rule" and "reign" between these two brothers—Ishmael versus Isaac.

In the next generation, this conflict would continue between Esau and Jacob and so on and so forth throughout all the generations that have come to pass throughout the *synergy of the ages.* And, it is for this very reason, the descendants of Ishmael and Esau will continually seek to destroy the descendants of Isaac and Jacob to "rule" and "reign" over them.

In addition, as it was in the beginning with the Ottoman Empire, we are now witnessing the re-emergence of the worldwide Islamic caliphate for those Muslims and Arabs who are practicing "radical" Islam.

Their primary goal is to annihilate both Christians and the Jewish people, who are all heirs according to the promises God gave to Abraham, based on the *everlasting* covenant God made with Abraham and his descendants. This came to pass through Abraham's son Isaac, and his grandson Jacob (Israel), who begot the patriarchs of the twelve tribes of Israel.

We will continue to carefully examine some of the underlying causes of this "ancient" jealousy and hatred between the descendants of the twelve tribes of Israel versus the twelve princes who are descendants of Ishmael and Esau in Chapters 26, 27, 28, 29, 30, 31, and 32 of this book.

But before we do, in the next chapter we will take a closer look at a couple of examples of how *Yehóvah* tested Abraham's faith and allegiance. God asked Abraham to leave everything behind—his country, his family, and his father's house and go to a place the Lord would show him.

However, the ultimate test of Abraham's faith is when God

would ask him to sacrifice his beloved son Isaac—the *Son of the Promise.* This was a prophetic shadow picture and enactment of what God would later do with His only *begotten* Son, Jesus Christ.

Who is Israel? Discovering our True Identity in Jesus Christ
and Why it Matters! The Root

CHAPTER 25

EXAMPLES OF HOW YEHOVAH TESTED ABRAHAM'S FAITH AND ALLEGIANCE

W e have already learned that Abraham inherited the promises from God because of his faith and obedience. Now we will look at a couple of examples based on God's Word of how specifically Abraham was "tested" to prove his faith in God, which was evidenced by his "obedience" to God's Voice.

ABRAHAM HAD TO BE WILLING TO LEAVE EVERYTHING BEHIND

One thing Abraham had to be willing to "do" was to leave everything behind—his country, his family, and his father's house.

This is substantiated in Genesis 12:1–3, which says the following:

> *"Now the LORD had said to Abram: 'Get OUT of your COUNTRY, From your FAMILY And from your FATHER'S HOUSE, To a LAND that I will SHOW you. I will make you a great NATION; I will BLESS you And make YOUR NAME GREAT; And you shall be a BLESSING. I will BLESS those who BLESS you, And I will*

CURSE him who CURSES you; And in you all the FAMILIES of the EARTH shall be BLESSED.'" (Gen. 12:1–3, NKJV) (emphasis added).

Therefore, Abraham had to choose whether or not to leave behind everything familiar and comfortable to him and go to an undisclosed location. Notice that God did not tell Abraham where he was going beforehand. Abraham had to leave in blind obedience, fully trusting God. Abraham did not know where he was going or what he would be doing once he got there.

How many of you reading this have to know ahead of time the full scope of an endeavor before you will "act" on what God has asked you to do? This is relying on our own reasoning, which is the direct opposite of us having faith and fully trusting God.

Like Abraham demonstrated for us all, to fulfill God's will for our lives, oftentimes we must leave behind people, places, and things to fully embrace new experiences and mandates from our heavenly Father.

We cannot hold onto the old and expect to fully embrace new mandates from God.

We may be required to endure being in the wilderness for a time. This will give us the necessary opportunity to prepare for what lies ahead. We will receive our new marching orders by seeking God's face, and we must follow His instructions step-by-step.

In this hour, we are entering into "unchartered" territory while God is on the move.

Therefore, we cannot rely on old mandates from the Lord. We must abide in His presence daily and be willing to act and focus *only* on those things that He has specifically told us to do. This is the only way that we will have His divine providence, provision, and protection in the days ahead.

ABRAHAM HAD TO BE WILLING TO GIVE UP HIS BELOVED SON ISAAC

Another example illustrating the depth of Abraham's faith and obedience to God occurred when God asked Abraham to do the unthinkable by sacrificing his beloved son Isaac—after waiting for this blessing for twenty-five long years.

It was all a test to see if Abraham would be "counted worthy" to inherit the promises and the blessings that God wanted to bestow on Abraham and his descendants throughout the *synergy of the ages.*

God asking Abraham to sacrifice his beloved son Isaac was an act of sacrificial love and obedience foreshadowing how Jesus, God's only *begotten* Son, would "become" the perfect "Passover Lamb" without spot or blemish. He had to prove Himself worthy by learning "obedience" from His suffering.

Again, this is based on Hebrews 5:8 which says, *"...though He [Jesus Christ] was a Son, yet He learned OBEDIENCE by the THINGS which He SUFFERED."* (NKJV) (emphasis added).

A servant is not greater than His Master. This is *Yehôvah's* requirement for all His sons and daughters. Who is our Master?

Adonai, our Lord, and our Master is Jesus Christ, who is our "King" and the "Ruler" (Lord) of our lives.

Our heavenly Father sent Him to the earth to die for the forgiveness of our sins and to "restore" and "reconcile" us back into "walking" in a covenant relationship Him.

Why was this necessary? Because both the House of Judah and the House of Israel committed "spiritual" harlotry against *Yehôvah,* our heavenly Father, and He issued them a *certificate of divorce.* I conveyed this fact in Chapter 12 of Book 1.

Jesus paid a very high price for us, His bride, with the shedding of His precious blood. Therefore, we are no longer our own, and we owe Him our *total* allegiance.

In addition, because we are Abraham's descendants, we would be wise to follow the example demonstrated by Abraham. Abraham's faith and commitment to *Yehôvah* are *severely* tested yet prevails.

This is substantiated in Genesis 22:1–19 where Abraham's

faith is challenged by God and confirmed by his willingness to "do" what God had asked him to do despite his trepidation!

As you read this passage of Scripture in Genesis 22:1–2, notice that *Yehovah* is telling Abraham to take Isaac his *only* son and offer him as a burnt sacrifice, even though Ishmael was Abraham's son too.

Genesis 22:1–2, says the following:

> *"Now it came to pass after these things that God tested Abraham, and said to him, 'Abraham!' And he said, 'Here I am.' Then He said, 'Take now YOUR SON, your only SON Isaac, whom you love, and GO to the land of MORIAH* (1) (2) [H4179: *Moriyah*: a hill in Palestine; which was the ancient name for Jerusalem where the Lord has written His name, Yahweh; H3050: *Yahh:* Jah, the sacred name; Jah, the Lord], *and OFFER him there as a BURNT OFFERING on ONE of the MOUNTAINS of which I shall TELL you.'"* (Gen. 22:1–2, NKJV) (emphasis added).

Before we continue, it is worth mentioning that the land of Moriah is a hill in Palestine we now know as the city of Jerusalem. The name of Yahweh is written on it. In fact, this very mountain where God showed Abraham *where* to sacrifice Isaac as a burnt offering is the *same* Mount Moriah located in Jerusalem—the city of our God in Israel where the Temple

111

Mount is located. As substantiated in Second Chronicles 3:1, this is the *same* city where Solomon, King David's son, built the house of the Lord (Solomon's Temple). This is also the *same* place where David prepared the threshing floor of Ornan the Jebusite.

Because of this, I believe this is also the *same* mountain where Jesus Christ would later be crucified. The New Testament describes the crucifixion site, Golgotha, as being *near* the city in John 19:20, and we are told that Jesus suffered outside the gate of the city in Hebrews 13:12.

When God called Abraham to sacrifice Isaac, this sacrificial offering was to be done on the altar of the sacrifice. So we must ask ourselves this question. Where did the priests of the Lord under the *first* covenant continually offer animal sacrifices for the sins of the people until Jesus Christ became the final sacrifice for all time forevermore?

The answer is the animal sacrifices were made on the altar of the sacrifice at the Temple which was located on Mount Moriah in Jerusalem where the Temple Mount is now located.

Therefore, when Abraham who represents God, the Father, offered his only begotten son Isaac, who represents God's only *begotten*—Son, Jesus Christ, as a sacrificial offering, he did so on Mount Moriah which is the same location where the Temple Mount in Jerusalem is currently located.

However, we are specifically told in Leviticus 1:10–11 that the sacrifice for the burnt offering shall be killed on the "north side" of the altar (the Temple Mount located on Mount Moriah).

Leviticus 1:10–11, says the following:

> *"If his offering is of the flocks—of the sheep or of the goats—as a burnt sacrifice, he shall bring a male without blemish. He shall KILL IT on the NORTH SIDE of the ALTAR* [The Temple Mount located on Mount Moriah] *before the LORD; and the priests, Aaron's sons, shall sprinkle its blood all around on the altar."* (Lev. 1:10–11, NKJV) (emphasis added).

As we all know Jesus Christ is our perfect male Passover Lamb who was without spot or blemish. He would be killed (sacrificed) on the "north side" of the altar where the burnt sacrifice was to be offered.

As such, there are currently two places in Jerusalem which people say is the location of Jesus' death, burial, and resurrection.

One site that claims to be the place of Jesus' death, burial and resurrection is the Church of the Holy Sepulchre which was founded by Constantine the Great and is now under the ownership of the Roman Catholic Church.

However, this cannot be the site of Jesus' death, burial, and resurrection for this reason: This site is located to the "west"

113

of the Temple Mount located on Mount Moriah.

However, the other site which claims to be the actual location where Jesus Christ was crucified, buried in the tomb for three days and three nights and was resurrected on the third day is The Garden Tomb. The location of The Garden Tomb is on the "north side" of the altar where the sacrifices were made at the Temple which is located on the Temple Mount located on Mount Moriah.

This location is in alignment with what God's Word specifically tells us according to Leviticus 1:10–11.

Shortly you will understand why I believe this is the *same* location that Jesus would be offered up as the final sacrifice for all time.

Now let's continue to see what happens next based on Genesis 22:3–5, as Abraham embarks on his painstaking journey to offer his *only* son Isaac as a burnt sacrifice based on what the Lord had told him to do in Genesis 22:1–2. Genesis 22:3–5, says the following:

> *"So Abraham ROSE early in the MORNING and SADDLED his DONKEY, and took two of his YOUNG MEN with him, and ISAAC HIS SON; and he SPLIT the WOOD for the BURNT OFFERING, and AROSE and WENT to the PLACE of which GOD HAD TOLD HIM. Then on the THIRD DAY, Abraham LIFTED his EYES*

and SAW the PLACE afar OFF. And Abraham
said to his young men, 'Stay here with the
donkey; the LAD and I will go YONDER and
WORSHIP, and WE [Abraham and Isaac] WILL
COME BACK to you.'" (Gen. 22:3–5, NKJV)
(emphasis added).

Based on Genesis 22:3–5, there are three "key" prophetic shadow pictures that I would like to briefly elaborate on which are as follows:

PROPHETIC SHADOW PICTURE # 1

The first prophetic shadow picture concerns the donkey Abraham used to ride to the place where God would require Abraham to offer a burnt offering to Him.

This was a prophetic enactment of what Jesus Himself would do when He made His triumphant entry into Jerusalem just prior to *that* particular Passover where He would become "the" perfect "Passover Lamb." This is based on John 12:12–15, Matthew 21:5, and Zechariah 9:9.

PROPHETIC SHADOW PICTURE # 2

The second prophetic shadow picture is this: It was not a coincidence that Abraham took two of his young men with him and his son Isaac.

Later in this chapter, you will learn the full significance of "who" these two men are symbolic of. One of the reasons why

Abraham took these two young men with him on his pilgrimage to sacrifice Isaac is for this reason: God always substantiates or confirms His Word based on the testimony of two or three witnesses.

This is based on Deuteronomy 17:6 which says, *"Whoever is DESERVING of DEATH shall be PUT to DEATH on the TESTIMONY of TWO or THREE WITNESSES; he shall not be PUT to DEATH on the TESTIMONY of one WITNESS."* (NKJV) (emphasis added). Moreover, Second Corinthians 13:1 states, *"...By the MOUTH of TWO or THREE WITNESSES, every WORD shall be ESTABLISHED."* (NKJV) (emphasis added).

You may be thinking, "Well, Isaac and Jesus was not deserving of death." Yet God required both of them to be offered as a *living* sacrifice because the "wages of sin" is death.

Therefore, when Jesus Christ would later die on the cross at Calvary, He took all of our sins upon Himself. He reaped the "curse" we would have received for not keeping *the letter* of God's law.

Hence, one of the reasons why Jesus had to die on the cross at Calvary is so that we would be "redeemed" by His precious blood, based on Hebrews 9:22.

This says that according to the law almost all things are purified with blood, and *without* the shedding of blood there is no remission (forgiveness or pardon) for our sins.

Jesus Christ was *willing* to die for us at Calvary so we would not have to die *spiritually* speaking, based on our inability to walk perfectly according to God's law.

Moreover, even though there were countless individuals who witnessed Jesus' crucifixion on the tree (cross) at Calvary, it is no coincidence that there were three "official" witnesses of His death.

The first two "official" witnesses of Jesus' death were the criminals who were crucified at the same time as Jesus. Have you ever wondered why on the day Jesus was crucified there were three crosses and two other men were being crucified at the same time Jesus was?

One reason why there were three crosses, with Jesus' cross in the middle, was to signify that with Jesus' crucifixion both the Jews from the House of Judah and those of us who were formerly Gentiles from the House of Israel became "one" *spiritually* speaking. At Calvary we became "one" New Man, "one" house, "one" kingdom, and "one" body of Christ under the headship of Jesus Christ, God's only *begotten* Son who was slain as our "Passover Lamb" during *that* particular Passover which took place over two thousand years ago.

Another reason why there were two other crosses was to signify that Jesus Christ shed His precious blood for both the sinner and the repentant man. This was illustrated by the one criminal who was forever lost and hardened by sin and chose not to repent even as he was dying. Whereas, the other criminal was saved at the last possible moment of his life because he decided to humble himself and repent by placing his faith in the *only* One who could save his soul.

The third reason why there were three crosses when Jesus shed His precious blood when He was crucified on the cross at Calvary is for this reason: He was fulfilling (consummating, executing, and ratifying [confirming]) the law which was given at the very first Feast of Weeks (*Shavuot* or *Pentecost*) through God's servant Moses. This is when the Father, the Son, and the Holy Spirit witnessed all the children of Israel enter into a "Covenant of Marriage" with God at the base of Mount Sinai.

The first five books of our Bible, written by Moses, are the terms and conditions of our "Covenant of Marriage" with our heavenly Father, which was "ratified," "confirmed," and "sealed" with the precious blood of our Lord and Savior, Jesus Christ, under the New Covenant.

In fact, the terms and conditions of the "Covenant of Marriage" serve the same purpose as the "ketubah" did in ancient times.

The "ketubah" used to be an integral part of a traditional Jewish marriage. It is a special type of Hebrew prenuptial agreement, which is a written "legal" contract that outlines the rights and responsibilities of the groom in relation to his bride and vice versa.

Under the New Covenant, Jesus also was fulfilling

118

(consummating, executing, and ratifying [confirming]) the *Spirit of Truth* witnessed by John the Baptist.

John saw the *Spirit of God* (symbolized by the dove) alight upon Jesus when John baptized Jesus with water based on Matthew 3:16–17. It was then John heard God, the Father, bear witness to *whom* Jesus was when a voice came from heaven saying, *"This is My beloved Son, in whom I am well pleased."*

Moreover, this prophetic enactment of what happened in Matthew 3:16–17 was a public prophetic declaration that those who were baptized with the Holy Spirit with fire under the New Covenant would also be crucified in Christ and die to their sins.

The resurrection power of the Holy Spirit would be "poured out" in great abundance on those who believed that Jesus was the Son of God after Jesus died, was resurrected, and ascended back into heaven.

And, speaking of John the Baptist, Jesus said that all the "prophets" and the "law" prophesied until John, and if we are willing to receive it, he (John the Baptist) is Elijah who is to come which is based on Matthew 11:13–15.

Therefore, the fact that there were three crosses at the time Jesus was crucified was a *symbolic* and *prophetic* representation of Jesus fulfilling both the "law" and the "prophets." Jesus Christ was and is the living Torah as His disciples should become as well after we became the One New

119

Man, *spiritually* speaking. Jesus' cross being in the middle of the two other crosses represents the bridge joining those things written about in the Old Testament with those things revealed in the New Testament. As a result, there would no longer be two "houses" or two "kingdoms."

Because Jesus fulfilled (consummated, executed, and ratified [confirmed]) the "law" and the "prophets," He did not abolish (demolish, disintegrate, or dissolve) the law based on what He says to us in Matthew 5:17–18. As such, with Jesus' death, resurrection, and ascension, we would all become a "new" creation in Him, and the old would pass away and all, not *some*, things would become new.

We would all become One New Man in Him just as God the Father, God the Son, and God the Holy Spirit are all one, *spiritually* speaking. Hence, another reason for three crosses on that particular day was to symbolize the Father, the Son, and the Holy Spirit.

In addition, you may be wondering why I am proclaiming that the two men who were crucified along with Jesus that day were two of the "official" witnesses.

It is because the two criminals who were hanging on the cross beside Jesus witnessed His death.

We know this is true based on the written testimony that the legs of the two criminals crucified with Jesus were broken by the Roman soldier so they would die a quicker death. The

Jews had requested that their bodies be taken down from the cross before sundown so they could get ready for the High Sabbath Day which would begin the Feast of Unleavened Bread during *that* particular Passover.

Before the legs of the two criminals crucified with Jesus were broken by the Roman soldier, Jesus had already given up His Spirit (died). Therefore, the two criminals who were crucified with Jesus both "officially" witnessed His death before they died. The Roman soldier was the third "official" witness of Jesus' death based on Mark 15:39 which says, *"So when the CENTURION, who stood opposite Him [Jesus], saw that He cried out like this and BREATHED HIS LAST, he said, 'Truly this MAN was the SON of GOD!'"* (NKJV) (emphasis added).

Moreover, this same Roman soldier did not break Jesus' legs, fulfilling John 19:36 which proclaims, *"For these THINGS were DONE that the SCRIPTURE should be FULFILLED, 'Not one of His BONES shall be BROKEN.'"* (NKJV) (emphasis added).

Instead, this Roman soldier pierced Jesus' side as a testimony that He was indeed already dead. Thus, His legs did not have to be broken.

In addition, the blood and water which came forth from Jesus' side when the Roman centurion pierced His side with a spear fell down to the earth.

This made the final atonement, *spiritually* speaking, for the shedding of innocent blood throughout the *synergy of the*

121

ages. Thus, when Jesus' blood spilled upon the ground when the Roman centurion pierced His side, this fulfilled the requirement of God's law.

This is based on Numbers 35:33, which says:

> *"So you shall not POLLUTE the LAND where you are; for BLOOD defiles the LAND, and no ATONEMENT can be made for the LAND, for the BLOOD that is SHED on it, EXCEPT BY the BLOOD of him who SHED it."* (Num. 35:33, NKJV) (emphasis added).

THE EARTH IS DEFILED DUE TO SHEDDING BLOOD AND BREAKING GOD'S EVERLASTING COVENANT

Since mankind has shed innocent blood continuously throughout the *synergy of the ages,* it has "polluted" and "defiled" the earth. And, based on Numbers 35:33, there is no atonement which can be made for the shedding of innocent blood except by the blood of him who shed it. As such, Jesus died for the salvation of the whole world, including its inhabitants.

Moreover, God's Word says that another reason why the earth is "defiled" under its inhabitants is because mankind, including God's people due to our ignorance of the *whole*

122

counsel of His Word, have transgressed His laws, changed His ordinance, and broken His *everlasting* covenant.

This is based on Isaiah 24:5, which says the following:

"The EARTH is also DEFILED [(3)] [H2610: *chânêph*: to soil, corrupt, pollute or to profane, especially in a moral sense] *under its INHABITANTS, Because THEY* [those who are "out" of covenant with God] *have TRANSGRESSED* [(4)] [H5674: *âbar*: to turn away from; to invalidate, make obsolete or cease to exist] *the LAWS* [(5)] [H8451: *tôrâh*: a *precept* or *statute*, especially the *Decalogue* or *Pentateuch*: direction or instruction based on the *Mosaic* or *Deuteronomic* Law], *CHANGED* [(6)] [H2498: *châlaph*: to slide by; hasten away, abolish; alter change; to pass away by striking through or cutting off] *the ORDINANCE* [(7)] [(8)] [H2706: *chôq*: an *enactment*, hence an *appointment* at a set time concerning a commandment, custom, decree, law, or statute (i.e.: our heavenly Father's seven holy convocations based on Leviticus 23, which begins with the *seventh* day Sabbath], *BROKEN* [(9)] [H6565: *pârar*: to break up, violate, frustrate, cause to cease, disannul, dissolve, divide; to make of non-effect or to make void] *the EVERLASTING* [(10)] [H5769: *'ôlâm*: properly concealed from the ancient time; and is continued for all eternity

from the beginning of the world and is without end] *COVENANT* (11) [H1285: *b'riyth*: in the sense of cutting as made by passing between pieces of flesh; a compact]." (Isa. 24:5, NKJV) (emphasis added).

Some believers are of the "opinion" that Jesus abolished the law God established through His servant Moses for all the children of Israel from all twelve tribes of Israel, not just the Jews from the House of Judah.

However, that law (the Torah) that God "decreed," "established," and "confirmed" with the precious blood of Jesus is based on His *everlasting* covenant with Abraham and his descendants.

So clearly based on Isaiah 24:5, Jesus did not abolish the law.

Rather, He set us free from the "curse" that we would receive for not keeping the *letter of the law* which I will cover in detail in Chapter 47 of Book 3.

Thus, on the cross at Calvary, Jesus Christ took all the sins of mankind upon Himself when He shed His innocent blood. He "redeemed" not only mankind—the inhabitants of the earth—He also made atonement for the earth. This is why John 3:16 says, *"For God so LOVED the WORLD* (12) [G2889: *Kosmos*: orderly arrangement, by implication the world, including its inhabitants] *that He GAVE His only begotten SON, that whoever BELIEVES in Him should not PERISH but have EVERLASTING LIFE."* (NKJV) (emphasis added).

However, the full manifestation of this redemption, *physically* speaking, has not come to pass until all things spoken from the mouths of God's holy prophets throughout the *synergy of the ages* are fulfilled.

PROPHETIC SHADOW PICTURE # 3

The third prophetic shadow picture is extremely significant. It is based on Genesis 22:4 which says, *"Then on the THIRD DAY Abraham LIFTED his EYES and SAW the PLACE afar off."* (NKJV) (emphasis added).

Do not dismiss the significance that it was on the "third" day that Abraham lifted his eyes and saw "the" place from afar off.

As I will shortly convey, Abraham saw what Jesus would later do on the cross at Calvary at the very *same* place that God led Abraham to in order to offer a burnt offering with his son Isaac.

Hence, Abraham prophetically enacted what would later come to pass at Calvary.

Also, God would reveal to Abraham that Jesus Christ would be raised up (resurrected) from death and the grave on the "third" day following His crucifixion and burial.

Jesus was raised (resurrected) on the "third" day. This is substantiated in Matthew 16:21; Matthew 17:23; Matthew 20:19; Mark 9:31; Mark 10:34; Luke 9:22; Luke 18:33; Luke

24:7; Luke 24:46; Acts 10:40, and First Corinthians 15:4.

Furthermore, based on Genesis 22:5, in which Abraham said to his young men, *"STAY HERE with the donkey; the lad and I will GO YONDER and WORSHIP, and WE* [Abraham and Isaac] *will COME BACK to you. "* (NKJV) (emphasis added).

Do not dismiss the significance of what Abraham professed out loud, despite the ominous dread and uncertainty he must have been feeling! Abraham, like Jesus, did not allow his emotions to keep him from obeying God's will without delay. Abraham essentially said, "We will worship and then we will come back to you." Abraham didn't say, "I will come back," he said, "we will come back to you."

Thus, Abraham trusted *Yehóvãh* so much that he had faith to believe that somehow *Yehóvãh* would come through for him by either not requiring him to kill his beloved son Isaac, or He would raise Isaac from the dead if Abraham had to follow through with what he was told to do.

In addition, we must remember that based on Galatians 3:8 we already know that the gospel was preached to Abraham before it was ever written.

Therefore, the specific reference to it being the "third" day in Genesis 22:4 (when Abraham lifted his eyes and *saw* "the" place "afar off") foreshadows what Jesus Christ would do when He defeated death on the "third" day. He would be resurrected from the grave after being in the heart of the earth for three days and three nights.

This is based on Matthew 12:40 which says, *"For as Jonah was three DAYS and three NIGHTS in the BELLY of the great FISH, so will the Son of Man be three DAYS and three NIGHTS in the HEART of the EARTH."* (NKJV) (emphasis added).

Hence, *Yehovah* gave Abraham a prophetic vision at the *same* place of what would take place "afar off" in the future concerning the death and resurrection of Jesus Christ. We are told in Genesis 22:4 that Abraham lifted his eyes.

Where did Abraham lift his eyes? Upwards towards *Yehovah* in heaven who unveiled the *prophetic* vision to Abraham of the re-enactment of a pilgrimage similar to the one Abraham was making now with his beloved son Isaac.

In addition, *Yehovah* showed Abraham that He would indeed provide a sacrificial lamb, without spot or blemish—His only *begotten* Son, Jesus Christ.

He would be "the" perfect "Passover Lamb," and this would come to pass "afar off" at the "appointed" time in the future.

Moreover, *Yehovah* was leading Abraham to take his son Isaac to Mount Moriah, the *same* exact location where Jesus would later be crucified on the cross at Calvary.

God's Word substantiates that Abraham did *prophetically* see Jesus Christ's death and resurrection. This is based on John 8:56 which proclaims, *"Your father Abraham rejoiced to SEE*

127

My DAY, and HE SAW IT and was GLAD." (NKJV) (emphasis added). This is exactly what happened! And, this is why the very next thing Abraham says to the young men who were with him is that he and Isaac would come back to them after they worshiped *Yehôvâh.*

God had revealed to Abraham that He would send His only *begotten* Son, Jesus Christ, to die on the cross as a sacrificial offering and He would be raised on the "third" day so Isaac wouldn't have to be sacrificed. Thus, this was indeed a reason for Abraham to rejoice to see His day "afar off" and want to worship *Yehôvâh* like never before!

Furthermore, this is why in the next passage of Scripture in Genesis 22:6–8, Abraham says to his son Isaac after Isaac asked where the lamb for the burnt offering was, that God Himself would provide the lamb for a burnt offering and indeed He did!

Therefore, *Yehôvâh* showed Abraham in a *prophetic* vision that He would indeed sacrifice His only *begotten* Son, Jesus Christ, "the" perfect "Passover Lamb" in the future.

Genesis 22:6–8, says the following:

> *"So Abraham took the WOOD of the BURNT OFFERING and LAID IT ON Isaac, his son; and he took the fire in his hand, and a knife and the two of them went together. But Isaac spoke to Abraham his father and said, 'My father!' And*

he said, 'Here I am, my son.' Then he said, 'Look, the FIRE and the WOOD, but WHERE is the LAMB for a BURNT OFFERING?' And Abraham said, 'My son, GOD will PROVIDE for HIMSELF the LAMB for a BURNT OFFERING.' So the two of them went together. " (Gen. 22:6–8, NKJV) (emphasis added).

Based on Genesis 22:6–8, there are two "key" prophetic shadow pictures I would like to briefly elaborate on which are as follows:

PROPHETIC SHADOW PICTURE #1

First, Abraham was prophetically declaring and enacting exactly what would happen in the future when God would indeed provide the sacrificial lamb—His only *begotten* Son, Jesus Christ.

As illustrated in this story, God always uses His people on the earth to *prophetically* "decree," "declare," and "enact" His will on the earth as it is in heaven before His will shall manifest in the *physical* (earthly) realm.

Therefore, Abraham was being used by God to prophetically "decree," "declare," and "enact" what *Yehôvâh* would later do when He sacrificed His only *begotten* Son, Jesus Christ. As a matter of fact, God showed Abraham in advance what would happen at Calvary when Jesus would become "the" perfect "Passover Lamb" and shed His precious blood for the forgiveness of our sins because Jesus would become the mediator of the New Covenant.

This would "confirm" (renew) the *everlasting* covenant God established with Abraham and his descendants at the very beginning!

God's Word substantiates this fact in Genesis 14:18–20. We are told that *the Word* who is Melchizedek, *king of Salem,* came and met with Abram long before His heavenly Father would send Him to the earth as the Son of Man in the Person of Jesus Christ in order to shed His blood at Calvary.

Why is this pivotal act that we read about in Genesis 14:18–20 so critical for us to understand? It is because God was renewing (re-confirming) the *everlasting* covenant He made with Abram at the very beginning. In fact, the *first* covenant that God established through Moses with all the children of Israel, as well as the New Covenant, was for the purpose of renewing (re-confirming) the *everlasting* covenant that God established with Abraham and his descendants which God swore by Himself to keep forever!

Notice as you read Genesis 14:18–20, *the Word* who is Melchizedek, *king of Salem*, and Abram were prophetically enacting the Passover Seder under the New Covenant.

The only two elements needed to "do" this in "remembrance" of the great sacrifice Jesus would fulfill, would be "bread" and "wine." Genesis 14:18–20, says the following:

"Then Melchizedek king of Salem brought out BREAD and WINE; he was the PRIEST of God Most High. And he [the Word who is Melchizedek the King of Salem] BLESSED him [Abram] and said: 'BLESSED be Abram of God Most High [El Elyon], POSSESSOR of HEAVEN and EARTH;And BLESSED be God Most High [El Elyon], Who has DELIVERED your ENEMIES into your HAND.' And he [Abram] gave him [the Word who is Melchizedek the King of Salem] a TITHE of ALL." (Gen. 14:18–20, NKJV) (emphasis added).

Yes, indeed *the Word* is commemorating with Abram what He would later do with His disciples on the night before He became "the" "Passover Lamb," when Jesus and His disciples prepared the Passover.

This is detailed in Matthew 26:17–30, Luke 22:7–23, and Mark 14:12–26 where the only two elements Jesus focused on for *that* particular Passover meal were "bread" and "wine" because Jesus would become "the" "Passover Lamb" at *this* particular Passover.

PROPHETIC SHADOW PICTURE #2

Second, when Abraham split the wood for the burnt offering, the wood symbolized the cross that Jesus would later be crucified on. When Abraham laid the wood on his son Isaac, this was a *prophetic* enactment of what *Simon the Cyrenian* would later do for Jesus Christ.

They laid the cross on Simon that he might bear it after Jesus as Jesus made His pilgrimage up to Calvary based on Matthew 27:32–37, Mark 15:21–22, Luke 23:26–32, and John 19:16–18.

Now let's see what happens next based on Genesis 22:9–12. As so often is the case, God waits until the very last minute to intervene on our behalf. God does this for several reasons:

1. To see if we fully trust Him by being obedient to do what He says.

2. To grow our faith and for us to know that we can trust Him to rescue us in perilous circumstances.

3. To elevate us to the next level because we have passed the test based on our obedience.

As such, Abraham passed the *ultimate* test, demonstrating to *Yehóvah* that Abraham *reverentially* feared Him and would do anything to obey Him when he chose not to withhold his *only* son Isaac from Him.

This is substantiated in Genesis 22:9–12, which says the following:

> *"Then they came to the PLACE of which God had TOLD him. And Abraham built an ALTAR there and PLACED the WOOD in order; and*

he BOUND Isaac his son and LAID him on the
ALTAR, upon the WOOD. And Abraham
STRETCHED out his HAND and took the
KNIFE to SLAY his son." (Gen. 22:9–10, NKJV)
(emphasis added).

"But the ANGEL of the LORD called to him
[Abraham] from heaven and said, 'Abraham,
Abraham!' So he said, 'Here I am.' And He
[*Yehôvâh*] said, 'Do not lay your hand on the
lad, or do anything to him; For NOW I KNOW
THAT YOU FEAR GOD, since YOU HAVE not
WITHHELD YOUR SON, YOUR only SON,
from ME.'" (Gen. 22:11–12, NKJV) (emphasis
added).

God tested Abraham's heart, evidenced by his willingness to
offer everything he had, including his beloved and *only* son
Isaac, to please the One he served. It was only then *Yehôvâh*
intervened as shown in Genesis 22:13–14, which says the
following:

"Then Abraham LIFTED HIS EYES and
LOOKED, and there behind him was a RAM
caught in a thicket by its horns. So Abraham
WENT and TOOK THE RAM, and OFFERED
IT UP for a BURNT OFFERING instead of HIS
SON. And Abraham called the NAME of the
PLACE, *THE-LORD-WILL-PROVIDE* (13)
[H3070: *Yehôvâh Yir'eh*: Jehovah will see (to

133

it); *Jehovah-Jireh*, a symbolical name for Mt. Moriah]; *as it is said to this DAY, 'In the MOUNT of the LORD* [Mount Moriah] *it shall be PROVIDED.'"* (Gen. 22:13–14, NKJV) (emphasis added).

At the last possible moment, *Yehôváh* provided a ram that had been caught in a thicket to be sacrificed to Him as a burnt offering.

Thus Isaac, the son to whom the promises God gave to Abraham would come through for all of Abraham's *spiritual* descendants forevermore, was indeed spared. *Yehôváh* Himself provided a substitute burnt offering in Isaac's place.

However, the story and the prophetic shadow picture of Abraham offering Isaac as a sacrifice, which was a prophetic enactment of what Jesus Christ would later fulfill after His crucifixion, burial, and resurrection does not end here. We need to take another look at Genesis 22:15–19, which says the following:

"Then the Angel of the LORD called to Abraham a second time out of heaven, and said: "By Myself I have sworn, says the LORD, because you have done this thing, and have not withheld your son, your only son— blessing I will bless you, and multiplying I will multiply your descendants as the stars of the heaven and

as the sand which is on the seashore; and your descendants shall possess the gate of their enemies. In your seed all the nations of the earth shall be blessed, because you have obeyed My voice." So ABRAHAM RETURNED TO HIS YOUNG MEN, and THEY ROSE and WENT TOGETHER TO BEERSHEBA; and ABRAHAM DWELT AT BEERSHEBA." (Gen. 22:15–19, NKJV) (emphasis added).

At this time I want you to focus your attention on the last verse of this passage of Scripture we just read in Genesis 22:15–19. We are specifically told in Genesis 22:19, *"So ABRAHAM RETURNED TO HIS YOUNG MEN, and they rose and went together to Beersheba; and Abraham dwelt at Beersheba."* (NKJV) (emphasis added).

Based on this Scripture we are specifically told *only* Abraham returned to his young men even though when they began this pilgrimage we are told in Genesis 22:5, *"And Abraham said to his YOUNG MEN, 'Stay here with the donkey; the LAD* [Isaac] *and I* [Abraham] *will go yonder and worship, and WE will COME BACK to YOU.'"* (NKJV) (emphasis added).

What happened to Isaac and why didn't he come back with Abraham when Abraham returned to his young men?

We are told the answer to what happened to Isaac, *figuratively* speaking, in Hebrews 11:17–19, which says the following:

"By faith Abraham, when he was tested, offered

135

up Isaac, and he who had received the promises offered up his only begotten son, of whom it was said, 'In Isaac your seed shall be called,' concluding that *GOD WAS ABLE TO RAISE HIM UP, EVEN FROM THE DEAD, FROM WHICH HE ALSO RECEIVED HIM IN A FIGURATIVE SENSE.'"* (Heb. 11:17–19, NKJV) (emphasis added).

In fact, the two young men Abraham took with him are the two witnesses that could attest that God would "raise up" Isaac from the dead and also received him in a *figurative* sense for this reason: The two young men represent the two angels we read about in John 20:12 that Mary saw when she went to the empty tomb because Jesus had already been resurrected. These two angels in white were sitting one at the head and the other at the feet where the body of Jesus had lain.

THE SIGNIFICANCE OF THE "THIRD" DAY

Since Isaac represents Jesus Christ, who was "raised" (resurrected) from the grave on the "third" day after His death and burial, and He (Jesus) was "received" by God as the *firstfruits* of the wave offering when Jesus ascended into heaven on Sunday, the day after the weekly Sabbath, the "third" day has many profound prophetic meanings.

One meaning is this: Since Jesus went back to His Father in

heaven, then God, the Father, sent His Holy Spirit to not only find a bride for His Son, the Holy Spirit has also given His bride spiritual gifts. Hence, the "third" day specifically relates to the *bride of Christ.*

Again, we are told in Genesis 22:4 that it was on the "third" day when Abraham lifted his eyes and saw the place afar off. This prophetic vision the Lord gave to Abraham has a dual fulfillment.

The first fulfillment of this vision is the fact that Abraham saw Jesus Christ's death and resurrection—which was why Isaac did not have to be killed. The second fulfillment of this vision is Abraham also saw the Day of the Lord when the "marriage supper of the Lamb" would take place as well.

In fact, the "third" day specifically refers to a wedding taking place.

And, it is for this very reason, based on Hebrews 11:17–19 after God, *figuratively* speaking, "raised" Isaac up—from the dead, and God "received" him because Isaac represents Jesus Christ, the next time we hear mention of Isaac, the *Son of the Promise,* being "seen" again is two chapters later in Genesis 24. Just like Jesus, Isaac, disappeared until he was ready to receive his bride.

Genesis Chapter 24 is about Abraham sending his servant to look for a bride for his beloved son Isaac. The servant in this passage of Scripture represents the Holy Spirit who is sent by God the Father after Jesus Christ was crucified and resurrected from the grave to look for a bride for God the Father's only *begotten,* Son. Again, Abraham represents God, the Father and Abraham's only *begotten* son—Isaac represents Jesus Christ who is God's only *begotten* Son.

When Isaac did not come back down from Mount Moriah with Abraham, it was because God *figuratively* speaking, "raised" Isaac up—from the dead, and God "received" him into heaven, *spiritually* speaking, because he was crucified with Christ and would be raised with Christ in the heavenly places.

We have the tendency to look at this great test of Abraham's faith from Abraham's perspective when God asked Abraham to sacrifice his only *begotten* son of his love—Isaac.

Yet God was also testing Isaac to see if he was willing to die for his faith based on his obedience to not only his earthly father Abraham but also based on his unwavering devotion and obedience to His heavenly Father as well.

Just as Jesus Christ would later do for all of us, Isaac was willing to give his life because this is what his father asked of him. As such, he was "counted worthy" because he, like Jesus, was willing to die so he could receive his bride. And, this is why after *Yehóvah* tested Isaac's obedience and willingness to give his life that we are told in Genesis Chapter 24 that his father Abraham knew it was time to find an acceptable wife for his beloved son because he was ready to receive her.

It is for this very reason, at the end of Genesis Chapter 24 we are told that Isaac brought Rebekah into the tent of his mother, Sarah. It was then Isaac took Rebekah, and she became his wife, and he loved her.

Therefore, Genesis Chapter 24 is a prophetic enactment of what would happen later on after Jesus Christ died and rose from the grave and ascended back up into heaven because God had received Him. God received Him because He did the will of His Father and was willing to die for His bride.

Jesus who is *the Word* that became flesh would go to His Father's house to prepare a place for His bride so that where He was, there she would also be in the Spirit until He physically came back for her at the "appointed" time.

As a result of Jesus Christ going to the Father after He died, was raised, and ascended into heaven, the Holy Spirit would be sent to abide with and in His bride until Jesus was done preparing a place for her at his Father's house.

Then when the Father decided it was time for His Son to go get His bride, then the Son would receive His bride unto Himself.

Hence, since Isaac represents Jesus Christ, God tested him to see if he was ready to die for his bride so he could receive her unto himself as his wife.

Again, the entire Bible is about God's betrothal to His beloved bride—the children of Israel who are all *spiritual* descendants of Abraham. And, it is for this very reason, why one of the prophetic meanings of the significance of the "third" day has to do with "when" the children of Israel entered into the "Covenant of Marriage."

They entered into a "Covenant of Marriage" on the "third" day with the Lord at the base of Mount Sinai when the law was given by His servant Moses. This is substantiated in Exodus 19:11, Exodus 19:15, and Exodus 19:16.

Therefore, as in the case of Isaac disappearing when Abraham came back to the young men when he came down from Mount Moriah, the next time we see Jesus Christ it will be when the "consummation" of our wedding takes place.

This will happen on the "third" day at the dawn of the third millennium since the time Jesus Christ died, was resurrected from the grave, and went back to His Father's house located in heaven to prepare a place for us.

He will come back for us when He sends His angels to gather together His elect at the dawn of the seventh millennium.

This is the total amount of time (based on the creation week) that God has allowed mankind to "rule" and "reign" on the earth since God formed the first Adam from the dust of the earth.

Following are examples of the relevance of the "third" day according to the whole counsel of God's Word:

❖ As it was in the beginning in Exodus 19:11, so it shall be in the end. The *bride of Christ* must be ready for the "third" day for on the "third" day the Lord will come down from heaven in a cloud, and every eye will see Him. This is when Jesus will once again "confirm" all of God's *everlasting* covenants based on Revelation 11:19.

Based on Exodus 19:16, it will come to pass that on the "third" day, in the morning, that there will be thunderings and lightnings, and a thick cloud on the mountain and the sound of the trumpet will be very loud.

At the sound of the last trump, the dead will be raised, and those few who are still alive and remain on planet earth shall be "caught up" (raptured) together with them (the dead in Christ) in the clouds to meet the Lord in the air.

Thus, we shall always be with the Lord. This is substantiated in First Thessalonians 4:15–17.

❖ It was on the "third" day that there was a wedding in Cana of Galilee based on John 2:1.

❖ We are specifically told it will be on the "third" day we

141

shall go up to the house of the Lord. This is based on Second Kings 20:5 and 20:8

❖ It was on the "third" day that Esther put on her royal *robes* and stood in the inner court of the king's palace, across from the king's house, while the king sat on his royal throne in the royal house. This is based on Esther 5:1.

❖ After two days, He will revive us, and on the "third" day He will raise us up so we may live in His sight based on Hosea 6:2.

It has been over 2,000 years since Jesus was crucified. 2,000 years equals two days based on Second Peter 3:8.

Therefore, when the dawn of 3,000 years occurs (which equates to the "third" day) since the time Jesus was crucified, buried, and resurrected, then we will be "raised up" or "caught up" to be with Him forevermore.

Again, the significance of the "third" day in all these examples is symbolic of "when" the children of Israel entered into a "Covenant of Marriage" with our heavenly Father as a nation because of His *everlasting* covenant with Abraham and his descendants. It is our wedding anniversary as the body of Christ, *spiritually* speaking! In fact, every time we keep the

Feast of Trumpets which is a memorial of the blowing of trumpets that first happened at the base of Mount Sinai when the law was given to the children of Israel, we are "renewing" our wedding vows we made with our heavenly Father as His *holy* nation and *royal* priesthood. We are commanded to commemorate the Feast of Trumpets, which is an *everlasting* ordinance, based on Leviticus 23:23–25.

Whereas, every year that we commemorate Passover in "remembrance" of what Jesus did on the cross at Calvary when He was willing to die for us, His bride, so we may be restored into a "covenant" relationship with our heavenly Father, we are "renewing" our individual marriage vows we entered into when we accepted Jesus Christ as our personal Lord and Savior.

When we commemorate Passover which is an *everlasting* ordinance based on Leviticus 23:4–8, we are acknowledging before the Father, the Son, and the Holy Spirit that Jesus Christ is our Passover Lamb and we have been made "righteous" and we are "justified" by His precious blood.

The last example I will use to substantiate the significance of the "third" day is this relevant truth: The "marriage supper of the Lamb" will take place at the dawn (in the morning) of the third millennium (which represents the "third" day since 3,000 years equals three days based on Second Peter 3:8) since Jesus Christ died for His bride whom He is coming back for so we can be where He now is. Jesus is currently at our heavenly Father's house preparing many mansions for us in the city of the living God—Mount Zion in the *heavenly* Jerusalem. This is based on Hebrews 12:22–24.

In summary, as disciples of Jesus Christ, we are Abraham's *spiritual* descendants. And, as such, we too shall be blessed along with Abraham *if* we seek after the *Lord of the harvest* for who He is, rather than for what He can do for us!

This truth is substantiated in Genesis 22:15–19. And, this includes us being willing to give up everything for His name's sake as Abraham did, including allowing "our" dreams to die so that God can resurrect them at the "appointed" time. Genesis 22:15–19, says the following:

> *"Then the ANGEL of the LORD* [Yehóvah] *called to Abraham a second time OUT of HEAVEN, and said: 'BY MYSELF I HAVE SWORN, says the LORD, BECAUSE you have DONE this THING, and HAVE not WITHHELD YOUR SON, YOUR only SON— blessing I will BLESS you, and multiplying I will MULTIPLY YOUR DESCENDANTS as the stars of the heaven and as the sand which is on the seashore; and YOUR DESCENDANTS shall POSSESS the GATE of their ENEMIES. In YOUR SEED all the NATIONS of the EARTH shall be BLESSED, Because YOU HAVE OBEYED My VOICE.' So Abraham returned to his young men, and they rose and went*

144

together to **BEERSHEBA** (14) [H884: *B'ér Sheba': well of an oath; Beer Sheba*, a place in Palestine]; and Abraham *dwelt* at **BEERSHEBA**." (14) (Gen. 22:15–19, NKJV) (emphasis added).

Based on Abraham's "obedience" to God which was proven when he did not withhold his only son, Isaac, from the Lord is why God told Abraham in Genesis 22:18, *"In YOUR SEED all the NATIONS of the EARTH shall be BLESSED, Because you have OBEYED My VOICE."* (NKJV) (emphasis added).

Therefore, if we want to "inherit" the promises God gave to Abraham and his descendants, we too must "obey" God's Voice and His Word.

THE SIGNIFICANCE OF BEERSHEBA

After this declaration of the Lord was made which is based on Genesis 22:15–19, we are told Abraham dwelt in Beersheba. This place called Beersheba is worth looking at more closely so we may discover why Abraham chose to dwell there.

Beersheba, the land of the Philistines, is the *same* place where Abraham made a covenant with Abimelech based on Genesis 21:22–34.

This covenant was the result of the kindness Abimelech showed Abraham when Abraham rebuked Abimelech because of a well of water which Abimelech's servants had seized.

Abimelech told Abraham that he did not know who had seized this well of water and he had not heard about it until Abraham mentioned it.

Abraham called this place Beersheba because the two of them swore an oath and made a covenant there.

Abraham would swear to Abimelech and his offspring (his posterity) that according to the kindness Abimelech had shown Abraham, he would return to him and to the land in which Abraham dwelt.

Now you know one of the reasons why Israel has always shown kindness to the Philistines who dwell in their land even as it is to this *very* day.

It was *after* Abraham and Abimelech made this covenant that Abraham planted a tamarisk tree in Beersheba and called on the name of the Lord as *El Olam,* which means "the Everlasting God" which is based on Genesis 21:33.

Also, Beersheba is the *same* place where Ishmael and Hagar wandered in the wilderness after God told Abraham to send them away, based on Genesis 21:14.

God promised Abraham that He would make a nation of his *firstborn* son Ishmael because he was Abraham's "seed."

Beersheba was also the *same* place where God told Hagar to arise and lift up the lad, Ishmael, and hold him with her hand for He would make Ishmael a great nation.

God "remembered" His promises to Abraham who called upon Him as *El Olam* (the Everlasting God) in this *same* location.

As a result, it was right after this that God unveiled Hagar's eyes so she could see the well of water that Abimelech's servants had seized earlier so that Hagar could give Ishmael a drink of water from that *same* well. Ishmael would not perish in the wilderness for God heard the lad's cry. He would bless Abraham's *firstborn* son Ishmael because God "remembered" His *everlasting* covenant with Abraham and his descendants.

This attests to the fact that our God is a covenant keeping God. He is faithful to His covenant promises to His people despite our wayward ways. It is all about fulfilling His "redemptive" *eternal* purposes, which shall come to pass so that His *eternal* Word shall accomplish that for which He has sent it.

In Chapter 33 of this book, I will cover in detail how Abraham inherited great wealth and prosperity while he still lived on the earth as a result of his devotion to the *Lord of the harvest,* which is a testimony to us all.

In Chapter 34 of this book, I will cover in detail how Abraham's son Isaac inherited great wealth and prosperity as God used almost the same set of circumstances as He did with Abraham.

In Chapter 35 of this book, I will cover in detail how we, as disciples of Jesus Christ can, like Abraham, reap financial blessings despite the coming worldwide economic collapse *if* we first *seek* God's Kingdom and His righteousness above all else.

In Chapter 36 of this book, I will cover in detail how, like Abraham, New Covenant believers must be "obedient" to God's Voice and His Word in order to inherit God's covenant promises that He gave to Abraham and his descendants.

These promises are "activated" by our "faith" but "inherited" by our "obedience" to God's Voice and Word.

In Chapter 54 of Book 3, I will cover in detail how we need to fully understand the "blessings" that we will reap for "keeping" God's covenants and the "curses" that we will reap for "breaking" God's covenants.

This determines whether or not we will inherit the promises given by God to Abraham and his descendants.

However, in the next few chapters, we will take a closer look at some of the underlying causes of this "ancient" jealousy and hatred between the descendants of Isaac and the descendants of Ishmael.

This animosity continues in the next generation with Esau and Jacob—Isaac's two sons and Abraham's grandsons.

All these things are extremely relevant to all believers in Jesus Christ, the Orthodox Jews, and the state of Israel for a time such as this.

CHAPTER 26

WHAT ARE SOME OF THE UNDERLYING CAUSES OF THIS "ANCIENT" JEALOUSY AND HATRED BETWEEN THE CHILDREN OF ISRAEL AND THE DESCENDANTS OF ISHMAEL AND ESAU?

There are many factors which have fueled this "ancient" jealousy and hatred between the descendants of Abraham, Isaac, and Jacob (Israel) versus the descendants of Abraham, Ishmael, and Esau.

Shortly we will closely examine what some of these factors are that have contributed to this "ancient" jealousy and hatred.

But before we do, I need to briefly clarify who Abraham's descendants are, what religion they adhere to, that determines which God they worship and serve.

There is a lot of confusion in the body of Christ which is leading many of God's people astray. Therefore, this must be addressed.

The descendants of Abraham, refer to, but are not limited to, the following people groups:

❖ Abraham's "physical" descendants include the Orthodox Jews who practice Judaism. This sect of Jews is still *spiritually* blinded to the truth that Jesus Christ is their Messiah who has already come. All they need to do to be saved is to receive the revelation Jesus Christ is their Messiah and receive Him as their Lord and Savior.

❖ Abraham's "physical" descendants include the descendants of Ishmael and Esau, otherwise referred to as the Edomites who predominantly adhere to the Islamic faith. All they need to do to be saved is to receive the revelation Jesus Christ is their Messiah and receive Him as their Lord and Savior.

❖ Abraham's "spiritual" descendants refer to both the Jews from the House of Judah and those of us who were former Gentiles from the House of Israel who believe in Jesus Christ and has received Him as their Lord and Savior.

Even though each of these people groups started out as being descendants of Abraham, the similarities end there. Because there is a BIG difference between the "spiritual" descendants of Abraham versus the "physical" descendants of Abraham which is this: The God they worship and serve.

When people due to their ignorance say there are "three" Abrahamic faiths (Judaism, Islam, and Christianity), they are essentially saying Abraham did not worship and serve the one and *only* true God which Abraham did, and he practiced monotheism. Monotheism is a religion or belief system that involves serving and worshiping just one God. Rather, they are erroneously insinuating Abraham practiced polytheism. Polytheism is the worship or belief in multiple deities or gods.

In fact, this is one of the reasons why God made Abraham leave his country, his family, and his father's house and go to a land that He would show him in the first place. Abraham refused to worship all the false idols and the false gods that were prevalent in his country, his family, and his father's house. See Joshua 24:2.

Instead, Abraham chose to follow a different path to worship the one and *only* true God.

Therefore, we must briefly examine this "major" difference concerning which God the descendants of Abraham serve and worship more closely. The three different religions of Judaism, Islam, and Christianity can be categorized as follows:

❖ The Orthodox Jews are "physical" descendants of Abraham who worship and serve *Yehóvah* (Yahweh [YHWH]), the God of Abraham, Isaac, and Jacob (Israel) but they are not "spiritual" descendants of Abraham for this reason: They deny Jesus Christ is the Son of God and that He has come in the flesh. They are still waiting for their Messiah.

❖ The descendants of Ishmael and Esau do not worship and serve *Yehóvah* (Yahweh [YHWH]), the God of Abraham, Isaac, and Jacob (Israel). Rather, they worship and serve Allah the ancient moon god. They say their God is the same God that Christians worship and serve—the God of Abraham. However, this is not true for the following three main reasons: 1) They deny Jesus Christ is the Son of God; 2) They deny He is God; 3) They deny Jesus Christ died on the cross.

❖ The Jews from the House of Judah and those of us who were formerly Gentiles from the House of Israel worship and serve *Yehóváh* (Yahweh [YHWH]), the God of Abraham, Isaac, and Jacob (Israel) and they acknowledge these truths: 1) Jesus Christ is the Son of God; 2) Jesus Christ is God; 3) Jesus Christ came in the flesh; 4) Jesus Christ was crucified on the cross at Calvary for the forgiveness of our sins as He shed His precious blood; and 5) He was resurrected from death and the grave.

Just the very fact that Judaism and Islam denies 1) Jesus Christ is the Son of God; 2) Jesus Christ is God, and 3) Jesus Christ did not come in the flesh, should be the end of all controversy regarding this subject of there being "three" Abrahamic faiths for disciples of Jesus Christ.

However, in Chapter 32 of this book, I will cover this indisputable truth in-depth for this reason: We are never to worship or participate in a joint-activity with "unbelievers" for the following four main reasons:

1. They deny Jesus is the Son of God.

2. They deny He is God.
3. They deny He came in the flesh.
4. They deny He was crucified and died on the cross at Calvary.

Those that practice Judaism and Islam have the *Spirit of Antichrist* because they deny Jesus Christ is the Son of God and He is God who came in the flesh.

Yet many evangelicals are participating in worship or in a joint-activity in our quest for peace and unity under the guise of love when God's Word clearly tells us we are not to do so in Second Corinthians Chapter 6. This chapter starts out with the apostle Paul pleading with believers to not receive the grace of God in vain!

Now let's focus our attention on the descendants of Ishmael and Esau who are often referred to as the Edomites. In fact, *some* of the modern day Edomites are the Palestinian people who came up into Jerusalem prior to 1967 when Jerusalem was given back to Israel.

Israel reacquired Jerusalem as their capital when the Arab nations lost the *Six Day War*. Yet the Palestinian people still want their own state, even though this is the land that God promised to Abraham as a result of the *everlasting* covenant God made with Abraham and his descendants.

Therefore, the Palestinian people remain a displaced people group since they are refugees of war who have settled predominately in the Gaza strip region of Israel and some parts of Jerusalem. After the fall of the Ottoman Empire in World War I, the name Palestine was revived and applied to the land falling under the British Mandate for Palestine. Arabs use the name "Falastin" for Palestine, an Arab pronunciation of the Roman word "Palaestina." [1]

It is also interesting to note that all three major world religions—Judaism, Christianity, and Islam, started with the God of Abraham. However, the God that Islam serves is Allah, the pagan moon god.

Therefore, the God that Islam serves and worships, Allah, is not the same God of Abraham, Isaac, and Jacob (Israel) that the Jews and the Christians believe in, serve, and worship.

For now, let's focus our attention on the five main reasons attributing to this underlying cause of this "ancient" jealousy and hatred between the Jews and Christians versus the Arab and Muslim people who for the most part practice Islam.

I will cover the five reasons in detail in subsequent chapters. However, the five main reasons are as follows:

1. Abraham was forced to abandon and reject his *firstborn* son Ishmael and his other sons as well; giving everything, he possessed to Isaac, the *Son of the Promise*.

2. God orchestrated the beginning of the "enmity" between the descendants of Esau and Jacob (Israel) as

two nations while they were still in their mother's womb.

3. Esau "despised" and "forfeited" his "birthright" as the *firstborn* son of Isaac; therefore, Jacob became the heir to the promises that God gave to Abraham.

4. Despite Jacob's lying, deception, and trickery, God still chose him to be the son through whom He would "confirm" the promises that He gave to Abraham and his descendants as an *everlasting* covenant to Israel.

5. Control and possession of the Promised Land.

For the remainder of this chapter, we will look at the first reason why *some* descendants of Ishmael and Esau have this "ancient" jealousy and hatred towards the children of Israel. These feelings are because of the "spirit of rejection" and the "orphan spirit" that Ishmael, Abraham's *firstborn* son, was plagued with after Abraham was forced to abandon and reject him.

REASON # 1: ABRAHAM WAS FORCED TO ABANDON AND REJECT HIS FIRSTBORN SON ISHMAEL

Think about how Ishmael must have felt when he was abandoned by his father, Abraham. Ishmael was a young teenager when he was sent away, based on the fact we are told in Genesis 17:25 that Ishmael was thirteen years old when he was circumcised.

Therefore, Ishmael was old enough to know what was going on and he must have been experiencing the bitter sting of rejection.

As is the case with all young boys, they need their father to teach them *how* to become a man. Yet in one day, Ishmael loses his dad, his family, his life, and his inheritance. In one day his life was changed forever!

Hence, the "spirit of rejection" and the "orphan spirit" that Ishmael was plagued with from long ago is still one of the underlying factors and a "root" cause of *some* Arab and Muslim people's "ancient" jealousy or hatred against God's "chosen" people.

Moreover, it is interesting to note that according to the excerpt below, taken from *Wikipedia,* that Muhammad, believed by Muslims to be a messenger and the last prophet sent by God, was also orphaned.[2]

> *"Who is believed by Muslims and Bahá'ís to be a messenger and prophet of God, Muhammad is almost universally[n 1] considered by Muslims as the last prophet sent by God to mankind.[2][n 2] While non-Muslims regard Muhammad as the founder of Islam,[3] Muslims consider him to have restored the unaltered original monotheistic faith of Adam, Noah, Abraham,*

Moses, Jesus, and other prophets.[4][5][6][7] Born in about 570 CE in the Arabian city of Mecca,[8][9] MUHAMMAD WAS ORPHANED AT AN EARLY AGE..." According to Muslim tradition, Muhammad himself was a Hanif and one of the descendants of Ishmael, son of Abraham.[46] "* [end of excerpt]

Therefore, do you believe it is a coincidence that Muhammad and Ishmael were both orphaned at an early age? Especially since according to Muslim "tradition" Muhammad is one of the descendants of Ishmael, the *firstborn* son of Abraham.

Now let's refocus our attention on Ishmael's plight, based on Genesis 21:9–16. This passage of Scripture details this pivotal sad story in the life of young Ishmael who was sent away and lost everything in one day due to Sarah's jealousy and intolerance of both Ishmael and Hagar. Sarah had finally reached her capacity to endure dealing with them any longer *when* she witnessed Ishmael scoffing (mocking) during a great feast that Abraham had made on the *same* day that Isaac was weaned.

Ishmael's mocking during this feast celebrating Isaac being weaned was *the straw that broke the camel's back* for Sarah. She not only demanded that her husband Abraham "cast out" her servant Hagar and Hagar's son Ishmael, but Sarah also insisted that Ishmael not be an "heir" with her son Isaac. As you can imagine, this matter was *very* displeasing in Abraham's sight because of his *firstborn* son Ishmael.

Nevertheless, God told Abraham to listen to Sarah.

This is substantiated in Genesis 21:12 which says, "...*Do not let it be displeasing in your sight because of the lad or because of your bondwoman. Whatever Sarah has said to you, listen to her voice; for in Isaac your seed shall be called.*" (NKJV)

As difficult as this was for Abraham, he obeyed God's instructions despite his feelings. He rose early the next morning, sending Hagar and his *firstborn* son Ishmael away with *only* bread and a skin of water for their provision.

Sometimes God will ask us to do painful things that we do not understand because of His *eternal* "redemptive" plan. We need to be obedient *despite* how we feel.

Now let's witness this drama unfold in Genesis 21:9–16, which says the following:

> "*And Sarah saw the SON of HAGAR the Egyptian, whom she had borne to Abraham, SCOFFING. Therefore she* [Sarah] *said to Abraham, 'CAST OUT this BONDWOMAN* [Hagar] *and her SON* [Ishmael]*; for the SON of this BONDWOMAN shall not be HEIR with my SON, namely with ISAAC.' And the matter was very DISPLEASING in Abraham's sight BECAUSE of his son* [Ishmael]*.*" (Gen. 21:9–11, NKJV) (emphasis added).

158

"But God said to Abraham, 'Do not let it be DISPLEASING IN YOUR SIGHT BECAUSE OF THE LAD [Ishmael] *or BECAUSE OF YOUR BONDWOMAN* [Hagar]. *Whatever SARAH HAS SAID to you, LISTEN to HER VOICE; For in ISAAC, YOUR SEED shall be CALLED. Yet I will also make a NATION of the SON* [Ishmael] *of the BONDWOMAN* [Hagar], *BECAUSE he* [Ishmael] *is YOUR SEED.'"* (Gen. 21:12–13, NKJV) (emphasis added).

"So Abraham rose early in the morning, and took BREAD and a SKIN of WATER; and putting it on her [Hagar] *shoulder, he gave it and the boy* [Ishmael] *to Hagar, and SENT HER AWAY. Then she DEPARTED and WANDERED in the WILDERNESS of BEERSHEBA. And the WATER in the SKIN was USED UP, and she PLACED the BOY under ONE of the SHRUBS. Then she went and sat down across from him* [Ishmael] *at a distance of about a bowshot; for she said to herself, 'Let me not SEE the DEATH of the BOY.' So she sat opposite him* [Ishmael], *and LIFTED her VOICE and WEPT."* (Gen. 21:14–16, NKJV) (emphasis added).

Now let's focus our attention on what happened when God intervened on behalf of Ishmael and Hagar. In Genesis 21:17–21, even though Ishmael was abandoned and rejected by his earthly father Abraham, his heavenly Father *Yehóvăh,* did not forsake Hagar or Ishmael. God heard Hagar's cry and the voice of the lad as well. As a matter of fact, Ishmael's name means "the Lord hears."

Genesis 21:17–21, says the following:

> *"And God heard the VOICE of the LAD* [Ishmael]. *Then the ANGEL of GOD called to Hagar OUT of HEAVEN, and said to her, 'What ails you, Hagar? FEAR NOT, for GOD has HEARD the VOICE of the LAD* [Ishmael] *where he is. Arise, LIFT UP the LAD* [Ishmael] *and HOLD him with your HAND, for I will make him* [Ishmael] *a great NATION.'"* (Gen. 21:17–18, NKJV) (emphasis added).

> *"Then God opened her* [Hagar] *EYES, and she* [Hagar] *SAW a WELL of WATER. And she* [Hagar] *went and FILLED the SKIN with WATER, and GAVE the LAD a DRINK. So God was with the LAD* [Ishmael]*; and he GREW and DWELT in the WILDERNESS, and became an ARCHER. He* [Ishmael] *dwelt in the WILDERNESS of **PARAN*** [3] [4] [5] [H6290: *pă'răn:* a desert of Arabia: an area of the Hejaz around Mecca in the western region of Saudi Arabia and is known for the Islamic holy cities of Mecca and Medina]*; and his MOTHER*

160

[Hagar] *took a WIFE for him* [Ishmael] *from the LAND of EGYPT."* (Gen. 21:19–21, NKJV) (emphasis added).

The first thing to take notice of based on Genesis 21:17–21, is that this pivotal scene takes place in the *wilderness of Beersheba*, the land of the Philistines. This is the *same* place where Abraham made a covenant with Abimelech based on Genesis 21:22–34.

As you may remember, this concerned the kindness Abimelech showed Abraham when Abraham rebuked Abimelech because of a well of water which Abimelech's servants had seized. Abraham and Abimelech swore an oath that Abraham would not deal falsely with Abimelech, his offspring, or his posterity and that Abraham would return the kindness that Abimelech had shown him and to the land in which he had dwelt.

Abraham planted a tamarisk tree in Beersheba and called on the name of the Lord, as *El Olam,* meaning "the Everlasting God" based on Genesis 21:33.

This is the *same* well of water that God showed to Hagar when He opened up her eyes so she could see the well in order to provide water for her and Ishmael when they wandered in the *wilderness of Beersheba.*

Genesis 21:14 attests to the fact God is a covenant keeping God, "remembering" His covenant with Abraham and his descendants. This is why God heard the voice of Abraham's son Ishmael. And, as in the case of Ishmael (and many children like myself who were abandoned by their earthly parents at a young age and experienced the sting of rejection), God's Word proclaims in Psalm 27:10, *"When my FATHER and my MOTHER forsake me, Then the LORD will TAKE CARE of ME."* (NKJV) (emphasis added).

I know from firsthand experience this is true! For those of us who have been abandoned and rejected by our earthly parents, we will grow up with deep wounds in our souls until we come to the saving knowledge of the *unconditional* "love" and "acceptance" of our heavenly Father.

He will never leave us nor forsake us as we place our faith and trust in His only *begotten* Son, Jesus Christ and we finally submit to the transforming power of the Holy Spirit within our hearts. Only then can we be healed of these deep "spiritual" and "emotional" wounds by us "receiving" our heavenly Father's great love for us!

Therefore, until we realize that nothing can separate us from the love of our heavenly Father, we may act "wild" and "rebellious" as Ishmael did after being abandoned and rejected by those who should love, protect, nurture, and guide us.

Yet only God can save our souls and make us whole by healing our broken hearts.

This is why God's Word tells us the characteristics of Ishmael in Genesis 16:11–12. The characteristics of those who feel rejected by their heavenly Father are often similar to the characteristics of people who have been rejected by their earthly parents, particularly their earthly father. Genesis 16:11–12, says the following:

> *"And the ANGEL of the LORD said to her [Hagar]: 'Behold, you are with CHILD, And you shall BEAR a SON. You shall CALL his NAME ISHMAEL, Because the LORD has HEARD your AFFLICTION. He shall be a WILD MAN; His HAND shall be AGAINST every man, And every man's hand AGAINST him. And he shall DWELL in the PRESENCE of all his BRETHREN.'"* (Gen. 16:11–12, NKJV) (emphasis added).

In addition, we are told in Genesis 25:5–6, that even though Ishmael was Abraham's *firstborn* son, it would be his second born son Isaac, the *Son of the Promise* who would inherit "everything" that Abraham owned, even though Abraham gave gifts to his sons who came from the "concubines" that Abraham had.

Also, notice that this verse says that Abraham sent *them* eastward, meaning it was not just Ishmael that was sent to the country of the east, but also the other sons Abraham had with his concubines. Genesis 25:5–6, says the following:

> *"And Abraham gave all that he HAD to Isaac.*

163

> But Abraham gave GIFTS to the SONS of the CONCUBINES which Abraham HAD; and while he [Abraham] was STILL LIVING, he SENT THEM EASTWARD, away from Isaac, his son, to the COUNTRY of the EAST." (Gen. 25:5–6, NKJV) (emphasis added).

In the next chapter, we will take a look at how God orchestrated the beginning of the "enmity" between the descendants of Esau and Jacob (Israel) while they were still in their mother's womb!

CHAPTER 27

GOD ORCHESTRATED THE BEGINNING OF THE ENMITY BETWEEN THE DESCENDANTS OF ESAU AND JACOB (ISRAEL) WHILE THEY WERE STILL IN THEIR MOTHER'S WOMB

T his "ancient" jealousy, hatred, and rivalry between God's chosen people and *some* Arabs and Muslims who adhere to the Islam faith began with the birth of Ishmael and Isaac, yet it continued with the birth of Isaac's twin sons Esau and Jacob. This feud between the two brothers who were two nations began while they were still in their mother's womb!

Isaac's *firstborn* son was named Esau and his second born son was named Jacob, whose name would later be changed to Israel by God.

This account of the feud between the two brothers, while they were still in their mother's womb is detailed in Genesis 25:21–26, which says the following:

> *"Now Isaac pleaded with the LORD for his wife, because she was barren; and the LORD granted his plea, and Rebekah his wife conceived. But the CHILDREN STRUGGLED TOGETHER* [1] [H7533: *ratsats* break, bruise, crush,

discourage, oppress] *within her; and she said, 'If all is well, why am I like this?' So she went to INQUIRE of the LORD. And the LORD said to her: 'TWO* **NATIONS** [(2)] [H1471: *gôy:* a foreign nation; hence a Gentile, heathen people] *are in your WOMB, Two* **PEOPLES** [(3)] [H3816: *l'ôm:* to *gather,* a *community,* nation, people] *shall be* **SEPARATED** [(4)] [H6504: *pârad:* to *break through* that is, *spread* or *separate* (oneself); disperse, divide, be out of joint, part, scatter (abroad)] *from your body; One* **PEOPLE** [(3)] *shall be* **STRONGER** [(5)] [H553: *'âmats:* to *be alert,* physically (on foot) or mentally (in courage); confirm, be courageous (of good courage, steadfastly minded, strong, stronger), establish, fortify, harden, increase, prevail, strengthen (self), make strong (obstinate, speed)] *than the OTHER, And the OLDER shall SERVE the YOUNGER.' So when her days were FULFILLED for her to give BIRTH, indeed there were TWINS in her WOMB. And the first came out* **RED** [(6)] [H132: *'admônîy:* reddish (of the hair or the complexion)]. *He was like a* **HAIRY** [(7)] [H8181: *sê'âr:* in the sense of *dishevelling;* hair (as if *tossed* or *bristling*)] **GARMENT** [(8)] [H155: *addereth:* mantle, glory, or robe] *all over; so they called his name* **ESAU** [(9)] [H6215: *'êsâv:* sense of *handling; rough* or "*hairy*"; *Esav*, a son of Isaac, including his posterity; who sold his *birthright* and became the progenitor of the Arab peoples]. *Afterward his brother, [Jacob] came out, and his HAND took HOLD of ESAU'S* [9] *HEEL; so his name was called JACOB* [10] [H3290: *Ya'ăqŏb*: heel-catcher (supplanter) Jaakob, the Israelitish patriarch]. *Isaac was SIXTY YEARS OLD when she bore them.*" (Gen. 25:21–26, NKJV) (emphasis added).

Therefore, this *spiritual* battle between the descendants of Jacob (Israelites) versus the descendants of Esau (Edomites) has been waging since the beginning of time. It was God who orchestrated the formation of these two *spiritual* nations while the babies were still in their mother's womb!

Again, as I have clearly conveyed according to God's Word, while Esau and Jacob were still in their mother's womb, it was God who orchestrated the beginning of the "enmity" between these two brothers.

They would eventually become two different "spiritual" nations, even though they were both conceived at the same time, by the same "seed" and from the same blood which came from their father, Isaac and their mother, Rebekah. And, they are both descendants of Abraham as well.

You may be thinking this is not fair; however, God wrote the script of how His *eternal* plan of "reconciliation," "restoration," and "redemption" would unfold for His *eternal* purposes and glory to prevail no matter what because *"it is written..."* And, as I say to my children, "Who told you that life is fair?"

The only thing fair in life is the fact that once we are born, we will all die a *physical* death.

Therefore, it doesn't matter the color of our skin, how much money we make, how special we think we are, what we do for a living, who we know, with the exception of Jesus. For we will all die a *physical* death.

The only exceptions, of course, are for those few who are still alive and remain (survive) the tribulation period, who will be "caught up" (raptured) like Enoch and Elijah *supposedly* were. I will cover this in Book 3.

We are all created equal, *spiritually* speaking, according to God's image and likeness.

However, as is truly apparent, God does not give each human being the same physical and intellectual attributes or talents to be used for His glory and His purposes to prevail.

Moreover, we each have a unique calling that only we can fulfill according to God's "eternal" purpose for creating us in the first place.

Thus, the same applies to God having a unique plan and purpose for both Jacob and Esau to fulfill. He foreknew what their choices would be before one of their days on this earth came to be. As such, God used them accordingly to fulfill His *eternal* plan for the "restoration," "reconciliation," and "redemption" of all mankind. Again, there are no "ifs" in God's "eternal" plan for His "eternal" Word will not return to Him void. It shall accomplish the very thing for which He sent it.

And, God uses every person He has ever created to bring His "eternal" plan to pass for His glory and His pleasure.

It is for this very reason; we are specifically told in Genesis 25:26, *"Afterward his brother* [Jacob] *CAME OUT, and his HAND took HOLD of Esau's HEEL; so his name was called Jacob..."* (NKJV) (emphasis added).

Again, the name Jacob in Hebrew means "deceiver" or "supplanter." The definition of the word "supplanter" means to take the place of (another), as through force, scheming, strategy, or the like.

In addition, as substantiated in Genesis 3:15, we must remember that God's Word proclaimed at the very beginning that the "seed" of a woman would bruise the heel of the "seed" of the serpent. We are also told God would put "enmity" between the "seed" of the serpent and the "seed" of the woman.

Therefore, eventually, a Child (Jesus Christ) would be born from the "seed" of the woman, not from the "seed" of a man. Jesus would "redeem" fallen men who were from the "seed" of the serpent based on the "curse" that entered in as a result of the first Adam's transgression. Genesis 3:15, says the following:

> "*And I will put ENMITY* (11) [H342: *'eybah*: hostility, hatred] *Between YOU and the WOMAN, And between YOUR SEED and HER SEED; He shall BRUISE your HEAD* (12) [H7218: *ro'sh*: to shake the head (as the most easily shaken); used in many applications of place, time, rank, etc.; captain, chief, principal, ruler], *And you shall BRUISE His HEEL* (13) (14) [H6119: *'aqeb*: a *heel* (as *protuberant*); hence a *track*; figuratively the *rear* (of an army); H6117: *'âqab*: to *swell* out or up; to *seize by the heel*; "circumvent" (as if *tripping* up the heels); also to "restrain" (as if holding by the heel); supplant]. *" (Gen. 3:15, NKJV) (emphasis added).

Therefore, with the birth of Isaac's twins, God began to set in motion the fulfillment of Genesis 3:15.

Each of the two children in Rebekah's womb represented a different nation in the *physical* sense in relation to their bodies, complexions, dispositions, lifestyle, etc.

Each child also represented a different nation *spiritually* speaking based on "which" God they would ultimately bow down to and worship.

170

This was the beginning of the fulfillment of Genesis 3:15 which would eventually result in the birth, death, resurrection, and ascension of Jesus Christ, a direct descendant of Abraham, Isaac, and Jacob (Israel) and King David.

It would be Jesus Christ who was wounded for our transgressions and bruised for our iniquities that would crush the head of the serpent, rendering the fatal blow forevermore. Hallelujah!

Therefore, Genesis 3:15 was God's prophetic decree concerning the two different "seeds" that would represent two distinct nations. One group of people would emerge from the "seed" of the serpent (Satan), resulting in rebellion and sinning against God and His Word.

Whereas, the other "seed" would be the "seed" of the woman which would eventually result in the *Son of the Promise* being born. Isaac was the first *Son of the Promise* until "the" *Son of the Promise,* Jesus Christ, would be born in a body of flesh and blood through the "seed" (egg) of a woman named Mary, who was highly favored by God.

It would also come to pass that the "seed" of the woman would rule over the "seed" from the serpent. God has already decreed in the *spiritual* realm that "the" *Son of the Promise,* Jesus Christ, has already prevailed and is the Victor! In John 19:30 when Jesus cried out on the cross just before He gave up His Spirit and said, *"It is finished!"* Satan was defeated *spiritually* right then and there!

However, until this victory fully comes to pass and manifests in the *physical* (earthly) realm, the children born from the two different "seeds" or "nations" will constantly be at war with one another.

Moreover, until we become "born again" *spiritually* speaking by our faith in Jesus Christ, we are all born into this world from the "seed" of the serpent in relationship to our "fallen" state or nature, due to the first Adam's sin and rebellion against God our Creator.

But the "good news" is that the first time Jesus Christ came to the earth as the Son of Man, He came to *seek* and to *save* that *which* was lost due to the transgression of the first Adam based on Luke 19:10.

Once we become "born again" *spiritually* speaking, we are "transferred" into the kingdom of light by the blood of Jesus.

We become "born again" *spiritually* speaking, by acknowledging Jesus Christ is God's only *begotten* Son, He is the Savior of the World, and we "invite" and "receive" Him into our heart as our personal Lord and Savior after we sincerely repent.

This is the *first* step to becoming sons and daughters of our heavenly Father *Yehóvãh*. We have been "redeemed," "reconciled," and "restored" back into a covenant relationship with our heavenly Father and God our Creator by the shed blood of His only *begotten* Son, Jesus Christ.

Hence, by faith, we become the "seed" of Abraham *spiritually* speaking, and heirs according to the *everlasting* covenant that God made with Abraham and his descendants.

As the apostle Paul tells us in Romans 9:6–8, those who come from the "seed" of Abraham are not all Israel who are of Israel. Nor, are we all children of God, *spiritually* speaking because we are from the "seed" of Abraham. Romans 9:6–8, says the following:

> *"But it is not that the Word of God has taken no effect. For they are NOT all ISRAEL who are of ISRAEL, NOR are they all CHILDREN because they are the SEED of ABRAHAM; but, 'In Isaac YOUR SEED shall be CALLED.' That is, those who are the CHILDREN of the FLESH, these are not the CHILDREN of GOD; but the CHILDREN of the PROMISE are COUNTED as the SEED."* (Rom. 9:6–8, NKJV) (emphasis added).

For it is through Isaac, the *Son of the Promise,* that we shall be "called" the children of God and Israel. For Ishmael and Esau are both from the "seed" of Abraham as children of the flesh. They are not the children of God because only the *children of the Promise* are "counted" as the "seed" of Abraham. And, the *children of the Promise* who are "counted" as the children of God also makes us sisters and brothers of Jesus Christ who came from the "seed" of a woman as decreed by God according to Genesis 3:15.

173

Who is Israel? Discovering our True Identity in Jesus Christ and Why it Matters! The Root

This was ultimately fulfilled by Jesus' mother Mary, who was overshadowed by the Holy Spirit when she conceived the Son of God, who was not from the "seed" of an "earthly" father.

Therefore, each individual and every generation is given the opportunity to decide for ourselves whether or not we will enter into a "covenant" relationship with *Yehôvah*, our heavenly Father, and become His sons and daughters.

Under the New Covenant, this is made possible by the blood of Jesus Christ, His only *begotten* Son, who is *the Word* whom He sent to the earth as the Son of Man in the Person of Jesus Christ.

This decision to be "redeemed," "reconciled," and "restored" back to "walking" in a covenant relationship with *Yehôvah*, our heavenly Father, and God our Creator, *begins* with those individuals who place their faith and trust in "the" *Promised Seed* of the woman—Jesus Christ, *Yehôvah's* only *begotten* Son.

In addition, the apostle Paul tells us in Romans 4:13–15, the following:

> *"For the PROMISE that he would be the HEIR of the WORLD was not to ABRAHAM or to his SEED through the LAW, but through the RIGHTEOUSNESS of FAITH. For if those who are of the LAW are HEIRS, FAITH is made VOID and the PROMISE Made of NO*

174

EFFECT, because the LAW brings about WRATH; for where there is NO LAW there is NO TRANSGRESSION." (Rom. 4:13–15, NKJV) (emphasis added).

Sin is the transgression of God's law. Without God's law, how would we know "when" we sin or "what" sin is?

And, when we are in Christ, we have died to our sins, or this is what is *supposed* to happen as we submit our will to the *sanctifying* process of the Holy Spirit.

For we have been crucified with Christ and it is *no* longer we who live, but Christ lives in us and the life which we now live in the flesh, we live by faith in the Son of God.

Therefore, when we learn to "walk" according to the terms and conditions of being in a covenant relationship with our heavenly Father once we "become" saved by being "obedient" to His Voice and His Word as we are led by the Holy Spirit, then we will "inherit" the covenant promises thereof.

The apostle Paul tells us in Galatians 3:13–14, that the blessing of Abraham *might* come upon the Gentiles in Christ Jesus so that we *might* "receive" the promise of "the Spirit" through faith. In other words, we do not "receive" the promise of "the Spirit" by the works of the law.

Galatians 3:13–14, says the following:

"Christ has REDEEMED us from the CURSE of the LAW, having BECOME A CURSE FOR US

> *(for it is written, 'Cursed is everyone who hangs on a tree'), that the BLESSING of ABRAHAM might COME UPON the GENTILES in Christ Jesus, that we might RECEIVE the PROMISE of the SPIRIT through FAITH.'"* (Gal. 3:13–14, NKJV) (emphasis added).

Again, the *children of the Promise* are those that place their faith and trust in Jesus Christ, and as such, they are "counted" as the children of God, and they are the children of Israel who are called Israel.

Moreover, they are "counted" as the "seed" of Abraham by their faith in Christ. And, as a result, they are God's sons and daughters who will "receive" through faith the promise of "the Spirit."

Yet at the same time, faith *without* works and producing the "proper" fruit is dead.

This is based on what Jesus tells us in John 8:39 which says, *"They answered and said to Him, 'Abraham is our father.' Jesus said to them, 'If you were Abraham's children, you would do the WORKS of Abraham.'"* (NKJV) (emphasis added).

So only those who are God's sons and daughters who "receive" the promise of "the Spirit" by faith in Christ and "do" the *works* of Abraham are "counted" as the "seed" of Abraham from God's perspective. However, for those

176

individuals who "choose" to rebel and sin against *Yehôvâh* our heavenly Father and reject *the Word* whom *Yehôvâh* sent to the earth as the Son of Man in the Person of Jesus Christ, then they will continue to be from the "seed" of the serpent and reap the curses thereof!

Again, after the flood, God gave mankind a "new" beginning through Noah and his family. Mankind would once again be faced with the "choice" to either serve God or to serve Satan.

For immediately preceding the flood, with the exception of Noah and his family, it seems like the majority of the people living on the earth at that time were from the "seed" of the serpent and chose to serve Satan.

Why do I say this? Because out of the entire world's population only eight people, Noah, and his family, were saved from perishing in the flood.

Because of Noah's *righteousness* and *godly fear,* he prepared an ark for the saving of his household.

By this act, Noah "condemned" the world and became an heir of "righteousness" which is according to faith.

If Noah had not chosen to be "obedient" as he took clear, decisive action by building the ark to save his household as instructed by God, then Noah and his family would have also perished. Therefore, faith without works is meaningless!

In addition, we are told in Genesis 6:4 that there were giants on the earth in those days and afterward, who were the

177

progeny of the fallen angels. These were *sons of God* who "came in" to the daughters of men who bore children to them. These offspring are called the Nephilim.

Ponder this truth for a moment. Think about how evil the actions of men must have been at this time for God to want to kill everyone with the exception of eight people who were "left behind" to start a "new" beginning!

Then it would come to pass that Noah and his descendants would "choose" whom they would serve in their succeeding generations.

Based on God's eternal plan of "redemption" for the entire world, God would choose to make an *everlasting* covenant with Abraham who was a descendant of Noah's son, Shem, based on Genesis 11:10–26 which lists all of Shem's descendants.

In Genesis 11:26 Shem's genealogy specifically says concerning Abram, *"Now Terah lived seventy years, and begot ABRAM, Nahor, and Haran."* (NKJV) (emphasis added).

On the following page is an illustration to help us understand who Abraham's descendants include since he had other children with Keturah. This was in addition to Isaac, the *Son of the Promise,* who was the *firstfruits* from Sarah's womb and his firstborn son Ishmael who was born to Hagar. This is why God changed Abram's name to Abraham. The name Abraham means the "Father of Many Nations."

178

Abraham's Progeny

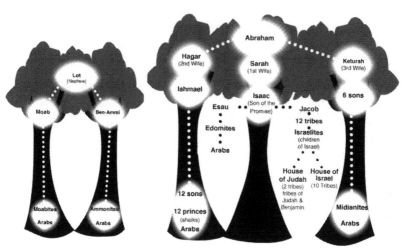

Notice in the illustration depicting Abraham's progeny that most of Abraham's descendants resulted in the formation of the Arab nations who are always warring with the descendants of Jacob—the Israelites.

The Israelites are comprised of the Jews from the House of Judah and those of us who were formerly Gentiles from the House of Israel (Jacob/Joseph/Ephraim) that were grafted into the commonwealth of Israel by our faith in Jesus Christ.

Moreover, this is why *some* Arab and Muslim people who are "radical" extremists of Islam want to annihilate the Jews and the Christians. There are "extremists" in any religion. More blood has been shed because of "religion" than from any other reason throughout the *synergy of the ages!*

179

Therefore, please do not have the mindset that all Arabs and Muslims want to cause harm and kill Jews and Christians, despite the fact they are deceived into "worshiping" and "serving" Allah—the moon god.

Furthermore, they deny that Jesus Christ is the Son of God, as do most of the Jews from the House of Judah because they are still *spiritually* blinded by God until the *fullness of the Gentiles* comes to its zenith.

The primary causes for the deception of the Muslim and Arab people who practice Islam are rooted in beliefs taught from childhood and regional customs.

The same can be said of many believers in the body of Christ who are deceived based on what we have been taught in Church or have inherited from our ancestors, especially from the early church fathers throughout the *synergy of the ages*.

Our heavenly Father's heart is that all mankind comes to the saving knowledge of Jesus Christ and that no man perishes. This includes Muslim and Arab people too, especially since they are also the descendants from the "seed" of Abraham in the flesh.

Based on the illustration depicting Abraham's "spiritual" and "physical" descendants, showing how greatly the Arab nations or peoples outnumber the Israelites, it is evident that God's ways are not our ways. He will always use a remnant, the least of a people group, to accomplish His agenda for the salvation of a "remnant" of Jews from the House of Judah and those of us who were formerly Gentiles who are from the House of Israel (Jacob/Joseph/Ephraim). This is based upon the *everlasting* covenant God established with Abraham, King David, and their descendants.

For there are no "ifs" in God's *eternal* plan of "redemption," "reconciliation," and "restoration" of the entire world, including its inhabitants! God's will shall indeed prevail no matter what, for His "spoken" Word that has gone forth from His mouth and the mouths of His servants the prophets, shall not return to Him void. But it shall accomplish *what* He pleases, and it shall prosper in the thing for which He sent it.

Therefore, it is for this reason that *spiritually* speaking, the "seed" of the serpent would continue with the descendants of Abraham through his *firstborn* son Ishmael and his grandson Esau and their descendants. And, the "seed" of the woman would continue through the *Son of the Promise* Isaac and continue through Isaac's son Jacob, whose direct lineage led to "the" *Son of the Promise*—Jesus Christ.

Again, each new generation will determine *which* "seed" it comes from and *which* God they will serve while they still live on the earth.

Will each individual "choose" to be in a covenant relationship with *Yehóvah*, the God of Abraham, Isaac, and Jacob (Israel) and His only *begotten* Son Jesus Christ? And, based on this choice they would be of the "seed" of the *Promise of the Spirit* which came from the "seed" of the woman.

Or, will each individual "choose" to continue to sin and rebel against their heavenly Father *Yehovah* and God their Creator, who is the God of Abraham, Isaac, and Jacob (Israel) and His only *begotten* Son Jesus Christ? Based on this choice they would remain to be part of the "seed" from the serpent who is Satan.

For there are *only* two choices which are based on two different paths each individual is given a choice to follow. Love is a choice which must come from our heart. And, it is for this very reason, God gives every one of us our own free will so we may "choose" *which* path we shall follow and *whom* we will serve. Our choice will determine the eternal destiny of our soul when we die a *physical* death.

Those who "choose" to place their faith and trust in Jesus Christ will receive the *Promise of the Spirit* to serve Abraham's God who is *El Elyon*, the *Most High God.*

They will become heirs according to the promises God gave to Abraham and his descendants *when* God made this *everlasting* covenant with Abraham. God swore by Himself to never break this *everlasting* covenant and to curse those who would.

These *children of the Promise* (of the Spirit) "received" through faith in Christ are those who are "counted worthy" as the children of God and they are called Israel.

For even Jesus tells us that we must be "counted worthy" in

Luke 20:35 concerning attaining that age and the resurrection from the dead. In addition, Jesus tells us that we must be "counted worthy" to escape all these things that will come to pass and to stand before Him, the Son of Man in Luke 21:36.

So obviously there is much more to *working out* our *own* salvation with fear and trembling than just *saying* that we believe in Jesus Christ. Even the demons believe in Jesus Christ, and they tremble at His name! See James 2:19.

Therefore, those who fear God, will obey His Voice and His Word, and practice "righteousness" after becoming "born again" *spiritually* speaking. As such, if we finish the race which is set before us, then we will be "counted worthy" and inherit these special promises from God as His sons and daughters, who are the children of the Holy One of Israel.

As the children of Israel, we are "transferred" from the *kingdom of darkness* into the *kingdom of light* since we have been transformed by the *sanctifying* power of the Holy Spirit. We have been "cleansed" and "justified" by the blood of our Passover Lamb to "walk" by the Spirit rather than our flesh in a covenant relationship with our heavenly Father.

As such, we will exhibit the characteristics and the nature of our heavenly Father and our Lord and Savior Jesus Christ. We will produce abundant "fruit" for the *kingdom of God* while we are still living on the earth for His glory. His *eternal* purposes will prevail based on why He created us in the first place as we fulfill our destiny as God's sons and daughters.

Yet if an individual "chooses" to continue to sin and rebel against their heavenly Father *Yehováh* and God their Creator, who is the God of Abraham, Isaac, and Jacob (Israel) and His only *begotten* Son Jesus Christ, then they are still "counted" from God's perspective to be from the "seed" of Satan.

And, if this is the "choice" they make, then they will serve Satan in the *kingdom of darkness*, and they will exhibit the characteristics and nature of their father—the Devil—who is the god of this age!

Satan has blinded many individuals who are the children of God because they are made in His image and in His likeness. Satan has done this so they will not believe the light of the gospel of the glory of Christ who is the image of God that He should shine His light upon them. This truth is based on Second Corinthians 4:4.

Sadly, because they have not received the truth of the light of the gospel, they will produce the "fruit" and inherit the eternal destination of the *kingdom of darkness* unless they repent and they come to the saving knowledge of Jesus Christ as their Lord and Savior.

For there is no such thing as "collective" salvation! *Every* person at the age of accountability (usually thirteen years old) who has ever been born and lived on this earth must decide for themselves "which" God they will serve.

Again, there are only two choices.

We will either serve or worship *Yehóvah*, the God of Abraham, Isaac, and Jacob (Israel) and His only *begotten* Son, Jesus Christ. Or, we will serve and worship Satan.

God has given all of Abraham's descendants the opportunity to "choose" the path they shall "walk" according to while they are still living on the earth.

This "choice" will ultimately determine their "eternal" destination as well based on the following two choices:

❖ Will we reap God's blessings for "walking" in a covenant relationship with *Yehóvah* the God of Abraham, Isaac, and Jacob (Israel) while we are still living on the earth? This decision also brings forth "eternal" consequences as well.

❖ Or, will we reap God's curses for not "walking" in a covenant relationship with our heavenly Father and Jesus Christ our Lord and Savior while we are still living on the earth? This decision also brings forth "eternal" consequences as well.

Again, *each* individual and *every* subsequent generation have the right to "choose" their own path and chart their own course. Each individual has been given their own sovereign will by God their Creator and can decide "who" they will serve while they are still living on the earth.

Our heavenly Father *Yehóvah* tells us in advance, based on Deuteronomy 28, what we will reap according to what we "choose" to do or "choose" not to do while we are still living on the earth. Love is not a feeling; it is a choice!

Therefore, our "choices" have "eternal" consequences for we will all have to give an account to God, our Creator and our Lord and Savior Jesus Christ based on what we have decided to "do" or not "do" on Judgment Day.

This is the day when the "blame" game stops and all excuses no longer matter. Everyone will have to give an account to the *Supreme Judge of the Universe* and reap the consequences of what we have sown while we were still living on the earth. It will be then that God will render His final judgment which will be solely based on what is written (recorded) in all the books (plural) that will be opened up in the *Courtroom of Heaven* on *that* fateful day.

In the next chapter we will discover that because Esau *despised* and *forfeited* his "birthright" as the *firstborn* son of Isaac, God hated Esau but loved Jacob. And, as a result, God chose Jacob to be the *Son of the Promise* that He would use to "confirm" the *everlasting* covenant He established with Abraham and his descendants as an *everlasting* covenant with all Israel.

CHAPTER 28

ESAU DESPISED HIS BIRTHRIGHT AS THE FIRSTBORN SON OF ISAAC. THEREFORE, JACOB BECAME THE HEIR OF THE PROMISES GOD GAVE TO ABRAHAM

I n the Bible, usually the *firstborn* son receives the double portion of the blessing and inheritance from the father. Therefore, in this instance, Esau, not Jacob, should have received his birthright because Esau was the *firstborn* son of Isaac.

However, in Genesis 25:29–34, we are told that Esau willingly sold his "birthright" for food to satisfy his carnal, fleshly appetite. Esau's choice to quickly satisfy his hunger for the things of this world resulted in him forfeiting the inheritance and the blessing from his earthly father, Isaac.

Ultimately, Esau's wrong choice would also cause him to lose his "spiritual" inheritance in the eyes of God, his heavenly Father. Notice this passage of Scripture ends with saying, *"Thus Esau despised his birthright."* Genesis 25:29–34, says the following:

> *"Now Jacob cooked a stew; and Esau came in from the field, and he was weary. And Esau said to Jacob, 'Please feed me with that same red stew, for I am weary.' Therefore his NAME*

187

[Esau] *was called* **EDOM** [(1)] [H123: *'ĕdốm:* *Edom*, the elder twin-brother of Jacob; hence the region (Idumaea) occupied by him; Edom, Edomites]. *But Jacob said, 'SELL me YOUR BIRTHRIGHT as of this day.' And Esau said, 'Look, I am about to die; so what is this birthright to me?' Then Jacob said, 'Swear to me as of this day.' SO HE SWORE TO HIM, and SOLD HIS BIRTHRIGHT TO JACOB. And Jacob gave Esau bread and stew of lentils; then he ate and drank, arose, and went his way. Thus ESAU* **DESPISED** [(2)] [H959: *bâzâh:* to *disesteem;* disdain, contemn (-ptible), + think to scorn; vile person] *his BIRTHRIGHT."* (Gen. 25:29–34, NKJV) (emphasis added).

In addition, based on the written accounts substantiated in Genesis Chapter 27, Jacob and his mother Rebekah "deceived" Isaac into giving his blessing to Jacob instead of Esau.

This deception and trickery of Jacob did not go unnoticed by God. It would come to pass that Jacob would, in turn, be deceived and tricked by his future father-in-law Laban.

This substantiates this truth: A man will reap what he sows!

Nevertheless, in regards to Esau, God did not forgive Esau and restore his "birthright" because Esau did not repent of despising his "birthright."

Also, Esau did not forgive his brother Jacob for his deception and trickery. Instead, Esau held onto his bitterness and hatred towards his brother Jacob in his heart.

This is substantiated in Genesis 27:41 which says, *"So Esau HATED Jacob because of the BLESSING with which his FATHER BLESSED him, and Esau said in his HEART, 'The days of mourning for my father are at hand; then I will KILL my brother Jacob.'"* (NKJV) (emphasis added).

WHY DID GOD LOVE JACOB, BUT HATE ESAU?

Now let's see what God's response to Esau was based on the following facts:

1. Esau "despised" and "sold" his "birthright" to his brother Jacob.

2. Esau did not confess his sins.

3. Esau did not forgive Jacob for his transgression against him.

4. Esau did not repent and turn back to God, his Creator until it was too late!

It is for all these reasons listed above that Esau forfeited his right to receive his inheritance as a "birthright" heir based on

189

the promises that God promised Abraham and his descendants who came after him. In fact, God said the following concerning Esau, in Malachi 1:3 below:

> *"But Esau I [Yehôvah] have* **HATED** [3] [H8130: *sâne*: to hate (personally); as an enemy or foe; odious], *And laid WASTE his MOUNTAINS and his HERITAGE For the JACKALS of the WILDERNESS."* (Mal.1:3, NKJV) (emphasis added).

And, in Romans 9:13, the apostle Paul reiterates the fact that God did not change His mind concerning Esau when he proclaims, *"As it is written, 'Jacob I have LOVED, but Esau I have* **HATED** [4] [G3404: *miseō*: (hatred); to detest (especially to persecute); by extension to love less].'"* (NKJV) (emphasis added).

Therefore, God has not changed His mind about Esau, whose descendants are referred to as the "Edomites." The Hebrew word "Edom" means "red." Edom is also used to describe the region (Idumaea) occupied by Esau's descendants, the Edomites.

God has a sense of humor. Based on Genesis 25:21–26, when Esau was born we are told that Esau was the first to be born and came out "red," referring to Esau's hair and complexion.

Listen to God's future judgment and plans for Edom and the descendants of Esau in the following Scriptures. Also worth mentioning is this fact: The final destruction of the "mighty" men of Edom by *Yehôvâh* precedes the destruction of Damascus, which we are beginning to witness now.

"Against Edom. *Thus says the* LORD *of hosts:* *'Is wisdom no more in* **TEMAN** [5] [The name *Teman* (Hebrew: תימן), was the name of an Edomite clan and the term is also traditionally applied to Yemenite Jews and is used as the Hebrew name of Yemen. There is other strong evidence that Teman could be identified as the site of the modern Ma'an. There is some information that says that the state which emerged in the south of the Arabian Peninsula is Yemen]*? Has counsel perished from the* *prudent? Has their wisdom vanished? Flee, turn* *back, dwell in the depths, O inhabitants of* **DEDAN** [6] [*Dedan* (Hebrew: דדן *Dədān*) means "low ground" and is a city of Arabia, in modern times it is called Al-'Ula and is located in northern Saudi Arabia]*! For I will bring the* *CALAMITY of ESAU upon him, The time that I* *will PUNISH him. If grape-gatherers came to* *you, Would they not leave some gleaning* *grapes? If thieves by night, Would they not* *destroy until they have enough? But I have* *made Esau bare; I have uncovered his secret* *places, And he shall not be able to hide himself.* *His descendants are plundered, His brethren*

and his neighbors, And he is no more. Leave your fatherless children, I will preserve them alive; And let your widows trust in Me." (Jer. 49:7–11, NKJV) (emphasis added).

"For indeed, I will make you [Esau=Edom] *SMALL among nations, DESPISED among MEN."* (Jer. 49:15, NKJV) (emphasis added).

*"The earth shakes at the NOISE of their FALL; At the cry its noise is heard at the Red Sea. Behold, He shall come up and fly like the eagle, And spread His wings over **BOZRAH** [7]* [Bozrah means "sheepfold" and was the capital city of the Edomites which is now located in modern day Jordan along the King's Highway]; *The HEART of the MIGHTY MEN of Edom in that DAY shall be Like the HEART of a WOMAN in BIRTH PANGS."* (Jer. 49:21–22, NKJV) (emphasis added).

Esau despised and forfeited his "birthright" and his "inheritance." Thus, he was rejected by God.

It is for this very reason that *Yehovah* is the God of Abraham, Isaac, and Jacob. He is not the God of Abraham, Isaac, and Esau.

Jesus substantiates this in Matthew 22:31–32, when He says,

"But concerning the resurrection of the dead, have you not read what was spoken to you by God, saying, 'I am the God of Abraham, the God of Isaac, and the God of Jacob? God is not the God of the DEAD, but of the LIVING.'" (NKJV) (emphasis added).

In the next chapter, I will convey how the story of Esau despising and forfeiting his "birthright" and "inheritance" is relevant to all disciples of Jesus Christ, particularly for those who are carnal Christians. Carnal Christians are those who have not "learned" to crucify their flesh and do not "obey" God's Voice and His Word.

CHAPTER 29

HOW IS ESAU DESPISING AND FORFEITING HIS INHERITANCE AND HIS BIRTHRIGHT RELEVANT TO ALL DISCIPLES OF JESUS CHRIST?

As we have seen in the case of Esau, contrary to what is taught, God does not love everybody. Anyone who is not for God is against Him and is His enemy. Moreover, God will repay with His vengeance those who hate Him because they are His enemies.

This is substantiated in Deuteronomy 32:41 which says, *"If I whet My GLITTERING SWORD, And My HAND takes HOLD on JUDGMENT, I will render VENGEANCE to My ENEMIES, And repay those who HATE Me."* (NKJV) (emphasis added).

As God's sons and daughters by our faith, trust, and obedience to our heavenly Father and His only *begotten* Son Jesus Christ, anyone who comes against us with persecution and hates us for His name's sake should listen to what God says He will do to our enemies. Deuteronomy 30:7 proclaims, *"Also the Lord your God will PUT all these CURSES on your ENEMIES and on those who HATE you, who PERSECUTED you."* (NKJV) (emphasis added).

Why would God put all these curses on our enemies who hate and persecute us? Since we are grafted into the commonwealth of Israel by our faith in Jesus Christ, we are heirs according to the promise given by God to Abraham and his descendants. This is based on Genesis 12:2–3, which says the following:

> *"I will make you* [Abraham] *a GREAT NATION; I will BLESS you* [Abraham] *And make your NAME* [Abraham] *great; And you* [Abraham] *shall be a BLESSING. I will BLESS THOSE WHO BLESS you* [Abraham]*, And I will CURSE him who CURSES you* [Abraham]*; And in you* [Abraham] *all the FAMILIES of the EARTH shall be BLESSED."* (Gen. 12:2–3, NKJV) (emphasis added).

Moreover, God's enemies should be His people's enemies too! However, Jesus tells us in Matthew 5:44–46, the following:

> *"But I say to you, LOVE YOUR ENEMIES, BLESS those who CURSE you, DO GOOD to those who HATE you, and PRAY for those who SPITEFULLY USE YOU and PERSECUTE YOU, that you may be SONS of YOUR FATHER in HEAVEN; for He makes His sun rise on the evil and on the good, and sends rain on the just and on the unjust. FOR IF YOU LOVE THOSE WHO LOVE YOU, WHAT REWARD HAVE YOU? Do not even the tax collectors do the*

same?" (Matt. 5:44–46, NKJV) (emphasis added).

Therefore, based on Matthew 5:44–46, we are told to do the following things so we *may* be sons and daughters of our heavenly Father:

1. To love our enemies.

2. Bless those who curse us.

3. Do good things to those who hate us.

4. Pray for those who spitefully use and persecute us.

Why does Jesus tell us to do all these things for our enemies? It is a test to see *if* we will be obedient to His Word so we *may* be "counted worthy" to be sons and daughters of our heavenly Father *Yehóvah* who is in heaven.

Because, *if* we do what we are commanded to do according to God's Word and we do not repay evil with evil, then guess what? Our heavenly Father will deal with our enemies on our behalf based on Romans 12:19, which says the following:

"Beloved, do not AVENGE [^(1)] [^(2)] [G1556: *ekdikeō:* to *vindicate, retaliate, punish;* take *revenge;* G1558: *ekdikos.* carrying *justice out,* that is, a *punisher*] *YOURSELVES, but rather give PLACE to WRATH; for it is written, 'VENGEANCE* [^(3)] [G1557: *ekdikēsis.*

vindication, retribution: (a-, re-) venge (-ance), punishment] *is MINE, I will REPAY,' says the Lord."* (Rom. 12:19, NKJV) (emphasis added).

This is why Jesus says to us in Matthew 5:46, *"For if you LOVE THOSE WHO LOVE YOU, what REWARD have you?..."* (NKJV) (emphasis added).

I have seen and experienced God do this on my behalf time and time again when people have been outright mean and nasty to me when I have done nothing wrong but be friendly and kind to them. And, this is why the apostle Paul proclaims in Romans 8:31, *"What then shall we say to these things? If God is for us, who can be AGAINST us?"* (NKJV) (emphasis added).

Or, as Psalm 118:6 proclaims, *"The LORD is on my side; I will not FEAR. What can MAN do to me?"* (NKJV) (emphasis added).

You may be thinking the following: We have the right to condemn every tongue that rises up against us in judgment which is based on Isaiah 54:17.

Yes, you do, and as King David did, we must take our grievances concerning our enemies and God's enemies to God in prayer, after we have prayed for them, blessed them and "done" good to them. Then God will condemn our enemies and render His judgment against them on our

198

behalf. Isaiah 54:17 says the following:

"No WEAPON FORMED against YOU shall PROSPER, And every TONGUE which RISES AGAINST YOU in JUDGMENT YOU shall CONDEMN. This is the HERITAGE of the SERVANTS of the LORD, And their RIGHTEOUSNESS is from Me,' Says the Lord." (Isa. 54:17, NKJV) (emphasis added).

However, sometimes we are put in situations where we have to act quickly. The Holy Spirit will come upon us. We shall operate in the authority that we have *already* been given as God's servants to condemn every tongue which rises against us right then and there. Yet we *must* be led by the Holy Spirit as to *when* to speak and *when* not to speak.

Now let's refocus our attention on Esau who became God's enemy based on his actions and his decisions.

As is the case with Esau despising his "birthright" as God's son, anyone who has rejected Jesus Christ is still under God's wrath.

This is based on John 3:36, which states the following:

*"He who **BELIEVES** [4] [G4100: pisteuō: to have faith* (in, upon, or with respect to, a person or thing), that is, *credit,* by implication to *entrust* (especially one's spiritual well-being to Christ)] *in the SON has EVERLASTING LIFE; and he*

199

who does *not* **BELIEVE** [4] the SON shall *not* SEE life, but the WRATH of GOD *abides* on him." (John 3:36, NKJV) (emphasis added).

Notice this Scripture does not say those who just "say" that they believe in Jesus Christ will have eternal life. Rather, it specifically says based on the Greek meaning of the word "believe" or "believes" it is referring to those who have faith in Jesus Christ which is evidenced by them entrusting their spiritual well-being to Christ. This is what gives us "eternal" life from the moment we "believe" and "receive" Jesus Christ as our Lord and Savior.

Our salvation is based on us committing our faith and trust in Christ's ability, not our own, to save us, since He is the One who "justified" us in the first place.

However, like Esau who forfeited his "birthright" and his "inheritance," there are many professed believers who will reap the same consequences.

This applies to all those who "say" with their mouths that they have accepted Jesus Christ as their Lord and Savior *BUT* they...

1. Refuse to confess their sins and ask our heavenly Father for His forgiveness on an ongoing, consistent basis.

We must humble ourselves and ask God to search our

heart for any secret sins we may not know about, based on us practicing things which do not please Him.

2. Continue to sin once we know God's *righteous* requirements for living holy because He is holy.

3. Refuse to be obedient to God's commandments found in His Word, or only honoring those commandments that will not require us to change the way we live our lives. In other words, we cannot pick and choose *which* commandments we have decided we will obey while discarding other commandments that we do not agree with because it would require us to change the way we live. In fact, this would be putting our own "opinion" *above* the knowledge of God's Word like Satan did.

4. Refuse to forgive others who have offended or transgressed against us. This is based on what Jesus says to us in Matthew 6:15 which proclaims, *"But if you do not FORGIVE men their TRESPASSES, neither will your Father FORGIVE your TRESPASSES."* (NKJV) (emphasis added).

Therefore, for those who "say" they are believers in Jesus Christ, yet their "fruit" says otherwise, if they do not repent, stop sinning, and return to God the Father, and His Son, Jesus Christ, like Esau, they will *forfeit* their "birthright" and "inheritance" as His sons and daughters.

As such, they will lose all their rights to His "covenant" promises *because* they have "chosen" to break "covenant" with God. Moreover, the apostle Paul says to us in Second Corinthians 7:10, *"For godly SORROW produces REPENTANCE leading to SALVATION, not to be REGRETTED; but the SORROW of the WORLD produces DEATH."* (NKJV) (emphasis added).

Based on what the apostle Paul says to us in Second Corinthians 7:10 above, if a new convert to the faith says a "sinner's prayer," yet they did not have *"godly* sorrow," resulting in *true* repentance leading to salvation, then are they truly saved? Not according to the whole counsel of God's Word!

As such, we can "say" that we repent all we want! Yet *true* repentance will be evidenced by *"godly* sorrow" which will propel us to first change our mind concerning a matter.

This will cause us to take the necessary actions to change our behavior, submitting to the Holy Spirit and coming into alignment with God's *eternal* Word.

For God, the Father has "exalted" Jesus to His right hand as Prince and Savior to give "repentance" to Israel and to grant "forgiveness" for our sins.

This is substantiated by the apostle Peter and the other apostles. Peter said to the high priest, the captain of the temple, and to the chief priests, that they *ought* to "obey" God rather than men and that God will give the Holy Spirit to those who "obey" Him. This is based on Acts 5:29–32, which says the following:

> *"But Peter and the other apostles answered and said: 'We ought to OBEY GOD rather than MEN. The God of our fathers raised up Jesus whom you murdered by hanging on a tree. Him [Jesus] God has EXALTED to His right hand to be Prince and Savior, to give REPENTANCE to ISRAEL and FORGIVENESS of SINS. And we are His witnesses to these things, and so also is the HOLY SPIRIT whom God has GIVEN to those who OBEY Him."*
> (Acts 5:29–32, NKJV) (emphasis added).

Next, based on Hebrews 12:14–17, God's people must *pursue* "peace" with all people, *without* compromising His Word and *pursue* "holiness," without which, *no one* will see the Lord. Otherwise, as in the case of Esau, we will "forfeit" our "birthright" and our "inheritance" as His sons and daughters.

We must not allow a "root of bitterness" to spring up in our heart, leading to resentment against those who spitefully use us, betray us, and hurt us. We must not become offended with people, and especially with God.

We must take an axe to sever and eradicate any "root of bitterness" in our hearts. If we do not deal with these issues, then *BEWARE—by this* many believers become "defiled." We will become "defiled" when we harbor unforgiveness in our hearts. Hebrews 12:14–17, says the following:

"Pursue [is a verb—action is required by us] **PEACE** [5] [G1515: *eirēnē*: (to join) as one in *quietness* and *rest*, to set at one again; *peace* (literally or figuratively); by implication *prosperity*] with all *PEOPLE*, and **HOLINESS** [6] [G38: *hagiasmos*: purification, that is, (the state) *purity*; sanctification (which is accomplished by submitting our will to the Holy Spirit and being led by Him], *without which NO ONE will SEE the LORD: looking carefully lest anyone FALL SHORT of the* **GRACE** [7] [G5485: *charis*: manner or act of the divine influence upon the heart and its reflection in the life of one by having graciousness, gratitude, favour, gift, grace, thanks, worthy, or pleasure] *of God; lest any ROOT of* **BITTERNESS** [8] [G4088: *pikria*: acridity (especially *poison*)] *springing up cause trouble, and by this MANY become* **DEFILED** [9] [G3392: *miainō*: to *sully* or *taint*, that is, *contaminate* (ceremonially or morally)]*; lest there be any* **FORNICATOR** [10] [G4205: *pornos*: to *sell*; (male) *prostitute* (as *venal*); (by analogy) a *debauchee* (*libertine*); whoremonger] *or* **PROFANE** [11] [G952: *bebēlos*: from the base of *bēlos*: (a *threshold*); *accessible* (as by *crossing the door way*), that is, (by implication of Jewish notions) *heathenish*, *wicked*] *PERSON* like

204

ESAU, who for one morsel of food SOLD his BIRTHRIGHT. For you know that AFTERWARD, when he wanted to inherit the BLESSING, he was **REJECTED** [12] [G593: *apodokimazo*: to *disapprove*, that is, (by implication) to *repudiate*; disallow, reject], *for he FOUND no PLACE for* **REPENTANCE** [13] **[G3341: *metanoia*:** *compunction* (for guilt, including *reformation*); by implication *reversal* (of another's decision)], *though he* [Esau] *SOUGHT IT DILIGENTLY WITH TEARS."* (Heb. 12:14–17, NKJV) (emphasis added).

How very sad that Esau found no place (opportunity) for repentance even though he sought it diligently with tears. For *without* repentance, there is *no* remission (pardon or freedom) from sins.

Therefore, when Esau wanted to *inherit* his "birthright" as a son of God and "receive" the covenant blessings thereof, as his "inheritance," it was too late.

God rejected him because he "despised" and "sold" (prostituted) his "birthright" for one morsel of food.

Unfortunately, many in the body of Christ are doing the *same* thing that Esau did by committing *spiritual* adultery (fornicating) with the things of this world.

Many have "profaned" what is *supposed* to be holy with the unholy! We are to have no idols or to serve any false gods because the *one* and *only* true God demands our *unwavering* faithfulness to Him and Him alone.

This is based on the first commandment of the Ten Commandments in Exodus 20:3 which says, *"You shall have no OTHER GODS before Me."* (NKJV) (emphasis added).

In fact, the first four commandments of the Ten Commandments have everything to do with "how" we are to "worship," "serve," and "walk" in a covenant relationship with our heavenly Father *Yehóvah* who is *E'lōhim*, God our Creator, the God of Abraham, Isaac, and Jacob who is also the Holy One of Israel.

It is for this very reason that in commandments one through four of the Ten Commandments, our heavenly Father *Yehóvah* specifically tells us *what* "love" looks like to Him from His perspective.

As such, if Esau's fate doesn't give us the *reverential* fear of the Lord, then what will?

Some believe that because we are under the New Covenant, we do not have to be concerned about God not accepting our repentance after we have "despised" or "forfeited" our "birthright" as His sons and daughters because we are "justified" by Christ because of what Jesus did on the cross at Calvary. Yet in the New Testament and under the New Covenant, this is exactly *what* the apostle Paul *warns* us about in Hebrews 10:26–39. The apostle Paul says to us that *if* we sin "willfully" *after* we have come to the saving knowledge of Jesus Christ as our Lord and Savior and we have "received" the knowledge of His truth, yet we continue to commit *spiritual* "adultery" or "fornication" whereby we become "defiled" and "profaned" as Esau did in the sight of God, then there *no* longer remains a sacrifice for sins, but a certain fearful expectation of judgment and fiery indignation, devouring the adversaries of God.

God, Himself will unleash His wrath upon His enemies who, like Esau, hate Him. This will happen *when* Jesus appears the second time and deals with the *unrepentant* wicked inhabitants on the earth at the brightness of His coming.

Again, Jesus deals *first* with the "tares" before His angels will gather His "wheat" into His barn, based on Matthew 13:24–30 and Matthew 13:36–43.

This is *when* God will "consume" or "destroy" those whom He has "cut off" from being His people because they have transgressed His laws, changed His ordinance, and broken the *everlasting* covenant that He established with Abraham and his descendants.

Again, according to *Strong's Hebrew Lexicon* #H3772, the word "cut off" is the Hebrew word "kârath" (pronounced "kaw-rath'"), which means: To "destroy" or "consume" specifically to covenant. Therefore, God will "destroy" or "consume" those who "break" the *everlasting* covenant that He established with Abraham and his descendants.

Who is Israel? Discovering our True Identity in Jesus Christ and Why it Matters! The Root

I will cover this fact in-depth in Chapter 56 of Book 3. If we *truly* love God with all of our mind, heart, soul, and strength, then we will keep His commandments and not grieve His Holy Spirit by practicing "unrighteousness" and committing "iniquity" against Him and His Word.

Again, without *sincere* repentance resulting in genuine "*godly* sorrow" which will lead to our salvation, there is *no* pardon for our sins. This is why Jesus and His early disciples always preached the *gospel of the kingdom* beginning with the message of the need to repent.

I cover this indisputable fact in Chapter 64 of Book 3 because any *gospel of the kingdom* which is preached, but does not declare the message of repentance is not the true *gospel of the kingdom*. The true *gospel of the kingdom* that Christ and His early disciples preached made *no* compromise with sin after someone "became" saved by grace through faith in Jesus Christ.

Therefore, if we have truly repented of our sins *when* the Holy Spirit "convicts" us of the sins in our heart and our lives, then it will lead to us having "compunction."

This is a feeling of guilt that usually follows when we do something bad that we know is against God and His Word.

Contrary to what some believe the Holy Spirit will bring "conviction" to us as we read or listen to the Word of God. This is the job of the Holy Spirit—He will convict the world of

Donna M. Rogers

sin based on John 16:5–10 which says the following:

> *"But now I go away to Him who sent Me, and none of you asks Me, 'Where are You going?' But because I have said these things to you, sorrow has filled your heart. Nevertheless I tell you the truth. It is to your advantage that I go away; for if I do not go away, the Helper will not come to you; but if I depart, I will send Him to you. And when HE HAS COME, HE WILL CONVICT THE WORLD OF SIN, AND OF RIGHTEOUSNESS, AND OF JUDGMENT: OF SIN, BECAUSE THEY DO NOT BELIEVE IN ME; of righteousness, because I go to My Father and you see Me no more; of judgment, because the ruler of this world is judged."* (John 16:5–10, NKJV) (emphasis added).

And, before you quickly point out the fact that this Scripture in John 16:5–10 is specifically talking to those in the world who do not know Jesus Christ as their Lord and Savior, let me ask you this question: Before you became saved by grace through faith in Jesus Christ what "convicted" you to receive Jesus Christ as your Lord and Savior? It was the Holy Spirit who "convicted" you of sin, righteousness, and judgment.

It is the work of the Holy Spirit to "guide" us into all truth based on John 16:13. God's truth is found in His "eternal" Word which is the plumb line. As such, do we truly believe

209

from the moment we become saved the Holy Spirit will no longer "convict" us when we are in sin, and we have fallen short of the glory God's grace?

The Holy Spirit will bring "conviction" if we are walking in sin and rebelling against God and His Word. This may feel like "condemnation" to some, but "reproofs" (chastisement or correction) of instructions are the way of life for disciples of Jesus Christ.

One way to tell if it is the Holy Spirit bringing "conviction" or the accuser of the brethren—Satan bringing "condemnation" is based on this indisputable truth: The Holy Spirit will "convict" you based on the truth of God's Word which is the plumb line.

Whereas, the devil will lie to you twisting the truth of God's Word, so you will be "deceived" into believing a lie. The Holy Spirit will tell you the truth but Satan will tell you a lie.

As the apostle Paul says to us in Romans 8:1, *"There is therefore now NO CONDEMNATION to those who are in Christ Jesus, WHO DO NOT WALK ACCORDING TO THE FLESH, but ACCORDING TO THE SPIRIT."* (NKJV) (emphasis added).

Therefore, we must carefully examine our "fruit" on a daily basis to determine if we are walking according to the flesh or according to the Spirit. The apostle Paul tells us what the "fruit" of the Spirit is based on Galatians 5:22–23, which says the following:

> *"But the FRUIT OF THE SPIRIT is love, joy,*
> *peace, longsuffering, kindness, goodness,*
> *faithfulness, gentleness, self-control. Against*
> *such there is NO LAW* [or condemnation]*."*
> (Gal. 5:22–23, NKJV) (emphasis added).

The apostle Paul identifies some of the "fruit" of the flesh in Galatians 5:19–21. This is based on the truth of God's Word—which is the plumb line concerning how we are *not* to walk and live as God's sons and daughters.

Because if we walk and live this way after we become saved, we can profess all that we want that we believe in Jesus Christ—but our "fruit" will be the deciding factor based on what is written in all the books (plural) that will be opened up on Judgment Day.

If we practice these *works of the flesh,* we will not inherit the *kingdom of God* while we still live on the earth. Nor, will we inherit eternal life once we pass away based on Revelation 21:8. This truth is based on the Word of God. Therefore, if you have an issue with this truth—take it to God. In other words, don't shoot the messenger. Galatians 5:19–21, says the following:

> *"Now the works of the flesh are evident, which*
> *are: adultery, fornication, uncleanness,*
> *lewdness, idolatry, sorcery, hatred, contentions,*
> *jealousies, outbursts of wrath, selfish ambitions,*

211

dissensions, heresies, envy, murders, drunkenness, revelries, and the like; of which I tell you beforehand, just as I also told you in time past, that those who PRACTICE SUCH THINGS WILL NOT INHERIT THE KINGDOM OF GOD." (Gal. 5:19–21, NKJV) (emphasis added).

The testimony of Jesus Christ as written by the apostle John in Revelation 21:8 says that if we have any of these "fruits" which are based on the *works of the flesh* if we do not repent, we shall perish in the *lake of fire* which is the second death.

Revelation 21:8 says the following:

"But the cowardly, unbelieving, abominable, murderers, sexually immoral, sorcerers, idolaters, and all liars SHALL HAVE THEIR PART IN THE LAKE WHICH BURNS WITH FIRE AND BRIMSTONE, WHICH IS THE SECOND DEATH." (Rev. 21:8, NKJV) (emphasis added).

Based on Revelation 21:8, we must hope and pray that the Holy Spirit will "convict" us if we are sinning against God and His Word for this reason: If after we become saved we should commit any of these *works of the flesh*, we simply repent and confess our sin to God, and He promises to forgive us and cleanse us from all unrighteousness.

The Holy Spirit will continue to "convict" us of our sins and lead us into all truth, especially God's truth, as long as His presence doesn't leave us because we have grieved the Holy Spirit by us *willfully* practicing "unrighteousness" and "lawlessness." The Holy Spirit will not dwell in a temple which has become "defiled" because of practicing unrighteousness.

In fact, one of the purposes of repenting is, so we will "think" differently, and feel "moral" compunction. The definition of "compunction" is a feeling of uneasiness or anxiety of the conscience caused by regret for doing wrong or causing pain; contrition; and remorse. There is something seriously wrong if we sin against God and His Word and we do not feel remorse for having done so.

This "compunction" should result in "reformation," the action or the process of "reforming" a practice of an individual or an institution such as the Church or a nation.

Reformation should change the way we "think" about *what* God requires of us according to the *whole* counsel of His Word to "walk" in a covenant relationship with Him.

In other words, repentance without "*godly* sorrow" will not result in changed behavior and changed lives. Therefore, if we have sincerely repented of a sin in our life or the iniquity in the Church or a nation that grieves God's Holy Spirit, then it will result in changed behavior.

Being a nation of people who have been "transformed" by the power of His love is the result of the *sanctification* process of the Holy Spirit. We will not remain the same!

Based on the *great* apostasy that is taking place in the body of Christ, many—the largest portion of people in the body of Christ who call themselves by His name, have not sincerely repented with "*godly* sorrow" which has resulted in changed behavior.

Unfortunately, many so-called believers are using the Lord's name in vain. They are the very ones, who have trampled the Son of God underfoot and have counted "the blood" of the covenant by which they became *sanctified* as a common thing.

Hence, many believers in the body of Christ have insulted the *Spirit of Grace* and, like Esau, many have "despised" and "forfeited" their "birthright" and "inheritance" as God's sons and daughters. And, as a result, many have "forfeited" their "birthright" to *receive* any of the covenant promises thereof as their inheritance unless they sincerely repent with "godly sorrow."

In the next chapter we will discover why despite Jacob's lying, deception, and trickery, God still chose Jacob to be the son through which the promises God gave to Abraham would be "confirmed" as an *everlasting* covenant to Israel.

In addition, we will look at a few examples in God's Word where God rewarded individuals who were not honest with those in authority because of His *righteous* cause.

CHAPTER 30

DESPITE JACOB'S LYING, DECEPTION, AND TRICKERY, GOD STILL CHOSE HIM TO CONFIRM AN EVERLASTING COVENANT WITH ISRAEL

N ow let's take a look at what God did concerning Jacob's character defect of lying, deceiving, and trickery. This was a generational *iniquity* Jacob inherited from his father Isaac and his grandfather Abraham.

They both lied saying their wives were their sisters in enemy territory so they would not be killed. See Genesis 26:6–9 and Genesis 20:1–18 respectively. In all three cases, despite Abraham, Isaac, and Jacob's lie, God still chose to reward them greatly.

You may be wondering why God would bless someone who lies because we all know that God's Word forbids lying.

Therefore, let me digress for a few minutes and address this issue because the Bible has some other examples where God decided to bless people who lied. Two other biblical examples are as follows:

EXAMPLE 1:

Rahab, the prostitute, lied to protect the lives of the two spies Joshua secretly sent out to spy on the fortified city of Jericho.

See Joshua 2:4–7. As a result, Rahab and her entire household were spared when the walls of Jericho fell after the Israelites encircled Jericho for a period of seven days.

God acted based on their faith in His ability to give them the city.

This is based on Hebrews 11:30 which says, *"By FAITH the walls of Jericho FELL DOWN after they were ENCIRCLED for SEVEN DAYS."* (NKJV) (emphasis added).

Also, Rahab's faith played a role in not only her entire family surviving the siege of Jericho, but also in the legacy that she would leave behind for all *eternity.*

First, she "believed" what the spies had told her and did as she was instructed to do, binding the scarlet cord, symbolic of the blood of the "Passover Lamb," in the window of her house.

Second, God chose to list Rahab in Jesus' genealogy because she was "justified" (converted) in the eyes of the Lord by her "faith" as she received the two spies for God's *righteous* cause with peace.

This is substantiated in Hebrews 11:31 which says, *"By FAITH the HARLOT RAHAB did not PERISH with those who did not BELIEVE, when she had RECEIVED the SPIES with PEACE."* (NKJV) (emphasis added).

Therefore, long before Cornelius, the Gentile, was saved by "faith" when Peter was sent to him as detailed in the Book of

Acts in Chapter 10, Rahab was the very first Gentile to be saved by "faith" in the Old Testament. Ruth was second.

Last, but certainly not least, it would be from Rahab's lineage that King David would eventually be born.

This is based on Matthew 1:4–6 which says, *"Ram begot Amminadab, Amminadab begot Nahshon, and Nahshon begot Salmon. Salmon begot BOAZ by RAHAB, Boaz begot OBED by RUTH, Obed begot JESSE, and JESSE begot DAVID the KING. David the king begot SOLOMON by her* [Bathsheba] *who had been the wife of Uriah."* (NKJV) (emphasis added).

EXAMPLE 2:

Another example in the Bible about people being rewarded despite the fact that they lied for the sake of God's *righteous* cause is found in Exodus 1:15–22.

We are told in this Scripture when the *king of Egypt* spoke to the Hebrew midwives and told them to kill the sons of the babies born to the Hebrew women because the midwives feared God they did not obey the *king of Egypt's* command.

This is substantiated in Exodus 1:18–19, when Pharaoh, *king of Egypt,* called for the midwives and said to them, *"Why have you done this thing and saved the male children?"* The midwives lied to Pharaoh and said, *"Because the Hebrew women are not like the Egyptian women; for they are lively and give birth before the midwives come to them."*

217

Who is Israel? Discovering our True Identity in Jesus Christ and Why it Matters! The Root

In Exodus 1:20–21 we are told how God responded. This Scripture says, *"Therefore God dealt WELL WITH THE MIDWIVES, and the people multiplied and grew very mighty. And so it was, BECAUSE THE MIDWIVES FEARED GOD THAT HE PROVIDED HOUSEHOLDS FOR THEM."* (NKJV) (emphasis added).

Thus, based on the two biblical examples that I have cited, God rewarded all of them despite the fact they had lied. What was the common denominator in all these examples? They all lied for the sake of God's *righteous* cause to save lives.

Please do not think that I am saying it is okay to lie because I am not, for our integrity is everything. Rather, I am citing specific examples from God's Word concerning those individuals who were still blessed by God despite lying.

God is the only One who is worthy to judge a person's true motives in their heart and will extend mercy to those who fear Him and to whoever He determines has been merciful to other people in return.

Another example of breaking free from a "legalistic" mindset of following the *letter of the law* versus walking in accordance to the *Spirit of Grace* is as follows: Jesus healed people on the Sabbath day although God's Word says absolutely no work is to be done on His Sabbath day.

Hence, the need to love others by healing them, setting people free from the enemy or saving a life outweighs

218

keeping the *letter of the law.* Don't take my word for it; let's look to the author and finisher of our faith, Jesus Christ, for the answer.

The answer is found in Mark 3:4–6 when Jesus asked the following question to the Pharisees whom Jesus often called a *brood of vipers* when He said to them the following:

> *"... 'Is it lawful on the Sabbath to DO GOOD or to DO EVIL, to SAVE LIFE or to KILL?' But they kept silent. And when He* [Jesus] *had looked around at them with anger, BEING GRIEVED by the HARDNESS of their HEARTS, He said to the man, 'Stretch out your hand.' And he stretched it out, and his HAND was RESTORED as WHOLE as the other. Then the Pharisees WENT OUT and IMMEDIATELY PLOTTED with the Herodians against Him, how they might DESTROY Him."* (Mark 3:4–6, NKJV) (emphasis added).

And, again, in Luke 6:9, Jesus said to the scribes and Pharisees who watched Him closely, as to whether or not He would heal on the Sabbath, that they might find an accusation against Him, *"I will ask you one thing: Is it lawful on the Sabbath to DO GOOD or to DO EVIL, to SAVE LIFE or to DESTROY?"* (NKJV) (emphasis added).

Therefore, even though God's law says that we are to keep His Sabbath day holy and rest from our labors by doing no work, Jesus often healed people on the Sabbath day.

So do you believe if we break God's law to save a life or to do good for another person, that God will hold us accountable for breaking His law due to extenuating circumstances?

When we choose to do something, our intent and motives are everything to God. In each of the aforementioned examples, their motives for lying was for the purpose of God's *righteous* cause by healing or saving lives during a time of extreme persecution, war, and famine.

Are you still not sure? Do you think God punished people during the Holocaust for lying to the authorities concerning hiding His chosen people—the Jews—in their homes when the enemy's intent was to torture and kill them? Of course not!

Furthermore, unlike during the Holocaust, in the end-times, both the Jews from the House of Judah and those of us who were formerly Gentiles from the House of Israel—Christians will be faced with this same scenario once again. The authorities will come knocking on our door to take our family members and us to the concentration camps during the Antichrist's reign of terror.

I am being led by the Holy Spirit to have you think about these types of scenarios now.

Come to your own conclusion based on what God tells you to do by the leading of the Holy Spirit *when*, not *if*, you are faced with life or death circumstances and must defy the authorities for God's *righteous* cause to prevail. This is based on what Jesus says to us in Mark 13:11, which says the following:

> *"But when they ARREST YOU and DELIVER YOU UP, do not WORRY BEFOREHAND, or PREMEDITATE WHAT YOU WILL SPEAK. But whatever is given you in that hour, SPEAK THAT; for it is not you who SPEAK, but the Holy Spirit."* (Mark 13:11, NKJV) (emphasis added).

Moreover, Jesus tells us how to act during perilous times when persecution is rising. In Matthew 10:16, He says to us, *"Behold, I send you OUT as SHEEP in the MIDST of WOLVES. Therefore be WISE* [discreet and cautious] *as SERPENTS* [sharpness of vision, sly or cunning] *and HARMLESS* [innocent] *as DOVES."* (NKJV) (emphasis added).

History always repeats itself, and God always calls the past to account. And, as it was in the beginning, so it shall be in the end. *Yehóvah's* Word declares the end from the beginning.

So if you want to know what will happen at the end of days, you must seek to understand what happened at the very beginning. This is substantiated in Isaiah 46:10 which proclaims, *"Declaring the END from the BEGINNING, And from ANCIENT TIMES things that are not YET DONE, Saying, 'My COUNSEL shall STAND, And I will DO all My PLEASURE...'"* (NKJV) (emphasis added).

221

Now let's refocus our attention on what God allowed to happen to Jacob because he was deceptive for his own selfish ambitions *before* Jacob's name was changed to Israel by God. Jacob, unlike Esau, eventually repented of his lies and deception and became a changed man.

However, as usually is the case, he finally fully submitted to God *after* he learned his lesson at the hands of his father-in-law Laban who gave Jacob a taste of his own medicine.

Jacob had to learn obedience and righteousness by suffering, and he had to work a total of fourteen years first to marry Leah and then his true love, Rachel.

When Jacob finally had enough of reaping the consequences of his actions, he decided to be set free from the bondage of Laban for whom he had worked for a total of twenty years based on Genesis 31:38. It was then Jacob decided it was time to return to his homeland despite the consequences he would have to face from his brother Esau.

This decision would result in a "new" beginning for Jacob and his family. Jacob received his inheritance from God that God swore an "oath" to his father Isaac, based on the *everlasting* covenant God made with his grandfather Abraham.

Again, God would "confirm" this *everlasting* covenant through Jacob, which would be an *everlasting* covenant with all Israel. As we already know, based on the written testimony of God's Word, Jacob was a deceiver, supplanter, and a conniver until Jacob wrestled with God and he became a new man. This is based on Genesis 32:28, which says the following:

> *"And He [Yehóvâh] said, 'Your NAME shall no longer be called JACOB* [1] [H3290: *Ya'ăqốb:* *heel catcher* (that is, supplanter); *Jaakob,* the *Israelitish* patriarch], *but ISRAEL* [2] [H3478: *Yisrã'ẽl:* *he will rule* as *God; Jisrael,* a symbolical name of Jacob; also (typically) of his posterity]; *for you have STRUGGLED with GOD and with MEN, and have PREVAILED.'*" (Gen. 32:28, NKJV) (emphasis added).

God changed his name from Jacob to Israel after Jacob wrestled with God at Peniel.

This is based on Genesis 32:30, which says, *"So Jacob called the name of the place PENIEL* [3] [H6439: *P'nú'ẽl:* *face of God; Penuel* or *Peniel,* a place East of Jordan]: *'For I have SEEN God FACE to FACE, and my life is PRESERVED.'*" (NKJV) (emphasis added).

As a result, God changed Jacob's name to Israel. This is substantiated in Genesis 35:10, which says the following:

> *"And God said to him, 'Your NAME is JACOB* [1] [H3290: *Ya'ăqốb:* *heel catcher* (that is, supplanter); *Jaakob,* the *Israelitish* patriarch]; *your NAME shall not be called JACOB* [1] *anymore, but ISRAEL* [2] [H3478: *Yisrã'ẽl:* *he will rule* as *God; Jisrael,* a symbolical name of

Jacob; also (typically) of his posterity] *shall be your NAME.' So He called his name ISRAEL."*
[2] (Gen. 35:10, NKJV) (emphasis added).

Therefore, Jacob finally understood his *true* identity as God's son only *after* he wrestled with God and with men and prevailed.

In other words, Jacob became a "changed" man and as such received a "new" name from God based on Jacob's *true* identity from God's perspective of who Jacob was as His son.

And, so it is with us. When we finally comprehend our *true* identity based on "who" we belong to rather than based on "what" we do, then we will receive our "new" name from God as substantiated in Revelation 2:17.

As such, we need to look to God and His Word in order to understand our *true* identity as God's sons and daughters rather than deriving our identity based upon what other people tell us or based on what we do.

Thus, God's plan of "redemption," "reconciliation," and "restoration" from the foundation of the world would indeed prevail.

It would come to pass that Jacob would have twelve sons who would be the princes of the twelve tribes of Israel.

This would eventually result in the birth of Jesus Christ from the *tribe of Judah,* who is the Holy One of Israel.

In the next chapter, we will take a look at the final reason for this "ancient" jealousy and hatred between the descendants of Isaac and Jacob (Israel) versus the descendants of Ishmael and Esau.

It is all about who will control and take possession of the Promised Land, the land that God promised Abraham's descendants as a result of His *everlasting* covenant with him.

CHAPTER 31

ANOTHER REASON FOR THIS "ANCIENT" JEALOUSY AND HATRED IS FOR CONTROL AND POSSESSION OF THE PROMISED LAND

Another reason for this "ancient" jealousy and hatred between the descendants of Jacob (Israel) and Esau (Edomites) concerns the *physical* land God promised to Abraham and his descendants.

This is based on the *everlasting* covenant *Yehóvah* established with Abraham, the "oath" that He swore to Isaac, and "confirmed" it through Jacob for an *everlasting* covenant with all Israel.

This "spiritual" battle still wages on. As we are currently witnessing, many of the descendants of both Esau and Ishmael *say* it is about the land that Israel stole from them and has no right to possess.

And, no matter what amount of land Israel gives up for the sake of "peace," they are never satisfied and care nothing about the land. When I was in Israel, you can immediately see the difference between those areas that are occupied by the Palestinians versus those areas which are under Israeli control. The areas that the Palestinians occupy are in deplorable conditions. In other words, they do not take care of the land or their houses. Their neighborhoods resemble a war zone for there is trash and graffiti everywhere.

Therefore, this epic "spiritual" battle is not truly about the land. God defined and gave both nations their own land according to His *eternal* Word.

In fact, the land is so important to God that the word "land" is mentioned 1,653 times in the Bible. God gave a specific designation of land to the Israelites as detailed in Genesis 15:17–21.

However, *Yehóvah* also gave a specific designation of land to Esau and his descendants.

Moreover, God specifically told the Israelites in the following Scriptures not to meddle with Esau's descendants and that He would not give the Israelites any of their land.

> *"Do not MEDDLE with them, for I will not GIVE you any of their LAND, NO, not so much as one footstep, because I have given MOUNT SEIR* (1) (2) [H8165: *Se'iyr*: rough; Seir, a mountain of Idumaea and its aboriginal occupants, also one in Palestine (thought to be located near Petra in Jordan)] *to Esau as a POSSESSION."* (Deut. 2:5, NKJV) (emphasis added).

> *"Then the Lord said to me, 'Do not HARASS*

228

Moab, *nor* CONTEND with them in BATTLE, for I will *not* GIVE you *any* of THEIR LAND AS A POSSESSION, because I have given *AR* [3] [4] [H6144: *'Ar*: a *city*; *Ar*, a place in Moab; which is in the southern part of the Arnon Valley, which is the present day Wadi Mujib gorge in Jordan] to the DESCENDANTS of LOT as a POSSESSION.' " (Deut. 2:9, NKJV) (emphasis added).

Furthermore, Genesis 36 substantiates the truth that long ago Esau chose to take his wives, his sons, his daughters, all the persons of his household, including his livestock and all his goods which he had gained in the land of Canaan, and go to a country away from the presence of his brother Jacob.

In Genesis 36:7–8 below, it tells us not only *why* Esau did this, but also *where* he settled which would bring to pass what God decreed and mandated in Deuteronomy 2:9 above.

"For their POSSESSIONS WERE TOO GREAT FOR THEM TO DWELL TOGETHER, *and* THE LAND WHERE THEY WERE STRANGERS COULD NOT SUPPORT THEM BECAUSE OF THEIR LIVESTOCK. *So Esau dwelt in* MOUNT **SEIR** [1] [2] [H8165: *Śē'yr*: *rough*; *Seir*, a mountain of Idumaea and its aboriginal occupants, also one in Palestine (thought to be located near Petra in Jordan)]. ESAU *is* **EDOM** [5] [H123: *'ĕdôm*: *Edom*, the

elder twin-brother of Jacob; hence the region (Idumaea) occupied by him; Edom, Edomites, Idumea]." (Gen. 36:7–8, NKJV)

Therefore, at this time in history, Esau's descendants were called the "Edomites." They dwelled at Mount Seir which was located in the lower third region of Petra, now modern day Jordan. The "Edomites" are a Transjordan tribe whose territory was between Petra and the Red Sea.

Petra represented an East-West boundary between Edom and Moab. This is substantiated based on the fact that Israel asked both Edom and Moab for permission to cross through their lands from Kadesh.

From the earliest time, Edom's geographic domain was Transjordan. The Edomites never lived in the Negev or the "land of Judah" until the Babylonian captivity in about 587 BC. [6]

Moreover, what I find to be extremely interesting concerning the fact that Esau was described as having "reddish" features when describing one's hair or complexion, this also is a *physical* attribute describing Petra.

Petra is referred to as the "Rose-Red City," describing the color of the rocks Petra was carved from which are "red" in their appearance.

Furthermore, another interesting fact is this: Jordan will be spared from succumbing to the Antichrist's attempted takeover of Jordan, even though the Antichrist will be successful in his quest to overthrow Egypt, Libya, and Ethiopia (the northern horn of Africa) based on Daniel 11:40–45. Why will God not allow Jordan to be overthrown by the Antichrist and his minions? Jordan will become a "place of refuge" for God's people at the time that they are forced to flee from Jerusalem into this region.

This shall take place *when* the Antichrist reveals himself at the fullness of their kingdom. He will sit in the rebuilt Temple on the Temple Mount in Jerusalem and claim he is the Messiah the Orthodox Jews are still waiting for to appear the first time. (7)

Now let's refocus our attention on the subject at hand. We must keep in mind that this rivalry between the descendants of Jacob (Israel) and Esau (the Edomites) has never ceased since the beginning of time. As we are now witnessing, it is still going on.

Who is considered to be the modern day Edomites? One description is as follows:

> *"The Edomites doubtlessly also exist among the various tribes of today's Middle East. Without question, over the last four millennia, Edomite blood has infiltrated into the tribes that descended from Abraham through his second wife Keturah, whose children inhabited the territory to the east of Israel. And also without a doubt, the Edomites intermarried with the sons*

231

of Ishmael, the titular head of today's Arab tribes."[8]

Another description of *who* the Edomites are is found in Psalm 83. As a matter of fact, at this time we are witnessing the Confederation of Arab and Muslim nations, descendants of Ishmael and Esau, conspiring and consulting together to annihilate Israel in what is referred to as the Psalm 83 War.

They have unanimously agreed to come against Israel based on the "crafty counsel" of the United Nations, the Vatican, the Council on Foreign Relations, and the Trilateral Commission.

These are only *some* of the think-tank organizations that are spearheading and leading the New World Order/One World Order/Revived Roman Empire/Antichrist kingdom.

Moreover, they do not care that they are coming against God Almighty Himself for breaking the *Abrahamic* Covenant! As such, God will turn their wicked schemes back on their own heads without mercy.

I believe that the Psalm 83 War will also result in the total destruction of Damascus, Syria, based on Isaiah 17:1. Again, this "confederation" of Arab and Muslim nations are descendants of Ishmael and Esau, as indicated in Psalm 83:1–8. This Scripture is also a prayer that God's people can pray to frustrate the conspiracy against Israel. Psalm 83:1–8, says the following:

> *"Do not KEEP SILENT, O God! Do not HOLD*
> *Your PEACE, And do not BE STILL, O God!*
> *For behold, Your enemies make a TUMULT;*
> *And those who HATE You have LIFTED UP*
> *their HEAD. They have taken CRAFTY*
> *COUNSEL against Your PEOPLE, And*
> *CONSULTED TOGETHER against Your*
> *SHELTERED ONES. They have said, 'COME,*
> *and let us CUT THEM OFF from being a*
> *NATION, That the NAME of ISRAEL may be*
> *REMEMBERED no more.'"* (Psalm 83:1–4,
> NKJV) (emphasis added).

> *"For they have CONSULTED TOGETHER with*
> *ONE CONSENT; They FORM a*
> *CONFEDERACY against You: The TENTS of*
> *EDOM* [Palestinians and Southern Jordanians]
> *and the ISHMAELITES* [Saudi's—Ishmael is
> the "Father of the Arabs"]; *MOAB* [Palestinians
> and central Jordan] *and the HAGRITES*
> [Egyptians–Hagarenes]; *GEBAL* [Hezbollah
> and North Lebanese], *AMMON* [Palestinians
> and northern Jordan], *and AMALEK* [Arabs of
> the Sinai area]; *PHILISTIA* [Hamas occupying
> the Gaza strip] *with the inhabitants of TYRE*
> [South Lebanon occupied by Hezbollah];
> *ASSYRIA* [Syrians and Northern Iraqis] *also has*

233

joined with them; They have helped the CHILDREN of LOT." Selah (Psalm 83:5–8, NKJV) (emphasis added).

However, based on Jeremiah 12:14, listen to what the Lord says will happen to those who touch the inheritance (the land), which He has caused His people to inherit as a result of the *everlasting* covenant that He established with Abraham. Jeremiah 12:14, says the following:

"Thus says the Lord: 'AGAINST all My EVIL NEIGHBORS who touch the INHERITANCE which I have caused MY PEOPLE ISRAEL to INHERIT—behold, I will PLUCK THEM OUT of their LAND and PLUCK OUT the HOUSE of JUDAH from AMONG THEM.'" (Jer. 12:14, NKJV) (emphasis added).

As I was writing this section on July 29, 2014, Israel is at war with Hamas in the Gaza region, and yet the United States of America and the world is condemning Israel for responding to the repeated launching of missiles into their land by Hamas.

How can the US and the world expect Israel to make peace with Hamas, a "terrorist organization," when Hamas clearly states in their Hamas Charter [9] [10] the following:

1. Israel will exist until Islam rises to annihilate her.

2. The land of Palestine is to be an Islamic consecrate to the future Muslim generations until Judgment Day.

3. There is only one solution to resolve the conflict, and that is Jihad.

Therefore, this epic "spiritual" battle between the descendants of Jacob (Israel) and the descendants of Esau (the Edomites) is really about oppression and control. This conflict is fueled by an "ancient" jealousy that turned into hatred of God's chosen people, including not only the Orthodox Jews but also all believers in Jesus Christ who are called by His name—Christians.

And, it is for all these reasons I have conveyed in this chapter why "radical" Islam wants nothing more than to crush and annihilate the existence of the Jewish people and believers in Jesus Christ, who mostly reside in Israel and America.

Moreover, this is also why the Communists; Socialists; Marxists; global elite; Illuminati, and the Islamic Caliphate are in "collusion" with one another. They are acting on directives coming from the Council on Foreign Relations, the Trilateral Commission, the Vatican and the UN's "crafty counsel" as they have formed a "coalition" with "one" consent to work together to fund and support the proliferation of the Muslim Brotherhood.

The intent of the Muslim Brotherhood is to form a worldwide Islamic Caliphate led by the Antichrist, who will be the 12th Imam—their Mahdi. He will use the False Prophet as a "front man" or the "mediator" between God and His people, and he will falsely proclaim that he serves as a "representative" of Jesus Christ. In John 5:43–44, Jesus warns us about believing another who will come in his own name, that we will receive him who seeks honor for himself, but does not receive honor from God. John 5:43–44, says the following:

> *"I have come in My FATHER'S NAME, and you do not RECEIVE Me; if ANOTHER comes in his OWN name, HIM YOU WILL RECEIVE. How can you believe, who RECEIVE HONOR from ONE ANOTHER, and do not SEEK the HONOR that COMES from the only GOD?"*
> (John 5:43–44, NKJV) (emphasis added).

The first "key" thing that I want you to focus your attention on at this time, based on John 5:43–44 above is this: Jesus specifically tells us that He has come in His Father's name. Therefore, what is Jesus' and our heavenly Father's name? It is *Yehóvah* (Yahweh [YHWH]).

Therefore, if Jesus Christ came in His Father's name, then *Yehóvah's* only *begotten* Son would be named *Y'hóshûa'* or *Yáhushá* or *Yéshûa'* rather than the name of Jesus because there are no "J's" in the Hebrew language.

Yet we have been taught to call Him by the name of Jesus. This is based on what our early church fathers have taught us and is based on the name used in our Bibles, translated by men. As such, the False Prophet will come in "another" name. Many people will receive and honor the one who will call himself by the title of the "Vicar of Christ" who is an earthly representative of God or Christ.

This title is used in Catholicism to refer to the bishops and more specifically to the Bishop of Rome (the Pope). In addition, this title is also used in the sense of a person acting as a parish priest in place of the *only* true God as well. [11]

I proclaim that the Antichrist will either be a Muslim or an Arab man who practices "radical" Islam for two reasons.

First, Islam's eschatology concerning end-time events discusses the 12th Imam, the Mahdi, who will be their end-time Messiah.

Some even believe Jesus will be the Mahdi, returning and proclaiming Islam as the true religion.

The majority of the *Shiite* Muslims believe the 12th Imam will come out of hiding at the end of days after they destroy the United States of America (*The Great Satan*) and Israel (*The Little Satan*).

To usher in the Mahdi's return, they must control the world through Jihad and kill all the infidels. This is based on the end-time eschatology of "radical" Islam.

Second, another reason why I believe the Antichrist will be a Muslim or an Arab man who practices "radical" Islam is because this would be the only way that a leader with a fierce countenance could be kept *hidden* until the *fullness* of the Antichrist kingdom comes to fruition.

In addition, only an Arab or Muslim man who adheres to the Islam religion would be able to get the "buy-in" of all the Arab and Muslim nations who have formed a "confederacy" (Caliphate) with "one" consent to come against Israel and the world.

The prophet Daniel tells us in Daniel 8:23 that in the *latter* time of their kingdom *when* the transgressors have reached their *fullness* that a king shall arise, having fierce features who understands sinister schemes. This is talking about the Antichrist who will lead this "coalition" comprised of mostly Arab or Muslim nations. Some of these Arab or Muslim nations who have all helped the children of Lot based on Psalm 83:5–8 will include the following nations or people groups:

1. Edom (Palestinians and Southern Jordanians)
2. Ishmaelites (the Saudi's [descendants of Ishmael])
3. Moab (Palestinians and central Jordan)
4. Hagarenes (Egyptians–Hagarenes)
5. Gebal (Hezbollah and North Lebanese)
6. Ammon (Palestinians and northern Jordan)
7. Amalek (Arabs of the Sinai area)
8. Philistia (Hamas occupying the Gaza strip)
9. Tyre (South Lebanon occupied by Hezbollah)
10. Assyria (Syrians and Northern Iraqis)

Do you think all these Arab and Muslim nations would come under the leadership of anyone who is not Arab or Muslim and who does not practice "radical" Islam?

It is my "opinion" that there is no way all these Muslim and Arab nations would follow the orders of anyone who is not Arab or Muslim and who does not practice "radical" Islam.

This is exactly one of the reasons why the Islamic Antichrist will need the False Prophet to "deceive" the masses who will follow him and actually believe that they are "practicing" Christianity. However, they have perverted the *gospel of the kingdom* which was once delivered to the saints.

Under *this* False Prophet—and many who follow in his footsteps—the vast majority of believers in the body of Christ will have been "deceived" into following *another* Jesus, rather than following the one and *only* true God's Son who came in His Father's name.

In fact, the False Prophet will be the one to lead many people in the body of Christ astray. This False Prophet has and will continue to "deceive" them into "worshiping" the Antichrist and becoming part of the One World "Harlot" Religious System.

It will be led by the "Mother" of all Harlots and the abominations of the earth, a "key" player of *Mystery Babylon the Great*, as it has been since the very beginning of the "organized" Church. In the very next chapter, I will present the truth, if you are willing to receive it, of the connection between the one who comes in "another" name and calls himself the "Vicar of Christ" and the Vatican's connection to Islam. This is based on many years of research I have personally done. I began this research based on the revelation I received from the Holy Spirit while I was in Israel and at the Vatican.

For all the reasons cited in this chapter, and in previous chapters, is it any wonder that *some* of the descendants of Esau and Ishmael, those Arab and Muslim people who practice "radical" Islam, are hostile and want to annihilate the Jews and the Christians?

And, if they cannot annihilate the Jews and the Christians through Jihad, then they will do it through "mass" deception.

In fact, we are told in Revelation 12:9 that the great dragon who was cast out, that serpent of old, called the Devil and Satan, will "deceive" the *whole* world with his angels who were cast out with him.

As such, both the Antichrist and the False Prophet will "deceive" the *whole* world, with the *exception* of those whose names are written in the Lamb's Book of Life from the foundation of the world.

So how will the Antichrist, the False Prophet, and their minions "deceive" the *whole* world? Because they will derive their "power" from Satan, and they will perform signs, wonders, and miracles designed to "deceive" even the elect *if* that is possible. Speaking of the elect being "deceived," I need to digress from the subject at hand for a few minutes and talk about the Lamb's Book of Life, based on the fact that our names were written in this book from the foundation of the world.

This is particularly relevant since many people in the body of Christ teach and believe that our names are written in the Lamb's Book of Life *when* a person receives Jesus Christ as our Lord and Savior.

THE LAMB'S BOOK OF LIFE

We often tell people we are trying to evangelize that they must accept Jesus Christ as their Lord and Savior for their names to be written in the Lamb's Book of Life. Otherwise, when they die, they will be thrown into the *lake of fire* and perish for all eternity.

However, this is not true or biblical at all for this reason: Every human being, before they are ever conceived in their mother's womb, *already* has their name written in the Lamb's Book of Life.

Their name has been written in this book *before* their first day on this earth ever came to be.

This is why Psalm 139:16 proclaims, *"Your eyes saw my substance, being YET UNFORMED. And in YOUR BOOK they all were WRITTEN, The DAYS fashioned for me,*

When as YET there were NONE of them." (NKJV) (emphasis added).

When babies are aborted, or children die before they are old enough to choose Jesus Christ as their Lord and Savior and live their lives for Him, they will still go to heaven. This is because their names are *already* written in the Lamb's Book of Life.

Before Jesus went to the cross at Calvary and shed His precious blood for the forgiveness of our sins, He clearly stated that our names are *already* written in heaven. This is substantiated in Luke 10:20 when Jesus says to us His disciples, *"Nevertheless do not rejoice in this, that the SPIRITS are SUBJECT to you, but rather REJOICE because your NAMES are WRITTEN in HEAVEN."* (NKJV) (emphasis added).

This is in accordance with God's eternal plan of "redemption," "reconciliation," and "restoration" of all mankind. God's eternal plan is only made possible through faith and trust in His only *begotten* Son—Jesus Christ.

Jesus shed His blood for the salvation of all mankind, no matter what ethnic group they may be from based on what region of the world they are born.

For it is God's will that no one should perish but all should come to repentance and have *everlasting* life by "believing" in His only *begotten* Son, Jesus Christ.

242

In fact, acknowledging and receiving God's only *begotten* Son, Jesus Christ, as our Lord and Savior is what prevents our names from being "blotted out" of the Lamb's Book of Life!

Yet we must also finish the race which is set before us by "overcoming" until the very end. I cover this fact in detail in Chapter 43 of Book 3. However, this truth is substantiated by Jesus who tells us in Revelation 3:5, that for those who "overcome" until the end, He will not "blot out" our name from the Lamb's Book of Life. He will confess our name before His Father and before His angels. Revelation 3:5 says the following:

> *"He who OVERCOMES* [to *subdue:* conquer, prevail, get the victory] *shall be CLOTHED in WHITE GARMENTS, and I will not BLOT OUT his NAME from the BOOK of LIFE; but I will CONFESS his NAME before My FATHER and before His ANGELS."* (Rev. 3:5, NKJV) (emphasis added).

As we are clearly told, based on what Jesus says to us in Revelation 3:5 above, our names can be "blotted out" of the Lamb's Book of Life. This includes us not finishing the race which has been set before us until we take our last breath or until Jesus returns the second time. We must "overcome" until the end of our lives by "occupying" and "doing" the will of our heavenly Father.

Our names can also be "blotted out" of the Lamb's Book of Life if we do not repent for sinning against God *after* we become saved by "worshiping" false gods and false idols.

One biblical example substantiating this truth concerns the time when the children of Israel worshipped the "Gold Calf" in Exodus 32:1–35. Listen carefully to what God said to Moses concerning His people who sinned against Him in Exodus 32:33–34. He specifically says to Moses that whoever sinned against Him He would "blot out" their name in His Book (the Lamb's Book of Life).

This happened long before Jesus Christ would be sent to the earth as the Son of Man in the Person of Jesus Christ. Exodus 32:33–34, says the following:

> *"And the LORD said to Moses, 'Whoever has SINNED against Me, I will BLOT HIM OUT of MY BOOK. Now therefore, go, lead the people to the place of which I have spoken to you. Behold, My Angel shall go before you. Nevertheless, in the DAY* [the Day of the Lord] *when I VISIT for PUNISHMENT, I will visit punishment UPON THEM for their SIN.'"* (Exod. 32:33–34, NKJV) (emphasis added).

Based on Exodus 32:33–34 above, before the children of Israel could receive Jesus Christ as their Lord and Savior, their names were *already* written in the Lamb's Book of Life!

The *Word* was (chosen, selected, and qualified) to be the Lamb who was slain from the foundation of the world based

244

on Revelation 13:8.

In addition, we are specifically told in Exodus 32:33–34, that *when* the "Day of the Lord" comes, it will be then that God will render His final punishment upon all those who have sinned against Him and have not repented and turned from their wicked ways.

Therefore, our names are *already* written in the Lamb's Book of Life before the foundation of the world.

However, it's important to understand our names can be "blotted out" by God for various reasons based on the following Scriptures:

> *"Then the LORD said to Moses, 'Write this for a MEMORIAL in the BOOK and recount it in the hearing of Joshua, that I will utterly BLOT OUT the REMEMBRANCE of Amalek from under heaven.'"* (Exod. 17:14, NKJV) (emphasis added).

> *"Yet now, if You will FORGIVE their SIN—but if not, I pray, BLOT me OUT of Your BOOK which You have WRITTEN."* (Exod. 32:32, NKJV) (emphasis added).

> *"And the LORD said to Moses, 'Whoever has SINNED against Me, I will BLOT him OUT of My BOOK.'"* (Exod. 32:33, NKJV) (emphasis added).

> *"Let Me alone, that I may DESTROY them and BLOT OUT their NAME from under HEAVEN; and I will make of you a nation mightier and greater than they."* (Deut. 9:14, NKJV) (emphasis added).

> *"The LORD would not spare him; for then the anger of the LORD and His jealousy would burn against that man, and every curse that is written in this book would settle on him, and the LORD would BLOT OUT his NAME from under HEAVEN."* (Deut. 29:20, NKJV) (emphasis added).

> *"You have rebuked the NATIONS, You have destroyed the WICKED; You have BLOTTED OUT their NAME forever and ever."* (Psalm 9:5, NKJV) (emphasis added).

> *"Let them* [the wicked] *be BLOTTED OUT of the BOOK of the LIVING, And not be WRITTEN with the RIGHTEOUS."* (Psalm 69:28, NKJV) (emphasis added).

As clearly seen based on the whole counsel of God's Word, God can and will "blot out" our name in the Lamb's Book of Life based on the following three things:

1. By us rejecting His only *begotten* Son as our Lord and Savior so that our sins may be forgiven. This is only

made possible by Jesus' precious blood which was shed at Calvary on the cross. Those who reject God's *only* plan of "redemption" for the forgiveness of our sins, planned by God from the foundation of the world, will have made their "choice" to be separated from their Creator for all eternity.

As such, they will be cast into the *lake of fire* based on what is written or not written in all the books (plural) which shall be opened up on Judgment Day when God's final judgment will be rendered, and His royal decree is carried out.

2. If once we come to the saving knowledge of Jesus Christ and have "received" Him as our Lord and Savior, yet we continue to "willfully" sin and do not "obey" God's Voice and His Word, then we can "say" all that we want that He is our Lord and we are His disciples.

Yet from God's perspective, we have broken the *everlasting* covenant with Him that His precious Son died to "restore" and "reconcile" us back to so we may "walk" in a covenant relationship with our heavenly Father.

3. Based on what is "recorded" in the Book of Remembrance which I will cover in more detail in Book 3, Malachi 3:16 says that a Book of Remembrance was written for those who "fear the

247

Lord" and who "meditate" on His name.

Do you know that God even "records" those who will keep His *everlasting* ordinances that are an *everlasting* "memorial" in His Book of Remembrance to record those who fear Him? This will be one of the books (plural) that will be opened up on Judgment Day.

Therefore, contrary to what is taught, there is no such thing as "unconditional" eternal security based on us simply saying a sinner's prayer, yet we refuse to "obey" God's Voice and His Word! In fact, many of God's covenant promises use the word "if" which makes what He says conditional based on what we "choose" to do or we "choose" not to do.

The only exception to this statement is this: If you repent and receive Jesus Christ as your Lord and Savior on your deathbed at the last possible moment before you take your last breath. This truth is substantiated by the criminal on the cross who repented as he was dying. This is based on Luke 23:42–44.

THERE IS NO SUCH THING AS "UNCONDITIONAL" ETERNAL SECURITY BASED ON THE WHOLE COUNSEL OF GOD'S WORD

Are you still not sure what I am proclaiming is true? If you believe there is "unconditional" eternal security, then let me ask you the following question as a believer who has repented and received Jesus Christ as your Lord and Savior.

What does God's Word say will happen to you as a believer in Jesus Christ *if* you cave in to pressure after experiencing great persecution for His name's sake during the Antichrist's reign of terror?

What will happen to you if you end up worshiping the beast, his image, or you receive his mark on your forehead or your hand because you fear for your life, or for the life of your loved ones? The answer is given to us in Revelation 14:11–13, which says the following:

> *"And the SMOKE of their TORMENT ascends FOREVER and EVER; and they have no REST day or night, who WORSHIP the BEAST and his IMAGE, and whoever RECEIVES the MARK of his NAME."* (Rev. 14:11, NKJV) (emphasis added).

> *"Here is the PATIENCE of the SAINTS; here are those who KEEP the COMMANDMENTS of GOD and the FAITH of JESUS."* (Rev. 14:12, NKJV) (emphasis added).

> *"Then I heard a voice from heaven saying to me, 'Write: 'BLESSED are the DEAD who DIE in the LORD from NOW on.' 'Yes,' says the Spirit, 'that they may rest from their labors, and their works follow them.'"* (Rev. 14:13, NKJV) (emphasis added).

As we can clearly see based on Revelation 14:11, *if* God's people worship the beast, his image, and receive the mark of his name, they will perish in the *lake of fire*! This is despite the fact that Jesus Christ shed His blood on the cross at Calvary.

As stated in Revelation 14:13, we must be willing to die for His name's sake rather than bowing down to Satan by worshiping the beast, his image, and receiving the mark of his name.

Also, do not dismiss the significance based on Revelation 14:12, for us to "overcome" until the end and be "counted worthy" in the sight of God we must "keep" His commandments and have "faith" in Christ—both are required!

Based on this one example alone, there is no such thing as "unconditional" eternal security.

To "receive" eternal life and "keep" it based on the whole counsel of God's Word, it is "conditional" concerning *some* of the requirements listed below and on the following page. And, this is not a comprehensive list by any means.

Receiving and keeping our eternal salvation is contingent based on what we "choose" to do or "choose" not to do. *Some* of God's requirements are as follows:

❖ We must place our faith and trust in God's only *begotten* Son Jesus Christ. This is "how" we become saved by grace through faith.

❖ We must repent, turn towards God, and stop "willfully" sinning. This is based on Hebrews 10:26.

❖ We must "know" on a personal, intimate basis our heavenly Father, the only true God and Jesus Christ whom He sent based on John 17:3.

❖ We must "keep" the commandments of God *after* we *become* saved. The commandments of God are based on the doctrine of Christ which is the full volume of Moses and the gospels.

This is based on John 7:16. Also, this is based on Second John 9 which says, *"Whoever transgresses and does not abide in the doctrine of Christ does not have God. He who abides in the doctrine of Christ has both the Father and the Son."*

❖ We must "do" the will of our heavenly Father based on what Jesus says to us in Matthew 7:21.

❖ We must stop practicing "lawlessness" based on what Jesus says to us in Matthew 7:22-23. If we practice "lawlessness" we are not doing the will of our heavenly Father based on Matthew 7:21.

This is why Isaiah 8:20 says, *"To the law* [the Torah] *and to the testimony! If they do not speak according to this word, it is because there is no light in them."*

251

Again, we must "obey" the commandments of our heavenly Father and Jesus Christ our Lord and Savior once we become saved. Jesus became the author of eternal salvation to those who "obey" Him based on Hebrews 5:9.

❖ We must "overcome" until the end and finish the race which is set before us. This is based on Revelation 2:7; 2:11; 2:17; 2:26; 3:5; 3:12; 3:21, and 21:7.

I could devote an entire chapter to this subject alone. Nevertheless, Jesus Christ, the Lamb of God, who was slain from the foundation of the world was and is God's *only* "eternal" plan of "redemption" period!

As such, *every* man is given the opportunity to become "born again" by coming to the saving knowledge of Jesus Christ, who is the Lamb that was slain from the foundation of the world.

Most individuals become "born again" *spiritually* speaking, once they receive the revelation that they need a Savior. This usually happens when they *finally* come to an end of themselves and doing what they deem right in their own eyes which has resulted in them reaping the consequences of their "bad" choices.

As a result, they make a "choice" to live for Jesus Christ and to serve *only* Him after they have "received" Him as their personal Lord and Savior and repented of their sins.

If they "choose" to receive Jesus Christ as their personal Lord and Savior by living for Him all the days of their life on the earth, then God will not "blot out" their names from the Lamb's Book of Life.

Jesus will confess their names before His Father and before His angels after they die a *physical* death when the resurrection of the dead in Christ takes place. This is when the books (plural) are opened up on Judgment Day, and they will receive their "eternal" rewards.

Although, as substantiated in the case of the criminal on the cross, some people never spend their lives living for Him. Instead, they repent and receive Jesus Christ as their Lord and Savior on their deathbed at the last minute. Yet they shall be saved and inherit eternal life!

Jesus addresses this fact in *The Parable of the Minas* beginning in Chapter 19 in the Book of Luke. He also talks about the fact that *some* believers who have served Jesus Christ all their lives *may* feel this is not fair. However, we should rejoice that these "last minute" converts to the faith shall not burn in the *lake of fire*.

Again, God's eternal plan of "redemption" was planned from the foundation of the world, offering *every* man, no matter what their sins may be, the opportunity to become "born again" by coming to the saving knowledge of Jesus Christ, the Lamb that was slain from the foundation of the world. As such, they receive Jesus Christ as their personal Lord and Savior.

Therefore, God's eternal plan of "redemption" also includes the Muslim and Arab people who are descendants of Abraham.

In addition, the descendants of Esau and Ishmael, the Arab and Muslim people are still dealing with the "spirit of rejection" and the "orphan spirit" that God desires to set them free from once He removes their *spiritual* blindness.

As such, they have fostered a "root of bitterness" in their hearts as Esau did. Yet God's will is to save, deliver, and to heal them *if* they will allow Him to.

Until they receive the revelation and come to the knowledge of Jesus Christ as their Lord and Savior, they are still *spiritually* blinded to the truth of God's plan for the "redemption," "reconciliation," and "restoration" of all mankind, especially for those who are descendants of Abraham.

Therefore, in the next chapter, I will cover "how" disciples of Jesus Christ should witness to the Muslim and Arab people who adhere to the Islam religion. Yet we must *never* come into agreement with them by "practicing" Chrislam or by becoming involved with the interfaith or the ecumenical movement that is currently gaining momentum which is ushering in the One World "Harlot" Religious System.

Please note: This next chapter is extremely long based on the content of what I am covering but it is extremely important.

So I apologize in advance for the length of this next chapter. However, I have put many subheadings in this next chapter so you can take a break at each section I am covering and resume reading each section as time permits. Thank you in advance for your understanding.

Chapter 32

How Should Disciples of Jesus Christ Witness to Muslim and Arab People Who Are Also Descendants of Abraham?

So how should we, as disciples of Jesus Christ, respond and witness to the Muslim and the Arab people who are descendants of Ishmael and Esau? We should pray to our heavenly Father that He hears the *cry of Ishmael* for his father and that He delivers and heals his descendants from the "spirit of rejection" and the "orphan spirit."

We should pray that God reveals His only *begotten* Son, Jesus Christ, to the descendants of Ishmael and Esau through visions and dreams. We should also pray that God removes their *spiritual* blindness so they can receive His truth.

As this happens and the Jews witness the Arab and Muslim people becoming reconciled to the God of Abraham, Isaac, and Jacob, the Jews will be provoked to jealousy.

The truth of the matter is this: Those of us who were formerly Gentiles from the House of Israel should be the ones who are provoking the Jews from the House of Judah to jealousy.

According to what the apostle Paul states in Romans 11:11, this is one of the reasons why salvation was offered to the Gentiles in the first place. Do you want to know the main reason why the body of Christ is not provoking the Orthodox Jews to believe in Jesus?

It is because the Messiah that they are still waiting on, based on all their studies of the Tanak would "be" the "living" Torah. And, as such, those who follow Him would be keeping *Yehóvǎh's* Sabbaths (plural) that *Yehóvǎh* commanded His people to keep based on His seven (7) holy convocations which are detailed in the Book of Leviticus beginning in Chapter 23.

Therefore, when the Orthodox Jews see Christians keeping the Sabbath Day on Sunday, the first day of the week instead of on Saturday, the seventh day of the week and celebrating Christmas instead of the Feast of Tabernacles when Jesus was actually born and Easter instead of Passover and the Feast of Unleavened Bread, they think there is no way that the Jesus we serve could ever be their Messiah that they are waiting for.

According to the Tanak, their Messiah would only do the will of His heavenly Father—the God of Abraham, Isaac, and Jacob (Israel) based on the "Book of the Law" or the "Book of the Covenant" which the prophets of the Old Testament said would point to their Messiah's coming as detailed in the Books of the Prophets.

During my most recent trip to Israel which occurred in September 2015, as I was witnessing to Orthodox Jews I was really confusing them when I told them that I was Christian and yet they witnessed that I honored the seventh day Sabbath and was there to celebrate the Day of Atonement (Yom Kippur) and the Feast of Tabernacles (Sukkot) with them.

What I had to learn to say when I was witnessing to our Jewish sisters and brothers is the following: I told them that I serve the same God that they do who is El Elyon (the Most High God), the God, of Abraham, Isaac, and Jacob (Israel) but I am redeemed by the blood of Yeshua our Jewish Messiah who has already come to the earth the first time to make atonement for our sins on the cross at Calvary.

The reason why I had to change the way I witnessed to our Jewish sisters and brothers is because when the Orthodox Jews hear us proclaim that we are Christians they automatically link us to the Roman Catholic Church, who throughout the *synergy of the ages* has persecuted and martyred countless Jews because of Anti-Semitism.

And, unfortunately, this includes the Anti-Semitism which spewed forth from the early reformers such as Martin Luther and many others who were quoted as saying many horrible things about the Jewish people.

Therefore, as disciples of Jesus Christ, we must pray that God removes the *spiritual* blindness off of our Jewish sisters and brothers who are still *spiritually* "blinded" by God until the *fullness of the Gentiles* comes to fruition. They are still waiting for their Messiah to appear for the first time. The *fullness of the Gentiles* is at hand, and God is removing the *spiritual* blindness off of His Jewish people for the set time to favor Zion is at hand.

What we should not do is compromise the Word of God under the "guise" of loving one another and for the sake of "peace" or "unity" as many evangelical Christians are now doing!

COME OUT FROM THEM AND BE SEPARATE

God's Word says to us in Second Corinthians 6:14–18, the following:

> *"Do not be UNEQUALLY YOKED TOGETHER with* **UNBELIEVERS** [1] [G571: *apistos:* disbelieving, that is, *without* Christian faith (specifically a heathen); faithless, untrustworthy person]. *For what* **FELLOWSHIP** [2] [3] [G3352: *metoche:* participation, sharing, communion; partnership; a close relation between partners, i.e. people sharing something held in common (used only in 2 Cor 6:14); joint-activity; G3348: *metecho:* to share or participate; by implication belong to, eat (or drink): to be a partaker] *has* **RIGHTEOUSNESS** [4] [G1343: *dikaiosune:* equity (of character or act); specifically (Christian) justification] *with* **LAWLESSNESS**

(5) (6) (7) [**G458:** *anomia:* violation of law or the condition of being without law which leads to unrighteousness, wickedness, or iniquity because of ignorance of the law or violating the law due to contempt of God's law; **G459:** *anomos:* lawless, that is, not subject to (the Jewish) law; a Gentile who is a transgressor of the law; **G3551:** *nomos:* (regulation), specifically (of Moses, including the volume; also of the gospel]*? And what **COMMUNION** (8) (9) [**G2842:** *koinōnia:* partnership, that is, (literally) participation, or (social) intercourse, or (pecuniary) benefaction; (to) communicate, communion, fellowship; **G2844:** *koinōnos:* a sharer, that is, associate; companion, partaker, partner] has LIGHT with DARKNESS?"* (2 Cor. 6:14, NKJV) (emphasis added).

*"And what **ACCORD*** (10) (11) [**G4857:** *sumphonēsis:* concord; **G4856:** *sumphōneō:* to be harmonious, that is, (figuratively) to accord (be suitable, concur) or stipulate (by compact): agree (together, with)] *has **CHRIST*** (12) (13) [**G5547:** *Christos:* anointed, that is, the Messiah, an epithet of Jesus; **G5548:** *chriō:* through the idea of contact; to smear or rub with oil, that is, (by implication) to "consecrate" to an office or religious service; anoint] *with **BELIAL*** (14) (15) [**G955:** *Belial:* of Hebrew origin [H1100];

worthlessness; Belial, as an epithet of Satan; H1100: *B'līya'al:* without profit, worthlessness; by extension destruction, wickedness; evil, naughty, ungodly (men), wicked]*? Or what part has a* **BELIEVER** [16] [G4103: *pistos:* objectively trustworthy; subjectively trustful; believe, (-ing, -r), faithful (-ly), sure, true] *with an* **UNBELIEVER** [17] [G571: *apistos:* (actively) disbelieving, that is, without Christian faith (specifically a heathen); that believeth not, faithless, incredible thing, infidel, unbeliever (-ing), untrustworthy person]*?"* (2 Cor. 6:15, NKJV) (emphasis added).

"And what **AGREEMENT** [18] [G4783: *sugkatathesis:* a deposition (of sentiment) in company with, that is, (figuratively) accord with or consent with] *has the* **TEMPLE** [19] [G3485: *naos:* naio̅ (to dwell); a fane, shrine] *of* **GOD** [20] [G2316: *theos:* a deity; the supreme Divinity or Magistrate] *with* **IDOLS** [21] [G1497: *eidōlon:* an image (that is, for worship); by implication a *heathen* god, or (plural) the *worship* of such]*? For YOU are the* **TEMPLE** [19] *of the LIVING* **GOD**. [20] *As God has said: 'I will DWELL in them And WALK among them. I will be THEIR God, and THEY shall be My PEOPLE.'"* (2 Cor. 6:16, NKJV) (emphasis added).

"Therefore COME OUT from AMONG THEM And BE **SEPARATE** (22) [G873: *aphorizo*: to *set off* by a boundary, that is, (figuratively) limit, exclude, appoint; divide, sever ties],' *says the Lord*. *'Do not TOUCH what is* **UNCLEAN** (23) [G169: *akathartos*: impure (ceremonially, morally (*lewd*) or specifically (*demonic*)], And I WILL RECEIVE YOU. I will be a FATHER to YOU, And YOU shall be My SONS and DAUGHTERS,' Says the LORD Almighty." (2 Cor. 6:17–18, NKJV) (emphasis added).

Thus, disciples of Jesus Christ are commanded to be holy because the God that we serve is holy. Based on Second Corinthians 6:14–18, the following is a commandment from God, not a suggestion:

1. Do not be unequally "yoked" together with **unbelievers** (*disbelieving*, that is, *without* Christian *faith* [specifically a *heathen*]; faithless and untrustworthy person) because of the following reasons:

    a. For what **fellowship** (which includes participation, sharing, communion, eating or drinking together, belonging to, having a partnership or a close relationship between partners, sharing something held in common like a joint-activity) has **righteousness** (*equity* [of character or act]; specifically [Christian] *justification*) with **lawlessness** (those who violate God's law or those who are without God's law which leads to "unrighteousness," "wickedness," or "iniquity" because of ignorance of the law or violating the law due to contempt of God's law. It is the state of one being "lawless" because one is not subjected to [the Jewish] law. This applies to Gentiles who are a transgressor of God's law, which is God's regulation for all His people which includes the volume of Moses' writings found in the Torah and also the gospel)?

b. And, what **communion** (to have a *partnership* in order to participate in a social *intercourse* [communication or dealings between individuals or groups], or *benefaction* [a *donation* or *gift*] in order to communicate or fellowship together) has "light" with "darkness"?

c. And, what **accord** (to be in a *harmonious* or *suitable* accord together in order to concur or stipulate [by compact] an agreement) has **Christ** (an anointed believer of the Messiah who is an epithet [expressing a *quality* or *characteristic* of the person] of Jesus) with **Belial** (an unprofitable, worthless, evil, wicked, ungodly person who is an epithet [expressing a *quality* or *characteristic* of the person] of Satan)?

d. Or, what "part" has a **believer** (a trustworthy, believing, faithful person who is sure and true) with an **unbeliever** (a disbelieving, faithless, unbelieving, untrustworthy infidel heathen who is without Christian faith)?

e. And, what "agreement" has the "temple" of the living God, in which God dwells in all *true* disciples of Jesus Christ, with **idols** (an *image* [that is, for worship]; by implication a heathen *god*, or [plural] the *worship* of such)?

f. For we are the "temple" of the living God. God dwells in us and walks amongst us, and the God of Abraham, **Isaac**, and Jacob (Israel) is our God, not the God of Abraham, **Ishmael**, and Jacob.

2. In the same Scripture, it is a commandment, not a suggestion that we are to "come out" from among them. As such, we are to "obey" and "do" the following:

a. We are to be **separate** (we are to be "set apart" by establishing boundaries, which limit, exclude, and divide in order to sever ties).

b. We are **not** to touch what is **unclean** (impure [ceremonially], or morally [lewd] or specifically [demonic]).

3. Only then, will the Lord do the following:

    a.   Receive us.

    b.   Be a Father to us.

    c.   And, we shall be His sons and daughters.

Therefore, as disciples of Jesus Christ, we are not to get into an agreement, worship, or fellowship for a "joint activity" or a "partnership" in any way, shape, or form at a house of worship with those "practicing" any religion other than Christianity.

These are "false" religions, and they are "unbelievers" because they do not believe Jesus Christ is God or the Son of God. Some of these "false" religions include, but are not limited to, the following religions:

Islam; Judaism; Bahá'í Faith; Hinduism; Taoism; Buddhism; Sikhism; Slavic neopaganism; Celtic polytheism; Heathenism (German paganism); Semitic Neopaganism; Wicca; Kemetism (Egyptian mysticism); Hellenism, and Italo-Roman Neopaganism.

At the same time, those who **practice** "lawlessness" are not considered to be *true* disciples of Jesus Christ from God's perspective either even though they "profess" to have the testimony of Jesus Christ for this reason: They are totally negating our heavenly Father's instructions found in the Torah. By the way, the full volume of Moses and the gospel is the doctrine of Christ based on what Jesus tells us in John

7:16, when Jesus answered them and said, *"My DOCTRINE is not Mine, BUT His who SENT me."* (NKJV) (emphasis added).

Who sent *the Word* as the Son of Man to the earth in the Person of Jesus Christ, to "redeem" us from our sins and to "restore" and "reconcile" us back into "walking" in a covenant relationship with Him? Our heavenly Father, *Yehôvâh.*

THE DECEPTION OF THE "INTERFAITH" MOVEMENT

Now I want us to focus our attention on the religion of Islam. There are many people within the body of Christ who are now embracing the following movements being spearheaded by many evangelical leaders:

1.   The Common Ground Movement.
2.   Jesus in the Quran Seminar.
3.   The Insider Movement.
4.   Chrislam Movement.
5.   Interfaith Movement.

The movement called *Chrislam* is embracing both Christianity and Islam.

Followers of *Chrislam* agree with those who have the *Spirit of Antichrist* based on Islamic beliefs, as I will convey shortly.

This is part of the postmodern movement currently

attributing to the great apostasy we are currently witnessing all over the world, particularly in America.

However, the most "insidious" and "deceptive" of all the movements that are currently being spearheaded is the "interfaith" movement.

This movement is being initiated worldwide by the Pope of the Roman Catholic Church, who calls himself "The Vicar of Christ."

For he is issuing a beckoning call for all Christian denominations to come back to their "mother" church at breakneck speeds. Many evangelical leaders are being wooed by the Pope for this very reason.

As a matter of fact, at a recent gathering called *Azusa Now,* held on April 9, 2016, Catholic leader Matteo Calisi, appointed by Pope Benedict XVI to serve on the Pontifical Council for the Laity, said the following during this event:

> "*...that the division between Christians and Catholics is a 'diabolical sin,' and that Jesus 'doesn't care' that Christians and Catholics disagree on biblical doctrine by saying. 'He doesn't care about our differences...'*" In addition, he said, "*We're not going to be known by our differences, but for the love, we have for one another.*"[24]

Nothing could be further from the truth when Calisi said Jesus doesn't care that Christians and Catholics disagree on "biblical" doctrine. By the time you have finished reading this chapter, you will understand why I am saying this.

Unbeknownst to many, this "interfaith" movement, led by the Pope of the Roman Catholic Church, is based on the "ancient" and "hidden" agenda of the Vatican that most people do not know about because most people do not take the time to investigate these matters.

I, like many others, have learned the truth by conducting years of research as a result of being led by the Holy Spirit to do so.

The job of the Holy Spirit is to lead us into all truth because He is the *Spirit of Truth*. God has unveiled His truth to us so we could warn others to come out of *mystery* or *spiritual* Babylon, so we will not share in her sins and receive her plagues based on Revelation 18:4.

True love for God, and for one another, reveals His truth because we are called to be *Purveyors of the Truth*. Anyone who truly loves God and His people will warn His sheep when they are being led astray and straight to the slaughter.

We are called to proclaim the whole counsel of God's unadulterated, uncompromised Word and testify of His truth.

In fact, Jesus answered Pilate in John 18:37 after being asked by Pilate if He is a king. Jesus responded and said, *"You say*

269

rightly that I am a KING. For this CAUSE I was BORN, and for this CAUSE I have COME INTO the WORLD, that I should BEAR WITNESS to the TRUTH. Everyone who is of the TRUTH hears My VOICE. " (NKJV) (emphasis added).

Jesus was born and came into the world to "bear witness" to the "truth" of His heavenly Father's instructions as written in the Torah. At the time of Jesus' earthly ministry, the New Testament was not written yet.

Again, Jesus was and is the "living" Torah whose Holy Spirit dwells in New Covenant believers.

This is why we are told in Isaiah 8:20, *"To the LAW* [the Torah] *and to the TESTIMONY! If they do not SPEAK ACCORDING TO THIS WORD, it is because THERE IS NO LIGHT IN THEM.* " (NKJV) (emphasis added).

God loves His people, and it is His desire that no one perishes due to a lack of knowledge, especially concerning His truth and the *gospel of the kingdom* which was once delivered to the saints.

Therefore, what I am about to convey is just one example of many concerning why God's people are perishing from a lack of knowledge or will perish if His truth is not made known to His *unsuspecting* sheep.

They are being led astray and scattered by their shepherds, who, for the most part, are nothing more than hirelings.

CONCERNING THE VATICAN'S INTERFAITH MOVEMENT TO EMBRACE ALL FAITHS, BRINGING THEM TOGETHER UNDER THE GUISE OF LOVE, PEACE, AND UNITY

We already know the Pope has welcomed and embraced the Grand Imam of Al-Azhar, the prestigious Sunni Muslim center of learning, in a historic bid to reopen dialogue between the two faiths. In addition, the Pope is allowing the Quran to be read and allowing Islamic prayers in the Vatican, based on some news stories substantiating this truth. [25] [26] [27] [28]

Yet Jesus says to us in the following Scriptures:

> *"...I am the WAY, the TRUTH, and the LIFE. NO ONE comes to the FATHER except THROUGH Me."* (John 14:6, NKJV) (emphasis added).

> *"Most assuredly, I say to you, he who BELIEVES in Me* [Jesus, not Allah, not Buddha, nor any other false god] *has EVERLASTING LIFE."* (John 6:47, NKJV) (emphasis added).

Everyone has their own God, even atheists, BUT the name of Jesus changes everything! And, the name of Jesus will cause division. In fact, Jesus tells us this truth in Matthew 10:34 when He says to us, *"Do not THINK that I came to bring PEACE ON EARTH. I did not COME to bring PEACE but a*

SWORD."(NKJV) (emphasis added).

Again, the apostle Paul says to us in Second Corinthians 6:14, *"Do not be unequally YOKED TOGETHER with UNBELIEVERS. For what FELLOWSHIP has RIGHTEOUSNESS with LAWLESSNESS? What COMMUNION has LIGHT with DARKNESS?"* (NKJV) (emphasis added).

Therefore, I pose the following questions to disciples of Jesus Christ: Why is the Pope, who is *supposedly* a Christian, meeting and praying with Islamic leaders in order to pursue "peace" and "unity" when we are not to be unequally yoked together with unbelievers?

Remember, Jesus said to us in Matthew 10:34 that He has come to cause division on the earth and to bring a sword not peace. And, He also said in John 14:6 that NO ONE comes to the Father except through Him because He is the WAY, the TRUTH, and the LIFE!

As such, why would any Christian get into "agreement" with Islam?

Why would disciples of Jesus Christ seek to have **communion** (to have a *partnership* in order to participate in a social *intercourse* [communication or dealings between individuals or groups], or *benefaction* [a *donation* or *gift*] in order to communicate or fellowship together) with those who have "darkness" instead of "light"? Especially, based on the fact we are adamantly commanded by God not to do so!

After all, isn't the Pope of the Roman Catholic Church *supposed* to pledge his total allegiance to Jesus Christ since he calls himself "The Vicar of Christ"?

And, as such, he should not compromise His *eternal* Word in order to pursue "peace" or "unity" under the guise of love.

So why would the Pope of the Roman Catholic Church extend an invitation to imams of the Islamic religion, allow readings from the Quran, and consent to Islamic prayers to be prayed at the Vatican? Moreover, I wonder if the Pope prayed with the Islamic leaders in the name of Jesus or the name of their god—Allah? If the Pope got into an agreement with them when they invoked the name of Allah in prayer, what does this tell us?

In fact, this is particularly worrisome when the Pope of the Roman Catholic Church states that the Quran and the Holy Bible are the same. [29]

In addition, why does the Roman Catholic Church use the Islamic symbol of the sun and the crescent moon, which are ancient Egyptian symbols of the "mother" of false gods—ISIS, when they perform the Catholic Eucharist? [30]

Where have we heard of the name ISIS before?

Isn't this the *same* name that the Islamic Caliphate that practices "radical" Islam uses as they wage Jihad in their quest for world dominance as they seek to annihilate the infidels who will not bow their knee to Allah?

You have probably heard the old saying, *"Birds of a feather flock together..."* which is in line with Amos 3:3 that poses the following thought-provoking question: *"Can two WALK TOGETHER, unless they are AGREED?"* (NKJV) (emphasis added).

The answer to this question is a resounding no!

What we see happening here between the Vatican and Islam is an "unholy" alliance! Read Second Chronicles 18 and 19 about the "unholy" alliance the *king of Israel* and Jehoshaphat, *king of Judah* made with Ahab instead of with the Lord. It did not end well!

But don't take my word for it. Do your own homework. However, I have provided links to some news stories that you will find to be very interesting regarding this "unholy" alliance between the Pope of the Roman Catholic Church and Islam. (31) (32)

The next topic I will address is regarding all the evangelical leaders who recently flew to Rome to meet with the Pope to discuss areas of "mutual agreement" concerning where they "respectfully disagreed." It was reported that the purpose of this gathering, which supposedly had no "official" agenda, was to build unity between Christian "traditions" that have a historical "enmity" against the Word of God. The word "enmity" means the following: The state or feeling of being actively opposed or hostile to someone or something.

Do not dismiss the significance of the "key" word "traditions" of Christians that have an ancient "enmity" against the Word of God. [33]

As I will cover in-depth in Book 3, many of the "traditions" that the body of Christ still embraces were inherited from our "mother"—the Roman Catholic Church. In fact, many of these "traditions" we have "inherited" from the Roman Catholic Church do indeed have "enmity" against the Word of God and are an abomination in the sight of God!

Now let's refocus our attention on this historic meeting between the evangelical leaders and the Pope.

Did any of the evangelical leaders who attended this gathering bother to ask the Pope why he embraces Islam and allows Islamic prayers and the reading of the Quran at the Vatican?

Although Mike Bickle did pointedly ask the Pope this question: "Is Jesus the only way of salvation?"

In addition, it is reported that Mike Bickle described Francis as being "very strong" in his agreement on Christ as the Savior of the World and emphasized his love for Jesus and the Scriptures. [34]

However, no matter what the Pope may have told these evangelical leaders about his belief that Jesus is the *only* way to have salvation, his "fruit" says otherwise! Don't take my

275

word for this. Instead, watch the video the Pope produced concerning his intentions for prayer for January 2016. [35]

This video should send chills up your spine, and it is absolutely deceptive! This video should say that in order to have *eternal* life, you must believe in Jesus Christ.

Yet it does not because it is sending a "hidden" message to those who know the true intent behind it which is this: We are witnessing the formation of the One World "Harlot" Religious System. Watch this video and discern what this message is really all about.

The evangelical leaders who recently met with the Pope in Rome should have instead asked the Pope, "Which Jesus is the only way to receive salvation for the forgiveness of our sins?"

The true answer to this question would have explained why the Pope is allowing the Quran to be read and Islamic prayers to be invoked at the Vatican. I will address this "other" Jesus that Islam believes in later on in this chapter.

Concerning this video that the Pope produced regarding his prayer intentions in 2016, I agree that we are all children of God created in His image and His likeness.

However, Jesus is the WAY, the TRUTH, and the LIFE and NO ONE comes to the Father except through Him.

As John 3:16 proclaims, *"For God so loved the world that He GAVE His only begotten SON, that whoever BELIEVES in*

276

Him should not PERISH but have EVERLASTING LIFE."
(NKJV) (emphasis added).

The Pope's "fruit" says that he is "the" False Prophet who is leading all the false prophets. By the time you finish reading this entire chapter, you will know that the Pope of the Roman Catholic Church is a "puppet" of the real "puppet master" who is none other than the "Black Pope" of the Roman Catholic Church who is a massive deceiver.

We cannot believe a thing that he says because he is a Jesuit.

If you do not know anything about the Jesuits and the "Black Pope" of the Roman Catholic Church, read this article by WordPress titled, *The Most Powerful Man in the World? The Black Pope?* This knowledge will help you on your quest for the truth. [36]

The Jesuits are a military, religious order of the Roman Catholic Church. In addition, the oaths of the *Knights of Columbus*, the *Knights of Malta,* and *Rhodes Scholars* are based on the oath of the Jesuits.

THE CONNECTION BETWEEN ISLAM AND THE ROMAN CATHOLIC CHURCH

We must ask ourselves the following thought-provoking question: Why would the Roman Catholic Church, specifically the Pope, have such an interest in the Islam religion and be willing to "fellowship" and "communion" with religious leaders who practice Islam and who openly declare Jesus Christ is not God or the Son of God?

Isn't the Islam religion diametrically opposed to Christianity? It all depends on what you call *true* Christianity.

As a matter of fact, in response to the recent breaking news story concerning US Lutherans approving a document recognizing agreement with the Catholic Church, [37] I emphatically stated the following when I posted a blog on Facebook concerning this FALSE "reformation" in which I wrote the following:

> *"WARNING! The One World "Harlot" Religious System is emerging, DO NOT BE DECEIVED! This ecumenical movement which is being spearheaded under the guise of love and peace is a FALSE unity movement. This is NOT the reformation that God is seeking to orchestrate in this hour. To the contrary! In fact, God is calling His people OUT of mystery or spiritual Babylon lest we share in her sins and receive her plagues. As such, when the Lutheran Church says there are no longer church-dividing issues on many points with the Roman Catholic Church it is because most of the body of Christ still follows the "customs," "traditions," and "doctrines" of men instituted by the RCC long ago under Constantine in lieu of following*

the commandments of God."

For you see the truth is this: Just as from the very beginning the Roman Catholic Church birthed many denominations in Christianity, they also are the very ones who birthed Islam! As such, I will provide the links for you to access many videos which will substantiate this truth later on in this chapter.

Yes, indeed! You heard me correctly. Islam was birthed from the Roman Catholic Church many moons ago.

This is why Muslims use Islamic prayer beads, called the *Misbaha* or *Tasbih*, while they are in prayer just like the Catholics do when they pray the Rosary. They use these prayer beads when they are chanting during *hikr,* which are Islamic devotional acts during which short phrases or prayers are repeatedly recited either silently or aloud. Also, like the Catholic nuns who cover their heads with veils, Muslim women also cover their head and veil their face with a *burqa*.

This "tradition" or "custom" which is practiced in both Catholicism and Islam is an outward act of the nuns in Catholicism and the women who practice Islam, wearing this head covering or veil for the purpose of showing their submission to their male superiors.

Those who practice the Islam religion also believe Mary is the mother of Jesus, but Jesus is not God's Son. And, the granddaddy of them all is this fact: This is why most of the places that they (the Vatican) control in the Holy Land in Israel also have a mosque on these sites. I witnessed this firsthand during my pilgrimages to Israel, asking the Holy Spirit why this is the case and this compelled me to start doing my research on this subject. The Holy Spirit unveiled His truth concerning this matter.

Here is another reason why the Pope is not the "Vicar of Christ" as he claims to be. The Vatican seeks to take control of the "Holy Land" in Israel in order to set up the Antichrist's headquarters in Jerusalem when they divide it. This is substantiated by the Pope who according to this news story announced to the world that Israel is to be divided when this is clearly against God's Word. [38]

As I have already covered in Book 1 and will continue to do so throughout these series of books, anyone who comes against the nation of Israel and seeks to divide Jerusalem is an enemy of God. God swore by Himself to give this land to Abraham's descendants.

This is one of the promises God made to Abraham and his descendants based on His *everlasting* covenant.

You will also want to watch this video revealing that the Pope of the Roman Catholic Church has also entered into a historic covenant with the Orthodox rabbis who do not believe that Jesus Christ is their Messiah and He has already come.

The purpose of this covenant between the Pope and Orthodox rabbis is to take control of the Temple Mount in

Jerusalem, where the Antichrist will set up his headquarters once Jerusalem has been divided. [39]

The Illuminati plan on rebuilding Solomon's temple on the Temple Mount [40] [41] [42] so the Antichrist can "deceive" the masses into thinking he is the Messiah whose arrival the Orthodox Jews are still waiting for to appear for the first time.

They will also deceive the majority of Christians who are waiting for Jesus to return the second time in order to set up His millennial kingdom on the earth.

In fact, in Chapter 69 of Book 3, I will go into detail substantiating the fact that there is no need to rebuild a third *physical* temple before Jesus Christ's second coming occurs.

Under the New Covenant, our bodies are the "temple" of the living God.

However, God will allow the third *physical* temple to be built so He can separate the "wheat" from the "tares."

God will mark those who are truly His people with the *spiritual* "mark of God" on their foreheads before His wrath is unleashed when the Antichrist sits in the "physical" temple and claims he is the Messiah and they (the Jews) resume the sacrifices of animals.

Thus, the Antichrist and his minions will "rebuild" the *physical* temple in Jerusalem in order to "deceive" the whole world into "worshiping" the beast and his image. As a result, they will receive his mark on their forehead or their hand.

281

Even the "elect" will be deceived into "worshiping" the beast unless they know the Word of God for themselves. Hence, one of the purposes of this series of books is to prevent this from happening by unveiling God's unadulterated, uncompromised truth to His people before it is too late to make a course correction for all eternity.

Now let's refocus our attention on the third temple that the Orthodox Jews and many Christians are clamoring to have rebuilt in Jerusalem. Tragically, some of these *same* Orthodox rabbis who are still waiting for their Messiah's first coming have been "deceived" into giving the Pope a written agreement.

This agreement will constitute Israel's capitulation to the Vatican's efforts to "Christianize" the holy site, similar to the building of a Catholic convent in Auschwitz." [43]

How about that for a "sign" foreshadowing the coming holocaust that will happen once again in Jerusalem after the Antichrist sets up his headquarters there?

Meanwhile, the Jews to whom the Temple Mount actually belongs to which is based on the Abrahamic covenant are not allowed to pray on the Temple Mount (with the exception of the Western Wall) in order to keep peace with the Muslims. What is wrong with this picture?

I'll tell you what is wrong with this picture based on years of research and the revelation that I have received from the

Holy Spirit concerning the Vatican and Israel.

This is the beginning of Satan and those who are in the *kingdom of darkness* joining forces in a "coalition" based on "one" accord and the "crafty" counsel of the UN, the Vatican, the Council on Foreign Relations, and the Trilateral Commission.

These are only a few of the "think tanks" or organizations who are in bed together as they move forward to bring forth the fourth and final beast system of the "Antichrist kingdom" or *Mystery* Babylon, otherwise referred to as the One World Order/New World Order/Revived Roman Empire.

THE ILLUMINATI PLANNED ALL THREE WORLD WARS IN ADVANCE

Satan's minions, who are his "change" agents for the Antichrist kingdom, are putting in place and orchestrating a series of events that will eventually lead to World War 3, which they have planned since the beginning of time.

For God uses all men, whether they are good or evil, in order to fulfill His Word, because *"it is written..."*

Unfortunately, Satan and his minions know God's Word and end-time prophecy better than most who profess to be Christians.

As a matter of fact, if you are willing to believe it, the minions and the global elite who comprise the Antichrist kingdom truly worship Lucifer (a.k.a. Satan).

And, as such, listen to what Albert Pike said in a letter he wrote to Mazzini, dated August 15, 1871. Albert Pike was a 19th century Freemason who established the framework for the establishment of the New World Order or One World Order.

Pike is also the Grand Master of a Luciferian cult. Giuseppe Mazzini was an Italian 33rd degree Freemason and the founder of the Mafia in 1860. The two worked closely together.

In this letter to Mazzini, Pike outlines the Illuminati's plans for all three world wars, necessary to bring about the One World Order! One can only marvel at the *chilling* accuracy of Pike's prediction about the events which led to World War 1 and 2. His predictions concerning the chain of events leading up to World War 3 are unfolding before our very eyes. [44]

Below and on the following pages are some of the excerpts from this letter, showing how all three world wars have been planned in advance for many generations.

> **"The First World War** *must be brought about in order to permit the Illuminati to overthrow the power of the Czars in Russia and of making that country a fortress of atheistic Communism. The divergences caused by the "agentur" (agents) of*

the Illuminati between the British and Germanic Empires will be used to foment this war. At the end of the war, Communism will be built and used in order to destroy the other governments and in order to weaken the religions."

"The Second World War *must be fomented by taking advantage of the differences between the Fascists and the political Zionists. This war must be brought about so that Nazism is destroyed and that the political Zionism be strong enough to institute a sovereign state of Israel in Palestine. During the Second World War, International Communism must become strong enough in order to balance Christendom, which would be then restrained and held in check until the time when we would need it for the final social cataclysm."*

"The Third World War *must be fomented by taking advantage of the differences caused by the "agentur" of the "Illuminati" between the political Zionists and the leaders of the Islamic World. The war must be conducted in such a way that Islam (the Moslem Arabic World) and political Zionism (the State of Israel) mutually destroy each other. Meanwhile, the other nations, once more divided on this issue will be*

285

constrained to fight to the point of complete physical, moral, spiritual and economical exhaustion. We shall unleash the Nihilists and the atheists, and we shall provoke a formidable social cataclysm which in all its horror will show clearly to the nations the effect of absolute atheism, the origin of savagery and of the most bloody turmoil. Then everywhere, the citizens, obliged to defend themselves against the world minority of revolutionaries, will exterminate those destroyers of civilization, and the multitude, disillusioned with Christianity, whose deistic spirits will from that moment be without compass or direction, anxious for an ideal, but without knowing where to render its adoration, will receive the true light through the universal manifestation of the pure doctrine of Lucifer, brought finally out in the public view. This manifestation will result from the general reactionary movement which will follow the destruction of Christianity and atheism, both conquered and exterminated at the same time."
[end of excerpt]

Notice that the vision of the Illuminati which shall lead to World War 3 is written about in God's Word. It is the Psalm 83 War which shall be initiated by a confederation of Arab and Muslim nations, who are descendants of Ishmael and

Esau, that are conspiring and consulting together to annihilate Israel. I already covered this in Chapter 31.

In addition, *mystery* or *spiritual* Babylon and the Antichrist, along with his False Prophet, will hijack what Jesus Christ is going to do, which is based on Daniel 9:27. It will be our Messiah who "confirms" a covenant with many that *already* exists.

This "existing" covenant that Jesus Christ will once again "confirm" at the very end of all the ages is the *everlasting* covenant God made with Abraham and his descendants. Again, Jesus fulfilled (consummated, executed, and ratified [confirmed]) this covenant when He became the "mediator" of the New Covenant by shedding His precious blood at Calvary for the remission (pardon and forgiveness) of our sins.

When Jesus returns the second time, He will once again "confirm" this *everlasting* covenant and all the *everlasting* covenants (plural) that God established with mankind and creation throughout the *synergy of the ages*. I cover this truth fully in Chapter 67 of Book 3.

MANY HAVE DRUNK THE WINE OF HER FORNICATION

Now let's refocus our attention back to the "insidious" and "deceptive" plans of the Vatican and the Pope of the Roman

Catholic Church. They plan to "deceive" the whole world into worshiping the Antichrist by being "deceived" into thinking that he is our Messiah who has returned to set up His millennial kingdom "rule" and "reign" on the earth.

This is why Jesus warns us ahead of time that we are not to be deceived when this happens. He says to us in Matthew 24:23–24, *"Then if anyone says to you, 'Look, HERE IS THE CHRIST!' or 'There!' DO NOT BELIEVE IT. For FALSE CHRISTS and FALSE PROPHETS will RISE and SHOW GREAT SIGNS and WONDERS to DECEIVE, if possible, EVEN THE ELECT."* (NKJV) (emphasis added).

Now let's refocus our attention on the "mother" of all harlots—the Roman Catholic Church.

Truly, if we are going to state that we believe in the "mother" church—the Roman Catholic Church, and we see the need to join in "unity" with her under the guise of love, then we *must* know what the "mother" of all "harlots" is truly all about!

Again, joining in "unity" under the guise of love with "unbelievers" who deny Jesus Christ is the Son of God is an abomination in the sight of God for all the reasons I will substantiate in this chapter. In addition, I will substantiate more reasons why the Roman Catholic Church is the "Mother of all Harlots" in Chapter 58 of Book 3.

Furthermore, we must also discover what their "hidden" agenda is for forming strategic partnerships with "unbelievers" of other faiths, such as the Orthodox rabbis in Israel and the imams of the Islam religion, who both do not believe that Jesus Christ is the Son of God or He is God.

In addition, we must also uncover the real reason why the Pope (the Vatican) is "wooing" many mainline evangelical Christian leaders in America for the sake of "unity" and "peace" under the guise of us "loving one another." This is the "catch" phrase that ensnares many Christians into getting involved with things that disciples of Jesus Christ should not be part of in any way, shape, or form.

We *must* always remember that one of Satan's favorite tactics is to deceive and snare God's unsuspecting sheep by masquerading as an *angel of light.* Many of God's people are ensnared by his web of lies and deceit by what appears to be a *righteous* and *noble* cause.

This is despite the fact, as I have already covered earlier in this chapter, God's Word says to us in Second Corinthians 6:14–18 that we should not be unevenly yoked with "unbelievers" or have fellowship with them for the purpose of a "joint" activity.

As such, take the time to watch all these videos by Professor Walter J. Veith who will systematically walk us through the history of the *synergy of the ages.* He will unveil the truth concerning the birth of Islam. [45] [46] [47] [48] [49] [50] [51] [52] [53] [54]

If you take the time to watch all these videos, you will learn that Islam was birthed from Catholicism a long time ago. Then you will understand why the Roman Catholic Church is so willing to embrace Islam, even though Islam denies Jesus Christ is God and especially that He is the Son of God. I will cover this later on in this chapter.

Again, if you actually take the time to watch these videos, you will understand why the Roman Catholic Church is not in any way, shape, or form to be associated with the true *gospel of the kingdom* which was once delivered to the saints.

Catholic doctrine is based on the "traditions," "customs," and "doctrines" of men who follow the dogma of the occult. It is not based on the doctrine of Christ, at all, as many believe that it is. I will cover this fact later in this chapter.

In Chapter 58 of Book 3, I will go into specific detail as to why the Roman Catholic Church and those who follow their "doctrines," "traditions," and "customs" of men, instead of following the commandments of God, are part of the apostate "harlot" church.

As such, they and those who follow the "doctrines," "traditions," and "customs" of the Roman Catholic Church that we have inherited from our early church fathers, are the very ones who have **transgressed** the laws of God. They have **changed** God's ordinances which are all *everlasting* ordinances (statutes).

In addition, the Roman Catholic Church has led many believers in the body of Christ to **break** the *everlasting* covenant that God established with Abraham and his descendants. And, to those who break this *everlasting* covenant they are going against Almighty God Himself and will reap the dire consequences for doing so.

Yes, indeed! Many have drunk the wine of her fornication through deception.

Tragically, as a result, because of our ignorance of the whole counsel of God's Word and understanding our "Hebraic" roots in Christianity, the vast majority of believers who claim the name of Christ, have broken the *everlasting* covenant God established with Abraham and his descendants.

So I pose the following question to my sisters and brothers in Christ: Are we following the "customs," "traditions," and "doctrines" of the Roman Catholic Church that Martin Luther, Calvin, and many other "reformers" tried to "liberate" God's people from following during the "reformation" that happened over 500 years ago? Unfortunately, the answer is yes.

Here we are—at the "midnight" hour, and the vast majority of Christians are still following the "customs," "traditions," and "doctrines" of men which were birthed from the Roman Catholic Church instead of following the commandments of God.

For all these reasons, God is calling His people to come out of *mystery* or *spiritual* Babylon lest we share in her sins and receive her plagues. Again, this is based on Revelation 18:4 which says, *"And I heard another voice from heaven saying,*

'COME OUT of HER [*mystery* or *spiritual* Babylon], *My PEOPLE, lest you share in HER SINS, and lest you RECEIVE of HER PLAGUES.'* " (NKJV) (emphasis added).

This goes right in line with what the apostle Paul tells us in Second Corinthians 6:17–18.

In this Scripture he says to us, *"Therefore COME OUT from AMONG THEM* [the unbelievers, those who practice "lawlessness" who are serving and worshiping Belial—Satan because they worship idols and false gods] *And BE SEPARATE,'* *says the Lord.* *'Do not TOUCH what is UNCLEAN* [impure (ceremonially), morally (lewd) or specifically (demonic)], *And I will receive you.'* *'I will be a Father to you, And you shall be My SONS and DAUGHTERS,' Says the LORD Almighty."* (NKJV) (emphasis added).

Therefore, God is certainly not calling His people to join in "unity" with the "mother" of all harlots under the guise of us loving one another. To the contrary! He is telling us to COME OUT of her and her ways NOW!

Again, do not take my word for it. I challenge you to do your own research. However, this website has done a stellar job in substantiating the fact that the god of the Roman Catholic Church is Baal. [(55)]

Now let's refocus our attention on this "interfaith" movement being spearheaded by the Pope of the Roman Catholic Church in the Holy Land (Israel). What is their overall objective and why do they have their sights set on Jerusalem?

UNIVERSALISM IS THEIR GOAL—UNITING ALL FAITHS TO WORSHIP THE SAME GOD BECAUSE ALL PATHS LEAD TO SALVATION

They have set their sights on Jerusalem to take control of that which seeks to bring the different religions together for the sake of "unity," "peace," and "love" as we all hold hands and sing the song, *"Let there be Peace on Earth."*

Listen very carefully to what the *Council of Religious Liberty Institute of the Holy Land* says based on their "mission statement" which is taken from their website. [56]

Their "mission statement" is as follows:

> *"As religious leaders of* **different faiths***, who share the conviction in the one Creator, Lord of the Universe; we believe that the essence of religion is to worship G-d and respect the life and dignity of all human beings, regardless of religion, nationality, and gender."* (emphasis added).

Again, this statement goes right in line with the new video that the Pope of the Roman Catholic Church just released entitled, *Pope Francis' Prayer Intentions for January 2016.*

So how do the religious leaders of different "faiths" share the conviction in one Creator, who is Lord of the Universe? What is the NAME of this one Creator and Lord of the Universe?

For Christians, Jesus is the WAY, the TRUTH, and the LIFE and NO ONE comes to the Father (*Yehováh,* the God of Abraham, Isaac, and Jacob [Israel]) except through the name of Jesus Christ.

This is substantiated in John 1:1–3, which says, *"In the BEGINNING was the WORD, and the WORD was with GOD, and the WORD was GOD. He was in the beginning with God. All THINGS were made THROUGH Him, and without Him, nothing was MADE that was MADE."* (NKJV) (emphasis added).

In addition, the apostle Paul talks about the "Preeminence of Christ" in Colossians 1:15–17, saying that *the Word* is in the image of the "invisible" God, the *firstborn* over all creation.

For by Him all things were "created" that are in heaven and that are on the earth, *visible* and *invisible,* whether thrones or dominions or principalities or powers. All things were created through Him and for Him. And, He is before all things, and in Him, all things consist. Also, He is the head of His body— the Church.

Furthermore, our heavenly Father *Yehováh* is *Elóhíym,* God our Creator and the *only* true Supreme God. His official title is the Creator of the heavens and the earth, based on Genesis 1:1. Again, the name *Elóhíym* is plural, and it refers to God the Father, God the Son, and God the Holy Spirit, who are all one in the Godhead. Also, *Yehóvàh* is the One who sent *the Word*—His only *begotten* Son of His love—as the Son of Man in the Person of Jesus Christ.

He did this to "redeem" the world, including its inhabitants, with His precious blood and to "restore" and "reconcile" mankind back into "walking" in a covenant relationship with our heavenly Father *Yehóvàh*.

Then they go on to say the following in their mission statement:

> *"We accordingly commit ourselves to use our positions and good offices, to advance these sacred values, to **prevent religion from being used as a source of conflict**, and to promote mutual respect, a just and **comprehensive peace** and **reconciliation** between people of **all FAITHS** in the **Holy Land** and **worldwide**."* (emphasis added).

First of all, the *only* **true** God who is worthy and was willing to die to bring "redemption," "reconciliation," and "restoration" to all mankind and the world is Jesus Christ, God's only *begotten,* Son.

In addition, it is obvious that these **different** religious leaders didn't read the Book of Revelation in the Bible. If they had, they would know there will not be a *just* **comprehensive** "peace" and "reconciliation" between people on the earth until Jesus Christ reigns on the earth as the *King of kings and Lord of lords.*

Furthermore, obviously, they did not read about Islam's version of the end-days either.

If they had, then they would know that the "infidels," namely Jews and Christians, who do not bow down and profess their allegiance to Allah, or the Antichrist, will be beheaded.

This will be the fate of many martyrs of the Christian faith based on Revelation 20:4.

In fact, this is already happening to Spirit-filled believers of Jesus Christ in Syria, Egypt, Iraq, and other Muslim and Arab nations located in the Middle East.

Does this sound like a *just* **comprehensive** "peace" and "reconciliation" between people of **all** "faiths" to you?

"SPIRIT" OF ANTICHRIST

Now let's talk about the fact that these "interfaith" and "ecumenical" movements are being orchestrated and embraced with those who have the *Spirit of Antichrist.*

They are bringing forth the One World "Harlot" Religious System, which is part of the One World Order/New World Order/Antichrist Kingdom.

Those with the *Spirit of Antichrist* are those individuals who deny the following three things:

1. Jesus is the Christ (the *Anointed* One).

2. The Father and the Son.

3. Jesus Christ has come in the flesh and is God.

This is based on the following Scriptures:

> *"Who is A LIAR but he who DENIES that JESUS is the CHRIST? He is ANTICHRIST who DENIES the FATHER and the SON."* (1 John 2:22, NKJV) (emphasis added).

> *"Beloved, do not BELIEVE every SPIRIT, but TEST the SPIRITS, whether they are of God; because many FALSE PROPHETS have GONE OUT into the WORLD. By this you KNOW the SPIRIT of GOD: Every SPIRIT that CONFESSES that JESUS CHRIST has COME in the FLESH is of GOD, and every spirit that DOES not CONFESS that JESUS CHRIST has COME in the FLESH is not of GOD. And this is the SPIRIT of the ANTICHRIST, which you have HEARD was COMING, and is NOW ALREADY in the WORLD."* (1 John 4:1–3, NKJV) (emphasis added).

> *"For many DECEIVERS have GONE OUT into the WORLD who do not CONFESS JESUS CHRIST as COMING in the FLESH. This is a DECEIVER and an ANTICHRIST."* (2 John 1:7, NKJV) (emphasis added).

THOSE WHO ARE ADHERENTS OF ISLAM AND JUDAISM HAVE THE "SPIRIT" OF ANTICHRIST

Adherents of Islam and Judaism have the *Spirit of Antichrist* based on all the reasons stated in First John 2:22, First John 4:1–3, and Second John 1:7.

Concerning the Orthodox Jews who practice Judaism, all they have to do to be saved is to receive the revelation that Jesus Christ is their Messiah, and He has come in the flesh.

Then they need to receive Him as their personal Lord and Savior.

They already keep our heavenly Father's commandments written in the Torah faithfully. As such, all they need is the "testimony" of Christ in order to become saved.

However, since they deny that Jesus (Yeshua) is the Son of God and is God, that He came in the flesh, and they proclaim that He was not crucified, we should not be joining in unity with the Orthodox Jews based on Second Corinthians 6:14–18.

Currently, there are many leaders in the body of Christ who are allowing some Orthodox Jews to take their pulpits and speak to their congregations because they want to show their support for Israel and help build the bridge to our Jewish sisters and brothers.

While this is a noble cause, I must ask these same leaders if they would invite an imam of the Islam religion to speak to their congregations. Hopefully, most pastors would say of course not!

Yet the undeniable truth is that both the Orthodox Jews and adherents of Islam have the *Spirit of Antichrist* because they deny that Jesus (Yeshua) is the Son of God and is God, that He came in the flesh, and they state He was not crucified.

Therefore, how can we justify joining in unity with either the Orthodox Jews or adherents of Islam when God's Word clearly tells us not to in Second Corinthians 6:14–18?

And, some of these same leaders who are joining in unity with the Orthodox Jews to show our support for Israel are "erroneously" saying that the Jews do not need to receive Jesus Christ as their Lord and Savior to be reconciled with our heavenly Father *Yehôvah.*

This is heresy based on the fact that our heavenly Father

established a New Covenant with both the Jews from the House of Judah and those of us who were former Gentiles from the House of Israel. See Jeremiah 31:31–33 and Hebrews 8:7–13.

Jesus Christ is the "mediator" between God and all men under the New Covenant that was (consummated, executed, and ratified [confirmed]) with His precious blood (1 Timothy 2:5).

God's eternal Word is very clear, and Jesus says to us in John 14:6, *"I am the way, the truth, and the life. No one comes to the Father except through Me."* (NKJV).

This Scripture does not say, that *"No one comes to the Father, with the exception of the Orthodox Jews, through Me."*

Hence, the Orthodox Jews must receive a revelation that Jesus is their Messiah, and they must receive Jesus Christ as their personal Lord and Savior in order to be saved and have everlasting life.

This is substantiated in John 3:16 which says, *"For God so loved the world that He gave His only begotten Son, that whoever believes in Him should not perish but have everlasting life."* (NKJV)

Therefore, there is no such thing as a "dual" covenant for God's covenant people. All of God's covenant people are reconciled to our heavenly Father through the New Covenant that God established for both the Jews from the House of Judah and former Gentiles from the House of Israel. This New Covenant can only be entered into by God's grace through faith in Jesus Christ.

WHAT DO ADHERENTS OF ISLAM BELIEVE?

Now let's refocus our attention on Islam. They believe that the God of Abraham, Isaac, and Jacob is not our heavenly Father—*Yehovah*. As a matter of fact, they do not believe God is a father at all. Rather, they believe that God is some distant, unloving God who would never take the time to love or be intimate with His children, let alone sacrifice His only *begotten* Son for them.

This belief system stems from the brokenness and the "orphan spirit" which was brought forth as a result of the inner *cry of Ishmael,* based on the "spirit of rejection" and being orphaned by Abraham, his earthly father.

Furthermore, Muslims who practice the Islamic faith believe God's name is Allah, the name of a pagan deity, who is the war god or the moon god. [57] [58] [59]

❖ Islam believes that Ishmael is the heir according to the promises that their God, Allah, gave to Abraham instead of Isaac, the *Son of the Promise.*

❖ Islam denies that Jesus Christ is God's Son who came to the earth as the Son of Man in the flesh even though they believe Jesus is the son of Mary.

A quote from Yusuf Ali...

*"In **blasphemy** indeed are those that **say** that **God is Christ, the son of Mary**. Say: 'Who then hath the least power against God, if His will were to destroy Christ, the son of Mary, his mother, and all every - one that is on the earth? For to God belongeth the dominion of the heavens and the earth, and all that is between. He createth what He pleaseth. For God hath power over all things.'"* (emphasis added).

Sahih International...

*"They have certainly disbelieved who say that **Allah is Christ, the son of Mary**. Say, 'Then who could prevent Allah at all if He had intended to destroy Christ, the son of Mary, or his mother or everyone on the earth?'*

And to Allah belongs the dominion of the heavens and the earth and whatever

302

is between them. He creates what He wills, and Allah is over all things competent." (emphasis added).

"They said, 'the most gracious has begotten a son!' You have uttered a gross blasphemy! The heavens are about to shatter; the earth is about to tear asunder." (Surah 19:88-92) (emphasis added).

"...the Christians call Christ the son of Allah. That is a saying from their mouth; in this they but imitate what the unbelievers of old used to say. Allah's curse be on them: how they are deluded away from the Truth!" (Surah 9:30) (emphasis added).

Therefore, if you believe Jesus is the Son of God, then Allah has cursed you! [60]

❖ Islam denies that Jesus was crucified on the cross.

Sahih International...

And [for] their saying, "Indeed, we have killed the Messiah, Jesus, the son of Mary, the Messenger of Allah."

And they did not kill him, nor did they

crucify him; *but [another] was made to resemble him to them. And indeed, those who differ over it are in doubt about it. They have no knowledge of it except the following of assumption.* **And they did not kill him, for certain.**" (Surah 4:157-8b) [61] (emphasis added).

❖ Islam denies that God has highly "exalted" Jesus above *every* name based on Philippians 2:9–11.

Sahih International...

"Rather, Allah raised him to Himself. And ever is Allah Exalted in Might and Wise."

❖ Islam denies the incarnation (a person who embodies in the flesh a deity or the Spirit) of God as Christ and that *the Word* was sent to earth by our heavenly Father to suffer for mankind.

Yet, believe it or not, there are some who claim to follow our Messiah that are saying and teaching that Jesus Christ (Yeshua) is not God as well.

If our Messiah is not God who manifested Himself in the flesh as the Son of Man to die for us on the cross at Calvary, then we are all in serious trouble if we hope to have eternal life! Can any of us who were created in God's own image and in His likeness die on a cross for the salvation of the entire world, including its inhabitants as the Savior of the World? Of course not! Therefore for us to insinuate that our Messiah was just a man like we all are and is not God Himself is heresy!

God's Word says in First Timothy 3:16, the following:

> *"And without controversy great is the mystery of godliness: **GOD** [G2316: **theos**: a deity, the supreme Divinity, or Magistrate] WAS **MANIFESTED** [G5319: **phaneroō**: to render apparent (literally or figuratively): appear, manifestly declare, (make) manifest (forth), shew (self)] IN THE FLESH, Justified in the Spirit, Seen by angels, Preached among the Gentiles, Believed on in the world, Received up in glory."* (NKJV) (emphasis added).

Yehôvah, our heavenly Father, is the One who (qualified, selected, and chose) the *Word*, as the *firstborn* over all creation based on Colossians 1:15, which says the following:

> *"He* [the Word] *is the IMAGE of the INVISIBLE **GOD*** [G2316: **theos**: a

305

> *deity*, the supreme *Divinity*, or *Magistrate*], *the* **FIRSTBORN** [G4416: *prototokos*: firstborn G4413: *protos*: foremost (in time, place, order, or importance): beginning, before, best] *over all CREATION.*" (Col. 1:15, NKJV) (emphasis added).

The Word existed at the beginning with God, and was and is God, as substantiated in John 1:1–3 below, where we are specifically told that all things were made through Him.

> *"In the beginning was the* **WORD** [G3056: *logos*: something said, or spoken (including the thought); utterance G3004: *lego*: (verb) to "lay forth," or to set discourse; call, speak, utter], *and the* **WORD** *was with* **GOD** [G2316: *theos*: a *deity*; the supreme *Divinity*, or *Magistrate*], *and the* **WORD** *was* **GOD**. *He was in the beginning with* **GOD**. *All things were made through Him, and without Him nothing was made that was made.*" (John 1:1–3, NKJV) (emphasis added).

❖ Islam denies the Godhead (the "plurality" of Elohim—

306

God the Father, God the Son, and God the Holy Spirit) otherwise referred to as the Trinity (in Catholicism). Yet God's Word talks about the "plurality" of Elohim and refers to the Godhead in Romans 1:20 and Colossians 2:8–10.

> *"They do blaspheme who say: Allah is one of three in a Trinity."* (Surah 5:73)

❖ Islam believes that Jesus is the Messiah. However, their meaning is different from the biblical definition of who the Messiah is.

Muslims believe that Jesus Christ is just one more prophet in a long line of prophets.

They deny that He is the "Anointed One" of God who will rule the world from Jerusalem. Jesus is seen in Islam as a precursor to Muhammad and is believed by Muslims to have foretold the latter's coming.

According to Wikipedia concerning the perception of Jesus in Islam, many evangelical believers are coming into agreement with the *Spirit of Antichrist* when they say they are a follower of Isa—the Jesus in the Quran. Below, and on the following page, is an excerpt from this article. However, I have also provided the link to this article in the reference section for those who wish to do a more in-depth study. [62]

Isa (Arabic: عيسى, Transliteration: *'Isā*

), known as **Jesus** in the New Testament, is considered to be a Messenger of God and the *Masih* (Messiah) in Islam[1] who was sent to guide the Children of Israel (*banī isrā'īl*) with a new Scripture, the *Injīl* or Gospel.[2] The belief in Jesus (and all other messengers of God) is required in Islam. The Quran mentions Jesus by name twenty-five times, while it only mentions Muhammad by name four times as Muhammad and once as Ahmad; making it a total of five times.[3][4]

It states that Jesus was born to Mary (Arabic: Maryam) as the result of virginal conception, a miraculous event which occurred by the decree of God (Arabic: Allah). To aid in his ministry to the Jewish people, Jesus was given the ability to perform miracles (such as healing the blind, bringing dead people back to life, etc.), all by the permission of God rather than of his own power.

According to the Quran, Jesus, although appearing to have been crucified, was not killed by crucifixion or by any other means, instead, "God raised him unto Himself." Like all prophets in Islam, Jesus is considered a Muslim (i.e., one who submits to the will of God), as he preached that his followers should adopt the "straight path" as commanded by God. Islam rejects the Trinitarian Christian view that Jesus was God incarnate or the son of God, that he was ever crucified or resurrected, or that he ever atoned for the sins of mankind. The Quran says that Jesus himself never claimed any of these things, and it furthermore indicates that Jesus will deny having ever claimed divinity at the Last Judgment, and God will vindicate him.[5] The Quran emphasizes that Jesus was a mortal human being who, like all other prophets, had been divinely chosen to spread God's message. Islamic texts forbid the association of partners with God (*shirk*), emphasizing a strict notion of monotheism (*tawhīd*).

Numerous titles are given to Jesus in the Quran and in Islamic literature, the most common being *al-Masīḥ* ("the Messiah"). Jesus is also, at times, called "Seal of the Israelite Prophets," because, in general,

Muslim belief, Jesus was the last prophet sent by God to guide the Children of Israel. Jesus is seen in Islam as a precursor to Muhammad and is believed by Muslims to have foretold the latter's coming.[6][7] Muslims believe that Jesus will return to earth near the Day of Judgment to restore justice and to defeat *Masih ad-Dajjal* ("the false messiah," also known as the Antichrist).[6][8] [end of excerpt]

❖ Islam does **not** believe Jesus Christ died for the atonement of mankind's sins.

❖ Islam does **not** believe in the resurrection of Jesus Christ.

In summary, for those of you who believe that Allah is just another name for the God of Abraham, Isaac, and Jacob (Israel), you are mistaken.

The God that believers in Jesus Christ serve, the *same* God who is our heavenly Father, is the God of Abraham, *Isaac*, and Jacob (Israel).

He is not the God of Abraham, *Ishmael*, and Jacob (Israel). And, our heavenly Father's name is *Yehóváh*, not Allah.

Therefore, we cannot be in agreement with those who

practice Islam and say Allah is our God when those who practice the Islamic religion deny the following things:

1.   Jesus Christ is the Son of God who came to the earth in the flesh.

In Islam, the *Sin of Shirk* describes how partners with God are unforgivable. In Islam, **shirk** (Arabic: شرك *širk*) refers to the sin of practicing idolatry or polytheism, i.e., the deification or worship of anyone or anything other than the singular God called Allah. Literally, it means the establishment of "partners" placed beside God.

If one is to convert to Islam, they must decree "The Shahada" in Arabic which says: *"There is no god but Allah and Muhammad is his Messenger."*

According to the Bible, Jesus Christ is the Son of God.

This is substantiated in the following Scriptures:

Hosea 11:1; Matthew 8:29; Matthew 14:33; Matthew 16:16; Matthew 27:43; Matthew 27:54; Mark 1:1; Mark 3:11; Mark 5:7; Mark 15:39; Luke 1:32; Luke 1:35; Luke 4:41; Luke 8:28; Luke 12:8; Luke 22:70; John 1:18; John 1:34; John 1:49; John 3:18; John 3:36; John 5:25; John 6:69; John 10:36; John 11:4; John 11:27; John 19:7; John 20:31; Acts 8:37; Acts 9:20; Romans 1:4; Romans 1:9; Romans 5:10; 1 Corinthians 1:9; 1

Corinthians 1:19; Galatians 2:20; Galatians 4:4; Galatians 4:6; Galatians 4:7; Ephesians 4:13; Hebrews 4:14; Hebrews 6:6; Hebrews 7:3; Hebrews 10:29; 1 John 3:8; 1 John 4:9; 1 John 4:15; 1 John 5:5; 1 John 5:9; 1 John 5:10; 1 John 5:12; 1 John 5:13; 1 John 5:20; 2 John 1:3; 2 John 1:9, and Revelation 2:18.

2. While they agree that Jesus Christ was born to Mary, they deny that Jesus Christ is the Son of God.

3. They deny that Jesus died on the cross, was resurrected, ascended into heaven, and He is seated at the right hand of His heavenly Father. God's Word says that Jesus Christ was crucified, resurrected, and He has ascended into heaven. He is now seated on the throne at the right hand of God, the Father, based on the following Scriptures:

Matthew 20:23; Matthew 22:44; Matthew 25:33; Matthew 25:34; Matthew 26:64; Mark 12:36; Mark 14:62; Mark 16:19; Luke 22:69; Acts 2:33; Acts 2:34; Acts 5:31; Acts 7:55; Acts 7:56; Romans 8:34; Ephesians 1:20; Colossians 3:1; Hebrews 1:3; Hebrews 1:13; Hebrews 8:1; Hebrews 10:12; Hebrews 12:2; 1 Peter 3:22; Revelation 5:1, and Revelation 5:7.

4. They deny that Jesus Christ shed His blood for the atonement of our sins. Jesus Christ shed His blood for our sins to be cleansed and forgiven. Only by the

blood of Jesus are we "redeemed" for our transgressions and sins. Moreover, Jesus Christ died for us so that our "covenant" relationship could be "reconciled" and "restored" with our heavenly Father.

The following Scriptures substantiate this truth:

Psalm 72:14 ; Matthew 26:28; Mark 14:24; Luke 22:20; John 6:53; John 6:54; John 6:55; John 6:56; Acts 17:26; Acts 18:6; Acts 20:28; Romans 3:25; Romans 5:9; 1 Corinthians 10:16; 1 Corinthians 11:25; 1 Corinthians 11:27; Ephesians 1:7; Ephesians 2:13; Colossians 1:14; Colossians 1:20; Hebrews 2:14; Hebrews 9:7; Hebrews 9:12; Hebrews 9:13; Hebrews 9:14; Hebrews 9:18; Hebrews 9:20; Hebrews 9:22; Hebrews 9:25; Hebrews 10:4; Hebrews 10:19; Hebrews 10:29; Hebrews 11:28; Hebrews 12:24; Hebrews 13:12; Hebrews 13:20; 1 Peter 1:2; 1 Peter 1:19; 1 John 1:7; 1 John 5:6; Revelation 1:5; Revelation 5:9, and Revelation 12:11.

5. Those who practice the Islamic faith deny that God has highly "exalted" Jesus above *every* name in the heavens, on the earth, and under the earth.

This is based on Philippians 2:9–11 which says, *"Therefore God also has highly EXALTED Him* [Jesus Christ] *and GIVEN Him the NAME which is ABOVE every NAME, that at the NAME of JESUS every KNEE SHOULD BOW, of those in HEAVEN, and of those on EARTH, and of those under THE EARTH, and that*

313

every TONGUE should CONFESS that Jesus Christ is LORD, to the GLORY of GOD the FATHER." (NKJV) (emphasis added).

6. God's Word emphatically states that anyone who denies God the Father and God the Son has the *Spirit of Antichrist.* Therefore, anyone who denies the Son has the *Spirit of Antichrist.* Moreover, those who practice Islam believe that Jesus Christ was not crucified, yet the Word of God says differently and talks about His crucifixion forty times in the Bible.

7. They deny that God the Father, God the Son, and God the Holy Spirit are one in the Godhead. Yet they are. This is substantiated in First John 5:7 which says, *"For there are THREE that BEAR WITNESS in HEAVEN: the FATHER, the WORD, and the HOLY SPIRIT; and these THREE are ONE."* (NKJV) (emphasis added).

This is talking about the "plurality" of *Elohíym* in the Godhead which refers to God the Father, God the Son, and God the Holy Spirit. All three are "one" in the Spirit even though they are each a distinct Person and Power in the Godhead.

The bottom line is this: No *true* disciple of Jesus Christ should in any way, shape, or form, embrace any other religion or come into agreement with those who practice other religions, including Islam.

If we do, then we are getting into agreement with the *Spirit of Antichrist,* and we will have rejected Jesus Christ who is God's only plan of "redemption," "reconciliation," and "restoration" for the world, including its inhabitants.

We can only become "saved" or "born again" by God's grace when we have placed our faith and our trust in God's only *begotten* Son, Jesus Christ.

We must acknowledge that He is the Savior of the World and make Him our personal Lord and Savior in every area of our lives.

Again, Jesus says to us in John 14:6, *"...I [Jesus] am the WAY, the TRUTH, and the LIFE. No ONE comes to the FATHER except through Me [Jesus]."* (NKJV) (emphasis added).

And, John 3:36 proclaims, *"He who believes in the SON has EVERLASTING LIFE; and he who DOES not BELIEVE the SON shall not SEE LIFE, but the WRATH of GOD abides on HIM."* (NKJV) (emphasis added).

COME OUT OF HER MY PEOPLE LEST YOU SHARE IN HER SINS AND RECEIVE HER PLAGUES

Most Christian denominations were birthed from the Roman Catholic Church long ago.

And, unfortunately, the vast majority of believers are still walking according to the perverted "traditions," "customs," and "doctrines" of men, that were inherited from our early church fathers whose origins were rooted in the occult.

Remember when I said earlier in this chapter regarding Calisi saying that Jesus doesn't care that Christians and Catholics disagree on "biblical" doctrine, to which I emphatically stated nothing could be further from the truth?

The reason why I said this is because the doctrine and the practices of the Roman Catholic Church are based on "sun" god worship and the occult.

Read all about the truth behind the "doctrine" and the practices of the Roman Catholic Church which is rooted in "sun" god worship and follows "Luciferian" doctrine. [63]

I can attest to what is presented on this website under the title, *Roman Catholic Sun (Baal) Worship—Lucifer Sun Worship Masquerading as True Christianity*, is true based on the years of research I have done as led by the Holy Spirit. This website has done a superb job in providing a chart comparing occult worship with the doctrine and practices of the Roman Catholic Church, which are one and the same.

Unfortunately, the majority of mainline Christian denominations are following the doctrine of the Roman Catholic Church instead of the commandments of God which are based on the doctrine of Christ.

Hence, we are embracing a "counterfeit" Christianity which

was invented by the trickery of men, in the cunning craftiness of deceitful plotting, led by the "mother" of all harlots—the Roman Catholic Church. And, instead of following Jesus and walking according to the doctrine of Christ, many believers in the body of Christ have laid aside the commandments of God, specifically our heavenly Father's commandments written in the Torah.

Again, the vast majority of believers in the body of Christ are walking according to the "traditions," "customs," and "doctrines" of the "mother" of all harlots—the Roman Catholic Church.

In Chapters 65, 66, and 67 of Book 3, I will fully cover the significance of why this knowledge matters to New Covenant believers and what the "eternal" ramifications are for those who have exchanged the truth of God's Word for a lie.

All because we have been "deceived" by our early church fathers, so we will walk according to the "doctrine" of the "mother" of all harlots, and we will worship the false "sun" god—Mithra—the Pagan Christ. [64] [65] [66]

In other words, ultimately we will worship Satan because we have been deceived.

Unless we repent and make an immediate course correction for drinking the wine of her fornication, then we will receive the spiritual "mark" of her fornication on our foreheads rather than the mark of God. The mark of the "harlot" of all the abominations of the earth is based on Revelation 17:5

which says, *"And on HER FOREHEAD a NAME was written: MYSTERY, BABYLON THE GREAT, THE MOTHER OF HARLOTS AND OF THE ABOMINATIONS OF THE EARTH."* (NKJV) (emphasis added).

In Book 3, I will also cover in-depth how the False Prophet (the Pope of the Roman Catholic Church) and the Islamic Mahdi will be attempting to orchestrate a fake millennial "rule" and "reign" of Jesus Christ on the earth. This will happen when they rebuild the "physical" temple which is based on the Illuminati's plan to rebuild Solomon's Temple.

The False Prophet (the Pope) and many Muslims leaders are already working with the Orthodox Jews in achieving their mutual goal which is to rebuild the temple in Jerusalem.

In fact, much to my dismay and horror, there are some Sanhedrin rabbis who are meeting with a certain influential Turkish Muslim leader, and they are saying that they would accept the Mahdi as their Messiah if he brings peace to Israel.

Take the time to watch this video titled, *Is the Pope and Israeli Rabbis Courting the Mahdi?* This video which is produced by Steven DeNoon with *Israeli News Live* [67] is collaborating what I am saying.

However, I do not agree with Steven when he alludes to the fact that the Pope may be the Mahdi. Rather, for all the reasons I have previously stated, I believe the Pope of the Roman Catholic Church, whether it be this current Pope or another one who will keep following their carefully planned agenda of a One World "Harlot" Religious System who will succumb to and be part of the One World Order/New World Order/Antichrist kingdom, is the "front man" for the Islamic Mahdi who will practice "radical" Islam.

Again, this is the only way they will get the "buy-in" of the ten Muslim and Arab nations based on Psalm 83.

The Pope of the Roman Catholic Church is the False Prophet who will unite the Jews, Muslims, and Christians who practice Judaism, Islam, and Christianity in order to deceive them into worshiping the false Messiah as they form an "unholy" alliance for world peace and unity.

At the time of the fullness of the Antichrist's kingdom when they have deceived the whole world into worshiping the Antichrist instead of the one true God, with the exception of those who know what is really going on because they know their God and His Word for themselves, then sudden destruction shall come.

When they proclaim "peace" and "safety," this is when God's wrath will be forthcoming. The apostle Paul talks about this in First Thessalonians 5:3, which says the following:

> *"For when they say, 'Peace and safety!' then sudden destruction comes upon them, as labor pains upon a pregnant woman. And they shall not escape."* (NKJV)

AVOID LIKE A PLAGUE THOSE WHO ARE CALLING FOR UNITY WITH THE ROMAN CATHOLIC CHURCH

Beware of leaders in the body of Christ such as Kenneth Copeland and others who are telling us they are signing an agreement to end the Protestant Reformation and that Christians should unite with the "Mother" of all "Harlots" for the sake of unity under the guise of love. [68] [69]

When you take the time to watch the video titled, *Kenneth Copeland Recants and Returns to Catholicism!,* you will hear Tony Palmer proclaim he is bringing this message to God's people in the Spirit of Elijah.

Yet he is twisting God's Word just like Satan did to deceive God's *unsuspecting* sheep to come back under the "mother" of all harlots. If, in fact, he is coming in the Spirit of Elijah he would tell God's people to remember the Law of Moses.

Let's take a look at Malachi 4:4–5, which talks about what shall take place before the coming of the *great* and *dreadful* day of the Lord.

This Scripture begins with, *"Remember the LAW of MOSES, My servant, Which I commanded him in Horeb for all Israel, With the statutes and judgments. Behold, I will send you Elijah the prophet Before the coming of the great and dreadful day of the Lord."* (NKJV) (emphasis added).

The reason why God is telling us to remember the Law of Moses is because this is what the doctrine of Christ is founded on for all Israel. See John 7:16. The doctrine of Christ is founded on the full volume of Moses and the gospel.

Our heavenly Father foreknew there would be great deception as the "Day of the Lord" was fast approaching and He is reminding us that the Law of Moses is not to be forgotten.

God is also revealing to us that those who come in the Spirit and power of the prophet Elijah will be teaching His people His statutes and judgments which are written in God's Law which is still in effect for all Israel.

God only has "one" law and "one" custom for all His covenant people who are called Israel. Israel refers to the land and to God's covenant people based on the *everlasting* covenant God established with Abraham and his descendants.

Therefore, do not be deceived any longer. There cannot be any true unity of our faith in Jesus Christ if it is not founded on the doctrine of Christ. Again, the doctrine of the Roman Catholic Church is a Luciferian doctrine which is based on "sun" god worship.

As such, this current "unity" movement which is being orchestrated by the trickery of men, in the cunning craftiness of deceitful plotting, is a FALSE unity movement.

321

In fact, on October 24-26, 2017, a pivotal event in history will take place where Catholics, Protestants, and Orthodox Leaders are scheduled to set aside their differences to "reconcile 500 years of Forgiveness." The event is entitled Kairos 2017 - Unity + Revival Conference, and Kenneth Copeland and Cardinal Daniel DiNardo will be the keynote speakers. This event will have a dramatic impact on the relations between the so-called Protestants and Catholics in the United States of America, and the implication are nothing short of prophetic. [70]

They are right about this event being prophetic because it is fulfilling what was prophesied about the final beast system and the apostate church.

There are many churches worldwide who are part of this "interfaith" and "ecumenical" movement which is a false unity movement. [71] Some of these churches include, but are not limited to, the following:

The World Baptist Alliance, the Disciples Ecumenical Consultative Council, the Ecumenical Patriarchate (Eastern Orthodox), General Conference of Seventh-Day Adventists, the International Old Catholic Bishops' Conference, the World Lutheran Foundation, the Mennonite World Conference, the Moravian Church Worldwide Unity Board, the Patriarchate of Moscow (Eastern Orthodox), the Pentecostals, the Pontifical Council for Promoting Christian Unity (Catholic Church), the Reformed Ecumenical Council, the Salvation Army, the Friends World Committee for Consultation (Quakers), the World Convention of Churches of Christ, the World Evangelical Alliance and the World Methodist Council. A representative of the World Council of Churches is also usually present.

Again, this is a false unity movement and is a snare from the enemy to entangle God's *unsuspecting* sheep who are being led straight to the slaughter!

And, it is for this very reason, as we commemorate the 500th anniversary of the Protestant Reformation, God is "raising up" a new breed of "reformers" who will finally take an ax to sever the "root" which has resulted in the great apostasy we have inherited from our early church fathers.

This new breed of "reformers" will completely finish the "reformation" which was started by Martin Luther, and continued by John Calvin, and Huldrych. And, they will expose the lies and the liars who are leading God's *unsuspecting* sheep right into the One World "Harlot" Religious System.

We are admonished by the apostle Paul in Ephesians 5:11, to have no fellowship with the "unfruitful" works of darkness, but rather expose them. As such, our silence is compliance to the "unfruitful" works of darkness if we do not speak up and take a stand against the works of darkness being devised by the trickery of men, in the cunning craftiness of deceitful plotting.

Mark my words. There will be a great divide coming into the body of Christ orchestrated by God Himself! Get ready for a revolutionary "reformation" as God separates the tares from the wheat and He exposes those who are serving and worshiping Him in vain versus those who are not.

In the next chapter, we will discover how Abraham inherited great wealth and was prosperous because of his devotion and obedience to the Word of God. And, so it shall be for all *true* disciples of Jesus Christ who "walk" in a covenant relationship with our heavenly Father because we "obey" His Voice and His Word once we become saved.

CHAPTER 33

ABRAHAM INHERITED GREAT WEALTH AND PROSPERITY WHILE HE STILL LIVED ON THE EARTH ONLY AS A RESULT OF HIS DEVOTION TO THE LORD OF THE HARVEST!

A s I have already conveyed in Chapter 25 of this book, Abraham was so devoted to God that he was willing to sacrifice everything, including his beloved son Isaac, in order to be obedient to God's Voice. As such, Abraham inherited great wealth and was prosperous.

Now let's discover what *Yehôva̓h* did when He transferred the wealth of Pharaoh to Abram. Because of Abram's unwavering devotion and obedience to God, He was with Abram wherever he went. God used *adverse* circumstances such as a famine in the land to bless Abram with great wealth as illustrated in Genesis 12:10–20, which says the following:

> *"Now there was a FAMINE in the LAND, and Abram went DOWN to EGYPT to DWELL THERE, for the FAMINE was SEVERE in the LAND. And it came to pass, when he was close to entering Egypt, that he said to SARAI his WIFE, 'Indeed I know that you are a WOMAN of BEAUTIFUL COUNTENANCE. Therefore it*

will happen, WHEN the Egyptians SEE you, that they will say, 'This is his WIFE'; and they will KILL me, but they will LET you LIVE. Please say YOU ARE MY SISTER, that it may BE WELL WITH ME FOR YOUR SAKE, and that I MAY LIVE BECAUSE OF YOU.' " (Gen. 12:10–13, NKJV) (emphasis added).

"So it was, WHEN Abram CAME into EGYPT, that the Egyptians saw the woman, that she was very beautiful. The princes of Pharaoh also SAW her [Sarai] *and COMMENDED her to Pharaoh. And the WOMAN was TAKEN to PHARAOH'S HOUSE. He TREATED ABRAM WELL FOR HER SAKE. He* [Abram] *had sheep, oxen, male donkeys, male and female servants, female donkeys, and camels."* (Gen. 12:14–16, NKJV) (emphasis added).

"But the LORD plagued PHARAOH and HIS HOUSE with GREAT PLAGUES BECAUSE of SARAI, Abram's wife. And Pharaoh called Abram and said, 'What is this you have done to me? Why did you not tell me that she was your wife? Why did you say, 'She is my sister'? I might have taken her as my wife. Now therefore, here is your wife; TAKE HER and GO YOUR WAY.' So Pharaoh COMMANDED his men

CONCERNING him [Abram]*; and they SENT
HIM AWAY, with his WIFE and all that he*
[Abram] *had."* (Gen. 12:17–20, NKJV)
(emphasis added).

What did Pharaoh give Abram for Sarai's sake? He gave
Abram sheep, oxen, male donkeys, male and female servants,
female donkeys and camels. And, when it was time for
Pharaoh to send Abram and his wife Sarai away, they went
with all that Pharaoh had given him based on Genesis 12:14–
16.

God always calls the past into account and history always
repeats itself. As a matter of fact, this same scenario is played
out concerning Abraham's son Isaac and King Abimelech of
the Philistines in Gerar as detailed in Chapter 26 in the Book
of Genesis. However, for the purpose of the subject at hand,
let's closely examine *how* God continued to bestow great
wealth on His servant Abraham as detailed in Genesis 20:1–
18, which says the following:

> *"And Abraham journeyed from there* [Egypt]
> *to the South, and* <u>dwelt</u> *between Kadesh and
> Shur, and stayed in Gerar. Now Abraham said
> of Sarah his wife, 'SHE IS MY SISTER.' And
> Abimelech king of Gerar SENT and TOOK
> SARAH. But God came to Abimelech in a
> DREAM BY NIGHT, and said to him, 'Indeed
> you are A DEAD MAN BECAUSE OF THE
> WOMAN WHOM YOU HAVE TAKEN, for SHE*

is a MAN'S WIFE.'" (Gen. 20:1–3, NKJV) (emphasis added).

"But Abimelech had not COME NEAR HER; and he said, 'Lord, will You SLAY a RIGHTEOUS NATION also? Did he not say to me, 'SHE IS MY SISTER'? And she, even she herself said, 'HE IS MY BROTHER.' In the INTEGRITY of my HEART and INNOCENCE of my HANDS I HAVE DONE THIS.'" (Gen. 20:4–5, NKJV) (emphasis added).

"And God said to him [Abimelech] *in a DREAM, 'Yes, I know that you did this in the INTEGRITY of your HEART. For I also WITHHELD YOU FROM SINNING AGAINST ME; therefore I did not LET YOU TOUCH HER. Now therefore, RESTORE THE MAN'S WIFE; for HE IS A PROPHET, and HE WILL PRAY FOR YOU, and YOU SHALL LIVE. But if you do not RESTORE HER, know that you shall SURELY DIE, YOU and all WHO ARE YOURS.'"* (Gen. 20:6–7, NKJV) (emphasis added).

"So Abimelech rose early in the morning, called all his servants, and told all these things in their hearing; and the men were very much AFRAID. And Abimelech called Abraham and said to

him, 'What have you done to us? How have I OFFENDED you, that you have BROUGHT ON ME and on MY KINGDOM a GREAT SIN? You have done DEEDS to me that ought not to be done.' Then Abimelech said to Abraham, 'What did you have in view, that you have done this thing?' And Abraham said, 'Because I thought, surely the FEAR of GOD is not in this PLACE; and they will KILL ME on account of MY WIFE. But indeed SHE IS TRULY MY SISTER. She is the DAUGHTER of my FATHER, but not the DAUGHTER of my MOTHER; and SHE BECAME MY WIFE. And it came to pass, when God caused me to wander from my father's house, that I said to her, 'This is your kindness that you should do for me: in every place, wherever we go, say of me, 'HE IS MY BROTHER.'" (Gen. 20:8–13, NKJV) (emphasis added).

"Then Abimelech took SHEEP, OXEN, and MALE and FEMALE SERVANTS, and GAVE them to Abraham; and he RESTORED Sarah his wife to him. And Abimelech said, 'See, MY LAND IS BEFORE YOU; DWELL WHERE IT PLEASES YOU.' Then to Sarah he said, 'Behold, I have GIVEN your BROTHER a THOUSAND PIECES OF SILVER; indeed this vindicates you before all who are with you and

before everybody.' Thus she was REBUKED." (Gen. 20:14–16, NKJV) (emphasis added).

"So Abraham PRAYED to God; and God HEALED Abimelech, his wife, and his female servants. Then they bore children; for the LORD had CLOSED UP all the WOMBS of the HOUSE of ABIMELECH because of Sarah, Abraham's wife." (Gen. 20:17–18, NKJV) (emphasis added).

Therefore, once again *Yehôvâh* uses almost the same set of circumstances to give the wealth of King Abimelech of Gerar to Abraham.

Again, because Abraham perceived King Abimelech to be unrighteous and to be his enemy once again, Abraham said Sarah was his sister. However, this time Abraham explains how Sarah is his step-sister. This is based on Genesis 20:12 which says, *"But indeed she* [Sarah] *is truly my SISTER. She is the DAUGHTER of my FATHER, but not the DAUGHTER of my MOTHER; and she became my WIFE."* (NKJV) (emphasis added).

As we have clearly witnessed by the written account of these passages of Scripture, the Lord took control of the situation and blessed Abraham greatly with the wealth of King Abimelech. This transference of wealth included Abraham receiving sheep, oxen, male and female servants, land and silver too. However, the favor of God does not end at this point. As a result of Abraham, who was a prophet, praying for the needs of others, God not only healed the wombs of Abimelech's wife and his female servants too, God also healed the womb of Abraham's wife, Sarah.

This substantiates that when we confess our trespasses to one another and pray for one another, *we* will be healed!

This is based on James 5:16 which proclaims, *"CONFESS your TRESPASSES to one another, and PRAY for one another, that YOU may be HEALED. The effective, FERVENT PRAYER of a righteous man AVAILS much."* (NKJV) (emphasis added).

As a result of Abraham confessing his trespass to King Abimelech, telling the king why he told him Sarah was his sister and praying to God concerning this whole situation, *Yehóváh* chose to heal Abimelech and to open up the womb of Abimelech's wife, and the wombs of his female servants as well as the womb of Abraham's wife, Sarah, too.

Moreover, do not dismiss the significance of *Yehóváh* choosing to use this unfortunate situation of a severe famine in the land to orchestrate the events that would bring to pass one of the most important promises God gave to Abraham which is this: That through Abraham's "seed" all the nations of the earth would be blessed and that his descendants would be as *numerous as the stars in the sky* and as the *sand on the seashore.*

This promise could not have come to pass without Sarah's

womb being opened up by the Lord. This fulfilled the long awaited promise of an heir from Abraham's loins with the birth of his beloved son Isaac, the son Sarah bore for Abraham as detailed in Genesis 21:1–5 below, when Abraham was one hundred years old no less!

> *"And the LORD VISITED Sarah as He had said, and the LORD did for Sarah as He had SPOKEN. For Sarah CONCEIVED and BORE Abraham a son in his old age, at the SET TIME of which God had SPOKEN to him. And Abraham called the name of his son who was born to him—whom Sarah bore to him—Isaac. Then Abraham CIRCUMCISED his son Isaac WHEN he was EIGHT DAYS OLD, as God had COMMANDED him. Now Abraham was ONE HUNDRED YEARS OLD when his son Isaac was BORN to him."* (Gen. 21:1–5, NKJV) (emphasis added)

In the next chapter, we will take a look at how *Yehóvǎh* used almost the same scenario to also bless Abraham's son, Isaac, with great wealth and prosperity.

CHAPTER 34

LIKE ABRAHAM, GOD BLESSED ISAAC, ABRAHAM'S SON, WITH WEALTH AND PROSPERITY WHILE HE STILL LIVED ON THE EARTH

In the last chapter, I conveyed how God used adverse circumstances like a famine in the land to bless Abraham with great wealth and prosperity while he lived on the earth. Therefore, now let's take a look at how God blessed Abraham's son, Isaac, by transferring King Abimelech's wealth, using circumstances similar to those He used with Abraham. This is based on Genesis 26:1–16, which says the following:

> *"There was a FAMINE in the LAND, besides the first FAMINE that was in the days of Abraham. And Isaac went to Abimelech king of the Philistines, in **GERAR** [1] [2] [3]* [H1642: *G'râr. rolling* country; *Gerar,* a Philistine city; today it is located in south central Israel; modern Wadi el-Jerdr in the valley of Nahal Gerar]. *Then the LORD appeared to him and said: 'DO NOT GO DOWN to EGYPT; live in the land of which I shall tell you. DWELL IN THIS LAND, and I will be with YOU and BLESS YOU; for to YOU and YOUR DESCENDANTS I give all these LANDS, and I will perform the **OATH*** [4]

333

[H7621: *shᵉbûʿah*: an oath or a curse which is sworn attesting of innocence (i.e.: Deuteronomy 28 blessings or curses)] *which I swore to Abraham your father.'"* (Gen. 26:1–3, NKJV) (emphasis added).

"And I will make YOUR DESCENDANTS multiply as the stars of heaven; I will give to YOUR DESCENDANTS all THESE LANDS; and in YOUR SEED all the NATIONS of the EARTH shall be BLESSED; because Abraham OBEYED My VOICE and KEPT My CHARGE (5) [H4931: *mishmereth*: watch, that is, the act (*custody*) or (concretely) the *sentry*, the *post*; objectively *preservation*, or (concretely) *safe*; figuratively *observance*, that is, (abstractly) *duty*], *My COMMANDMENTS* (6) [H4687: *mitsvah:* a *command*, whether human or divine (collectively the Law); (which was) commanded (-ment), law, ordinance, precept], *My STATUTES* (7) [H2708: *chuqqah:* appointed, *custom, manner* or *ordinance*], *and My LAWS* (8) [H8451: *torah:* a *precept* or *statute*, especially the *Decalogue* or *Pentateuch:* direction or instruction based on the *Mosaic* or *Deuteronomic* Law]." (Gen. 26:4–5, NKJV) (emphasis added).

"So Isaac dwelt in **GERAR** (1) (2) (3) [H1642: *G'rär: rolling* country; *Gerar*, a Philistine city; today it is located in south central Israel; modern Wadi el-Jerdr in the valley of Nahal Gerar]. *And the MEN of the place ASKED about his WIFE. And he said, 'SHE is my SISTER'; for he was AFRAID to say, 'SHE is my WIFE,' because he thought, 'lest the MEN of the place KILL me for REBEKAH, because she is BEAUTIFUL to BEHOLD.' Now it came to pass, when he had been there a long time, that Abimelech king of the Philistines looked through a WINDOW, and SAW, and there was Isaac, SHOWING ENDEARMENT to REBEKAH his WIFE. Then Abimelech called Isaac and said, 'QUITE OBVIOUSLY SHE IS YOUR WIFE; so how could you say, 'SHE is my SISTER?' Isaac said to him, 'Because I said, 'LEST I DIE on ACCOUNT of HER.'"* (Gen. 26:6–9, NKJV) (emphasis added).

"And Abimelech said, 'What is this you have DONE to us? ONE of the PEOPLE might soon have LAIN with your WIFE, and YOU WOULD HAVE BROUGHT GUILT ON US.' So Abimelech CHARGED all his PEOPLE, saying, 'He who TOUCHES this MAN or his WIFE shall surely be PUT to DEATH.'" (Gen. 26:10–11, NKJV) (emphasis added).

> *"Then Isaac SOWED in that LAND, and REAPED in the same YEAR a HUNDREDFOLD; and the LORD blessed him. The man began to PROSPER, and CONTINUED PROSPERING until he became VERY PROSPEROUS; for he had POSSESSIONS of FLOCKS and POSSESSIONS of HERDS and a great NUMBER of SERVANTS. So the Philistines envied him. Now the Philistines had STOPPED UP all the WELLS which his father's servants had dug in the days of Abraham his father, and they had filled them with earth. And Abimelech said to Isaac, 'GO AWAY FROM US, for you are much MIGHTIER than we.'"* (Gen. 26:12–16, NKJV) (emphasis added).

Notice in Genesis 26:1–3 how God used similar circumstances to give great wealth to Abraham's son, Isaac, as He did with Abraham.

There was a famine in the land so God told Isaac to go to a land that He would show him rather than going to Egypt as He had instructed Abraham to do. The land God told Isaac to go to was the land God swore an oath to Isaac's father–Abraham that his descendants would possess.

Based on Genesis 26:4–5, we see God's promise to Abraham

coming to pass with his son Isaac, because his father—Abraham did the following:

1. Abraham "obeyed" God's Voice.

2. Abraham kept God's "charge," meaning that he acted as God's sentry (a soldier stationed at a place to stand guard) and he kept his post, keeping him safe and preserving him while he carried out his duty for God's "eternal" purposes and glory to prevail.

3. Abraham kept God's "commandments" (collectively the Law) that refer to God's divine *laws*, *ordinances*, and *judgments* that God "decreed" and "established" from the beginning of the world; they are without end for all "eternity."

4. Abraham kept God's "statutes" which are God's "appointed" *customs*, *manners*, or *ordinances*, which are all *everlasting* statutes God "decreed" and "established" from the beginning of the world; they are without end for all "eternity."

5. Abraham kept God's "laws" found in the Torah. These are God's instructions or directions for "how" we are to "walk" and "live" which are based on God's "precepts" and "statutes" found in the *Mosaic* or *Deuteronomic* Law.

So if we want to be blessed with believing Abraham and "inherit" the covenant promises that God gave to Abraham and his descendants, perhaps we need to "do" what Abraham did by "obeying" God's Voice and His Word. This will be evidenced by us "keeping" God's *charge, commandments, statutes,* and His *laws* to "receive" God's covenant blessings, including prosperity and receiving great wealth.

In Genesis 26:6–9 we are told the following: Isaac, like Abraham, obeyed God and went to the land that God showed him. Also, Isaac continues the generational *iniquity* of being afraid and lying just like his father did when Isaac states that his wife Rebekah is his sister, rather than his wife.

In Genesis 26:12–16 we are told the following: That God has kept His promise to bless both Abraham and his son Isaac. God blessed Isaac so much that God's Word declares that as Isaac "sowed" in that land, then he "reaped" in the *same* year a hundredfold and became very prosperous as he inherited *great* wealth.

The "key" thing we need to realize is that we cannot expect to "reap" great wealth if we refuse to "sow" in the land where God has placed us for God's kingdom purposes to prevail. And, we must also be "obedient" and "go" where He tells us to go as well.

The last example I will use to convey "how" God transfers the wealth of the Gentiles to His chosen people concerns God blessing the Hebrew people in the land of Goshen with the wealth of the *wicked* Egyptians just before their exodus to the

Promised Land. This example has special significance to the children of Israel in *this* last generation—those who have already made their exodus from living according to the lusts and desires of the things of this world.

It will be those who do not care about the things of this world that will inherit the great wealth transfer prior to the return of Jesus Christ. God will give His *faithful* remnant great wealth for the purpose of establishing God's Kingdom and His *everlasting* covenant so that we can further the *gospel of the kingdom* and help bring in the end-time harvest of souls.

However, to understand what will happen in the end times, then we must look to the Torah, the first five books of the Bible, written by God's servant Moses. History always repeats itself, and as such, as it was in the beginning, so it shall be in the end.

This is substantiated in Ecclesiastes 3:15 which says, *"That WHICH IS has ALREADY BEEN, And WHAT IS to BE has ALREADY BEEN; And God requires an ACCOUNT of WHAT is PAST."* (NKJV) (emphasis added).

Just as God transferred the wealth of the wicked from Pharaoh and the Egyptian people to the Hebrew children *before* they started their exodus to the Promised Land, this same scenario will happen again. Furthermore, we will be supernaturally protected just like the Hebrew people were while they were dwelling in the land of Goshen as God released His wrath upon Pharaoh, the Egyptian people (which represents the wicked, *unrepentant* inhabitants on the earth), and the land of Egypt (which represents the world).

In other words, His "chosen" people were not "raptured" when God was releasing His judgments (plagues) upon Egypt which will be quite similar to what shall happen according to the Book of Revelation when God releases the following judgments just prior to the return of Jesus Christ: [9]

1. Seven "Seal" Judgments.
2. Seven "Trumpet" Judgments: 7 angels, 7 trumpets.
3. Seven "Bowl" Judgments.

This same supernatural protection will save (protect and preserve) us from the *wrath of God* that He will be releasing against His enemies during the tribulation period that we will witness while we are still living on the earth as the "kingdoms of this world" become the "kingdoms of our Christ" *physically* speaking.

As such, we will witness the *kingdom of darkness* clashing with the *kingdom of light.* As God's covenant children, we will be looking forward to our redemption drawing nigh, *physically* speaking, with great joy, despite the calamity that is taking place all around us.

Now back to the subject at hand concerning the end-time transfer of wealth that God will orchestrate so His people have the necessary resources to do what He has called us to do for His Kingdom and His glory. God tells Moses in Exodus 3:20–

22 below, that His people will not leave Egypt empty-handed before they begin their exodus to the Promised Land.

> *"So I will STRETCH OUT MY HAND and STRIKE EGYPT with all My WONDERS which I will do IN ITS MIDST; and AFTER THAT he* [Pharaoh] *will LET YOU GO. And I will GIVE this people FAVOR in the SIGHT of the EGYPTIANS; and it shall be, WHEN you GO, that YOU shall not GO EMPTY-HANDED. But every WOMAN shall ASK of HER NEIGHBOR, namely, of HER WHO DWELLS NEAR HER HOUSE, articles of SILVER, articles of GOLD, and CLOTHING; and YOU shall PUT THEM ON your SONS and on your DAUGHTERS. So YOU shall PLUNDER the EGYPTIANS."* (Exod. 3:20–22, NKJV) (emphasis added).

Therefore, based on Exodus 3:20–22 above, God will give us "favor" with the wicked people who have great wealth and so we shall plunder the wealth of the Egyptians!

The Egyptians are symbolic of the Gentiles who are not in a "covenant" relationship with God. Therefore, they are the wicked, *unrepentant* inhabitants of the world.

Just like our ancestors did, we shall ask our neighbors, mainly those who dwell near our houses, to give us their resources, and because God has given us His favor in their sight, they will gladly do so. Furthermore, do not dismiss the significance

341

that God tells us that *after* He stretches His hands and strikes the earth with His judgments, showing His great wonders; it will be then that the enemy will let us go as we enter into "our" Promised Land.

Also, we will not receive the kingdom resources that we need to "do" what God has called us to do until we "go." In other words, we must step out in faith and "go" (move forward) and then we will receive the resources we need so that we may "do" what God has called us to do. Remember, Abraham had to "go" before the Lord showed him the land to which he was going. God required the same of Abraham's son Isaac.

Next, in Exodus 12:31–36, we are told "how" the Hebrew children did, in fact, plunder the wealth of the Egyptians on their way out of Egypt. Exodus 12:31–36, says the following:

> *"Then he* [Pharaoh] *called for Moses and Aaron by night, and said, 'Rise, GO OUT from AMONG MY PEOPLE, both YOU and the CHILDREN of ISRAEL. And GO, serve the LORD as you have said. Also take your FLOCKS and your HERDS, as you have said, and BE GONE; and BLESS ME also.' "* (Exod. 12:31–32, NKJV) (emphasis added).

> *"And the Egyptians urged the people, that they might SEND THEM OUT of the LAND in HASTE. For they said, 'WE shall all be DEAD*

[the Egyptians had a fear of the Lord based on all the plagues that God had already unleashed upon them].' *So the people took their DOUGH before it was LEAVENED, having their KNEADING BOWLS bound up in THEIR CLOTHES on their shoulders. Now the CHILDREN of ISRAEL had DONE ACCORDING to the WORD of MOSES, and they had ASKED from the EGYPTIANS articles of SILVER, articles of GOLD, and CLOTHING. And the LORD had given the people FAVOR in the SIGHT of the EGYPTIANS, so that they GRANTED THEM WHAT THEY REQUESTED. Thus they PLUNDERED the EGYPTIANS."* (Exod. 12:33–36, NKJV) (emphasis added).

We are specifically told in Exodus 12:31–32 that we will have to do the following seven things:

1. Rise
2. Go Out
3. Go
4. Serve the Lord
5. Take our possessions (resources)
6. Leave
7. Bless those we leave behind

Also, do not dismiss the fact that as God was releasing His judgments, the Egyptian people wanted to get the children of Israel out of there quickly because they feared if they didn't leave in haste, they (the Egyptians) would all be dead. And, we are told specifically that the children of Israel had *done* according to the words of Moses, not allowing their dough to be leavened ("unleavened" bread is symbolic for getting all the sin out of our houses).

It was only *after* the children of Israel "did" according to the words of Moses, which included getting rid of all the sin in their houses, it was then that God instructed them through His servant Moses to ask the Egyptians for articles of silver, gold, and clothing. The Egyptian people gladly gave it to them when asked because God had given the children of Israel favor in the sight of the Egyptians. So the children of Israel plundered the wealth of the Egyptians when they *went out* in haste to "go" and serve the Lord.

Therefore, when God's Word tells us that He is going to do something, He always follows through on His promises. The question which remains to be answered is this: Will we be obedient to "do" what He tells us to "do" to inherit His promises? Are we willing to "do" what God tells us to "do" according to the words of Moses as written in the Torah, which are our heavenly Father's instructions for all His people? And, if we are willing to "do" what He tells us to "do" according to the words written by His servant Moses, then it will result in us getting all the sin out of our houses (bodies) and our lives!

Because *if* the children of Israel had not been obedient to "do" as the Lord had instructed them to "do" through His servant Moses, then they would never have "received" God's favor and "received" articles of silver, articles of gold, and articles of clothing from the Egyptians. Also, notice that they had to ask to receive. Because the Lord gave them His favor, they received what they had requested.

And, just like our ancestors did long ago when they removed the leaven from their house which represents sin before their exodus took place, we also have to remove the sin out of our lives before God will grant us favor concerning the petition that we have asked of Him and others. We have to ask the Lord first and foremost to receive anything from Him. We also need to stop sinning as is substantiated in James 4:2 which says, *"You LUST and DO not HAVE. You MURDER and COVET and cannot OBTAIN. You FIGHT and WAR. Yet YOU do not HAVE because you DO not ASK."* (NKJV) (emphasis added).

I cannot stress the importance of believers needing to "stand" firm and "obey" what God says in His Word and what He tells us to do through the Holy Spirit by listening to His Voice. This is the *only* way we will be able to "overcome" and "prosper" in the days ahead despite the *global* economic collapse and calamity which shall surely come to pass because *"it is written…"*

Therefore, *if* we, like Abraham, first seek God's *Kingdom* and His *Righteousness*, which will be evidenced by our "obedience" to His Voice and His Word, then we too shall plunder the wealth of the Gentiles.

Last, but certainly not least, the apostle Paul tells us in Galatians 3:8 that the Scripture, foreseeing that God would justify the Gentiles by faith, preached the "gospel" to Abraham beforehand.

Hence, we are told what the "gospel" is when God's Word tells us in Genesis 26:4–5, that Abraham kept God's *charge, commandments, statutes,* and His *laws* as written in the Torah. And, this is why Jesus tells us in John 7:16, *"My doctrine is not Mine, but His who sent Me."* Jesus is referring to His and our heavenly Father's instructions written in the Torah.

I hear Christians say all the time that doctrine does not matter and we can agree to disagree on doctrine. Yet God's Word says otherwise in Second John 9 which says, *"Whoever transgresses and does not abide in the doctrine of Christ does not have God. He who abides in the doctrine of Christ has both the Father and the Son."* (NKJV)

In fact, we must know both the Father and the Son because this is eternal life based on John 17:3 which says, *"And this is eternal life, that they may know You, the only true God, and Jesus Christ whom You have sent."* (NKJV)

Again, we may claim to have the testimony of Jesus Christ. However, if we do not obey our heavenly Father's commandments which the doctrine of Christ is founded on, then we do not know both the Father and the Son based on Second John 9. This is why God's Word explicitly tells us in Isaiah 8:20, *"To the law* [the Torah] *and to the testimony! If they do not speak according to this word, it is because there is no light in them."* (NKJV)

Again, the "gospel" was preached to Abraham, way before the law would be given to the children of Israel during the very first Feast of Weeks (*Shavuot* or *Pentecost*) by His servant Moses. After all God's commandments, statutes, and laws as written in the Torah are the terms and conditions of the "Covenant of Marriage" once we become saved through grace by faith.

Like us, Abraham was "justified" by faith, yet his faith in God was evidenced by him keeping God's *charge, commandments, statutes,* and His *laws.* This is why Abraham inherited God's covenant promises.

And, as Abraham's "spiritual" descendants, we too will inherit the covenant promises as long as we keep God's *charge, commandments, statutes,* and His *laws.* This includes inheriting great prosperity and receiving great wealth from the Lord.

This is God's covenant promise to those who follow in the steps of Abraham, who had faith which was evidenced by his obedience. God's covenant promise of wealth is based on Deuteronomy 8:18, which says, *"And you shall remember the LORD your God, for it is He who gives you power to get wealth, that He may establish His covenant which He swore to*

347

your fathers [Abraham, Isaac, and Jacob (Israel)]*, as it is this day."* (NKJV) (emphasis added).

God wants to bestow great wealth to His "covenant" people which includes Him giving us beautiful cities we did not build, houses filled with all good things which we did not fill, hewn-out wells which we did not dig, and vineyards and olive trees that we did not plant. However, this promise is "conditional," and it comes with a very serious warning that His "covenant" people must heed. Deuteronomy 6:10-15, says the following:

> *"So it shall be, when the LORD your God brings you into the land of which He swore to your fathers, to Abraham, Isaac, and Jacob, to give you large and beautiful cities which you did not build, houses full of all good things, which you did not fill, hewn-out wells which you did not dig, vineyards and olive trees which you did not plant—when you have eaten and are full— then beware, lest you forget the LORD who brought you out of the land of Egypt, from the house of bondage. You shall fear the LORD your God and serve Him, and shall take oaths in His name. You shall not go after other gods, the gods of the peoples who are all around you (for the LORD your God is a jealous God among you), lest the anger of the LORD your God be aroused against you and destroy you from the face of the earth."* (Deut. 6:10-15, NKJV)

348

In the next chapter, I will cover how, as in the case of Abraham, *true* disciples of Jesus Christ can reap financial blessings *despite* the coming worldwide economic collapse!

CHAPTER 35

LIKE ABRAHAM, TRUE DISCIPLES OF JESUS CHRIST CAN REAP FINANCIAL BLESSINGS DESPITE THE COMING WORLDWIDE ECONOMIC COLLAPSE

In Chapters 33 and 34 of this book, I substantiated "how" God blessed Abraham and his son Isaac with great wealth and prosperity because of their faith, devotion, and obedience to *Yehóvăh*, their God. And, it is for this reason in this chapter we will take a look at how we, as New Covenant believers, can be blessed as heirs of this *everlasting* covenant while we are still on the earth, inheriting all of God's covenant promises.

We will have the opportunity to receive great wealth as Abraham, and his descendants did despite the coming worldwide economic collapse.

Therefore, we will first take a look at how our faith plays a significant role for us as it did for Abraham in receiving all of God's covenant promises, including financial prosperity, while we are still living on the earth.

In Genesis 15:6, we are told that Abraham believed in the Lord and He accounted it to Abraham for righteousness. Moreover, the apostle Paul tells us in Hebrews 11:6, *"But without FAITH it is IMPOSSIBLE to please Him, for he who comes to God must BELIEVE that He is and that He is a*

REWARDER *of those who* diligently *SEEK Him.*" (NKJV) (emphasis added).

Then the apostle Paul tells us "who" he is referring to when he states *"...for he who comes to God must* believe *that He is..."*

According to *Strong's Greek Lexicon* #G4100, the word "believe" as used in this passage of Scripture is the Greek word "pist-yoo'-o," (pronounced "pist-yoo'-o"), which means: To entrust one's spiritual well-being to Christ.

Therefore, having faith in God the Father and God the Son does not only believe that He exists, but it is also placing our trust in His ability rather than our own to bring to pass what we envision for our lives. In other words, just as Abraham did, we must show God that we trust Him by our commitment to "obey" His Voice and His Word *despite* how we feel and what we see based on our limited understanding.

God views all things from an "eternal" perspective. Sometimes He allows what we "perceive" to be a "bad" thing which happens to good people for His eternal purposes to prevail. Yet we cannot even begin to understand "why" God allows these "bad" things to happen because of our limited perspective.

One such example is the case of God using a famine in the land to compel Abraham and Isaac to go to a "new" place that He would show them so that ultimately God would use this unfortunate situation to bless them.

Therefore, do we truly believe that God is good all the time until something that we "perceive" as being "bad" happens to us or to those we love?

This is why we must know beyond a shadow of a doubt that God is good without question all the time so that we can truly trust Him with our very lives.

We must not become offended with God when we "perceive" something "bad" has happened to us because we will never totally understand God's "eternal" plan while we are still living on the earth.

Think about the fate of John the Baptist who was hoping and believing he would be set free from prison. In fact, he sent two of his disciples to Jesus, to ask, *"Are You the Coming One, or do we look for another?"*

Why would John the Baptist ask this question of Jesus? Especially, based on the fact that he said in John 1:29, concerning Jesus: *"Behold! The Lamb of God who takes away the sin of the world!"*

John had his messengers ask Jesus this question because John could not believe he was still in prison facing a death sentence all because he boldly confronted sin.

King Herod had laid hold of John, bound him, and put him in prison for the sake of Herodias, his brother Philip's wife. All because John had not been "politically" correct when John said to him that it was not lawful for him to have her according to God's law.

However, John the Baptist was not released from prison, and he was beheaded for standing on the truth of God's Word. Jesus did not want John to be "offended" at Him because he did not act to save him from being martyred.

This is why Jesus said in Luke 7:22–24, *"Go and tell John the things you have seen and heard: that the blind see, the lame walk, the lepers are cleansed, the deaf hear, the dead are raised, the poor have the gospel preached to them. And BLESSED IS HE WHO IS NOT OFFENDED BECAUSE OF ME."* (NKJV) (emphasis added).

This is a lesson for all of us. As such, no matter what God requires us to "walk" through for His eternal purposes to prevail we must not allow ourselves to become "offended" with God. If we become "offended" with God and others, then we will allow a "root of bitterness" to defile our heart which will poison our entire being. And, unless we repent we shall perish for all eternity.

We must believe with all our mind, heart, soul, and strength that He who began a good work in us will be faithful to complete it.

Also, God is a rewarder of those who diligently seek Him. For if we truly believe this in our hearts, it will result in us desiring Him more than anything or anyone else. This is what it means for us to love the Lord our God with all our mind, heart, soul, and strength. Furthermore, God's Word says to us in Hebrews 11:1 that faith is the substance of things hoped for, yet the evidence of things not seen.

As such, do we have enough faith to believe that we will receive what we have petitioned God for in prayer?

- ❖ Are you still asking God to heal you or someone else?

- ❖ Are you still asking God for a breakthrough in your finances?

- ❖ Are you still asking God for a loved one to be saved?

- ❖ Are you still crying out to Him to restore your marriage or to bring reconciliation to your severed relationships with family members?

Can I tell you a secret? Stop asking God for these things over and over again when you pray! Instead, begin to thank Him with worship and praise because Jesus says to us in Mark 11:24, *"Therefore I say to you, whatever THINGS you ASK when you PRAY, BELIEVE that you receive THEM, and YOU will have THEM."* (NKJV) (emphasis added).

However, this Scripture is conditional based on the very next passage of Scripture in Mark 11:25–26 which says, *"And whenever YOU STAND PRAYING, if you have anything AGAINST anyone, FORGIVE HIM, that YOUR FATHER in HEAVEN may also FORGIVE YOU YOUR TRESPASSES. But if YOU DO not FORGIVE, neither WILL YOUR FATHER IN*

HEAVEN FORGIVE YOUR TRESPASSES." (NKJV) (emphasis added).

Therefore, if you have already asked God for whatever things you have petitioned Him for *when*, not if you have prayed, and you have no unforgiveness in your heart towards anyone, then you *must* believe that you have *already* received whatever things you have asked for. For this is what faith is! It is the substance of things hoped for, YET the evidence of things NOT seen.

MANY OF US ARE INVALIDATING GOD'S BLESSINGS BASED ON WHAT WE SPEAK FORTH WITH OUR MOUTHS

The Lord says according to His "eternal" Word that we can have whatever we are asking for in prayer, yet what are we asking for? What are we professing out loud with our mouths? For Proverbs 18:21 says, *"DEATH and LIFE are in the POWER of the TONGUE, And those who love it will EAT its FRUIT."* (NKJV) (emphasis added).

While it may seem like I am about to go on a "rabbit trail" concerning what I am about to share, it is extremely relevant concerning having the faith to believe that we will have what we have petitioned our heavenly Father about when we pray.

Unfortunately, many of us are invalidating God's blessings

based on what we talk about and speak into existence with our mouths.

Our heavenly Father wants to bless His covenant children superabundantly above all that we can think or ask. Yet when we *truly* "walk" in faith we will believe and then "speak" forth that which is not as though it already is!

In addition, what we "speak" forth with our tongue has the power of life and death and will manifest itself in our lives by either bringing forth "life" or bringing forth "death!"

Now let's substantiate this truth based on the following examples:

❖ *E'lōhim,* God, our Creator, "spoke" forth *the Word*—His only *begotten* Son—who is in the bosom of the Father when He "declared" Him when *E'lōhim* said in Genesis 1:3, "... *'Let there be light'; and THERE WAS LIGHT."* (NKJV) (emphasis added).

When the *Light of the World* was brought forth by *E'lōhim's* "spoken" Word, which was *the Word*, then the *Light of the World* "dispelled" the darkness that was on the *face of the deep* when the earth was still without form and void.

❖ Then *E'lōhim,* God, our Creator, "spoke" and said, "... *'Let there be a FIRMAMENT in the MIDST of the WATERS, and LET it DIVIDE the*

WATERS from the WATERS.'" (Gen. 1:6, NKJV) (emphasis added).

❖ Then *E'lōhim*, God, our Creator, "spoke" and said, "... *'Let the WATERS under the HEAVENS be GATHERED TOGETHER into one PLACE, and LET the DRY LAND APPEAR,' and IT WAS SO.*" (Gen. 1:9, NKJV) (emphasis added).

❖ Then *E'lōhim*, God, our Creator, "spoke" and said, "... *'Let the EARTH bring forth GRASS, the HERB that yields SEED, and the FRUIT TREE that yields FRUIT ACCORDING to ITS KIND, whose SEED is in ITSELF, on the EARTH'; and IT WAS SO.*" (Gen. 1:11, NKJV) (emphasis added).

❖ Then *E'lōhim*, God, our Creator, "spoke" and said, "... *'Let there be LIGHTS in the FIRMAMENT of the HEAVENS to DIVIDE the DAY from the NIGHT; and LET them be for SIGNS and SEASONS, and for DAYS and YEARS; and LET them be for LIGHTS in the FIRMAMENT of the HEAVENS to give LIGHT on the EARTH'; and IT WAS SO.*" (Gen. 1:14–15, NKJV) (emphasis added).

❖ Then *E'lōhim*, God, our Creator, "spoke" and

said, "... '*Let the WATERS abound with an ABUNDANCE of LIVING CREATURES, and LET BIRDS FLY above the EARTH across the FACE of the FIRMAMENT of the HEAVENS.' So God created GREAT SEA CREATURES and every LIVING THING that MOVES, with which the WATERS abounded, ACCORDING to THEIR KIND, and every WINGED BIRD ACCORDING to ITS KIND. And God saw that it was GOOD.*" (Gen. 1:20–21, NKJV) (emphasis added).

❖ Then *E'lōhim,* God, our Creator, "spoke" and said, "... '*Let the EARTH BRING FORTH the LIVING CREATURE ACCORDING to ITS KIND: cattle and creeping thing and beast of the earth, each ACCORDING to ITS KIND'; and IT WAS SO.*" (Gen. 1:24, NKJV) (emphasis added).

❖ Then *E'lōhim,* God, our Creator, "spoke" and said, "... '*Let Us make MAN in Our IMAGE, ACCORDING to Our LIKENESS; Let THEM have DOMINION OVER the fish of the sea, over the birds of the air, and over the cattle, over all the earth and over every creeping thing that creeps on the earth.' So God created MAN in HIS OWN IMAGE; in the IMAGE of GOD He created him; MALE and FEMALE He*

359

created THEM." (Gen. 1:26–27, NKJV) (emphasis added).

❖ Then *E'lōhim,* God, our Creator, blessed them and "spoke" and said to them, *"... 'Be FRUITFUL and MULTIPLY; fill the EARTH and SUBDUE it; have DOMINION OVER the fish of the sea, over the birds of the air, and over every living thing that moves on the earth.'"* (Gen. 1:28, NKJV) (emphasis added).

Therefore, since *E'lōhim,* God our Creator "spoke" all creation into existence, including us, His created, when He said, *"'Let there be'...,"* then do you suppose since we were created in *E'lōhim,* God our Creator's image, according to His likeness, that we too have been given His power and authority to "speak" forth things which are not as though they are?

WHAT WE "SPEAK" FORTH WILL BE BASED ON WHAT WE "MEDITATE" ON IN OUR MIND AND WILL BE BASED ON WHAT WE TRULY BELIEVE IN OUR HEART

God has given us, His created, His power and authority to "speak" forth in faith those things which are *not* as though they already *are.* Jesus says to us in Mark 11:23, *"For assuredly,*

I say to you, whoever says to this mountain, 'Be removed and be cast into the sea,' and does not DOUBT in his HEART, but BELIEVES that those THINGS he SAYS will be DONE, he will have WHATEVER he SAYS." (NKJV) (emphasis added).

Listen carefully. The Lord really wants His people to get this indisputable truth: What we "speak" out loud will be based on what we *truly* "believe" in our hearts.

As such, if we think "good" thoughts about ourselves and others, then we will "speak" forth "good" things (blessings) which will bring forth LIFE. Yet if we think "evil" thoughts about ourselves and others, then we will "speak" forth "evil" things (curses) which will bring forth DEATH. Out of the abundance of our heart, our mouth "speaks" forth what we are *truly* "meditating" on in our mind and what we *truly* "believe" in our heart.

This truth is substantiated by Jesus in Matthew 12:33–37 where Jesus is teaching about the fact that a tree is known by the "fruit" it produces.

He also says that we will be judged for *every* "idle" word we may "speak" forth. Then He says that by our "words" that we "speak" forth, we will be "justified" and by our "words" that we "speak" forth, we will be condemned.

Yikes! If this doesn't cause us to have a fear of the Lord, nothing will!

You may be thinking, that we are "justified" in Jesus based on what Jesus did on the cross at Calvary. Yes, this is true. However, do we *truly* have "faith" in His ability to bring to pass what He has said according to His "eternal" Word? Do we *truly* "believe" what the Holy Spirit has spoken over our lives through the prophetic Word?

Because *if* we *truly* have "faith" in Jesus' ability, rather than our own, then what we "speak" forth from our mouths will be in accordance with His "eternal" Word which shall not return to Him void. His "eternal" Word shall perform that for which God has sent it. And, so it is with us, His children.

The words we "speak" forth from our mouths will not return to us void, but they shall accomplish exactly what we have said. In fact, what we "speak" forth will manifest itself in the *physical* earthly realm, and the "fruit" of our words will bring forth either "blessings" and "life" or, our words shall bring forth "curses" and "death."

Thus, if we *truly* "believe" what Jesus says according to His "eternal" Word in our hearts, then the evidence of this will be heard by God and others based on what we "speak" forth from our mouths! After all, having *true* "faith" in God is for us to "believe" *without* doubting in His ability to bring those things we have petitioned Him for to come to pass, even if those things are not YET evident in the *physical* earthly realm.

As such, based on what many Christians are "speaking" forth, it does not seem as though we *truly* "believe" God is a rewarder of those who diligently seek Him, or that He will do what He has said He would do because of who He is!

Now let's take a closer look at Matthew 12:33–37. Jesus is explaining what the "root" cause of us either producing "good" or "bad" fruit is all about when He says that out of the abundance of the heart, our mouth speaks.

Matthew 12:33–37, says the following:

> *"Either make the TREE good and its FRUIT good, or else make the TREE bad and its FRUIT bad; for a TREE is known by its FRUIT. Brood of vipers! How can you, being EVIL, speak GOOD things? FOR OUT of the ABUNDANCE of the HEART THE MOUTH SPEAKS. A GOOD man out of the GOOD TREASURE of his HEART brings forth GOOD THINGS, and an EVIL man out of the EVIL TREASURE brings forth EVIL THINGS. But I say to you that for every IDLE WORD MEN may SPEAK, they will GIVE ACCOUNT OF IT in the DAY of JUDGMENT. For BY YOUR WORDS you will be JUSTIFIED, and BY YOUR WORDS you will be CONDEMNED."* (Matt. 12:33–37, NKJV) (emphasis added).

Again, a lot of us are negating God's blessings from coming to pass in our lives because what we are "speaking" out of our mouths is contrary to God's Voice and His Word.

Moreover, if we keep asking God over and over for the same things when we pray because His answer to us hasn't yet manifested in the natural *earthly* realm, how is this having faith in Him?

Remember that His "eternal" Word in Mark 11:24 says to us that *whatever* things we ask our heavenly Father for *when* we pray, we must believe and act as if we have *already* received them, and then we will have them.

I learned this lesson one day when once again I was crying out to the Lord in prayer for a breakthrough in my finances. I desperately needed a new vehicle because my current car was over thirteen years old and frequently breaking down, leaving me stranded. In addition, my master bedroom bathroom needed to be remodeled so I could actually use it, the roof on my house had a leak and the septic tank needed to be replaced, naming only some of the things I needed money for. These things were needs, not wants! God's Word says to us in Philippians 4:19, *"And my God shall SUPPLY all your need ACCORDING to His RICHES in GLORY by Christ Jesus."* (NKJV) (emphasis added).

Yet I was not receiving the money I needed to get all of these things taken care of. I knew that I had to rely on the Lord because for the past ten years I have worked for Him without pay, doing the work of my ministry solely off my husband's income, which is not going as far as it once did with the costs of goods and services rising exponentially.

Then one day while I was in prayer, I clearly heard God say to me to stop telling Him I needed money! Then He said to me the following:

> *"I want to bless you in this area, but you keep **negating** my blessing by what you are **speaking forth** because you can only **activate** My promises by **operating** in **faith**. As long as you keep saying that you need money, guess what? You will need money! Instead, believe that I have heard your prayer and start thanking me for your financial breakthrough."*

Wow! Needless to say, I repented right there and then and from that point on I started to thank Him for a breakthrough in my finances and began to profess out loud Scriptures found in His Word concerning prosperity.

As such, I began to get into agreement with what God's Word said concerning this lack of finances I was experiencing in my life rather than getting into agreement with what my checking account or my budget said. BUT this was not enough.

I had to "act" on what I believed! I had to "walk out" in "faith," rather than by sight, by finding the vehicle I wanted to take possession of. I had to find a contractor to remodel my bathroom. I had to shop for the materials I wanted to use for this project. Long story short, God orchestrated many different things concerning my finances. I finally received the brand new car, which by the way was the car of my dreams that I had believed Him for, and all these other things were finally taken care of as well. Praise the Lord! All glory goes to our *King of Glory*. Hallelujah!

Therefore, instead of listening to the bad report we receive from the doctor, our checkbooks, or whatever "exalts" itself *above* the knowledge of God's Word, we *must* stop getting into agreement with the enemy and instead "activate" our faith by coming into agreement with God's Word and His Voice. For the apostle Paul tells us in Hebrews 10:38, *"Now the JUST shall LIVE by FAITH; But if anyone draws BACK, My SOUL has no PLEASURE in him."* (NKJV) (emphasis added).

As Abraham did, we *must* be willing to "walk out" by "faith" rather than by sight and "act" on whatever we have believed for. We must stop listening to the enemy and getting into agreement with him!

Speaking of the enemy, how many of you have been dealing with a tremendous amount of spiritual warfare from the enemy lately? How would you like to be set free from all the ploys of the enemy? Well, then I have some "good news" for you today. Allow me to share the "good news" of the *gospel of the kingdom* with you. Let's take a closer look at Luke 10:17–20, which says the following:

> *"Then the seventy returned with joy, saying, 'Lord, even the DEMONS are SUBJECT to US in YOUR NAME.' And He* [Jesus] *said to them,*

366

'I saw Satan fall like lightning from heaven. Behold, I give YOU the AUTHORITY to TRAMPLE on SERPENTS and SCORPIONS, and over all [not some] the POWER of the ENEMY, and NOTHING shall by any MEANS HURT YOU. Nevertheless do not REJOICE in this, that the SPIRITS are SUBJECT to YOU, but rather REJOICE because YOUR NAMES are WRITTEN in HEAVEN.''' (Luke 10:17–20, NKJV) (emphasis added).

Do not dismiss the significance of this occurring *before* Jesus Christ went to the cross at Calvary.

Jesus gave His disciples the authority in His name to trample on serpents and scorpions and over all the power of the enemy! This indisputable truth applies to us, His disciples, in the twenty-first century as well.

Again, Jesus says that He has *already* given us the authority in His name—the same authority that was transferred from the first Adam to Satan in the fall.

In fact, Jesus came the first time to seek and to save that *which* was lost because of the fall. Jesus came to the earth the first time to restore our power and authority back to us so we could establish His government on the earth.

As a result, in Jesus' "matchless" name we have His authority and His power to trample on serpents, scorpions, and over all the power of the enemy! So are we "activating" and "using" the power and authority we have already been given?

DO WE HAVE THE FAITH TO BELIEVE WHAT GOD TELLS US ACCORDING TO HIS WORD OR NOT?

The early disciples who walked with Jesus believed what Jesus told them. They had faith. This is one of the reasons why they walked in His power and authority, turning the world upside down with the *gospel of the kingdom.*

So I ask each of you who are reading this the following question: *"Do we have the faith to believe what Jesus said or not?"* Because most Christians are not "living" the victorious life, Jesus Christ died to give us because we do not know who we are in Christ or what great exploits we are capable of achieving in Him!

Unfortunately, many Christians are living "defeated" lives because we do not "act" according to God's Word and we are not properly prepared for battle.

You must know beyond a shadow of a doubt that if you decide to live for God to establish His "kingdom" and His "righteousness" you will be experiencing *spiritual* warfare regardless of whether you want to or not.

Therefore, are you properly dressed for battle, so you will be victorious despite all the ploys of the enemy?

WE MUST "PUT ON" THE WHOLE ARMOR OF GOD TO STAND AGAINST THE WILES OF THE DEVIL

We all know that in order to stand against the wiles (deception) of the devil, we must "put on" the *full* "armor of God" based on Ephesians 6:10–20.

However, how many of us actually "put on" our armor when we begin our day? Just like we brush our teeth, comb our hair and get dressed every morning we must be determined we will "put on" on the full armor of God. This is the only way we will be prepared for battle when, not if, we encounter the ploys of the enemy when we go about our day.

The first piece of our armor the apostle Paul tells us to "put on" is this: He says we are to gird our waist with truth. Whose truth? The *only* absolute truth there is—the Word of God.

Thus, as we "walk out" in faith, rather than by sight, we must "profess" out loud what God says in His Word *despite* how we feel or what we see in the natural.

When we "profess" God's Word out loud, God's angels hearken to perform the Word of God that they hear us speak forth from our mouths.

Moreover, Psalm 91 reiterates this fact that we must stand on God's truth.

Psalm 91:4 says, *"He shall cover you with His feathers, And under His wings you shall take refuge; HIS TRUTH shall be*

369

your SHIELD and BUCKLER. " (NKJV) (emphasis added).

Then the apostle Paul tells us in Ephesians 6:16, *"... above ALL, taking the SHIELD of FAITH with which you will be able to quench ALL the fiery darts of the wicked one."* (NKJV) (emphasis added).

Therefore, no matter what other armor we "put on" (action required), *above* all else we must "lift up" the "shield of faith" in order to quench all the fiery darts of the wicked one, but *only* after we gird our waist with God's truth.

The main darts that the devil uses to derail our faith in God is fear and doubt, the opposite of having faith in God who is love. And, this is why God's perfect love casts out all fear. God has not given us the "spirit of fear"—but of power and of love and of a sound mind.

Always remember that everything we are battling against always begins as a thought in our mind. This is why I have the following motto under my signature line on my emails as a reminder of this truth: *Watch your thoughts because they become your actions, character, and ultimately your destiny...*

The "strongholds" which the apostle Paul speaks of in Second Corinthians 10:3–6, are the thoughts we meditate on in our mind.

Second Corinthians 10:3–6, says the following:

"For though we walk in the flesh, we do not war according to the flesh. For the WEAPONS of our WARFARE are not carnal but MIGHTY in GOD for pulling down STRONGHOLDS, casting down ARGUMENTS and every HIGH THING that EXALTS itself against the KNOWLEDGE of GOD, bringing every THOUGHT into CAPTIVITY to the OBEDIENCE of CHRIST, and being ready to PUNISH all DISOBEDIENCE when YOUR OBEDIENCE is FULFILLED." (2 Cor. 10:3–6, NKJV) (emphasis added)

Therefore, the weapons of our warfare are the Word of God. We must "speak" out loud God's Word as we come against every high thing that "exalts" itself against the knowledge of God, bringing every thought into captivity to the obedience of Christ.

Also, do not dismiss the fact that God shall only bring to pass what we "speak" out loud when our obedience is fulfilled!

When we sin we give Satan and his demons the "legal" right to penetrate our "breastplate of righteousness" and wreak havoc in our lives.

Yet because the battle always begins in our mind, if the enemy comes against your mind with fear concerning anything, say, *"it is written…"* after you look up all the Scriptures, you can find in God's Word addressing the area of fear that you are having. Then you must "speak" out loud these Scriptures until the fear leaves your mind. Be forewarned. The enemy will try to bring these thoughts back into your mind from time to time, and when he does then you simply say out loud, *"No! This affliction or* (whatever) *will NOT rise up a second time!"* as stated in Nahum 1:9.

If the enemy comes against your body with sickness or infirmities, and you are experiencing pain or do not feel well say, *"it is written..."* after you look up all the Scriptures you can find in God's Word for healing. Then you must "speak" out loud these Scriptures until you receive your *physical* healing in the natural realm.

Do not say out loud what your current infirmity is again or you will be negating your healing that God wants to bring forth in the *physical* realm. Rather, you can say to people the following: "While it is true you were diagnosed with (whatever), then immediately say out loud, *'BUT the truth is, By His stripes, I am healed.'* "And, keep saying you are healed in the name of Jesus until your healing manifests in the *physical* realm.

If the enemy comes against you and says you will never achieve (whatever), say *"it is written..."* after you look up all the Scriptures, you can find in God's Word addressing the area of lack or insecurities you are having. Then you must "speak" out loud these Scriptures until you know that you know "who" you are in Christ Jesus based on the "attributes" or the "inheritance" that God's Word says that you *already* have as His son or daughter.

After all, God "spoke" to Abraham and "said" that he would be the "Father of Many Nations" long before the *Son of the Promise,* Isaac, was ever conceived. The Angel of the LORD appeared to Gideon and "said" to him, *"The LORD is with you, you mighty man of valor..."* long before Gideon would be victorious in battle.

In other words, "speak" forth that which is *not* as though it *is,* based on what God's Word says rather than based on your reality. This is what it means to "activate" our faith in God's ability to bring to pass what He has said based on His Word.

Then *when* we "do" what we are supposed to "do" and we "speak" forth His Word out loud, then God must and will keep His Word. He will bring what we have "spoken" to pass in our lives according to what He has already said in His Word. This is based on Isaiah 55:11 which says, *"So shall MY WORD be that GOES FORTH FROM MY MOUTH; It shall not RETURN to Me VOID, But IT SHALL ACCOMPLISH WHAT I PLEASE, And IT SHALL PROSPER in the THING FOR WHICH I SENT IT."* (NKJV) (emphasis added).

Yet there are some believers in the body of Christ who are calling teachers of the "Word of Faith" movement, such as Joyce Meyer and many others, false teachers.

Obviously, these believers do not really understand what having faith really is. Having faith means that believers will "speak" and "walk out" what is *not* as though it *is* based on what God's Word says.

When we, as Jesus' disciples, *literally* "believe" what the Word of God says in our hearts, not in our minds on an intellectual level, but rather according to the *spiritual* eyes of our heart, then we will "speak" the Word of God forth. We will "do" what God says to "do" according to His Word and His Voice.

This is what it means to have *true* faith in God's ability to bring what He has said in His Word to pass in our lives.

Read Chapter 11 in the Book of Hebrews about all the great heroes of the Bible who were operating, walking, and speaking based on their faith in God and His Word.

The apostle Paul begins this entire chapter by defining what faith is when he says, *"...FAITH is the substance of THINGS HOPED FOR, the EVIDENCE of THINGS not SEEN."*

Every passage of Scripture in Hebrews Chapter 11 begins with the words *"By faith..."* In addition, everything that the great heroes of the Bible did and said was based on their faith in God's ability rather than on their own ability to "do" what He created them to do.

They would have *never* been able to fulfill their destinies by achieving what God asked them to "do" if they did not believe.

Furthermore, if God's people really had *true* faith in Him and

His "eternal" Word, and we actually "believed" what the Bible says, I can guarantee you we would be "acting" and "living" a lot differently than we currently are.

We would be living the abundant life the apostle Paul tells us about in Ephesians 3:20–21 below:

> *"Now to Him who is able to do <u>exceedingly</u> <u>abundantly</u> ABOVE ALL that we <u>ask</u> or <u>think</u>, ACCORDING to the POWER that WORKS in US, to Him be glory in the church by Christ Jesus to all generations, forever and ever. Amen."* (Eph. 3:20–21, NKJV) (emphasis added).

TRUE PROSPERITY MEANS MORE THAN HAVING RICHES AND WEALTH

What does all this mean that I have shared with you so far? It means that if we are not standing on God's truth by our faith in His ability to "do" exceedingly abundantly above all that we *ask* or *think* according to the POWER that works in us, then we have nothing to stand on and the enemy will defeat us!

Satan will have the "legal" right to kill, steal, and destroy everything that Jesus Christ died to give us.

In fact, you can have all the financial wealth possible but what good is it if your health is failing, your children are addicted to drugs and traversing the highway to hell, and your marriage is falling apart?

What good is having all the money in the world if you do not have true contentment and peace which can only come from knowing the *Prince of Peace* on a personal, intimate basis and trusting in Him?

Why is it that when we think of having prosperity, we think of only money?

Satan wants to kill, steal, and destroy your "birthright" and your "inheritance" as God's son or daughter.

Furthermore, the apostle Paul tells us in Romans 12:3 that God has dealt to each one of us a measure of faith. Yet he also tells us in Romans 10:17, *"So then FAITH comes by HEARING, and HEARING by the WORD of GOD."* (NKJV) (emphasis added).

The word "hearing" as used in this passage of Scripture is *Strong's Greek Lexicon* #G189. It is the Greek word "akoë" (pronounced "ak-o-ay'"), which means: To "act" on what we have heard.

Many of you reading this are parents. Therefore, when we tell our children to clean their rooms or to do whatever, how do we know they have heard us? We know when they "do" what we have told them to "do" correct?

The same holds true concerning our obedience to God's Voice and His Word. We must act on what we have heard.

WE "ACTIVATE" THE PROMISES OF GOD FOUND IN HIS WORD BY OUR FAITH. YET WE WILL ONLY "INHERIT" AND "RECEIVE" HIS PROMISES BY OUR OBEDIENCE

The analogy I just used with our children hearing what we say will be evidenced by them doing what we have said to do is applicable to believers who "hear" God's Word. As such, we may be able to fool those around us, but we cannot fool God. He knows when we truly believe what He has told us to do when we "act" on it!

We "activate" the promises found in God's Word by our faith. Yet we will *only* "inherit" and "receive" His promises by our "obedience" to His Voice and His Word when we "act" in response to what we have heard. Then we must step out in faith, not by sight, and "do" what He has told us to do.

I experienced this for myself the first time the Lord told me to go to Israel, and the Lord confirmed this through a couple of individuals in the body of Christ.

I didn't want to travel 6,744 miles away from home by myself in order to go to Israel. I didn't want to travel without my husband and my son going with me, and all of our passports were expired. Not to mention the fact that I wanted to go to Israel with Perry Stone and it would cost us a whopping $12,000 for the three of us to do so for ten days.

Yet in a very short period of time, all of our passports were renewed because of a special offer my husband's company was offering to their employees for a nominal price. In addition, I was able to effortlessly get my son excused from school for ten days. Everything else we needed to actually go on this trip quickly fell into place except for the money.

At the time we didn't have a lot of extra money saved up because, as I said earlier, I have been doing the work of the ministry without pay, using my husband's salary for the work of the ministry since God closed the door on my lucrative career on October 5, 2007.

Spending the $12,000 was pretty much going to wipe out our entire savings! Since the Lord was telling me to go to Israel, I expected Him to bring the provision that I needed in order to go. Therefore, I kept asking the Lord where the money was because my husband and I didn't want to use all of our savings to go.

However, to my dismay, the Lord told me to be obedient and go, and then He would bring the provision.

I had to "act" on what He told me and have faith that He would bring the provision. And, God was indeed faithful because I was "obedient" by "doing" what He instructed me to do. As such, about a month after we returned from Israel, my husband received a $20,000 bonus at work that more than paid for the trip and then some. Praise God!

Thus, when we *truly* "believe" what God has said based on His written (logos) Word and His spoken (Rhema) Word, then we will "do" according to what we have heard—we will obey.

Moreover, when we pray we must believe that God will not only answer our prayers, we must also believe that He has *already* answered them as we remain expectant, anticipating that we will receive what we have petitioned Him for.

Therefore, *if* we, like Abraham, truly believe in God's ability to provide everything that we need according to His glorious riches in Christ Jesus, and *if* we seek first His *Kingdom* and His *Righteousness* above all else, only then will God provide whatever resources we need to "do" what He has called us to do.

And, mark my words, God will test us as He did Abraham *before* He will give us the power to get great wealth. This is based on Deuteronomy 8:18, which says the following:

> *"And you shall REMEMBER the Lord your God,*
> *for it is He who gives you POWER to get wealth,*
> *that He may ESTABLISH* [1] [H6965: *qûm*: to
> *rise*; accomplish, confirm, ordain, strengthen,
> continue; get up; perform; stand up and make
> sure] *His COVENANT which He swore to your*
> *fathers* [Abraham, Isaac, and Jacob (Israel)]*, as*
> *it is this day."* (Deut. 8:18, NKJV) (emphasis
> added).

Our heavenly Father *Yehôvâh* is indeed our *Jehovah-Jireh*! And, as Abraham discovered when *Yehôvâh* provided a ram, caught in a thicket by its horns, so he would not have to

379

sacrifice his son Isaac, *Jehovah-Jireh* means, "The Lord will provide."

Yehôvâh will always provide everything we need based on Philippians 4:19 which proclaims, *"And my God shall SUPPLY all your NEED according to His RICHES in GLORY by Christ Jesus."* (NKJV) (emphasis added).

However, we must first seek the *kingdom* of God and His *Righteousness* as Jesus exclaimed in Matthew 6:33 in which He said to us, His disciples, *"But SEEK first the KINGDOM of GOD and His RIGHTEOUSNESS, and all THESE THINGS shall be ADDED to YOU."* (NKJV) (emphasis added).

The bottom line is this: *Yehôvâh*, our *Jehovah-Jireh,* is our source for everything we need in our lives, whether we need healing, deliverance, an increase in our finances, being able to overcome trials and tribulations, etc.

GOD WANTS US TO PROSPER FINANCIALLY SO WE CAN ESTABLISH AND EXPAND HIS KINGDOM

Contrary to what many teach and believe, God wants us to prosper "financially" and be in health even as our soul prospers.

This is substantiated in Third John 2, which says the following:

"Beloved, I pray that you may __PROSPER__ [(2)] *[G2137: euodoō: help on the road, that is, (passively) succeed in reaching; figuratively to succeed in business affairs: have a prosperous journey] in all THINGS and BE in HEALTH, just as your SOUL __PROSPERS__."* [(2)] (3 John 2, NKJV) (emphasis added).

Moreover, God's Word says to us that His people *should* have wealth and riches in our house.

This is the blessed state of the *righteous* based on Psalm 112:1–3, which says the following:

"Praise the LORD*! BLESSED is the man who FEARS the LORD, Who DELIGHTS greatly in His __COMMANDMENTS__* [(3)] *[H4687: mitsvāh: a command, whether human or divine (collectively the Law); (which was) commanded (-ment), law, ordinance, precept]. His descendants will be mighty on earth; The GENERATION of the UPRIGHT will be blessed. __WEALTH__* [(4)] *[H1952: hone: wealth; by implication enough: enough, + for nought, riches, substance] and __RICHES__* [(5)] [(6)] *[H6239: 'ōsher: wealth; H6238: 'āshar: to accumulate; chiefly (specifically) to grow (causatively make) rich] will be in his __HOUSE__* [(7)] *[H1004: bayith: a house (in the greatest variation of applications, especially family, etc.): palace, place, temple],*

And his *RIGHTEOUSNESS* endures *FOREVER.*" (Psalm 112:1–3, NKJV) (emphasis added).

Therefore, it is obvious based on Scripture, that the Lord desires to bless His people superabundantly above all that we could ask or think because Jesus Himself said in John 10:10, *"...I have come that they may have LIFE, and that they may have it more ABUNDANTLY."* (NKJV) (emphasis added).

Jesus is talking about us having life more abundantly while we are still living on earth! However, these promises from God are conditional, and they are based on us, His people, having the reverential fear of the Lord and delighting greatly in His commandments as specifically stated in Psalm 112:1–3.

Again, as Abraham demonstrated for all of us, we "activate" God's promises found in His Word by our "faith." However, we "inherit" and "receive" His promises by our "obedience" to His Voice and His Word as we "walk" by the Spirit, rather than our flesh, our carnal minds.

Moreover, it is one thing to have great wealth, but it is an entirely different matter for God to bless us so that we will be able to eat the fruit of it.

In fact, Ecclesiastes 5:19 proclaims, *"As for every man to whom God has given RICHES and WEALTH, and given him POWER to eat of it, to receive his HERITAGE and rejoice in his LABOR—this is the GIFT of GOD."* (NKJV)

In addition, Proverbs 10:22 proclaims, *"The BLESSING of the Lord makes one RICH, And He adds NO SORROW with it."* (NKJV) (emphasis added).

Have you ever known someone who is extremely wealthy, yet was the most miserable person you have ever met because they did not have their health or their family, they did not enjoy their labor, and hence, they did not enjoy their life?

Again, the enemy is the one who wants to kill, steal, and destroy everything that Jesus died to give us.

This is based on John 10:10 which says, *"The THIEF [Satan] does not come except to STEAL, and to KILL, and to DESTROY. I [Jesus] have come that they may have LIFE, and that they may have it more ABUNDANTLY."* (NKJV) (emphasis added).

Yet God in His infinite wisdom knows that the "love of money" is the root of all evil and if we are focused mainly on money, then we will fall away from the true faith.

For we *cannot* serve both God and money based on the following Scriptures:

> *"For the LOVE of MONEY is a root of all KINDS of EVIL, for which some have STRAYED from the FAITH in their GREEDINESS, and PIERCED THEMSELVES through with many SORROWS."* (1 Tim. 6:10, NKJV) (emphasis added).

> *"No one can serve TWO MASTERS; for either he will HATE the ONE and LOVE the OTHER, or else he will be LOYAL to the ONE and DESPISE the OTHER. You cannot SERVE God and MAMMON* [8] [G3126: *mammōnas: avarice:* extreme greed for wealth or material gain; greed, greediness, materialism]." (Matt. 6:24, NKJV) (emphasis added).

In addition, we need to realize that not all people who are wealthy are blessed by God. The enemy uses his ploys to give great wealth to people under his influence.

Remember how Jesus was tempted by Satan in the wilderness while he was under duress? Satan offered to give Him all the kingdoms of the world and their splendor if Jesus would bow down and worship him.

Read the story for yourselves in Matthew 4:1–11. Unfortunately, many *wicked* people prosper financially because they have sold their souls to the *prince of this world*—Satan for profit. Woe to them if they do not repent!

God wants us to know the "fruit" and ploys of the enemy. The proof of those who *truly* serve God is illustrated by their "fruit."

If they do not exhibit the "fruit of the Spirit" by the way they live their lives and they are not using their money and their time to further God's kingdom, then you have your answer.

However, there are some of God's people who are "deceptively" fleecing His sheep using the gifts that God has given them to help equip the saints in the body of Christ for the work of the ministry and to set the captives free.

MANY OF GOD'S PEOPLE ARE PROSTITUTING THEIR GIFTS BECAUSE OF THEIR LOVE FOR MONEY RATHER THAN FOR GOD'S PEOPLE

Many have prostituted the name of Jesus Christ for their own profit. Leading the pack are many leaders in the body of Christ. And, woe to them if they do not repent!

I am constantly amazed that many leaders in the body of Christ are misusing their gifts, given freely to them by Jesus and intended to be used to set people free. Instead, these leaders are charging people money for a prophetic word or for their deliverance. Show me one time in God's Word where Jesus or His disciples healed someone or cast out demons from them and asked for money to do so.

Yet at the same time, many of God's people in the ministry are working for virtually nothing, because many of God's people think that they should work for free. This is one of the reasons why God requires us to give our *tithes* and *offerings*.

We are commanded based on God's Word, even in the New Testament (Hebrews 7:5), to give our *tithes* and *offerings* so that those whom God calls into the ministry can devote their undivided attention to doing the work of the ministry and not focus on earning money. Rather, their entire focus should be on serving God without compromise and then serve His people.

Let me put this in the proper perspective for you if you desire to inherit financial prosperity from God. *Every* believer has a ministry regardless of what vocation God has called you to "do."

You are called to put the talents (giftings) that He has freely given to you to work for His kingdom and for His glory.

Again, Ecclesiastes 5:19 proclaims, *"As for every man to whom God has given RICHES and WEALTH, and given him POWER to eat of it, to receive his HERITAGE and rejoice in his LABOR—this is the GIFT of GOD."* (NKJV) (emphasis added).

Therefore, it does not matter if you are a businessman, a teacher, an artist, a hair dresser, or an engineer—whatever.

Do you believe God has given you your giftings (talents) to be used *only* for your own financial gain and to pay your bills?

Show me in the Bible where God has said the purpose for you existing is just for you to work and to pay your bills. Or, are you supposed to use the talents that you have freely received from God to help establish His kingdom and make a difference in the life of others while you are still living on the earth for all eternity?

And, with the talents that God has given you, enabling you to earn money in your "chosen" vocation, do you suppose God requires you to use *some* of your money to sow into His Kingdom as a *firstfruits* offering to the One who gives you the ability to produce wealth in the first place?

Would you go to work every day if you never got paid for what you did? Of course not! You would not be able to provide financially for yourself and for your family. Yet you earn a paycheck using the talents (giftings) that you have freely received from God, correct?

Then why is it that God's people think that people in the ministry should work for free?

Furthermore, God's people have no problem spending their money to go see a movie, to eat at a restaurant, to go to a sporting event or to go shopping at the mall.

They sow their money into *worldly* things which shall shortly pass away.

Yet when the offering plate is passed around, or a ministry asks that you consider sowing a seed into God's Kingdom, affecting people's lives for all eternity, many people have a propensity to not want to give financially.

This is an act of worship to God, not man. And, then we wonder why we live paycheck to paycheck and God is not giving us a breakthrough in our finances?

Another point I need to address is this: Why is it we believe God wants us to live paycheck to paycheck, barely getting by, when His Word says that Jesus died so we could live our lives superabundantly, above all that we could think or ask?

When His *eternal* Word says, we are to lend to nations and not borrow. In other words, we are not to be in debt. When His *eternal* Word says that the "blessed" state of the *righteous* is for wealth and riches to be in our houses!

Therefore, if we are just barely getting by *financially* speaking, how in the world can we give away what we do not first possess for ourselves?

How can we help meet the needs of the widows, the orphans, and the poor if we do not have the resources to do so?

Or, how can we even meet the needs of our own family members, if we are barely getting by ourselves? We cannot!

And, according to God's *eternal* Word we are supposed to provide for our own, especially for those in our own household.

This is based on First Timothy 5:8 which says, *"But if anyone does not PROVIDE for his OWN, and ESPECIALLY FOR THOSE OF HIS HOUSEHOLD, he has DENIED the FAITH and is WORSE than an UNBELIEVER."* (NKJV) (emphasis added).

Hence, we really insult God and negate Him blessing us when we doubt that He will not provide for His own sons and daughters who are part of His own household!

As such, do we really believe that God will require us to do something based on His Word, yet He will not give us the financial resources to do what He has called us to do?

If Satan gives great wealth to the people who have sold their souls for his purposes to be accomplished in the *kingdom of darkness,* then why do we believe that God will not provide His children in the *kingdom of light* with more than adequate "kingdom" resources?

Our heavenly Father's will is to bless His people with great wealth and prosperity so His "kingdom" purposes will be accomplished on the earth as it is in heaven.

God knows we need money in this world to live and do what He has called us to do for His glory and His purposes to prevail.

Therefore, God's people must eradicate and be delivered from the "spirit of poverty" and the "religious spirit" which has deceived us into believing that we are pious and holy when we are poor and destitute!

For those who are deceived into believing God wants His people to be poor in order for them to be holy, then guess what?

You will reap according to what you believe! As I have

conveyed, being poor and living in lack is contrary to God's Word.

WHY DO GOD'S PEOPLE WHO HAVE MINISTRIES WANT TO BE NON-PROFIT?

I do not know why God's people want to be part of or be a non-profit organization (business) when we would be wise to read and heed *The Parable of the Talents* as detailed in Matthew 25:14–30.

Jesus ends this parable by saying to the "wicked" and "lazy" servant the following in Matthew 25:26-28:

> *"...you knew that I REAP where I have not SOWN, and GATHER where I have not SCATTERED SEED. So you OUGHT to have DEPOSITED MY MONEY WITH THE BANKERS, and AT MY COMING I WOULD HAVE received BACK MY OWN WITH INTEREST. Therefore TAKE the TALENT from him, and GIVE IT to him who has ten TALENTS."* (NKJV) (emphasis added).

In the Scripture above, Jesus is talking about us using the talents we have freely been given by God to earn money (finances) so that we can sow some of it back into His kingdom for the furtherance of the gospel to all the nations of the world. We are called to establish His kingdom and His righteousness first in everything we do. And, since we live in the world it takes money to expand His kingdom.

Then Jesus says to all of us in Matthew 25:29–30, *"For to everyone who HAS, more will be GIVEN, and he will have ABUNDANCE; but from him WHO DOES not HAVE, even what he HAS will be TAKEN AWAY. And CAST the UNPROFITABLE SERVANT into the OUTER DARKNESS. There will be weeping and gnashing of teeth."* (NKJV) (emphasis added).

Yet we prefer to do the work of the ministry and be "non-profit" which limits us from earning the most "profit" in order to expand and proliferate His Kingdom? Especially, since Jesus tells us that *when* He comes back, He will settle all His accounts, and He will cast the "unprofitable" servant into the outer darkness where there will be weeping and gnashing of teeth.

In addition, if we set our sight on earning a tremendous profit, then we would yield a greater harvest by allowing us to sow the money earned back into God's kingdom.

Again, we would rather be non-profit instead of "multiplying" at least a hundred fold the great harvest that we would be able to produce by "multiplying" the money we were given based on the talents God has freely given us?

Especially, based on the fact that He wants us to "expand" and "multiply" His kingdom on the earth for the furtherance of the *gospel of the kingdom,* resulting in a greater harvest of souls!

Just imagine if we had more "kingdom" resources to work with like the devil's children do how we could influence the Media and Arts & Entertainment Mountains or pillars in our society for the advancement of the Christian faith for the glory of God to all the nations of the world.

We could make a tremendous difference concerning the "indoctrination" of our children being exposed to filth and the "evil" agenda of the *kingdom of darkness* just by funneling "kingdom" resources into these two mountains alone.

Yet many Christian organizations and ministries would rather be "non-profit," so they will not have to pay taxes. This mindset is contrary to God's Word, based on the following Scripture:

> *"For RULERS are not a TERROR to GOOD WORKS, but to EVIL. Do you want to be UNAFRAID of the AUTHORITY? Do WHAT is GOOD, and you will have PRAISE from the SAME. For HE is GOD'S MINISTER to you for GOOD. But if you DO EVIL, be AFRAID; for he does not BEAR the SWORD in VAIN; for HE is God's MINISTER, an AVENGER to EXECUTE WRATH on him WHO practices EVIL.*

*Therefore you must be SUBJECT, not only because of WRATH but also for CONSCIENCE' SAKE. For **BECAUSE OF THIS YOU ALSO PAY TAXES**, for they are God's ministers attending continually to this very thing. RENDER therefore to all their DUE: TAXES TO WHOM TAXES ARE DUE, customs to whom customs, fear to whom fear, honor to whom honor."* (Rom. 13:3–7, NKJV) (emphasis added).

Also, based on Romans 13:3–7 above, it is worth mentioning that this substantiates Proverbs 8:15 in which God says to us, *"By me KINGS reign, And RULERS decree JUSTICE."*

As such, if you want to know why the leaders in America are perpetuating "lawlessness" and our judges are decreeing "unrighteous" rulings leading to injustice, it is because God's people in America are "unrighteous." We are practicing "lawlessness" because our rulers are not a terror to "good works," but to "evil" for they are God's ministers, an avenger to execute wrath on those who "practice" evil!

This substantiates the truth that as a man sows, he shall also reap!

Notice that Proverbs 21:1 says, *"The KING'S HEART is in the HAND of the Lord, Like the rivers of water; He TURNS it* [the king's heart] *WHEREVER He WISHES."* (NKJV) (emphasis added).

Now let's refocus our attention on what Jesus says about us

paying our taxes to the civil authorities and giving our *tithes* and *offerings* to God.

We are to do both because those whom God has placed in authority in the civil government are God's ministers just like those whom God has placed in their position of authority in the Church are.

Matthew 22:15–21, says the following:

> *"Then the Pharisees went and plotted how they might entangle Him in His talk. And they sent to Him their disciples with the Herodians, saying, 'Teacher, we know that YOU ARE TRUE, and TEACH THE WAY of GOD in TRUTH; nor do You care about anyone, for You do not regard the person of men. Tell us, therefore, what do You think? Is it LAWFUL to PAY TAXES to CAESAR, or NOT?' But Jesus perceived their wickedness, and said, 'Why do you test Me, you hypocrites? SHOW ME THE TAX MONEY.' So they brought Him a denarius. And He said to them, 'Whose image and inscription is this?' They said to Him, 'Caesar's.' And He said to them, 'RENDER THEREFORE to CAESAR the THINGS that are CAESAR'S, and to GOD the THINGS that are GOD'S.'"* (Matt. 22:15–21, NKJV) (emphasis added).

As clearly indicated in the Scriptures I have already covered, we are commanded by God to pay our taxes to the rulers who are God's ministers that He has put in their place of authority in the civil government, and we are to pay our *tithes* and *offerings* to God. We are to do both!

Therefore, this mindset of the body of Christ of being a "non-profit" business and not paying their taxes is not from God. It is not according to His Word.

In fact, there are some ministries that are honoring and keeping God's Word who are not tax-exempt. Yet how many of you reading this would be willing to give to these ministries if you would not receive a tax deduction for doing so?

And, if this is why you choose not to give to these ministries who are not tax-exempt, are you truly giving your money to God's ministers who are serving Him faithfully without compromise?

Or, are you giving your money to a ministry so you can reap the benefit by paying fewer taxes on your tax return?

Some of you may be thinking it is okay for churches to be "tax -exempt" because our laws allow it.

However, if a "law" goes against what we are told in God's Word, then as Peter and the other apostles said in Acts 5:29, *"We ought to OBEY God rather than men."* (NKJV) (emphasis added).

In addition, if we have this "mindset" because it is permissible by the laws of our state or nation, even though it opposes God's Word, then I guess some believers in the body of Christ could "justify" having an abortion since it is lawful to have an abortion in almost every state in our nation.

However, does this mean that God's people should have abortions and approve of those who do so because it is legal when abortion is an abomination to the Lord? Of course not!

Therefore, just because something is "legal" according to the world's standards does not make it right in God's sight when it is contrary to His Word.

Thus, this "tax-exempt" status that churches and ministries take advantage of is not from God because it is contrary to His Word.

In fact, Satan has used it for his purposes, based on man's propensity to serve mammon rather than God, leading to all kinds of evil.

If you will take the time to read this article titled, the *501c3: The Devil's Church,* [9] then you will understand why many good honest people in the ministry *unknowingly* do not fully realize the full ramifications of what they are doing when they choose to become a "corporation" as a 501c3 organization.

Furthermore, this "tax-exempt" status muzzles the mouths of *some* of God's people who fall into the error of not proclaiming and preaching the uncompromised, unadulterated Word of God. They fear men in our government and those who sit in their pews rather than having a fear of the Lord!

This happens when pastors are afraid they will lose their "tax exempt" status and lose the people who pay their bills if they preach what their flocks "need" to hear rather than what they "want" to hear.

THE "NAME IT" AND "CLAIM IT" PROSPERITY MESSAGE

These "name it" and "claim it" prosperity messages being preached by many in the body of Christ is a lie from the pit of hell.

As I have clearly substantiated based on the Word of God, God will require His people to be obedient to His Voice and His Word, especially in the area of *tithes* and *offerings*, before He will bless us with great wealth.

Moreover, God will never bless His people with great wealth until they have proven themselves worthy and strong enough to not allow their wealth to shipwreck their faith.

God will always test our obedience to do His will for years before we will see the rewards of our devotion.

God knows we cannot give away what we do not first possess ourselves and this includes money.

The truth is without money there is not much that we can do in this world, and this is no surprise to God.

Our heavenly Father desires to bless His children superabundantly above all that we could think or ask to not only meet the desires of our hearts but the needs of others as well.

As we serve God with all our mind, heart, soul, and strength, the desires of our hearts will be in line with the desires of His heart. It is only then that God will bless us with great wealth when He knows we are ready to receive it and will use it to establish His Kingdom for His purposes and glory to prevail rather than using wealth only for our own purposes.

THE END-TIME TRANSFER OF WEALTH

In this "kairos" season as the "Day of the Lord" is fast approaching, the Lord will be transferring the wealth of the wicked to His faithful remnant.

He will reward those who have passed through the fiery furnace of trials and tribulations, yet they have prevailed and have not wavered in their devotion to Him.

This is based on Isaiah 61:6, which says the following:

> *"But you shall be named the PRIESTS of the LORD, They shall call you the SERVANTS of*

our *GOD. You shall EAT the RICHES of the GENTILES, And in their GLORY you shall BOAST.*" (Isa. 61:6, NKJV) (emphasis added).

The word "Gentiles" as used in Isaiah 61:6 above, is referring to heathen (wicked) people or nations who are out of covenant with God and practice or follow pagan rituals or false gods (idols).

Also, do not dismiss the significance that we, as disciples of Jesus Christ, are priests of the Lord based on First Peter 2:9–11.

Therefore, we are the servants of our heavenly Father and God our Creator, whose name is *Yehôvăh* and His only *begotten* Son, Jesus Christ, who is the *firstborn* over all creation.

Speaking of the priests of the Lord that shall eat the riches of the Gentiles, *Yehôvăh* is about to orchestrate the end-time wealth transfer for His *faithful* remnant, those who favor His *righteous* cause.

This is based on the following Scriptures:

> *"Let them shout for joy and be glad, Who FAVOR My RIGHTEOUS CAUSE; And let them SAY continually, 'Let the LORD be MAGNIFIED, Who has PLEASURE in the PROSPERITY of His SERVANT.'"* (Psalm 35:27, NKJV) (emphasis added).

"He also brought them OUT with SILVER and GOLD, And there was none FEEBLE (10) *[H3782: kâshal: to totter or waver (through weakness of the legs, especially the ankle); to falter, stumble, faint, fall or be weak or decayed] among His tribes."* (Psalm 105:37, NKJV) (emphasis added).

"I will PUNISH Bel in Babylon, And I will BRING OUT of his MOUTH what he has SWALLOWED; And the NATIONS shall not STREAM to him ANYMORE. Yes, the WALL of BABYLON shall FALL." (Jer. 51:44, NKJV) (emphasis added).

"Then you shall SEE and become RADIANT, And your HEART shall swell with joy; Because the ABUNDANCE of the SEA [people] shall be TURNED to you, The WEALTH of the GENTILES shall come to you." (Isa. 60:5, NKJV) (emphasis added).

"Therefore your GATES shall be OPEN continually; They shall not be SHUT day or night, That men may bring to you the WEALTH of the GENTILES, And their kings in procession." (Isa. 60:11, NKJV) (emphasis added).

"And Ephraim said, 'Surely I have become RICH, I have found WEALTH for myself; In all my LABORS They shall FIND in ME NO INIQUITY that is SIN.'" (Hos. 12:8, NKJV) (emphasis added).

"Judah also will fight at Jerusalem. And the WEALTH of all the surrounding NATIONS Shall be GATHERED TOGETHER: Gold, silver, and apparel in great ABUNDANCE." (Zech. 14:14, NKJV) (emphasis added).

In conclusion, we may be on our way to heaven because we have the faith to believe in Jesus, but do we have the faith necessary to "live" the exceedingly abundant life, above all that we could ask or think, while we are still living on the earth that Jesus died to give us?

Yet it all begins with us having faith in God's ability, not our own, to bring His promises to pass based on our "obedience" to His Word and His Voice.

As such, we, like Abraham, must learn to be "obedient" to God's Word and His Voice.

Again, we "activate" God's promises by our faith. However, we will "receive" and "inherit" His "covenant" promises based on our obedience.

In the next chapter, we will discover this truth: From God's perspective, we are a "living" sacrifice—holy and acceptable to

God which is based on our "obedience" to His Voice and His Word. Our "obedience" is a reasonable sacrifice that shall be acceptable to the Lord.

Please note: This next chapter of this book is extremely long but critically important if we hope to be "counted worthy" to escape all these things that shall come to pass and to stand before the Son of Man.

So I apologize in advance for the length of this next chapter. However, I have put many subheadings in this next chapter so you can take a break at each section I am covering and resume reading each section as time permits. Thank you in advance for your understanding.

CHAPTER 36

LIKE ABRAHAM AND JESUS, WE MUST LEARN TO BE OBEDIENT. FROM GOD'S PERSPECTIVE, OUR OBEDIENCE IS OUR SACRIFICE!

To help you understand the process of learning to become obedient to God's will I will use myself as an example. I have been through God's refining fire in this area and have passed many tests. And, I am quite sure before all things pass away, there will be many more trials and tribulations that you and I will have to "walk" through.

At the beginning of my walk with the Lord, I used to always ask, "Why God, why?" and "When God, when?" I did not have much patience—and you never want to ask the Lord to give you patience. If you do, He will give you many situations to test you in this area. Trust me on this! I have been around this mountain longer than necessary, learning to be patient and waiting on God's timing.

Furthermore, I have never been one to believe everything I read and hear. This is good because it propelled me to start digging deeper into His Word, needing to know His truth for myself through the revelation of the Holy Spirit. I am the type of individual with an "inquiring mind."

And, as such, I question *everything* with boldness and do my own investigative work. My prayer every day was for God to show me His truth and no one else's truth. Also, I prayed that He would show me the areas in my life where I was deceived. The truth is very important to me because if we are not standing on God's truth, then we are living according to a lie. And, if we are living according to a lie, then we will be serving and worshiping Him in vain.

I was even contemplating going to Bible school or to the Seminary, but the Holy Spirit emphatically told me no. The Lord told me to get in His Word, and His Holy Spirit would reveal His truth to me.

I have spent many years and countless hours meditating on His Scriptures, and the Holy Spirit would illuminate His truth to me so I could, in turn, teach others God's unadulterated, uncompromised truth based on the whole counsel of His Word.

In fact, my first trip to Israel coincided with the time the Lord told me to study the Torah. At this time, I had no desire to go to Israel at all, but the Lord told me to go, so I went. Looking back on my decision to be "obedient," I am so thankful that I chose to go and I did not lean on my own understanding.

The revelation and the impartations I received from the Holy Spirit while I was in Israel were life-changing. God established His love for His land and His Jewish people firmly in my heart forever. My walk with God would never be the same.

Studying the Torah and going to Israel would take me down a

road I never anticipated traveling, and it totally challenged everything I had ever heard taught at church. And, based on the truths the Holy Spirit was revealing to me, it turned my entire world upside down.

I was faced with a choice now that the Lord answered my prayer to only know His truth which is this: Now that I knew His truth I had a choice to make as to whether or not I would walk according to only His truth or walk the wide, easy path most follow which ultimately leads to destruction.

In fact, the Lord asked me one day if I was sure I wanted to continue with Him on this journey because my life would never be the same.

Of course, I said yes because He is everything to me.

Yet at the time I did not realize it would cost me everything to follow God and walk this narrow path that is very difficult and few find.

I have lost many relationships with friends and family because I chose to walk with God according to only His truth.

And, God has required me to give up many things that most Christians still practice, embrace, and do.

How could I teach God's people His truth if I did not walk according to His truth myself in the first place? That would make me a hypocrite like the Pharisees were, and that was not a road I was going to walk. I had to draw that line in the sand and make up my mind that I would be totally sold out to God

405

so I could fulfill the destiny He had in mind for me for His glory and His eternal purposes to prevail. We all need to do the same if we hope to fulfill God's "eternal" destiny for the very purpose that He created us for in the first place.

You will never be able to fulfill your destiny by straddling the fence—by living a double life—being part of the world by "conforming" to the world while at the same time trying to serve God. I know because I played this game for many years until God used adverse circumstances to finally get my full attention which I will share with you later on in this chapter.

God will require your total allegiance to only Him, and He will test you in your faith to see if you are ready to be used for "a cause greater than yourself."

Therefore, my journey to discover our "Hebraic" roots in Christianity truly began when I kept questioning the Lord about my true identity in Him because He would call me His little Hadassah since I was an orphan due to being abandoned by both parents at an early age.

As such, He is truly the only Father I have ever known and loved with all my heart, mind, soul, and strength. And, as my Abba Father, He has always taken care of me true to His Word based on Psalm 27:10.

I was inquiring of the Lord concerning my true identity when I was taking Torah classes because all I heard about was the Jews from the House of Judah. I asked the Lord, *"What about those of us who were Gentiles from the House of Israel? Are we not your "chosen" people too?"* God answered this question for me when the Holy Spirit revealed His truth to me which compelled me to thoroughly research this subject for myself based on the whole counsel of God's Word.

Moreover, I have always come to God with childlike faith, and as a result, I am very inquisitive. Any parent of a small child knows how they constantly ask us, "why?" This is how they learn.

As long as we live, we should never stop learning to grow deeper in our walk with the Lord. We are God's children, and He wants us to come to Him as "inquisitive" children, seeking answers according to His Word and not taking everything at face value that we hear preached by men.

At first, the Lord was very patient with me always needing to know why. Then one day He told me to stop asking why and trying to figure things out and just to obey Him.

Every time I would forget and ask Him, "why?" I heard Him say to me, *"Obedience is better than sacrifice!"*

He then explained to me to always hold onto, believe, and profess out loud the promises He has given me. Then He added, *"You will have to trust and fully rely on me."*

Therefore, in God's sight, our obedience is the "final exam" of how much we really trust and rely on Him.

Also, I had to let go of the tendency to try to figure out "how" what He told me would come to pass. If He gave us the whole picture all at once, then we would get ahead of His timing, and we would not be under His divine providence.

He wants us to depend and abide in Him every step of the way, allowing Him to bring His will to fruition in and through us. I learned this the hard way when the promise He gave me that He was going to close the door on my lucrative secular career and begin my prophetic ministry came to pass.

For the record, being in the ministry and being an author was not on my list of the top ten things I wanted to do with my life. My list of the things I wanted to do with my life changed drastically in 2004 when the Lord began to give me a prophetic revelation about America and He had me write my first book.

While I was writing about the testimony of my childhood in this book to help others, it was then that God gave me His dream of His government for America. It is the section in my book titled; "I Have a Dream."

I have always had God's government on my heart ever since I was a little girl when I envisioned what the world would be like if love, righteousness, and justice prevailed before I ever knew the true meaning of these things. While I was living a nightmare as a small child, God gave me a vision for my future that gave me hope at a time when I had no hope.

Therefore, I have always yearned and dreamed of making a

positive difference in the lives of people. This just proves the truth of Proverbs 16:9 which says, *"A man's heart plans his way, but the Lord directs his steps."* (NKJV) Now let's refocus our attention on God telling me in advance He was calling me into the ministry and closing the door on my secular career.

This promise that God gave to me began to unfold in early 2007, three years after He initially told me He was going to close the door on my secular career and bring me into full-time ministry in 2004. During this season, He would wake me up every morning promptly at 3:00 a.m.

It was during this time that I would write my first book for Him titled, *Shattered Dreams—Wake Up America Before it is Too Late!* The revelation for this book that I would receive from the Holy Spirit was flowing when I spent time writing it in the wee hours of the morning before I would begin my ten hour work day.

The only specific set of instructions He gave me concerning my secular career coming to an end was He told me to, *"Wait for the package."*

I knew God was referring to the Forced Management Package my employer gave to employees whose jobs were being outsourced overseas, a common practice for major corporations these days. In other words, I would not be resigning from my job.

At the time this happened, my husband would never have allowed me to walk away from making almost $60,000 per year with salary, benefits, and bonuses. As you can imagine, the loss of my income would make a huge financial impact to our way of life and severely impact our budget.

However, because of the stress of the situation I was in at my job and the stress I was under at home (due to my brother living with me at the time because he was at death's door and my husband's daughter progressing down the highway to hell), I got ahead of God's plan and resigned from the company twice.

During this whole ordeal, with God's help, I was able to exhibit the "fruit of the Spirit" to my co-workers and my family despite my dire circumstances.

For God had me in the palm of His hand through this whole ordeal. I prayed and cried out to God like I never did before.

And, as a result, Human Resources would not accept my resignation both times I quit because of how bad things were at work.

My brother, who should have died on the operating table, was spared; and I became his caretaker during this time.

And, my husband's daughter, who was on the highway to hell, ended up going back to live with her mother, with whom she had been living when we took her into our home due to the many issues she was dealing with at that time.

As I clung to God because He was my only hope, as time

progressed He ordered my steps, giving me further instructions for bringing about His will in a way I would never have imagined. The end result was that I did indeed receive one of the last Forced Management Packages offered to management employees. However, the process I had to "walk" through to get the package was unbelievable, and it was only by the grace of God that I survived this ordeal.

Therefore, when my secular career finally came to a close on October 5, 2007, and I received "the package" after resting for a few weeks, I thought I was ready to blaze a trail for Jesus and the *gospel of the kingdom*! However, God had other plans.

Before I knew God, I had been abandoned by both of my parents and suffered verbal, sexual, and physical abuse during the foundational years of my life.

As a result, I had learned that if I was going to survive, then it was up to me. Therefore, for the majority of my life, I based "who" I was on "what" I did, working very hard to excel at everything I undertook to be loved and accepted by people.

However, God was trying to teach me that I did not have to do anything to be valuable in His sight. He wanted me to learn to value myself as His daughter and to know who I am in Christ. He wanted me to know that I am valuable because of "who" I am, not based on "what" I do.

Still, I was striving to go through doors that God did not want to be opened up in the ministry. He just wanted me to learn to rest and do nothing while I waited on His timing.

Up until this time, telling me to rest was like telling a bear not to hunt in the woods—it was impossible! I had no clue what God meant when He said to rest, be still, and do nothing. Therefore, one by one all the doors to ministry opportunities were closed by God.

In addition, because I was wired with a "type A" personality, I have a natural propensity to be driven to "do" something. This was my normal operating mode for most of my life and helped me excel in my secular career.

People with a "type A" personality are individuals who are ambitious, highly organized, highly status-conscious, sensitive, impatient, take on more than they can handle, want other people to get to the point, anxious, proactive, and concerned with time management.

Moreover, people with a "type A" personality are often high-achieving "workaholics" who multitask, push themselves with deadlines, and hate to be delayed concerning anything.

Yes, indeed! This described me perfectly. Therefore, I got tired of waiting on God, and I decided I would take matters into my own hands, based on what I thought was right in my own eyes and based on my own plans. Like Abraham and Sarah, I was about to give birth to an Ishmael!

On the very day, I had a job interview for a position that would have been perfect for me until the right "ministry" opportunity opened up; I woke up in the morning with open, oozing sores covering my entire body, including my face and hands. This is one interview which never happened!

God has a way of causing us to see things His way. When the pain of remaining the way we are becomes greater than the pain it will take to change, it is usually only then that we will finally submit fully to Him in surrender.

For this very reason, in 2008 God fully stripped me of everything that I thought I was to give me a "new" identity in Him. As a result, I went through an entire year that I call "the dark night of my soul," which at that time, I didn't think I would survive.

I finally learned that the open, oozing sores covering my entire body were caused by systemic lupus after going to several specialists who didn't have a clue what was wrong with me.

Needless to say, even my own family members were afraid to get near to me because they thought I might be contagious.

The doctors were finally able to bring my systemic lupus under control with the use of steroids.

The anxiety and depression I suffered with for most of my life, before God delivered me, returned with a vengeance. Most days, I couldn't leave the house even to drive my son to school.

So for well over a year, I spent eleven to fifteen hours in bed most days.

In addition, suddenly a giant lump appeared on my neck. The doctors thought I had cancer; I even had to undergo surgery.

As so often is the case, God will send someone to you at the exact time you are finally ready to listen!

Right before I went into surgery, a dear friend of mine in the ministry told me two things. She told me I would be fine, and I would be working with her ministry in the near future. Then she asked me if I wanted to spend another year laid up in bed? Or, was I going to finally stop wrestling with God?

Like many of you reading this, I spent many years running from God's call on my life, totally understanding what Jacob endured and overcame when he wrestled with God in Genesis 32:24–32 and prevailed with God and with men.

Then my friend started telling me what God had originally told me—that God just wanted me to rest and to do nothing while I waited for Him. Wow. Talk about a "eureka" moment!

Long story short, I repented for being disobedient, asked God for His forgiveness, and then suddenly my breakthrough happened!

Everything I was afflicted with disappeared as quickly as it had come upon me.

The anxiety and depression that I was being plagued with completely left, the lump on my neck was benign, and the doctors were dumbfounded because there was no longer a trace of systemic lupus in my body.

And, just like God gave Jacob a "new" name when he wrestled with God and yet prevailed, God gave me a "new" name based on "how" He saw me because I had never liked the name of Donna May that my parents had given me.

God decided I needed to receive my "new" name which He gave me. He told me His name for me would now be Bella which means "devoted to God" in the Hebrew and Spanish language. In French it means beautiful. And, in the Latin, Bella is a diminutive of Annabella and Arabella meaning yielding to prayer.

You may be wondering why I had to go through this period of testing when I wanted to answer God's call on my life and fulfill my destiny.

It was because I wanted to do things my way based on what I deemed right in my own eyes!

And, even though I loved God with all my heart, mind, soul, and strength, this type of behavior is not acceptable to Him.

When we walk according to what we deem right in our own eyes, contrary to God's Voice and His Word, we are rebelling against Him by thinking that we know better than He does.

This is what pride does and is the very thing which caused Lucifer's rebellion and Adam's disobedience. We need to know that if we rebel against God's Voice and His Word we will reap the dire consequences for doing so until we repent.

GOD WILL AFFLICT HIS PEOPLE DUE TO OUR DISOBEDIENCE SO WE WILL REPENT AND NOT PERISH FOR ALL ETERNITY

For those of you who do not believe that God will afflict His people with diseases due to our disobedience, even though He is also the same God who will heal us, I beg to disagree for the following two reasons.

First, because of what I experienced. As soon as I sincerely repented everything that came upon me for my disobedience to God's Voice suddenly left as quickly as it had come upon me.

Second, based on what God's Word says to us in Exodus 15:25–26, which says the following:

> *"So he* [Moses] *cried out to the LORD, and the LORD showed him a tree. When he cast it into the waters, the waters were made sweet. There He made a* **STATUTE** [1] [H2706: *chóq:* an enactment; hence an appointment at a set time; law or ordinance] *and an* **ORDINANCE** [2] [H4941: *mishpất:* divine law, individual or collectively, including the act or the place of a ceremony] *for them, and there He TESTED them, and said, 'If you diligently* **HEED** [3] [H8085: *shâma':* to *hear* intelligently (often with implication of attention, obedience, etc.;*

consent, discern; obey; regard and understand]
*the VOICE of the LORD your God and DO what
is RIGHT in His SIGHT, give EAR to His
COMMANDMENTS* [4] [H4687: *mitsvâh*: a
command, whether human or divine
(collectively the Law): law, ordinance, precept]
and KEEP all His STATUTES, [1] *I* [the Lord]
*will put NONE of the DISEASES on YOU which
I HAVE BROUGHT on the EGYPTIANS. For I
am the LORD who HEALS you.'"* (Exod. 15:25–
26, NKJV) (emphasis added).

Notice that God is saying that He is the one who will put
diseases on us if we do not heed His Voice and we do not do
what is right in His sight, which will be evidenced by us
heeding His commandments by doing them and keeping all,
not some, of His statutes.

Moreover, Deuteronomy 32:39 says, *"Now see that I* [the
Lord], *even I, am He, And there is no GOD* [5] [H430:
'Elôhîym: the Supreme God] *besides Me; I KILL and I make
ALIVE; I WOUND and I HEAL; Nor is there any who can
DELIVER from My HAND."* (NKJV) (emphasis added).

Do you know why many believers in the body of Christ have
lost the *reverential* fear of the Lord and we do not truly know
the God we proclaim to serve?

It is because the leaders in the body of Christ feel as though
they need to do a public relations job for God and they
preach and teach only about the loving and merciful God.

417

They hardly ever present God in His role as a just *righteous* Judge who will "chasten" His sons and daughters so we will not be condemned with the world on Judgment Day (1 Corinthians 11:32).

In fact, read all of Hebrews 12:5–11, on your own. This Scripture talks about the discipline of our heavenly Father, and we are specifically told that whom the Lord loves He "chastens" and "scourges" every son whom He receives.

Reflect on what Jesus had to endure before He died on the cross when He was "scourged" beyond imagination and what He was required to suffer to be received by His heavenly Father. A servant is not greater than His Master.

In Hebrews 12:8, we are told that if we are not chastised by our heavenly Father, then we are illegitimate and not His sons and daughters.

I am thankful my heavenly Father loved me enough to "chasten" and "scourge" me in my disobedience to Him so I would learn to have the *reverential* fear of God and truly know my heavenly Father and Lord and Savior on a personal, intimate basis based on who He truly is and what He requires from His sons and daughters.

Therefore, I had to "experience" His truth that it is only when we place our hope and trust in the Lord, evidenced by our total "obedience," that we will inherit His promises based on

Isaiah 40:31, which says the following:

> *"But those who WAIT on the LORD Shall RENEW their STRENGTH; They shall MOUNT UP with wings like eagles, They shall RUN and not be WEARY, They shall WALK and not FAINT."* (Isa. 40:31, NKJV) (emphasis added).

Another thing worth mentioning at this time, based on Isaiah 40:31 above, is this truth: First, eagles do not fly in flocks. In other words, if we are doing what the majority of the people in the world are doing, more than likely we have drifted off the "narrow" path which leads to life.

Second, eagles do not flap their wings to get where they are going—they glide *effortlessly* on the wind that the Lord provides. Therefore, to achieve the purpose and the destiny that the Lord has for *every* one of us, we must learn to wait on God's timing, rely on the Holy Spirit's daily guidance, crucify our flesh, and be obedient.

What do I mean by crucifying our flesh? Let's suppose we feel led by the Holy Spirit to get physically fit. Will we achieve this goal by wishing it will happen? No. It will require us to deny our flesh by making up our mind to eat the right foods, reducing the amount of food we eat, and exercising. Can we do this in our own strength? No.

We must pray and ask God for His grace to help us. Then when situations arise where we are tempted to give up or not do what we know we need to do, we should say out loud something like, *"No. I have made up my mind, and I can do all things through Christ who strengthens me."*

WE HAVE TO LEARN TO CRUCIFY OUR FLESH AND DEMOLISH THE STRONGHOLDS KEEPING US CAPTIVE IN OUR MIND

The first step in crucifying our flesh is that we must make up our mind and be determined to "do" what we know is the right thing to do.

Then we must rely on the grace of God, to empower us and enable us to persevere to complete the goal. Moreover, having discipline is doing "what" we do not want to do "when" we do not want to do it.

In other words, we must renew our "carnal" mind with the washing of God's Word and begin walking according to the Spirit to do the things that God's Word says that we can achieve in Christ. We must stop doing things the way we have always done them, based on what we learned *before* we became saved.

The apostle Paul tells us to take *every* thought captive to the obedience of God's Word in Second Corinthians 10:3–6. Do we realize that every action we will ever "do" is first based on a "thought" that we have entertained in our mind?

The battle begins in our mind.

Second Corinthians 10:3–6, says the following:

> *"For though we WALK in the FLESH, we do not war ACCORDING to the FLESH. For the WEAPONS of our WARFARE are not CARNAL but MIGHTY in GOD for pulling down STRONGHOLDS, casting down ARGUMENTS and every HIGH THING that exalts itself AGAINST the KNOWLEDGE of GOD, bringing every THOUGHT into CAPTIVITY to the OBEDIENCE of CHRIST, and being READY to PUNISH all DISOBEDIENCE when YOUR OBEDIENCE is FULFILLED."* (2 Cor. 10:3–6, NKJV) (emphasis added).

Again, these "strongholds" that the apostle Paul is talking about are in our mind.

Also, notice that in God, we will "pull down" these strongholds; we will "cast down" arguments and every high thing that exalts itself against the knowledge of God when we bring *every* "thought" into captivity to the obedience of Christ.

However, as I said before, but it bears repeating, God will punish all disobedience *when our* "obedience" to His Word and His Voice is fulfilled.

In Second Corinthians 10:3–6, the apostle Paul defines "strongholds" as arguments, pretensions, or thoughts that set themselves against the knowledge of God.

421

However, I like Edgardo Silvoso's definition of a spiritual stronghold. He states: *"A spiritual stronghold is a mindset impregnated with hopelessness that causes us to accept as unchangeable, situations that we know are contrary to the will of God."* [Silvoso 1994: 155]

Therefore, any belief system which is entrenched in our "thinking" that is contrary to God's Word is a "stronghold" that we have formed as a result of our upbringing since our childhood, or by what we have inherited from generational *iniquities* in our family's bloodline.

In addition, some "strongholds" are the result of what we are "indoctrinated" with in our educational system, what we view on television, or read in books, or on the internet.

These "strongholds" are based on what our "society" deems right in their own eyes, usually in direct opposition to the Word of God.

These "strongholds" keep us from fully knowing God and stop us from receiving all the blessings that God wants to bestow on us so that we can fulfill our destiny. Therefore, we must choose to "think" and "walk" in the Spirit, rather than our flesh, which is our carnal minds. But how do we do this?

We can be victorious in our "thinking" and thus "walk" in the Spirit rather than the flesh by invoking this analogy I once heard which is as follows: Whatever we allow our "imagination" in our mind to see, is what we shall achieve.

In other words, if we take the word "imagination" and form two separate words, consisting of "imagine" and "nation," we can then ask ourselves for every situation we need to "overcome" the following question: "What nation am I currently "thinking" and "walking" in?"

There are only two nations—God's nation or Satan's nation.

If we are "thinking" and "walking" according to the Spirit, we are serving God's nation and will produce the "fruit" thereof. Whereas, if we are "thinking" and "walking" according to our carnal mind, we are serving Satan's nation (the world), and we will reap curses rather than the blessings God wants to bestow on us.

Therefore, as soon as a thought comes into our mind that we know is contrary to God's Word, we are not to entertain this thought or dwell on it at all. We are to immediately stop thinking about it and replace it with a Scripture from God's Word. Jesus invoked this technique when He was being tempted by the enemy in the wilderness. Every time Satan tempted Jesus, Jesus immediately quoted Scripture negating what the enemy said. In other words, Jesus refused to get into agreement with Satan!

Rather, He immediately got into agreement with what was written in God's Word. This is what believers must do if we want to be victorious in the battle for our souls, which always begins in our mind.

Furthermore, when we hear the Lord, we must obey what He

instructs us to do regardless of our flesh resisting every step of the way. I can guarantee you when you are attempting to get rid of any stronghold or sin from your life; the enemy will rear his ugly head and seek to derail you.

Satan knows that it is only by us being obedient to "do" what we hear from God based on His Word or His Voice, only then will we be able to fulfill our destiny and be a threat to his kingdom.

The Holy Spirit gave me a revelation which may help you to understand how the process of our obedience works. It is based on the words of Jesus in Matthew 7:24–25, which says:

> *"Therefore everyone who **HEARS** these WORDS of MINE and PUTS them into PRACTICE is like A WISE MAN WHO BUILT HIS HOUSE ON THE ROCK. The rain came down, the streams rose, and the winds blew and beat against that house; yet it did not FALL, because it had its FOUNDATION on the ROCK."* (Matt. 7:24–25, NIV) (emphasis added).

Hence, when we are building a fortified house which is built upon the Chief Cornerstone, Jesus Christ, two "key" ingredients are needed—stones and mortar.

In this analogy, the mortar is symbolic of our obedience, doing what the Lord told us to do.

The stones, unlike bricks, are not formed by human hands or effort. They represent the instructions we have received from the Lord.

As we listen, which will become evident when we "obey" His instructions, He will give us another stone. Our obedience is the mortar needed to firmly secure the stone in place.

Each time we are obedient, we are able to build the stone wall higher and higher.

Eventually, we will have accomplished the building of a fortified house of stones, which is symbolic of us achieving the dream or the mandate God has placed upon our hearts which is founded on Jesus Christ, the Chief Cornerstone.

Based on this analogy, we have built our house, ministry, or achieved our mandate based on God building it because we have been obedient to do only those things He instructed us to do.

If we allow God to build our ministries or accomplish our mandates, then there is no devil in hell that will stop us from achieving great things for God's kingdom.

The question we must ask ourselves is this: *"Is my ministry being done for Jesus, but not being built by Jesus?*

Many believers are building their own kingdoms, by their own will and efforts, rather than allowing Jesus to build His Kingdom *through* us. The bottom line is this: We will never achieve God's will for us on our own.

425

Many have accomplished their goals based on their own will and efforts, but they have built their house on sand, and it shall not last. For Jesus says to us in John 15:5, *"I am the VINE, you are the BRANCHES. He who ABIDES in Me, and I in him, BEARS MUCH FRUIT; for WITHOUT Me you can DO NOTHING."* (NKJV) (emphasis added).

Therefore, the foundation that we build our "houses" on must be built upon the rock, Jesus Christ. Furthermore, our authority and anointing, given to us by God, is always a result of our alignment with His will and based on our obedience.

OUR FAITH WALK AND OBEDIENCE IMPACTS OTHERS FOR ALL ETERNITY

Here is another fact to consider. Do we realize that our obedience to God's Voice and His Word will impact other people's lives and may alter their eternal destiny as well?

Usually, God will ask us to do some things that we would rather not do. We tend to look at these things that He asks us to do which is based on our limited perspective of how it will impact us or interrupt our plans.

We need to get over ourselves and realize that our walk with Jesus is not about our comfort, our convenience, or even our happiness. We must be willing to die to ourselves so that He can use us for a "cause greater than ourselves," and He usually requires us to "walk" *through* many trials and tribulations because countless souls are at stake for all eternity.

We also need to realize that the race which is set before us so that we can overcome and be found faithful until the very end is not a sprint! Rather, it is a marathon.

As such, order and authority are critical to God. He will not promote us to the next level all at once—it happens step-by-step based on our obedience. Following are some of the reasons why God chooses to do it this way:

❖ We must "walk" *through* trials and tribulations so that our character becomes more like Christ. We must submit to God's refining fire and allow Him to burn away anything which hinders us from walking fully in His presence. This is substantiated in Hebrews 12:1–2, which says the following:

> *"Therefore we also, since we are surrounded by so great a cloud of witnesses, let us LAY ASIDE every WEIGHT, and the SIN which so easily ENSNARES us, and let us RUN with ENDURANCE the RACE that is SET before us, LOOKING UNTO JESUS, the AUTHOR and FINISHER of our FAITH, who for the joy that was set before Him ENDURED the CROSS, DESPISING the SHAME, and has SAT DOWN at the*

427

> *RIGHT HAND of the THRONE of GOD."* (Heb. 12:1–2, NKJV) (emphasis added).

❖ We must go through a season of preparation by "applying" what we have learned to see if we are ready for more responsibility. In other words, we must pass the "final exam" which is based solely on our obedience.

❖ If God promoted or rewarded us too quickly, pride would be our downfall. He wants us to be successful in achieving the mandates He has given us. This is for His glory, not for ours!

It is critical that we allow Jesus to build our ministries, for only then will we be guaranteed to achieve and succeed in everything we put our hands to for His glory to prevail.

The last thing we want is for our anointing or giftings to take us where our character cannot keep us.

As such, God must develop and refine our character by allowing us to "walk" through various trials and tribulations, so we will learn "obedience" from what we suffer as Jesus had to do.

God will not promote us before He develops and refines our character so that we will be conformed to the image of His

428

Son. It is for this reason why we are told in James 1:2–4, that the "testing" of our faith produces "patience." Therefore, we need to let God develop our "patience" so we may be perfect and complete, lacking nothing. James 1:2–4, says the following:

> *"My brethren, count it all JOY when you FALL into various TRIALS, knowing that the TESTING of your FAITH produces PATIENCE. But let PATIENCE have its perfect WORK, that you may be PERFECT and COMPLETE, lacking NOTHING."* (James 1:2–4, NKJV) (emphasis added).

Last, but certainly not least, if we do not learn to "crucify" our flesh and be "obedient" to God's Voice and Word, then we can rest assured that God will not give us great wealth to establish His Kingdom for His glory and purposes.

Nor, will we "do" the will of our heavenly Father and fulfill our eternal destiny.

Every blood-bought disciple of Jesus Christ has a ministry to be accomplished for God's glory and purposes to prevail no matter what your chosen vocation happens to be.

Tragically, the graveyard is full of people who never fulfilled their destiny because they "chose" to live their lives for themselves and did not answer the call that God predestined and created them for before one of their days on this earth ever came to be.

Moreover, God's promise found in Galatians 3:5–9, *may* be claimed by *Yehóváh*'s children, who are disciples of Jesus Christ and, like Abraham, are *willing* to give up everything for His name's sake and use their wealth for God's kingdom purposes to prevail. Galatians 3:5–9, says the following:

> *"Therefore He who SUPPLIES the SPIRIT to you and works MIRACLES among you, does He do it by the WORKS of the LAW, or by the HEARING of FAITH?—just as Abraham 'BELIEVED God, and it* [Abraham's faith] *was ACCOUNTED to him* [Abraham] *for RIGHTEOUSNESS.' Therefore know that only those who are of FAITH are SONS of ABRAHAM. And the Scripture, foreseeing that God would JUSTIFY the GENTILES by FAITH, preached the GOSPEL to Abraham BEFOREHAND, saying, 'In you* [Abraham] *all the NATIONS shall be BLESSED.' So then those who are of FAITH are BLESSED with BELIEVING Abraham."* (Gal. 3:5–9, NKJV) (emphasis added).

Accordingly, based on Galatians 3:5–9 above, we are told the following:

1. *Yehóváh* who gives us His Holy Spirit and works miracles among us does so by us hearing (by "doing" what His Word says because we come into "agreement"

with what He says in His Word) and by us placing our faith in God's ability, rather than our own ability.

The bottom line is this: We must believe that *Yehôvâh* will bring to pass what He says that He will do according to His *eternal* Word! And, like Abraham, we will demonstrate our faith and trust in God by our "obedience" to His Voice and His Word.

Again, Abraham was obedient to God long before the law was given through God's servant Moses to the children of Israel. Our faith in "believing" God's Word as we "obey" His Voice will be accounted to us as *righteousness* just like it was with "believing" Abraham.

In other words, we practice *righteousness* by "living" and "walking" according to what our heavenly Father *Yehôvâh* tells us to do in accordance with His *eternal* Word and His Voice.

Therefore, know that *only* those who are of "faith" are sons of Abraham.

2. *Yehôvâh* our heavenly Father and our Lord and Savior Jesus Christ knows the end from the beginning. Thus, He foreknew that He would "justify" both the Jews from the House of Judah and those of us who were formerly Gentiles from the House of Israel (Jacob/Joseph/Ephraim) who have now been grafted into the commonwealth of Israel.

431

We are grafted into the commonwealth of Israel, when we place our faith and trust in His only *begotten* Son, Jesus Christ.

This is based on Romans 8:28–30, which says the following:

> *"And we know that all things WORK TOGETHER for good to those WHO LOVE GOD, to those who are the CALLED according to His PURPOSE. For whom He FOREKNEW, He also PREDESTINED to be CONFORMED to the IMAGE OF HIS SON, that He might be the FIRSTBORN among many BRETHREN. Moreover whom He PREDESTINED, these He also CALLED; whom He CALLED, these He also JUSTIFIED; and whom He JUSTIFIED, these He also GLORIFIED."* (Rom. 8:28–30, NKJV) (emphasis added).

According to *Strong's Greek Lexicon* #G4309, the word "predestined" as used twice in Romans 8:28–30, is the Greek word "proorizo" (pronounced "pro-or-id'-zo"), and means: To predetermine or determine before, ordain. Therefore, from the foundation of the world, God "predetermined" or "ordained" that all

432

men *might* be "conformed" to the image of His Son, once they received Jesus Christ as their Lord and Savior.

This was and is God's *only* plan of "redemption" for the forgiveness of our sins so that all mankind could be "restored" and "reconciled" back into "walking" in a covenant relationship with our heavenly Father, who is also God, our Creator.

However, this does not mean that all men will "choose" to answer the call.

In addition, since God knows the end from the beginning, He foreknew ahead of time those individuals who would reject Him and His only *begotten* Son, Jesus Christ.

And, He also foreknew ahead of time those who would love Him and answer the call according to His purposes for His glory.

It would be those who "chose" to love Him and answer the call that He has "chosen" to be predestined to be conformed to the image of His Son, so He would also "justify" and "glorify" us. Jesus tells us in Matthew 22:14, *"For many are CALLED, but few are CHOSEN."* (NKJV)

In other words, love is a choice. And, since God is love,

433

He has given all men the opportunity to "choose" whether or not we would answer the call to be conformed to the image of His Son after we acknowledge and receive Him as our personal Lord and Savior. Moreover, God still uses those who would reject Him for His purposes and glory to prevail as substantiated by Proverbs 16:4 which says, *"The LORD has made ALL for Himself, Yes, even the WICKED for the DAY of DOOM."* (NKJV) (emphasis added).

Yes, indeed! God will even use the "wicked" to carry out His plans, culminating in the day of doom when the "Day of the Lord" takes place at the end of all the ages.

An example of God using evil men so that His Word will be fulfilled is substantiated by Judas' betrayal of Jesus for thirty pieces of silver which led to the crucifixion of Jesus. Everything that was done which led to Jesus being crucified was God's will. This is according to His eternal Word based on Matthew 26:56 which says, *"But all THIS WAS DONE that the SCRIPTURES of the PROPHETS might be FULFILLED..."* (NKJV) (emphasis added).

As I covered in Book 1, God "foreknew" us when we were glorified spirits *when* He created us in His image and His likeness *before* He manifested our "spirit man" in these bodies of flesh and blood, which is the temple of the living God.

This is why God told the prophet Jeremiah in Jeremiah 1:5, that *before* He formed him in his mother's womb, He knew him and He "sanctified" him and "ordained" him as a prophet to the nations.

This is based on Jeremiah 1:5, which says the following:

> *"Before I FORMED you in the WOMB I KNEW you; Before you were BORN I SANCTIFIED you; I ORDAINED you a PROPHET to the NATIONS."* (Jer. 1:5, NKJV) (emphasis added).

As is true for all of us, even though God "ordained" him as a prophet to the nations, Jeremiah still had to "choose" to answer the call.

3. Do not dismiss the significance of the apostle Paul's words in Galatians 3:8, which says the following:

> *"And the Scripture, FORESEEING that God would JUSTIFY the GENTILES by FAITH, preached the GOSPEL to Abraham BEFOREHAND, saying, 'In you all the NATIONS shall be BLESSED.'"* (Gal. 3:8, NKJV) (emphasis added).

Remember, this is one of the reasons why Jesus Christ's genealogy begins with Abraham, the "Father of Many Nations" based on Matthew 1:1.

4.   Therefore, those who are of "faith" are blessed with "believing" (through our faith in Jesus Christ) as Abraham did. In other words, we are heirs according to the promises that God gave to Abraham *if* we have faith evidenced by our obedience to *Yehôvâh's* Word and His Voice.

If we refuse to be obedient to God's Word and His Voice, then we cannot claim to be "walking" in a covenant relationship with our heavenly Father that Jesus died to "reconcile" and "restore" us to. And, as a result, we are "choosing" to *despise* and *forfeit* our "birthright" and "inheritance" just as Esau did.

HOW TO PROSPER FINANCIALLY AND OVERCOME TRIALS AND TRIBULATIONS

If we want to prosper financially and "overcome" the trials and the tribulations in the days ahead, then we must be willing to "do" what Abraham did. We must step out in faith and be obedient to the Lord by "doing" *only* those things that He instructs us to do according to His eternal Word as we are led by the Holy Spirit.

This includes, but is not limited to, the following things:

1. Honoring the Lord by not breaking His *everlasting* covenant that He established with Abraham and his descendants. This *same* covenant that God "renewed" with all the children of Israel through His servant Moses at the base of Mount Sinai and Horeb. These covenants build upon each other and were confirmed by the blood of Jesus Christ when Jesus became the "mediator" of the New Covenant with both the House of Judah and the House of Israel.

2. Being focused on the needs of people rather than on making money.

3. Not withholding our *tithes* and *offerings* so the *gospel of the kingdom* can be preached in the entire world to every nation.

As I have already conveyed, Abraham had great faith in God's ability to bring what He had said to pass. Therefore, Abraham "walked" by faith not by sight according to Hebrews 11:1 which proclaims, *"Now FAITH is the SUBSTANCE of THINGS HOPED FOR, the EVIDENCE of THINGS not SEEN."* (NKJV) (emphasis added).

HOW TO GROW IN OUR FAITH

How do we exercise and grow in our faith as Abraham did? We follow his example. Abraham did not fully understand "how" the promises that God gave him would come to fruition. With the exception of Ishmael, Abraham allowed God to handle the outcome of "how" these promises would come to pass.

All Abraham had to do was believe, trust, and obey God which he was able to do because he had a personal, intimate relationship with *Yehôvâh.*

In fact, as I have already conveyed, but it bears repeating, Abraham walked so closely with *Yehôvâh* that God called Abraham His friend based on Second Chronicles 20:7, Isaiah 41:8, and James 2:23.

This is another reason why it is critical for all believers in Jesus Christ to have a personal, intimate relationship with our heavenly Father, *Yehôvâh,* and His only *begotten* Son, Jesus Christ. We do so by abiding in their presence—for this is "eternal" life based on John 17:3.

It is only by us cultivating this personal, intimate relationship with them that we will hear and understand what our heavenly Father's will is for our life. Then we must obey what the Holy Spirit tells us to do.

God's Holy Spirit will never contradict His written Word—the Bible, which contains all of *Yehôvâh's* general instructions for how we are to live our lives as His sons and daughters while we are still living on the earth. However, it is only when we humble and submit ourselves to the Holy Spirit, evidenced by us "doing" what He tells us to "do," that God will tell us what specifically we should do in our individual lives on such matters as our vocation, who we should marry, and where we should live.

You may be wondering how you can be certain it is God speaking to you and not your own voice or that of the enemy. We are told in God's Word to test the spirits based on First John 4:1 which states, *"Beloved, do not BELIEVE every SPIRIT, but test the SPIRITS* [plural]*, whether they are of God; because many FALSE PROPHETS have gone out into the world."* (NKJV) (emphasis added).

Notice that the word "spirits" is plural, meaning there are many different spirits that will attempt to influence our decision-making process.

I have learned that God will usually confirm what He tells us to "do" by the testimony of two or three witnesses. This is based on Second Corinthians 13:1 which states, *"This will be the third time I AM COMING TO YOU. By the MOUTH of two or three WITNESSES every WORD shall be ESTABLISHED."* (NKJV) (emphasis added).

God will always confirm what He tells us to do either through His Word or other people. And, as I have already conveyed, He will never tell us to do anything contrary to His Word.

In addition, we will usually feel a sense of peace and have a "knowing" deep down inside that we are hearing from God. What do I mean by this? Have you ever had a "gut feeling" about something, but your mind and your circumstances in the natural paint a different story? This is usually the Holy Spirit leading you in the direction of going with your "gut feeling."

However, as I have also experienced, sometimes God will require us to get out of the boat and do something totally outside our comfort zone. Therefore, we will not feel peaceful at first. Then after a while, after we have walked out by faith, not by sight or according to our feelings, it will become apparent that we did indeed hear from God.

At first, it is very difficult to know for sure how to discern which spirit is speaking to us, and like anything else in life, hearing the voice of God takes practice. As we learn to trust the Holy Spirit's leading, we are then to cautiously step out in faith once we have received confirmation from God.

This is why we need to get into agreement with God's Word and thank the Holy Spirit for ordering our steps daily.

We do not ask the Lord to order our steps because His Word already tells us that He does. This is based on the following Scriptures:

> *"The STEPS of a GOOD MAN are ORDERED by the LORD, And He DELIGHTS IN HIS WAY. Though he FALL, he shall not be utterly CAST DOWN; For the LORD UPHOLDS HIM with His hand."* (Psalm 37:23–24, NKJV) (emph. added).

"A man's heart PLANS his WAY, But the LORD DIRECTS his STEPS." (Prov. 16:9, NKJV) (emphasis added).

"There are many PLANS in a MAN'S HEART, Nevertheless the LORD's COUNSEL—that will STAND." (Prov. 19:21, NKJV)

"COMMIT your WORKS to the Lord, And your THOUGHTS will be ESTABLISHED." (Prov. 16:3, NKJV) (emphasis added).

Therefore, as you walk by faith rather than by sight if you somehow miss God, then He knows how to bring you back to the proper path *if* you seek Him with all your heart, soul, mind, and strength, and continue to abide in His presence and His Word.

We also need to ask the Lord to show us the doors of opportunity that are not from Him. Oftentimes an opportunity is not from God—it is a counterfeit orchestrated by Satan. As such, we must ask the Holy Spirit to show us the door or doors that He wants us to step through.

Once the Holy Spirit tells us which doors are to be shut and which doors are to be opened our action is required.

Then we are to use our power and authority in Jesus' name and decree and declare what doors are to be shut and what doors are to be opened. This is exercising our authority in Christ based on Isaiah 22:22.

After we thank the Lord for ordering our steps, then we must learn to place more trust in Him doing so in accordance with His "eternal" Word rather than fret about being deceived by the enemy. As we step out in faith, we will become more confident in this area.

Furthermore, it helps to keep a written journal of what you hear from the Lord. Each year, I take the time to go back to these journals that I have kept, and I date those things that the Lord has told me would come to pass, that have been fulfilled. This will help build your faith. Also, it will reassure you that you are not crazy after all—that you really do hear from God.

Every blood-bought believer should hear from God for themselves. Jesus tells us in John 10:27, *"My sheep hear My voice, and I know them, and they follow Me."* (NKJV)

Moreover, when you are going through a season of trials and tribulations, you can look back to those times in the past when God brought you through other difficult scenarios so you can know beyond a shadow of a doubt that He will never leave you or forsake you.

In addition, if you thought you heard from God, but after a while, you realize you made a mistake, do not fret.

Again, God knows how to find you and bring you back into alignment with His will as long as you are seeking His direction by abiding in His presence and His Word.

It is critical for us to fully trust and rely on God to order our steps. This will lead us to fulfill the destiny that He has for each of us, preordained by Him before one of our days on the earth ever came to be.

Stepping out in faith and being obedient to "do" His will begins by our willingness to submit to His Lordship in every area of our lives, not only those areas that we think we can handle on our own.

This is substantiated by Proverbs 3:5–6 which states, *"Trust in the LORD with all your HEART, And LEAN not ON YOUR OWN UNDERSTANDING; In ALL YOUR WAYS ACKNOWLEDGE Him, And He shall DIRECT your PATHS."* (NKJV) (emphasis added).

BE ANXIOUS FOR NOTHING BY PRAYING AND MAKING SUPPLICATIONS TO GOD WHO WILL GUARD YOUR HEART AND MIND WITH HIS PEACE

If you find yourself feeling anxious about your circumstances no matter what they may be, this indicates a lack of trust in God's ability to deliver you, provide for you, and to protect you.

A lot of what we are troubled about is directly related to what we meditate on. Therefore, change what you "choose" to think about.

Moreover, God's Word instructs us on what to do so that we are not anxious concerning anything.

This is based on Philippians 4:6–7 and Philippians 4:8–9, which says the following:

> *"Be ANXIOUS for nothing, but in everything by PRAYER and SUPPLICATION, with THANKSGIVING, let your REQUESTS be made KNOWN to God; and the PEACE of GOD, which SURPASSES all UNDERSTANDING, will guard your HEARTS and MINDS through CHRIST JESUS."* (Phil. 4:6–7, NKJV) (emphasis added).

> *"Finally, brethren, whatever THINGS are TRUE, whatever THINGS are NOBLE, whatever THINGS are JUST, whatever THINGS are PURE, whatever THINGS are LOVELY, whatever THINGS are of GOOD REPORT, if there is any VIRTUE and if there is anything PRAISEWORTHY—MEDITATE ON THESE THINGS. The THINGS which you LEARNED and RECEIVED and HEARD and SAW in me, these DO, and the GOD of PEACE will BE*

WITH YOU. " (Phil. 4:8–9, NKJV) (emphasis added).

I witness many Christians spending more time paying attention to and agreeing with the "bad" reports the news is full of instead of spending more time meditating on God's Word and praiseworthy things.

This is why many believers are feeling anxious and are becoming fearful. When we feel anxious and worry, we are sinning. God's Word commands us to be "anxious" for nothing.

When we are concerned about some things, then God tells us to pray and make supplication to Him with thanksgiving as we allow our requests to be made known to God and share with Him what is on our mind and our heart. This is "how" we are to guard our mind and heart, so we will receive the peace of God which surpasses all understanding through Christ our *Prince of Peace.*

Again, it is only by the blood of Jesus that we are "justified" period! It is not by us keeping the *letter of the law.* If we are trying to keep the *letter of the law,* then we are insulting His *Spirit of Grace.* We are putting our faith in "our" ability rather than in God's ability to "sanctify" us as we submit our will to God's Holy Spirit.

Therefore, we *must* humble ourselves and submit our will to the obedience of Christ based on His eternal Word. We may "become" saved through grace by faith in Jesus Christ. However, we must also *work out* our *own* salvation by submitting to the "sanctification" process of the Holy Spirit and by "believing" the truth of God's Word, which will be evidenced when we "obey" His Word and His Voice.

This truth is substantiated in Second Thessalonians 2:13, where the apostle Paul specifically says we have been "chosen" by God from the beginning for salvation *through* "sanctification" and "belief" in the truth. Both are required. Second Thessalonians 2:13, says the following:

> *"But we are bound to give thanks to God always for you, brethren beloved by the Lord, because God from the beginning CHOSE you for* **SALVATION** [6] [G4991: *sōtēria: rescue* or *safety* (physically or morally); deliver, health, save, saving] *through* **SANCTIFICATION** [7] [G38: *hagiasmos: purification,* that is, (the state) *purity;* concretely (by Hebraism) a *purifier;* holiness] *by the SPIRIT and* **BELIEF** [8] [G4102: *pistis: persuasion,* that is, *credence;* moral *conviction* (of *religious* truth, or the truthfulness of God or a religious teacher), especially *reliance* upon Christ for salvation; having fidelity which is faithfulness to a person, cause, or belief, demonstrated by continuing loyalty and support] *in the* **TRUTH** [9] [G225:

alētheia: truth; truly and verity of a true principle or belief, especially one of fundamental importance]..." (2 Thess. 2:13, NKJV) (emphasis added).

As substantiated in Second Thessalonians 2:13, God "chose" us for salvation. As such, for those who believe in His truth, then we become "sanctified" by the *Spirit of Truth.*

In addition, as clearly substantiated in this Scripture, our salvation is for a lot more than "fire insurance" when we die.

Jesus Christ died to save us, heal us, and deliver us while we are still living on the earth.

We all "become" saved by placing our faith in Jesus Christ. He came to testify to the truth of His heavenly Father's instructions written in the Torah and spoken by the mouths of God's holy prophets.

WE NEED TO DEFINE WHAT "TRUTH" IS ACCORDING TO GOD'S WORD.

Since salvation is for those who "believe" in the truth then perhaps we need to define what truth is, based on "religious" truth, which will result in us having "credence" which means: Belief in or acceptance of something as being true.

Salvation must also result in us having a *moral* "conviction" based on the truthfulness of God and His truth, in which we place our firm reliance upon Christ for our salvation.

447

And, as we place our firm reliance on Christ for our salvation, we will keep our fidelity and be loyally faithful to only our Lord and Savior Jesus Christ.

We will not worship and serve any false gods, based on the "traditions," "customs," and "doctrines" of men.

So let's consult God's Word to define what "religious" truth is.

God's Word is truth based on what Jesus says to us in John 14:6 as He proclaims, *"...I [Jesus] am the WAY, the TRUTH, and the LIFE. No one COMES to the Father EXCEPT through Me."* (NKJV) (emphasis added).

And, we are told in John 1:1, *"In the BEGINNING was the WORD, and the WORD was with GOD, and the WORD was GOD."* (NKJV) (emphasis added).

Therefore, *the Word*, who was with God in the beginning and who is God is the truth.

As such, *the Word* is the One who gave us His *Spirit of Truth,* who will lead us into all truth. He is also the One who gave us His instructions written in the Torah.

Yet many Christians think that the only commandments Jesus gave us are those that are highlighted in red in the New Testament.

However, these believers do not realize Jesus was speaking about the Torah which He came to "bear witness" to because this was the only Scripture which was written at the time of

Jesus' earthly ministry. The New Testament was not written yet.

Again, Jesus was born and came into the world to "bear witness" to His heavenly Father's truth. At least this is what Jesus said to Pontius Pilate when Jesus was questioned by him in John 18:37. Pontius Pilate asked Jesus, "... *'Are You a king then?' Jesus answered, 'You say RIGHTLY that I AM a KING. For this CAUSE I was BORN, and for this CAUSE I have COME into the WORLD, that I should BEAR WITNESS to the TRUTH. Everyone WHO is of the TRUTH hears My VOICE.'"* (NKJV) (emphasis added).

In fact, in John 8:31–32 we are told, *"Then Jesus said to those JEWS who BELIEVED Him, 'If you ABIDE in My WORD, you are My DISCIPLES indeed. And you shall KNOW the TRUTH, and the TRUTH shall make you FREE.'"* (NKJV) (emphasis added).

Unfortunately, there are many believers in the body of Christ who claim to be Jesus' disciples, yet they are not because they do not believe or follow His truth—even though they claim the name of Jesus and call themselves Christians.

To believe in the truth and the one *true* God, then we need to obey God's instructions written to all His people.

They are detailed in the Torah, written by God's servant Moses because Jesus Christ was and is the "living" Torah and He is the WAY, the TRUTH, and the LIFE. Furthermore, based on Psalm 119:142, God's law which came from *the*

449

Word is the truth. Psalm 119:142, says the following:

> *"Your RIGHTEOUSNESS is an everlasting RIGHTEOUSNESS, And Your **LAW**[10] [H8451: tôrâh: a precept or statute, especially the Decalogue or Pentateuch: direction or instruction based on the Mosaic or Deuteronomic Law] is TRUTH."* (Psalm 119:142, NKJV) (emphasis added).

Some believers are of the "opinion" that the law has been abolished and we do not have to obey God's law.

However, under the New Covenant God has now put His laws in our mind and written them on our heart by His *Spirit of Truth,* who is the One that "sanctifies" us for salvation. Thus, those believers who do not obey God's commandments are not His covenant people despite what they profess.

This is based on the fact that Jesus tells us He is the Way, the Truth, and the Life.

He also says, according to His *eternal* Word, that the Torah is truth and the doctrine of Christ is founded on this truth.

Again, the doctrine of Christ is based on our heavenly Father's instructions written in the Torah.

This is substantiated in John 7:16, when Jesus says to us, *"...My DOCTRINE is not MINE, but His* [our heavenly Father] *who SENT Me."* (NKJV) (emphasis added).

Therefore, for those believers in the body of Christ who claim the name of Jesus Christ, yet they do not obey the commandments of God written in the Torah, then they have the *Spirit of Antichrist,* deceiving them, so they do not "receive" the love of His truth.

If we claim to have God's *Spirit of Truth,* but do not obey His commandments, ordinances, statutes, or judgments as written in the Torah, then we are deceived.

The *Spirit of Truth* will *never* lead us to negate our heavenly Father's commandments, statutes, ordinances, and judgments for they are *everlasting* from the beginning of the world for all eternity.

You may be thinking that we are no longer under the law. And, you would be correct because "the" Lawgiver now lives inside of us.

We have His Holy Spirit to empower us and give us God's grace and power to obey God's Word and His Voice.

This includes obeying His law which He has now put in our mind and written on our heart under the New Covenant.

Thus, since Jesus says to us in John 14:15 that *if* we love Him, then we will keep His commandments *if* we truly love God, then we will obey His law—which is His truth that the doctrine of Christ is based on.

In addition, for us to *work out* our *own* salvation with fear and trembling, we must continue to have unwavering loyalty (fidelity) to *only* Jesus by putting our firm reliance for our salvation upon Christ.

Moreover, we must also have a *moral* "conviction" of His truth as we undergo the process of becoming holy by submitting ourselves to the "sanctification" process of the Holy Spirit.

As such, if we do not or will not submit our will and our lives to the Holy Spirit, who will "convict" us when we sin and unveil God's truth to us, then we will not finish the race which is set before us. We will not remain faithful to God until death or Jesus returns, whichever comes first.

The bottom line is this: We will "obey" the *essence of the law* when we love the Lord God with all our heart, mind, soul, and strength.

This is why "love" essentially fulfills the law—because God so loved the world that He sacrificed His only *begotten* Son, Jesus Christ, for the redemption of our sins.

Jesus also came to *seek* and to *save* that *which* was lost because of the transgression of the first Adam based on Luke 19:10.

However, this does not mean that we are to not to keep God's law. Jesus Christ did not do away with the law that God has now put in our minds and written on our hearts under the New Covenant.

Rather, Jesus did away with the "curse" of the law, which is sin and death that we would reap by not keeping the *letter of the law.* Again, when Jesus says to us in John 14:15, *"If you LOVE me, KEEP My COMMANDMENTS..."* (NKJV) (emphasis added), the New Testament had not been written yet.

According to *Strong's Greek Lexicon #G1785*, the word "commandments" as used in John 14:15, is the Greek word "entole" (pronounced "en-to-lā'"), which means: 1) an order, command, charge, precept, injunction; 1a) that which is prescribed to one by reason of his office; 2) a commandment; 2a) a prescribed rule in accordance with which a thing is done; 2a1) a precept relating to lineage, of the Mosaic precept concerning the priesthood; 2a2) ethically used of the commandments in the Mosaic law or Jewish tradition.

All of God's commandments found in the Old Testament came from *the Word* who was sent by our heavenly Father as the Son of Man in the Person of Jesus Christ which is substantiated in John 1:1. All the Ten Commandments are reiterated in the New Testament.

Yet, believe it or not, there are some Christians who say the Ten Commandments and the law are only for the Jews. And, many believers are of the "opinion" that we do not need to follow them because we are to be led by the Spirit under the New Covenant. This is absolute heresy!

Moreover, if we do not keep at least the Ten Commandments *after* we "become" saved—then we are definitely not being led by the Holy Spirit. The Holy Spirit would *never* lead anyone to practice "lawlessness" against God and His Word. This is especially significant because Jesus will say to many believers (the vast majority) on Judgment Day, *"I never knew you."*

This is what Jesus will say to those who practice "lawlessness" when it is too late to repent and make a course correction for all eternity. Now that you know we are Israel, you will realize how ridiculous and fatal this thinking is.

One purpose of receiving the *Spirit of Truth,* based on John 16:13, is that He will guide us into all truth, especially God's truth, based on the *whole* counsel of His *eternal* Word. Again, the Holy Spirit will *never* lead us to do anything contrary to God's Word.

Abraham loved the Lord so much that he was willing to give up his only son to be obedient and "do" the will of his heavenly Father, *Yehôvâh.* This act of *willing* "obedience" foreshadowed what God planned to do for all of us with His only *begotten* Son, Jesus Christ.

Therefore, can we truly say that we would be willing to give up everything as Abraham and Jesus did to "do" the will of our heavenly Father?

Moreover, if we say we are following the doctrine of Christ, yet we forsake our heavenly Father's instructions found in the Torah, then we are deceived.

In fact, we are specifically told in Proverbs 4:2, *"For I GIVE you good DOCTRINE: Do not FORSAKE My **LAW*** (10)

[H8451: *tôrâh*: a *precept* or *statute*, especially the *Decalogue* or *Pentateuch*: direction or instruction based on the *Mosaic* or *Deuteronomic* Law]. " (NKJV) (emphasis added).

The word "doctrine" as used in the Old Testament, according to *Strong's Hebrew Lexicon* #H3948, is the Hebrew word "leqach" (pronounced "leh'-kakh"), which means: Something received, that is, (mentally) instruction (whether on the part of the teacher or hearer); also (in an active and sinister sense) *inveiglement*; doctrine, learning, fair speech.

Whereas, the word "doctrine" as used in the New Testament according to *Strong's Greek Lexicon* #G1322, is the Greek word "didachē" (pronounced "did-akh-ay'"), which means: Instruction (the act or the matter); doctrine, which has been taught.

The doctrine of Christ is based on our heavenly Father's instructions, given to all His people so we may be discipled (taught) "how" or "the way" that we are to "live" and "walk" while we are still living on the earth. We must follow "the way" that is pleasing to God as we show Him that we love Him because He first loved us. Thus, we will love one another as we have been commanded to do.

In fact, many believers in the body of Christ have left their first love, and this is why we see an increase of "lawlessness" in our society!

For Jesus tells us in Matthew 24:12, *"And because LAWLESSNESS* [11] [G458: *anomia*: *illegality*, that is, violation of law or (generally) *wickedness; iniquity; unrighteousness]* *will ABOUND, the LOVE of many will grow COLD."* (NKJV) (emphasis added).

Again, this is the "root" cause of why we are witnessing an increase of "lawlessness" in our society.

It is because many believers in the body of Christ do not love God with all our heart, mind, soul, and strength. Because *if* we loved God with all our heart, mind, soul, and strength, then we would keep His commandments as Jesus tells us to do in John 14:15. And, we would love one another as we are commanded to do.

However, there is no way that we will love each other without first loving God and having a fear of the Lord so that we will obey Him and His Word.

In fact, Jesus tells us in John 13:35, *"By this ALL will KNOW that you are My DISCIPLES, if you have LOVE for ONE ANOTHER."* (NKJV) (emphasis added).

As the tribulation period accelerates, we can expect to see "lawlessness" increase, not decrease, and we will continue to witness the great falling away.

Therefore, in the days ahead, when the *kingdom of darkness* comes in like a flood, our faith will be severely tested by God's refining fire, evidenced by our total reliance, trust, and obedience to Jesus Christ alone.

And, like Abraham and many other saints who have walked in their footsteps, we may have to sacrifice our lives, our fortunes, and our sacred honor for His name's sake as well!

We need to realize that God will not ask us to do anything that Jesus Christ has not done Himself. This is substantiated in John 15:20, when Jesus says to us, His disciples, *"REMEMBER the WORDS that I SAID TO YOU, 'A SERVANT is NOT greater than HIS MASTER.' If they PERSECUTED Me, they will also PERSECUTE you. If they KEPT My WORD, they will KEEP yours also."* (NKJV) (emphasis added).

Jesus warns us ahead of time that we must pledge our total "fidelity" to Him above all else. This is based on the following Scriptures:

> *"He who LOVES father or mother MORE than ME is not WORTHY of Me. And he who LOVES son or daughter MORE than ME is not WORTHY of Me. And he who does not TAKE his CROSS and FOLLOW after Me is not WORTHY of Me."* (Matt. 10:37–38, NKJV) (emphasis added).

> *"Then He said to THEM all, 'If anyone DESIRES to COME after Me, LET HIM DENY HIMSELF, and TAKE UP HIS CROSS DAILY, and FOLLOW Me. For WHOEVER desires to SAVE HIS LIFE will LOSE IT, but WHOEVER*

loses HIS LIFE for MY SAKE will SAVE IT.'"
(Luke 9:23–24, NKJV) (emphasis added).

Notice based on the Scriptures we just read, Jesus is telling us that we must follow after Him, not our pastor, our priest, or our rabbi. And, as such, being a *true* disciple of Jesus Christ may cost us everything, even our life. Therefore, we must be willing to share in His "cup of suffering" as well as in His glory.

Beginning with John the Baptist, all of the early disciples, with the exception of the apostle John, were martyred for their faith. The apostle John survived being thrown into a cauldron of boiling oil before he was exiled to the Isle of Patmos where it is believed that he died of natural causes.

This is the true meaning of Jesus' commandment to His disciples, when Jesus said, *"DO this in Remembrance of Me..."* when we celebrate Passover. We are commanded to commemorate Passover and the Feast of Unleavened Bread as an *everlasting* "memorial" to honor what Jesus did for us all.

THE SIGNIFICANCE OF THE SACRIFICE OF OUR "PASSOVER LAMB" FOR NEW COVENANT BELIEVERS

When God's people commemorate and keep Passover in remembrance of what Jesus our "Passover Lamb" did for us at

Calvary, we are proclaiming to God and to the great cloud of witnesses that we are "redeemed" by our "Passover Lamb" who was willing to shed His blood for the forgiveness of our sins.

In fact, this "act of worship" of honoring our "Passover Lamb" who was slain from the foundation of the world, is recorded in God's Book of Remembrance because Passover is to be an *everlasting* "memorial" for all eternity. I will cover this fact in Book 3.

The apostle Paul elaborates further on *Yehóvah's* second holy convocation of Passover, called the Feast of Unleavened Bread in First Corinthians 11:23–29, which says the following:

> *"For I received from the Lord that which I also delivered to you: that the Lord Jesus on the same night in which He was betrayed TOOK BREAD; and when He* [Jesus] *had GIVEN THANKS, He BROKE IT* [the bread] *and said, 'Take, EAT; this is My BODY which is BROKEN for you; DO this in REMEMBRANCE* (12)(13) [G364: anamnēsis: recollection; G363: anamimnēskō: to remind; reflexively to recollect: call to mind] *of Me.' In the same manner He also took the CUP* (14) [G4221: potērion: a drinking vessel; lot or fate] *after SUPPER* [the Passover Seder where the only elements that Jesus focused on were bread (representing His body) and wine (representing His blood)], *saying, 'This CUP*

459

(14) *is the NEW COVENANT in My BLOOD. This DO, as often as YOU DRINK IT, in* **REMEMBRANCE** (12) (13) *of Me.'"* (1 Cor. 11:23–25, NKJV) (emphasis added).

"For as OFTEN as you EAT this BREAD [symbolic of *the Word* which is the *Bread of Life*] *and DRINK this* **CUP** (14) [G4221: **potērion**: *lot* or *fate* by crucifying our flesh, by dying to ourselves, our wants, our needs, our desires, and the things of this world and by learning obedience by what we suffer], *you PROCLAIM the Lord's DEATH till He COMES."* (1 Cor. 11:26, NKJV) (emphasis added).

"Therefore whoever EATS this BREAD or DRINKS this **CUP** (14) [G4221: **potērion**: *lot* or *fate*] *of the Lord in an UNWORTHY MANNER will be GUILTY of the BODY and BLOOD of the Lord. But let a man EXAMINE himself, and so let him EAT of the BREAD and DRINK of the* **CUP**. (14) *For he who EATS and DRINKS in an UNWORTHY MANNER eats and drinks JUDGMENT TO HIMSELF, not DISCERNING the Lord's BODY."* (1 Cor. 11:27–29, NKJV) (emphasis added).

460

Notice the significance of what God is saying through the apostle Paul in First Corinthians 11:26. This is not talking about only taking communion, a *symbolic* public practice like baptism. When we are baptized, we *symbolically* declare that we have died to our sins, our wants, our needs, our desires, and the things of this world.

As such, when we are baptized with water, we are publically declaring before the whole assembly of believers and God that we promise we will *no* longer live according to the fallen nature of Adam and Satan, as we did *before* we accepted Jesus Christ as our Lord and Savior and we became "born again" *spiritually* speaking.

When we accept Jesus Christ as our Lord and Savior, we enter into the New Covenant that Jesus Christ established with His precious blood. We are no longer our own. We were bought with an extremely high price paid in full by Jesus when He sacrificed His own blood and body for us, setting us free from the wages of sin which are death and the grave.

Jesus has "justified" us by His blood to a new life in Him NOW. Jesus Christ is the *Captain of our Salvation* for the whole man—body, soul, and spirit NOW.

Yet many Christians live defeated lives because we must not truly believe that the POWER of the Holy Spirit living in us is the *same* Spirit who raised Christ from the dead.

Do we believe that the resurrection of Jesus Christ happened or not? Because if we do not believe that the resurrection of

461

Jesus Christ really happened and that God raised Him from the grave—which no other religion in the world offers this "blessed" hope of LIFE eternally—then our faith in Jesus Christ is utterly in vain. This is what the apostle Paul tells us in First Corinthians 15:14–15.

Moreover, by Jesus' blood, we would also be set free from the *wages of sin* which is death. Therefore, when we *symbolically* partake in the practice of communion when we commemorate Passover, then we are "remembering" the great sacrifice Jesus Christ paid for all of us for the forgiveness of our sins and "restoring" and "reconciling" us back into "walking" in a covenant relationship with our heavenly Father *Yehôvah.*

However, commemorating Passover by taking communion is so much more than this.

First, we are to commemorate and keep Passover, and the Feast of Unleavened Bread as Jesus and His disciples did because our heavenly Father, *Yehôvah,* commands us to do so in Leviticus 23:4–8.

This commandment is an *everlasting* ordinance from the beginning of the world and is without end for all eternity. I will cover this fact in detail in Chapter 59 of Book 3.

In addition, the apostle Paul tells us the keep Passover and the Feast of Unleavened Bread in the New Testament in First Corinthians 5:8. In fact, the apostle Paul emphatically states in

Acts 18:21, that he must, but all means, keep this upcoming feast in Jerusalem. In Acts 20:6, we are told that he (they) sailed away from Philippi after the Days of Unleavened Bread and in five days joined others at Troas where they stayed seven days. Thus, Paul kept this feast.

Second, the "bread" that Jesus is telling us to eat is not His *literal* body or the symbolic wafer, cracker, or piece of bread representing His body that we use when we take communion. Rather, the bread that we are to eat as often as we can is God's Word, including the Torah.

The Torah details the terms and conditions of us "walking" in a covenant relationship with our heavenly Father and our Lord and Savior Jesus Christ. This "Covenant of Marriage" between God and all His people was fulfilled (consummated, executed, and ratified [confirmed]) by Jesus with His own blood when He became the "mediator" of the New Covenant.

This is the *same* covenant we made a vow before God, witnessed by the Holy Spirit, to obey as we follow only Jesus in a "worthy" manner.

Again, the apostle Paul talks about those who eat *this* "bread" or drinks *this* "cup" (*lot* or *fate*) of the Lord in an "unworthy" manner.

Doing so brings judgment upon ourselves because we have not discerned the Lord's body. As a result, we will be "guilty" of "the body" and "the blood" of our Lord because we are crucifying Jesus all over again.

Therefore, *if* we are like the five *wise* virgins Jesus talks about in *The Parable of the Wise and Foolish Virgins*, then we would want to know "why" the apostle Paul is saying this.

The apostle Paul tells us the answer in Hebrews 10:26–31, which says the following:

> *"For if we SIN willfully AFTER we have received the KNOWLEDGE of the TRUTH, there no LONGER REMAINS A SACRIFICE FOR SINS, but a CERTAIN FEARFUL EXPECTATION of JUDGMENT, and FIERY INDIGNATION which will DEVOUR the ADVERSARIES. Anyone who has REJECTED MOSES' LAW DIES WITHOUT MERCY on the TESTIMONY of two or three WITNESSES. Of how much WORSE PUNISHMENT, do you suppose, will HE BE THOUGHT WORTHY WHO HAS TRAMPLED the SON of GOD underfoot, COUNTED the BLOOD of the COVENANT by which he was SANCTIFIED a COMMON THING, and INSULTED the SPIRIT of GRACE? For we KNOW Him who said, 'VENGEANCE IS MINE, I WILL REPAY,' says the Lord. And again, 'The LORD will JUDGE His PEOPLE.' It is a fearful THING to FALL into the HANDS of the LIVING GOD."* (Heb. 10:26–31, NKJV) (emphasis added).

464

THE HIGH COST OF BEING A DISCIPLE OF JESUS CHRIST

Jesus warns us ahead of time in Matthew 10:37–38 and Luke 9:23–24 concerning the high cost we would have to be *willing* to pay to be His disciples. We *must* be willing to drink from the *same* "cup of suffering" that He was willing to drink from in "remembrance" of what He did for us at Calvary. Every time we drink from *this* "cup" (*lot* or *fate*) of the New Covenant, we are not only proclaiming the Lord's death until He comes again, but we are also proclaiming our death in Christ as well. We are proclaiming we have been "crucified" in Christ.

Jesus says to us in Matthew 10:37–38 and Luke 9:23–24 that anyone who desires to come after Him *must* deny ourselves by picking up our own cross daily to "walk" in our Master's footsteps as we follow *only* Him.

This is why Jesus also told us that anyone who loves their father, their mother, their son, or their daughter more than Him is not "worthy" of Him. Jesus also said that whoever desires to follow in His footsteps must be *willing* to drink from the *same* "cup of suffering" that He did, even to the point of whoever loses his life for His name's sake will save it and whoever desires to save his life will lose it.

In other words, we are "dead" in Christ because we have been "crucified" with Him and for Him.

Again, the "bread" that Jesus is telling us to eat that was

465

broken for us is referring to our daily bread, the Word of God. For Jesus is *the Word,* who became the Son of Man in the flesh in the Person of Jesus Christ whose body was broken for us.

Whereas, the "cup" that Jesus is talking about us drinking from is not His *literal* blood or the symbolic wine or grape juice that we use when we practice communion or commemorate Passover and the Feast of Unleavened Bread.

Rather, Jesus is telling His disciples that we *must* be willing to drink from the same "cup of suffering" as Jesus did before He went to the cross and also when He was crucified on the cross.

This truth is substantiated in the gospel of Matthew beginning in Chapter 20 when the mother of Zebedee's sons asks Jesus that He grant that her two sons may sit, one on His right hand and the other on the left, in His kingdom.

Jesus tells us specifically in Matthew 20:22 that those who want to follow Him must be willing to drink from His "cup" and "experience" the same *lot* or *fate* that He did when He said to her and to us, *"...You do not KNOW what you ASK. Are you ABLE to DRINK the **CUP** (14) [G4221: poterion: lot or fate] that I am ABOUT TO DRINK, and BE BAPTIZED with the BAPTISM that I am BAPTIZED WITH...?"* (NKJV) (emphasis added).

What "cup" is Jesus saying He is about to drink from? Read Matthew 26:36–46 and you will see that Jesus was sorrowful and deeply distressed as He prayed, wept, pleaded, and begged His heavenly Father to remove the "cup of suffering" He was about to experience as He headed to the cross at Calvary for you and me.

Yet Jesus would "do" what His heavenly Father required of Him *despite* His feelings.

This is substantiated in Matthew 26:42, which proclaims, *"Again, a second time, He went AWAY and PRAYED, saying, 'O My Father, if this CUP* [(14)] *[G4221: potērion: lot or fate] cannot PASS AWAY from Me unless I DRINK IT, Your WILL be DONE.'"* (NKJV) (emphasis added).

Moreover, Jesus learned "obedience" from "what" He suffered.

This is substantiated in Hebrews 5:7–9, which says the following:

> *"During the days of Jesus' LIFE on EARTH, he offered up PRAYERS and PETITIONS with fervent CRIES and TEARS to the ONE who could SAVE him from DEATH, and he was HEARD because of his reverent SUBMISSION. Son though he was, HE LEARNED OBEDIENCE FROM WHAT HE SUFFERED and, ONCE made PERFECT, he became the SOURCE of eternal SALVATION for all who OBEY Him..."* (Heb. 5:7–9, NIV) (emph. add.)

467

Therefore, we were bought with a high price, and we are not our own. And, as His "bondservants," we too must often eat from the Word of God and drink from His "cup of suffering" as Jesus did *until* He appears the second time.

The only way we will be able to "endure" and "overcome" our trials and tribulations, that we must "walk" through in order for us to "Pass over" into the Promised Land, is to offer up prayers and petitions with fervent cries and tears to the only One who can help us and save our soul from death— *Yehovah,* our heavenly Father.

In Hebrews 5:7–9, it is critically important to pay special attention to the part of the verse which says, *"Son though he was, he learned OBEDIENCE from what he SUFFERED and, ONCE made PERFECT, he became the SOURCE of eternal SALVATION..."* (NIV) (emphasis added).

In other words, even though Jesus was God's only *begotten* Son, Jesus had to learn to be "obedient" from what He suffered to be made (remain) perfect *before* He could become the source of eternal salvation.

This drives home the point that Jesus had to learn to crucify His flesh as the Son of Man *before* His flesh was crucified on the cross.

It was only then that Jesus could become the source of eternal salvation for all who would "obey" Him. After all, Jesus had to "choose" to willingly submit Himself to die on the cross at

Calvary to "do" the will of His heavenly Father. Therefore, does Hebrews 5:7–9 say that Jesus would become the source of eternal salvation to those who *only* "believe" in Him? No, it does not. Rather, it specifically says that Jesus would become the source of eternal salvation to all who "obey" Him.

LIKE JESUS, DISCIPLES OF JESUS CHRIST MUST LEARN OBEDIENCE BY WHAT WE SUFFER

As disciples of Jesus Christ, we are not greater than our Master that we profess to follow. Therefore, all *true* disciples of Jesus Christ *must* be willing to crucify our flesh, by dying to ourselves, our wants, our needs, our desires, and the things of this world by learning "obedience" by what we suffer just as Jesus did.

Just like our *Kinsman Redeemer*, we must learn "obedience" from what we suffer *before* we can become the source of sharing the true *gospel of the kingdom* with the lost by the words of our testimony.

As such, when we finally reach the point in our life that we are finally willing to "do" whatever it takes, "give up" whatever He asks us to give up, or "go" wherever He sends us, then we have reached the point where God can use us, so His kingdom purposes and glory will prevail.

This means that each day, we must be willing to crucify our flesh and pick up our cross to follow *only* Him. Again, this is

469

based on what Jesus said to us in Matthew 10:37–38 and Luke 9:23–24.

However, in exchange for the high cost involved in being a "bondservant" to Jesus Christ, we will inherit the promises of God which are based on all His *everlasting* covenants (plural) that He has established throughout the *synergy of the ages*, including having eternal life.

This includes us inheriting some of the promises God gave to Abraham while we are still living on the earth because we are sons and daughters of God Almighty because we are "walking" in a *covenant* relationship with Him.

As such, we will "obey" His Voice and His Word because we are willing to be crucified in Christ and drink from His *same* "cup of suffering" for a "cause greater than ourselves."

Why do you think God's Word repeatedly says that we *must* "overcome" until the end? For the vast majority of Christians in America, what exactly have we had to "overcome" yet?

For this reason, I will cover in detail in Chapter 43 of Book 3 exactly what "overcoming" to the end really means for us all.

Because if we think things are really horrible now, we haven't seen anything yet.

This is based on what the prophet Daniel tells us in the Book of Daniel when he says to us there shall be a time of trouble, such as there *never* was since there was a nation, that shall come upon the whole world, including America, to test those who dwell on the earth.

The truth is that many Christians do not even take the risk of being ridiculed by speaking out and standing up for what God says according to His uncompromised, unadulterated *whole* counsel of His Word. We are fearful because we would rather please people and seek their approval rather than seek God's approval. We want to "receive" and "inherit" our "birthright" as His sons and daughters, but we don't want to please God?

God *always* keeps His promises based on all His *everlasting* covenants (plural) that He has established with us throughout the *synergy of the ages*. The question which we must answer is this: *"Will we do what God requires according to the whole counsel of His Word to "receive" our inheritance as His sons and daughters?"*

Therefore, based on the many examples of God's favor and blessings in the life of Abraham, the same holds true for us— his descendants as well.

We need to take a stand on Romans 8:31 which states, *"What then shall we say to these THINGS? If GOD is for US, who can be AGAINST US?"* (NKJV) (emphasis added).

Furthermore, we need to get the mindset of God plus "me" equals the majority. If we are doing what God has told us to "do" and we will put our faith and trust in Him to accomplish it, then nothing will keep us from receiving all that God has promised us. We will fulfill the destiny He created us for before one of our days on this earth ever came to be. Also, worth pointing out is the truth that God will use great adversity to transfer the wealth of the wicked to His righteous, faithful remnant.

Many believers blame the enemy when things such as drought, famine, and cataclysmic events come to pass. However, God is sovereign, and often it is God Almighty orchestrating these adverse conditions so that His Word will be fulfilled for His glory and purposes. In other words, it is not about us.

Yet God will bless us despite these unfortunate situations *if* we stand on His Word and "do" what He tells us to do.

Another example of what I am referring to is substantiated in Psalm 105 where God is releasing His judgment against Egypt (which represents the "unsaved" world). In the beginning, God is purposely allowing the destruction of the world's food supply, resulting in famine, so that His will shall prevail and the promises that He gave to Abraham and his descendants will come to pass because *"it is written..."*

In addition, if you want God to move mightily on your behalf despite the trials and tribulations of what lies ahead as we progress through the tribulation period, then we must praise and worship Him and seek His face *despite* our circumstances, just as Abraham and King David did. Equally important, we must "keep" His *everlasting* statutes and "obey"

His laws that He has now put in our minds and written on the tablets of our hearts under the New Covenant.

As His people, we should give Him our thanks simply because of who He is. We should praise Him because He alone is worthy of our praise. His people should declare what He has done for us in our lives.

The truth of the matter is we do not even begin to realize what God has not allowed to come on us that could have occurred *if* His hand was not upon us because of His mercy and love for us.

Last, but certainly not least, this praise-worthy fact which cannot be overlooked—we have eternal life in Him NOW by "knowing" our heavenly Father and our Lord and Savior Jesus Christ on a personal, intimate basis so that we will not perish in the *lake of fire* when we die a *physical* death.

This truth in itself is worthy of all our thanks and praise to Jesus Christ who is our *King of kings and Lord of lords* who was willing to become our "Passover Lamb" because of His *everlasting* love for His beloved bride.

In fact, shortly He will return for His glorious, beautiful bride, who has made herself ready because she has arrayed herself in fine white linen without spot or blemish. She is fully mature in Him, and lacking nothing.

Jesus is coming back soon for His triumphant, glorious bride to "consummate" our wedding vows at the "marriage supper of the Lamb" which shall be held in the *kingdom of heaven* at our heavenly Father's house located in Mount Zion—the city of the living God in the *heavenly* Jerusalem. This is based on Hebrews 12:22–24.

Are you arrayed in fine white linen without spot or blemish and ready for your bridegroom's return?

Will you be "counted worthy" to escape all these things that shall come to pass to stand before the Son of Man? See Luke 21:26.

Will you be "counted worthy" to attain that age (the Messianic age—the seventh millennium) and the (first) resurrection of the dead if you pass away before Jesus returns? See Luke 20:35 and Revelation 20:6.

Always remember Jesus' words in Matthew 22:14 when He says to us, *"For many are called, but few are chosen."* (NKJV)

If you "choose" to be driven by eternity rather than the temporal things of this world which shall shortly pass away and you "obey" God's Voice and His Word, then you shall be "counted worthy" at your bridegroom's return.

Jesus, the author and finisher of your faith will be faithful to finish the great work He has started in you *if* you continue to abide in Him and He abides in you.

EPILOGUE

I n conclusion, based on what I have conveyed in Book 1 and Book 2 of this series, there should be no doubt in your mind, based on the whole counsel of God's Word, "who" Israel is.

I clearly conveyed in this book, and in Book 1, the following indisputable truth: Not all the children of Israel, who are of Israel, are God's sons and daughters because they are from the *physical* "seed" of Abraham.

Rather, the *children of the promise* are "counted" as Abraham's *spiritual* "seed" and are "heirs" according to the covenants (plural) of promise. This is made possible by grace through faith in God's only *begotten* Son, Jesus Christ.

As such, Israel, *spiritually* speaking, is comprised of both the Jews from the House of Judah and those of us who were formerly Gentiles from the House of Israel. We are the One New Man in Christ. And, if we are in Christ, then we are Abraham's "seed" and "heirs" according to the promises God gave to Abraham and his descendants.

Therefore, since we are "heirs" according to the "covenant" promises God gave to Abraham and his descendants, we are also God's "covenant" people. This is based on all of His *everlasting* covenants (plural) that our heavenly Father *Yehôvah* has established with mankind and creation throughout the *synergy of the ages.* All these *everlasting* covenants (plural) were fulfilled (consummated, executed,

475

and ratified [confirmed]) by the precious blood of Jesus Christ, our heavenly Father's only *begotten,* Son. God, our Creator, so loved the world, including its inhabitants that He gave His only *begotten* Son—Jesus Christ so that whoever believes in Him shall not perish but have everlasting life.

However, this series of books will not have served its intended purpose unless I convey in detail "why" this truth matters to New Covenant believers who were born for a time such as this.

Hence, in Book 3, I will convey many reasons "why" discovering our true identity in Jesus Christ as descendants of Abraham matters now that we know that we are Israel.

Many (the vast majority) of believers in the body of Christ have been led astray and are deceived due to the prevalent false teachings coming out of pulpits all over the world, particularly in America.

In addition, due to this great apostasy, many of us are *unknowingly* breaking the *everlasting* covenants (plural) that God has established throughout the *synergy of the ages* with mankind based on what we have been taught in the body of Christ. These false teachings are not the *gospel of the kingdom* as it was once delivered to the saints.

Therefore, never before throughout the *synergy of the ages,* has the need been greater for God's people to worship *Yehôvǎh,* our heavenly Father, and His Son, Jesus Christ, in both Spirit and according to His truth. However, before we can do this, we must know God's truth based solely on what His Word says, rather than based on the "doctrines," "customs," and "traditions" of men.

You will be shocked to learn that the body of Christ has been deceived and led astray concerning the "basic" tenets of our faith.

Furthermore, contrary to what most teach and believe, the *bride of Christ* will be only the *faithful* remnant—those who "obey" God's commandments, both the volume of Moses and the gospel and have the testimony of Jesus Christ.

In addition, we must finish the race which is set before us and "overcome" until the end of our lives or Jesus returns—whichever comes first.

In Book 3, I will substantiate this indisputable truth based on the *whole* counsel of God's unadulterated, uncompromised Word.

Let me close out this book based on the fact that we must "know" God on a personal, intimate basis, which will be evidenced by us "walking" according to the *whole* counsel of His Word.

We must be "obedient" to His Voice and His Word and produce the proper "fruit" which is worthy of repentance.

In fact, the clean, bright—fine linen His bride is arrayed in is based on the "righteous" acts of the saints. This is based on

Revelation 19:8 which says, *"And to her it was granted to be arrayed in fine linen, clean and bright, for the FINE LINEN is the RIGHTEOUS ACTS of the SAINTS."* (NKJV) (emphasis added).

This will "set apart" those who will be "counted worthy" to escape all these things which shall shortly come to pass and to stand before the Son of Man. When Christ appears a second time, apart from sin, it will be for the "consummation" of salvation for His bride who has made herself ready and is eagerly waiting for her bridegroom's return.

All others will be "consumed" or "destroyed" at the brightness of Jesus' second appearing because they rejected God's only *begotten* Son, Jesus Christ. This will also include those who do not obey the gospel of God.

This is based on First Peter 4:17 which says, *"For the TIME HAS COME FOR JUDGMENT to BEGIN at the HOUSE of GOD; and if it BEGINS WITH US FIRST, WHAT will be the END of THOSE who DO not OBEY the GOSPEL of GOD?"* (NKJV) (emphasis added).

Unfortunately, those who will be "consumed" or "destroyed" at Jesus Christ's second appearing will also include those who were "deceived" and did not know His truth, either because of their "ignorance" concerning His laws or because of their "contempt" of God's laws.

This truth is substantiated by the apostle Paul in Second

478

Thessalonians 1:3–10, which says the following:

> *"We are bound to thank God always for you, brethren, as it is fitting, because your faith grows exceedingly, and the love of every one of you all abounds toward each other, so that we ourselves boast of you among the churches of God for your PATIENCE and FAITH in all your PERSECUTIONS and TRIBULATIONS that YOU ENDURE, which is MANIFEST EVIDENCE of the RIGHTEOUS JUDGMENT of GOD, that you may be COUNTED WORTHY of the KINGDOM of GOD, for WHICH YOU ALSO SUFFER; since it is a RIGHTEOUS THING WITH GOD TO REPAY WITH TRIBULATION THOSE WHO TROUBLE YOU, and to give you who are troubled REST with us WHEN the LORD JESUS is REVEALED from HEAVEN with His MIGHTY ANGELS, in FLAMING FIRE taking VENGEANCE on THOSE who DO not KNOW GOD, and on THOSE who DO not OBEY the GOSPEL of OUR LORD JESUS CHRIST. These shall be PUNISHED with EVERLASTING DESTRUCTION from the PRESENCE of the LORD and from the GLORY of His POWER, WHEN He COMES, in that DAY [the "Day of the Lord"], to be GLORIFIED in His SAINTS and to be ADMIRED among all those who*

479

BELIEVE, because our TESTIMONY among
you was BELIEVED." (2 Thess. 1:3–10, NKJV)
(emphasis added).

Do not dismiss the significance of what the apostle Paul says to us concerning God's final judgment and glory.

He specifically says to us in Second Thessalonians 1:7–9, *"...and to give YOU who are troubled REST with us WHEN the Lord Jesus is REVEALED from HEAVEN with His mighty angels, in flaming fire taking VENGEANCE on THOSE who DO not KNOW GOD, and on THOSE who DO not OBEY the GOSPEL of our LORD JESUS CHRIST. These shall be punished with EVERLASTING DESTRUCTION from the PRESENCE of the LORD and from the GLORY of His POWER..."* (NKJV) (emphasis added).

When Jesus Christ is revealed the second time from heaven, it will be at this time that God's final judgment will be poured out, and He will take "vengeance" on those who:

1.   Do not know God.
2.   Do not "obey" the gospel of our Lord Jesus Christ.

From God's perspective, we may "claim" to know the Lord and say that we have placed our faith in Jesus Christ, but the truth of this "claim" will be evidenced by us "obeying" the gospel of our Lord Jesus Christ. This will include our heavenly Father's instructions written in the Torah for all His people—

for this is the doctrine of Christ.

Therefore, will we be "counted worthy" to stand before the Son of Man because of our patience and our unwavering faith during all the persecutions and tribulations that we must endure until the end, which is the manifest evidence of the *righteous* judgment of God?

Will we be "counted worthy" because we "know" God on a personal, intimate basis because we love Him? If so, then we will "obey" His Voice and the *whole* counsel of His unadulterated, uncompromised Word.

All these things are required *after* we "become" saved, for Jesus says to us in John 14:15, *"If you LOVE Me, KEEP my COMMANDMENTS."* (NKJV) (emphasis added). And, Hebrews 5:9 says that Jesus having been perfected *became* the author of eternal salvation to all who "obey" Him.

So will you prayerfully consider continuing on this journey with me by being willing to purchase and read Book 3 so you can understand "how" and in "what" ways we have been led "astray" and "deceived" by all the false teachings currently so prevalent in the body of Christ?

I hope and pray that you will. We *must* make a course correction now to be "counted worthy" to escape all these things that will come to pass and to stand before the Son of Man. Jesus is coming back for His bride who is without spot or blemish, who is fully mature in Him and lacking nothing.

The "meat" of this entire series of books will be conveyed in Book 3 (Volume I and Volume 2) and is not for the faint-hearted Christian or those who only want to hear what their itching ears "want" to hear, rather than what they "need" to hear. Because once you know God's truth, then He will hold you accountable.

At the same time, He will also hold us accountable for our ignorance of His truth based on the *whole* counsel of His unadulterated, uncompromised Word.

We are supposed to *work out* our *own* salvation with fear and trembling as we meditate on His Word day and night so that we can "do" the will of our heavenly Father.

I am quite certain you do not want to wait until Judgment Day, when it is too late to repent and to make a course correction for all *eternity*, to hear Jesus say to you, as He will say to many believers in the body of Christ who were deceived, led astray, and have used His name in vain the following:

> *"Not everyone who says to Me, 'Lord, Lord,' shall ENTER THE KINGDOM OF HEAVEN, BUT HE WHO DOES THE WILL OF MY FATHER in heaven. Many will say to Me in THAT DAY* [Judgment Day], *'Lord, Lord, have we not PROPHESIED IN YOUR NAME, CAST OUT DEMONS IN YOUR NAME, and DONE MANY WONDERS IN YOUR NAME?' And then*

I will declare to them, 'I NEVER KNEW YOU; DEPART FROM ME, you who PRACTICE LAWLESSNESS!'" (Matt. 7:21–23, NKJV) (emphasis added).

Jesus will say to many believers in the body of Christ on Judgment Day when it is too late to repent for all eternity that He never knew them because He will "blot out" their name from the Lamb's Book of Life because of the following two reasons:

1.   They practiced lawlessness.
2.   They did not do the will of their heavenly Father.

Notice based on Matthew 7:21–23, the very ones that Jesus will say this to are those who have been using the gifts of the Spirit to do the work of the ministry. Those who have done the following in His name in vain: Prophesied in His name, cast out demons in His name, and done many wonders in His name all in vain because they practiced lawlessness.

Therefore, if we do not repent and make an immediate course correction then Jesus will "blot out" our names from His Book of Life, and it will be as if we were never born, or in this case "born" again.

This is why Jesus will say to many believers on Judgment Day that He NEVER knew us.

If this truth does not cause us to have the reverential fear of the Lord, then I do not know what will!

Until we continue our journey together in Book 3, receive this blessing in the mighty "matchless" name of our Lord and Savior Jesus Christ who is the Holy One of Israel and the "tree of life."

> *May the Lord bless you and protect you and yours.*
>
> *May the Lord smile on you and be gracious to you.*
>
> *May the Lord show you His favor and give you His peace.*
>
> *May you walk in the fullness of your divine calling as you love the Lord your God with all your mind, heart, soul, and strength.*
>
> *May the God of peace Himself sanctify you completely; and may your whole spirit, soul, and body be preserved blameless at the coming of our Lord Jesus Christ.*

I pray this blessing for you in the name of the Father, the Son, and the Holy Spirit. Amen.

References

Chapter 19

No references

Chapter 20

[1]According to *Strong's Hebrew Lexicon* #**H567**, the word *Amorites* is the Hebrew word *'ĕmôrîy* (pronounced **"em-o-ree'"**), which is probably a patronymic from an unused name derived from H559 in the sense of *publicity*, that is, prominence; thus a *mountaineer*, an *Emorite*, one of the Canaanitish tribes: - Amorite. The Amorites were one of the Canaanitish tribes who practiced following and *worshiping* false idols or gods based on 1 Kings 21:26 which says, *"And he behaved very abominably in following idols, according to all that the Amorites had done, whom the Lord had cast out before the children of Israel."*

[2]According to *Strong's Hebrew Lexicon* #**H1285**, the word *covenant* is the Hebrew word *b'rîyth* (pronounced **"ber-eeth'"**), which is from H1262 (in the sense of *cutting* (like H1254)); a compact (because made by passing between *pieces* of flesh): - confederacy, [con-]feder[-ate], covenant, league.

Chapter 21

[1]According to *Strong's Hebrew Lexicon* #**H1285**, the word *covenant* is the Hebrew word *b'rîyth* (pronounced **"ber-**

eeth'"), which is from H1262 (in the sense of *cutting* (like h1254)); a *compact* (because made by passing between *pieces* of flesh): - confederacy, [con-]feder[-ate], covenant, league.

(2)According to *Strong's Hebrew Lexicon* #H1471, the usage of the word **nations** is translated from the Hebrew word *gôy* (pronounced **"go'ee"**), which is apparently from the same root as H1465 (in the sense of *massing*); a foreign *nation*; hence a *Gentile*; also (figuratively) a *troop* of animals, or a *flight* of locusts. As used in KJV: Gentile, heathen, nation, or people. Therefore, the word **Gentile** is referring to heathen people or nations that practice or follow pagan rituals or false gods. In other words, they are not in covenant with *Yehôvâh*.

(3)According to *Strong's Hebrew Lexicon* #H85, the name **Abraham** is the Hebrew name *'Abrâhâm* (pronounced **"ab-raw-hawm'"**), contracted from H1 and an unused root (probably meaning to *be populous*); *father of a multitude*; *Abraham*, the later name of Abram: - Abraham.

(4)According to *Strong's Hebrew Lexicon* #H6509, the word **fruitful** is the Hebrew word *pârâh* (pronounced **"paw-raw'"**), a primitive root; to *bear fruit* (literally or figuratively): - bear, bring forth (fruit), (be, cause to be, make) fruitful, grow, increase.

(5)According to *Strong's Hebrew Lexicon* #H4428 the word **Kings** is the Hebrew word **melek** (pronounced **"meh'-lek"**), which is from H4427; a *king:* - king, royal.

[6]According to *Strong's Hebrew Lexicon* #**H4427**, the word *kings* is taken from the root Hebrew word *mâlak* (pronounced "**maw-lak'**"), a primitive root; to *reign*; inceptively to *ascend the throne*; causatively to *induct* into royalty; hence (by implication) to *take counsel:* - consult, X indeed, be (make, set a, set up) king, be (make) queen, (begin to, make to) reign (-ing), rule, X surely.

[7]According to *Strong's Hebrew Lexicon* #**H6965**, the word *establish* is the Hebrew word *qûm* (pronounced "**koom**"), a primitive root; to *rise* (in various applications, literally, figuratively, intensively and causatively): - abide, accomplish, X be clearer, confirm, continue, decree, X be dim, endure, X enemy, enjoin, get up, make good, help, hold, (help to) lift up (again), make, X but newly, ordain, perform, pitch, raise (up), rear (up), remain, (a-) rise (up) (again, against), rouse up, set (up), (e-) stablish, (make to) stand (up), stir up, strengthen, succeed, (as-, make) sure (-ly), (be) up (-hold, -rising).

[8]According to *Strong's Hebrew Lexicon* #**H2233**, the word *descendants* or the word *seed* as used in the KJV is the Hebrew word *Zera'* (pronounced "**Zeh'-rah**"), which is from H2232; *seed*; figuratively *fruit, plant, sowing time, posterity:* - X carnally, child, fruitful, seed (-time), sowing-time.

[9]According to *Strong's Hebrew Lexicon* #**H2232**, the word *descendants* or the word *seed* as used in the KJV is from the root Hebrew word *zâra'* (pronounced "**zaw-rah'**"), which is a primitive root; to *sow*; figuratively to disseminate, plant,

fructify: - bear, conceive seed, set with, sow (-er), yield.

(10)According to *Strong's Hebrew Lexicon* #H5769, the word *everlasting* is the Hebrew word *'ôlâm* (pronounced "o-lawm'"), from   H5956; properly *concealed*, that is, the *vanishing* point; generally time *out of mind* (past or future), that is, (practically) eternity; frequentative adverbially (especially with prepositional prefix) *always*: - always (-s), ancient (time), any more, continuance, eternal, (for, [n-]) ever (-lasting, -more, of old), lasting, long (time), (of) old (time), perpetual, at any time, (beginning of the) world (+ without end). Compare H5331, H5703.

(11)According to *Strong's Hebrew Lexicon* #H272, the word *possession* is the Hebrew word *'ǎchuzzâh* (pronounced "akh-ooz-zaw'"), and is the feminine passive participle of H270; something seized, that is a possession (especially of land).

(12)According to *Strong's Hebrew Lexicon* #H4135, the word *circumcised* or *circumcision* is the Hebrew word *mûl* (pronounced "mool"), and is a primitive root; to *cut* short, that is, *curtail* (specifically the prepuce, that is, to *circumcise*); by implication to *blunt*, figuratively to *destroy*: - circumcise (-ing, selves), cut down (in pieces), destroy, X must needs.

(13)According to *Strong's Hebrew Lexicon* #H226, the word *sign* or *token* as used in the KJV is the Hebrew word *'ôth* (pronounced "oth"), which is probably from H225 (in the sense of *appearing*); a *signal* (literally or figuratively), as a flag, beacon, monument, omen, prodigy, evidence, etc.: - mark, miracle, (en-) sign, token.

(14) According to *Strong's Hebrew Lexicon* #H3772, the word *cut off* as used in these passages of Scripture is the Hebrew word *kârath* (pronounced "kaw-rath'"), and is a primitive root; to *cut* (off, down or asunder); by implication to *destroy* or *consume*; specifically to covenant (that is, make an alliance or bargain, originally by cutting flesh and passing between the pieces): - be chewed, be con- [feder-] ate, covenant, cut (down, off), destroy, fail, feller, be freed, hew (down), make a league ([covenant]), X lose, perish, X utterly, X want.

(15) According to *Strong's Hebrew Lexicon* #H6565, the word *broken* is the Hebrew word *pârar* (pronounced "paw-rar'"), which is a root; to *break* up (usually figuratively, that is, to *violate, frustrate*): - X any ways, break (asunder), cast off, cause to cease, x clean, defeat, disannul, disappoint, dissolve, divide, make of none effect, fail, frustrate, bring (come) to naught, x utterly, make void.

(16) According to *Strong's Greek Lexicon* #G1242, the word *covenant* is the Greek word *diathēkē* (pronounced "dee-ath-ay'-kay"), which is from G1303; properly a *disposition*, that is, (specifically) a *contract* (especially a devisory *will*): - covenant, testament.

(17) According to *Strong's Greek Lexicon* #G4061, the word *circumcision* is the Greek word *peritomē* (pronounced "per-it-om-ay'"), which is from G4059; *circumcision* (the rite, the

condition or the people, literally or figuratively): - X circumcised, circumcision.

(18) According to *Strong's Greek Lexicon* #**G4059**, the word *circumcision* is the Greek word *peritemnō* (pronounced **"per-ee-tem'-no"**), and is from G4012 and the base of G5114; to *cut around*, that is, (specifically) to *circumcise:* - circumcise.

(19) According to *Strong's Greek Lexicon* #**G2424**, the name *Jesus* in the Greek is the name *Iēsous* (pronounced **"ee-ay-sooce'"**), which is of Hebrew origin [H3091]; *Jesus* (that is, *Jehoshua*), the name of our Lord and two (three) other Israelites: - Jesus.

(20) According to *Strong's Hebrew Lexicon* #**H3091**, the name *Jesus* is the Hebrew name *Yĕhôshûaʻ* (pronounced **"yeh-ho-shoo'-ah"**), which is from H3068 and H3467; *Jehovah-saved;* *Jehoshua* (that is, Joshua), the Jewish leader: - Jehoshua, Jehoshuah, Joshua. Compare H1954, H3442. This name *Yĕhôshûaʻ* means "Jehovah is salvation." And, indeed He is! This is Jesus' name given to Him by the angel before He was conceived in Mary's womb when the Holy Spirit overshadowed her.

(21) According to *Strong's Hebrew Lexicon* #**H8451**, the word *law* is the Hebrew word *tôrâh* (pronounced **"to-raw'"**), which is from H3384; a *precept* or *statute*, especially the Decalogue or Pentateuch: - law.

(22)According to *Strong's Hebrew Lexicon* #H8549, the word *perfect* is the Hebrew word *tâmîym* (pronounced "taw-meem'"), which is from H8552; *entire* (literally, figuratively or morally); also (as noun) *integrity, truth:* - without blemish, complete, full, perfect, sincerely (-ity), sound, without spot, undefiled, upright (-ly), whole.

(23)According to *Strong's Hebrew Lexicon* #H7725, the word *converting* is the Hebrew word *shûb* (pronounced "shoob"), which is a primitive root; *to turn* back (hence, away) transitively or intransitively, literally or figuratively (not necessarily with the idea of *return* to the starting point); generally to *retreat*; often adverbially *again:* - ([break, build, circumcise, dig, do anything, do evil, feed, lay down, lie down, lodge, make, rejoice, send, take, weep]) X again, (cause to) answer (+ again), X in any case (wise), X at all, averse, bring (again, back, home again), call [to mind], carry again (back), cease, X certainly, come again (back) X consider, + continually, convert, deliver (again), + deny, draw back, fetch home again, X fro, get [oneself] (back) again, X give (again), go again (back, home), [go] out, hinder, let, [see] more, X needs, be past, X pay, pervert, pull in again, put (again, up again), recall, recompense, recover, refresh, relieve, render (again), X repent, requite, rescue, restore, retrieve, (cause to, make to) return, reverse, reward, + say nay, send back, set again, slide back, still, X surely, take back (off), (cause to, make to) turn (again, self again, away, back, back again, backward, from, off), withdraw.

[24] According to *Strong's Hebrew Lexicon* #H5715, the word **testimony** is the Hebrew word *'êdúth* (pronounced "**ay-dooth'**"), which is feminine of H5707; *testimony:* - testimony, witness.

[25] According to *Strong's Hebrew Lexicon* #H5707, the word **testimony** is from the root Hebrew word *'êd* (pronounced "**ayd**"), which is from H5749 contracted; concretely *a witness;* abstractly *testimony;* specifically a *recorder,* that is, *prince:* - witness.

[26] According to *Strong's Hebrew Lexicon* #H5749, the word **testimony** is also from the root Hebrew word *'ûd* (pronounced "**ood**"), a primitive root which means to *duplicate* or *repeat;* by implication to *protest, testify* (as by reiteration); intensively to *encompass, restore* (as a sort of reduplication): - admonish, charge, earnestly, lift up, protest, call (take) to record, relieve, rob, solemnly, stand upright, testify, give warning, (bear, call to, give, take to) witness.

[27] According to *Strong's Hebrew Lexicon* #H6490, the word **statutes** is the Hebrew word *piqqûd* (pronounced "**pik-kood'**"), which is from H6485; properly *appointed,* that is, a *mandate* (of God; plural only, collectively for the *Law*): - commandment, precept, statute.

[28] According to *Strong's Hebrew Lexicon* #H4687, the word **commandment** is the Hebrew word *mitsvâh* (pronounced "**mits-vaw'**"), and is from H6680; a *command,* whether human

or divine (collectively the Law): - (which was) commanded (-ment), law, ordinance, precept.

[29]According to *Strong's Hebrew Lexicon* #H3374, the word *fear* is the Hebrew word *yir'âh* (pronounced "yir-aw'"), the feminine of H3373; *fear* (also used as infinitive); morally *reverence:* - X dreadful, X exceedingly, fear (-fulness).

[30]According to *Strong's Hebrew Lexicon* #H4941, the word *judgments* is synonymous with the word *law* and is the Hebrew word *mishpât* (pronounced "mish-pawt'"), which is from H8199; properly a *verdict* (favorable or unfavorable) pronounced judicially, especially a *sentence* or formal decree (human or (particularly) divine *law*, individual or collectively), including the act, the place, the suit, the crime, and the penalty; abstractly justice, including a particular *right*, or *privilege* (statutory or customary), or even a *style:* - + adversary, ceremony, charge, X crime, custom, desert, determination, discretion, disposing, due, fashion, form, to be judged, judgment, just (-ice, -ly), (manner of) law (-ful), manner, measure, (due) order, ordinance, right, sentence, usest, X worthy, + wrong.

CHAPTER 22

[1]According to *Strong's Hebrew Lexicon* #H4135, the word *circumcised* or *circumcision* is the Hebrew word *mûl* (pronounced "mool"), and is a primitive root; to *cut* short, that is, *curtail* (specifically the prepuce, that is, to *circumcise*);

by implication to *blunt;* figuratively to *destroy:* - circumcise (-ing, selves), cut down (in pieces), destroy, X must needs.

(2)According to *Strong's Hebrew Lexicon* **#H1285**, the word *covenant* is the Hebrew word *b'riyth* (pronounced "ber-eeth'"), from H1262 (in the sense of *cutting* (like h1254)); a *compact* (because made by passing between *pieces* of flesh): - confederacy, [con-]feder[-ate], covenant, league.

(3)According to *Strong's Hebrew Lexicon* **#H5769**, the word *everlasting* is the Hebrew word *'ôlâm* (pronounced "o-lawm'"), from H5956; properly *concealed,* that is, the *vanishing* point; generally time *out of mind* (past or future), that is, (practically) eternity; frequentative adverbially (especially with prepositional prefix) *always:* - always (-s), ancient (time), any more, continuance, eternal, (for, [n-]) ever (-lasting, -more, of old), lasting, long (time), (of) old (time), perpetual, at any time, (beginning of the) world (+ without end). Compare H5331, H5703.

(4)According to *Strong's Hebrew Lexicon* **#H3772**, the word *cut off* is the Hebrew word *kârath* (pronounced "kaw-rath'"), and is a primitive root; to *cut* (off, down or asunder); by implication to *destroy* or *consume;* specifically to covenant (that is, make an alliance or bargain, originally by cutting flesh and passing between the pieces): - be chewed, be con-[feder-] ate, covenant, cut (down, off), destroy, fail, feller, be freed, hew (down), make a league ([covenant]), X lose, perish, X utterly, X want.

[5]According to *Strong's Hebrew Lexicon* #H6565, the word **broken** is the Hebrew word *pârar* (pronounced "paw-rar'"), which is a root; to *break* up (usually figuratively, that is, to *violate*, *frustrate*): - X any ways, break (asunder), cast off, cause to cease, x clean, defeat, disannul, disappoint, dissolve, divide, make of none effect, fail, frustrate, bring (come) to naught, x utterly, make void.

CHAPTER 23

[1]According to *Strong's Hebrew Lexicon* #H3045, the word **known** is the Hebrew word *yâda'* (pronounced "yaw-dah'"), a primitive root; to *know* (properly to ascertain by *seeing*); used in a great variety of senses, figuratively, literally, euphemistically and inferentially (including *observation*, *care*, *recognition*; and causatively *instruction*, *designation*, *punishment*, etc.): - acknowledge, acquaintance (-ted with), advise, answer, appoint, assuredly, be aware, [un-] awares, can [-not], certainly, for a certainty, comprehend, consider, X could they, cunning, declare, be diligent, (can, cause to) discern, discover, endued with, familiar friend, famous, feel, can have, be [ig-] norant, instruct, kinsfolk, kinsman, (cause to, let, make) know, (come to give, have, take) knowledge, have [knowledge], (be, make, make to be, make self) known, + be learned, + lie by man, mark, perceive, privy to, X prognosticator.

[2]According to *Strong's Hebrew Lexicon* #H2706, the word **statutes** or **ordinances** is the Hebrew word *chôq* (pronounced

"khoke"), is from H2710; an *enactment*; hence an *appointment* (of time, space, quantity, labor or usage): - appointed, bound, commandment, convenient, custom, decree (-d), due, law, measure, x necessary, ordinance (-nary), portion, set time, statute, task. This is referring to God's law that He decreed through His servant Moses, particularly with regards to his seven holy convocations/feasts based on Leviticus 23.

[3]According to *Strong's Hebrew Lexicon* #H4941, the word *judgments* is the Hebrew word *mishpất* pronounced *mish-pawt'* from H8199; properly a *verdict* (favorable or unfavorable) pronounced judicially, especially a *sentence* or formal decree (human or (particularly) divine *law*, individual or collectively), including the act, the place, the suit, the crime, and the penalty; abstractly *justice*, including a particular *right*, or *privilege* (statutory or customary), or even a *style:* - + adversary, ceremony, charge, X crime, custom, desert, determination, discretion, disposing, due, fashion, form, to be judged, judgment, just (-ice, -ly), (manner of) law (-ful), manner, measure, (due) order, ordinance, right, sentence, usest, X worthy, + wrong.

[4] According to *Strong's Hebrew Lexicon* #H8451, the word *law* is the Hebrew word *tôrâh* (pronounced **to-raw'**), which is from H3384; a *precept* or *statute*, especially the Decalogue or Pentateuch: - law.

[5]According to *Strong's Hebrew Lexicon* #H226, the word

sign is the Hebrew word *'óth* (pronounced **oth**), probably from H225 (in the sense of *appearing*); a *signal* (literally or figuratively), as a *flag, beacon, monument, omen, prodigy, evidence,* etc.: - mark, miracle, (en-) sign, token.

[6]According to *Strong's Hebrew Lexicon* #**H3789**, the word *write* or *written* is the Hebrew word *kâthab* (pronounced "kaw-thab''), a primitive root; to *grave*; by implication to *write* (describe, inscribe, prescribe, subscribe): - describe, record, prescribe, subscribe, write (-ing, -ten).

[7]According to *Strong's Greek Lexicon* #**G3809**, the word *training* is the Greek word *paideia* (pronounced "**pahee-di'-ah**"), from G3811; *tutorage*, that is, *education* or *training*; by implication disciplinary *correction:* - chastening, chastisement, instruction, nurture.

[8]According to *Strong's Greek Lexicon* #**G3559**, the word *admonition* is the Greek word *nouthesia* (pronounced "**noo-thes-ee'-ah**"), from G3563 and a derivative of G5087; calling *attention* to, that is, (by implication) mild *rebuke* or *warning:* - admonition.

[9]According to *Strong's Hebrew Lexicon* #**H3327**, the name *Isaac* is the Hebrew name *Yitschâq* (pronounced "**Yits-khawk'**"), from H6711; *laughter* (that is, *mockery*); *Jitschak* (or Isaac), son of Abraham: - Isaac. Compare H3446.

[10]According to *Strong's Hebrew Lexicon* #**H6965**, the word *establish* or *rise* is the Hebrew word *qûm* (pronounced "**koom**"), a primitive root; to *rise* (in various applications,

literally, figuratively, intensively and causatively): - abide, accomplish, X be clearer, confirm, continue, decree, X be dim, endure, X enemy, enjoin, get up, make good, help, hold, (help to) lift up (again), make, X but newly, ordain, perform, pitch, raise (up), rear (up), remain, (a-) rise (up) (again, against), rouse up, set (up), (e-) stablish, (make to) stand (up), stir up, strengthen, succeed, (as-, make) sure (-ly), (be) up (-hold, -rising).

[11]According to *Strong's Hebrew Lexicon* **#H1285**, the word *covenant* is the Hebrew word *bᵉrîyth* (pronounced **"ber-eeth'"**), from H1262 (in the sense of *cutting* (like h1254)); a *compact* (because made by passing between *pieces* of flesh): - confederacy, [con-]feder[-ate], covenant, league.

[12]According to *Strong's Hebrew Lexicon* **#H5769**, the word *everlasting* is the Hebrew word *'ôlâm* (pronounced **"ōlām'"**), from H5956; properly *concealed*, that is, the *vanishing* point; generally time *out of mind* (past or future), that is, (practically) eternity; frequentative adverbially (especially with prepositional prefix) *always*: - always (-s), ancient (time), any more, continuance, eternal, (for, [n-]) ever (-lasting, -more, of old), lasting, long (time), (of) old (time), perpetual, at any time, (beginning of the) world (+ without end). Compare H5331, H5703.

[13]According to *Strong's Hebrew Lexicon* **#H4150**, the word *set time* or *seasons* is the Hebrew word *môʻêd* (pronounced

"mo-ade'"), which is from H3259; properly an *appointment*, that is, a fixed *time* or season; specifically a *festival*; conventionally a *year*; by implication, an *assembly* (as convened for a definite purpose); technically the *congregation*; by extension, the *place of meeting*; also a *signal* (as appointed beforehand): - appointed (sign, time), (place of, solemn) assembly, congregation, (set, solemn) feast, (appointed, due) season, solemn (-ity), synagogue, (set) time (appointed).

(14)According to *Strong's Hebrew Lexicon* #**H6485**, the word *visited* is the Hebrew word *pâqad* (pronounced "**paw-kad**'"), a primitive root; to *visit* (with friendly or hostile intent); by analogy to *oversee, muster, charge, care for, miss, deposit*, etc.: - appoint, X at all, avenge, bestow, (appoint to have the, give a) charge, commit, count, deliver to keep, be empty, enjoin, go see, hurt, do judgment, lack, lay up look, make X by any means, miss, number, officer, (make) overseer have (the) oversight, punish, reckon, (call to) remember (-brance), set (over), sum, X surely, visit, want.

(15)According to *Strong's Hebrew Lexicon* #**H4135**, the word *circumcised* or *circumcision* is the Hebrew word *mûl* (pronounced "**mool**"), and is a primitive root; to *cut* short, that is, *curtail* (specifically the prepuce, that is, to *circumcise*); by implication to *blunt*; figuratively to *destroy:* - circumcise (-ing, selves), cut down (in pieces), destroy, X must needs.

CHAPTER 24

(1)According to *Strong's Hebrew Lexicon* #**H3458**, the name

Ishmael is the Hebrew name *Yishmāʿēʾl* (pronounced "yish-maw-ale'"), from H8085 and H410; *God will hear; Jishmael,* the name of Abraham's oldest son, and of five Israelites: - Ishmael.

(2)According to *Strong's Hebrew Lexicon* #H5387, the word *princes* is the Hebrew word *nāśîyʾ* (pronounced "naw-see'"), which is from H5375; properly an *exalted* one, that is, a *king* or *sheik;* also a rising *mist:* - captain, chief, cloud, governor, prince, ruler, vapour.

CHAPTER 25

(1)According to *Strong's Hebrew Lexicon* #H4179, the name *Moriah* is the Hebrew name *Môrîyāh* (pronounced "mo-ree-yaw'"), from H7200 and H3050; *seen of Jah; Morijah,* a hill in Palestine; Moriah.

(2)According to *Strong's Hebrew Lexicon* #H3050, the name *Moriah* is from the root Hebrew word *yāhh* (pronounced "yä"), *yaw* contracted for H3068, and meaning the same; *Jah,* the sacred name: - Jah, the Lord, most vehement. Cp. names in "-iah," "-jah."

(3) According to *Strong's Hebrew Lexicon* #H2610, the word *defiled* is the Hebrew word *chânêph* (pronounced "khaw-nafe'"), a primitive root; to *soil,* especially in a moral sense: - corrupt, defile, x greatly, pollute, profane.

(4) According to *Strong's Hebrew Lexicon* #H5674, the word

transgressed is the Hebrew word *'ābar* (pronounced "aw-bar'"), a primitive root; which can mean to *cross* over; used very widely of any *transition* (literally or figuratively; transitively, intransitively, intensively or causatively); specifically to *cover* (in copulation): - alienate, alter, X at all, beyond, bring (over, through), carry over, (over-) come (on, over), conduct (over), convey over, current, deliver, do away, enter, escape, fail, gender, get over, (make) go (away, beyond, by, forth, his way, in, on, over, through), have away (more), lay, meddle, overrun, make partition, (cause to, give, make to, over) pass (-age, along, away, beyond, by, -enger, on, out, over, through), (cause to, make) + proclaim (-amation), perish, provoke to anger, put away, rage, + raiser of taxes, remove, send over, set apart, + shave, cause to (make) sound, X speedily, X sweet smelling, take (away), (make to) transgress (-or), translate, turn away, [way-] faring man, be wrath.

(5) According to *Strong's Hebrew Lexicon* #H8451, the word *laws* is the Hebrew word *tôrāh* (pronounced "to-raw'"), from H3384; a *precept* or *statute*, especially the Decalogue or Pentateuch: - law.

(6) According to *Strong's Hebrew Lexicon* #H2498, the word *changed* is the Hebrew word *châlaph* (pronounced "khaw-laf'"), a primitive root; properly to *slide* by, that is, (by implication) to *hasten* away, *pass* on, *spring* up, *pierce* or *change:* - abolish, alter change, cut off, go on forward, grow up, be over, pass (away, on, through), renew, sprout, strike

through.

(7)According to *Strong's Hebrew Lexicon* #H2706, the word **ordinance** is the Hebrew word *chôq* (pronounced **"khoke"**), from H2710; an enactment; hence an appointment (of time, space, quantity, labor or usage): - appointed, bound, commandment, convenient, custom, decree (-d), due, law, measure, x necessary, ordinance (-nary), portion, set time, statute, task.

(8) Note: These *everlasting* ordinances are a prophetic enactment of God's appointed times that He has commanded that we meet with Him at a "set time" every week and every year based on our heavenly Father's seven holy convocations which are detailed in Leviticus 23.

(9) According to *Strong's Hebrew Lexicon* #H6565, the word **broken** is the Hebrew word *pârar* (pronounced **"paw-rar'"**), a root; to *break* up (usually figuratively, that is, to *violate, frustrate*): - X any ways, break (asunder), cast off, cause to cease, X clean, defeat, disannul, disappoint, dissolve, divide, make of none effect, fail, frustrate, bring (come) to naught, X utterly, make void.

(10)According to *Strong's Hebrew Lexicon* #H5769, the word **everlasting** is the Hebrew word *'ôlâm* (pronounced **"o-lawm'"**), from H5956; properly *concealed*, that is, the *vanishing* point; generally time out of mind (past or future), that is, (practically) eternity; frequentative adverbially (especially with prepositional prefix) *always:* - always (-s), ancient (time), any more, continuance, eternal, (for, [n-]) ever (-lasting, -more, of old), lasting, long (time), (of) old (time), perpetual, at any time, (beginning of the) world (+ without end). Compare H5331, H5703.

(11)According to *Strong's Hebrew Lexicon* #H1285, the word *covenant* is the Hebrew word *b'rîyth* (pronounced "ber-eeth'"), from H1262 (in the sense of *cutting* (like h1254)); a *compact* (because made by passing between *pieces* of flesh): - confederacy, [con-]feder[-ate], covenant, league.

(12)According to *Strong's Greek Lexicon* #G2889, the word *world* is the Greek word *kosmos* (pronounced "kos'-mos"), probably from the base of G2865; orderly arrangement, that is, *decoration*; by implication the *world* (in a wide or narrow sense, including its inhabitants, literally or figuratively [morally]): - adorning, world.

(13) According to *Strong's Hebrew Lexicon* #H3070, the name of the place, *The-LORD-Will-Provide* is the word *Jehovah Jireh* as used in the KJV which is the Hebrew word *Yehôvâh Yir'eh* (pronounced "yeh-hōvä' yireh'"), which is from H3068 and H7200; *Jehovah will see* (to it); *Jehovah-Jireh*, a symbolical name for Mt. Moriah: - Jehovah-jireh.

(14)According to *Strong's Hebrew Lexicon* #H884, the name *Beersheba* is the Hebrew name *B''êr sheba'* (pronounced "be-ayr' sheh'-bah"), which is from H875 and H7651 (in the sense of H7650); *well of an oath*; *Beer Sheba*, a place in Palestine: - Beer-shebah.

CHAPTER 26

[1] *Origin of the Name Palestine:*
http://www.palestinefacts.org/pf_early_palestine_name_origin.php

[2] *Muhammad:* http://en.wikipedia.org/wiki/Muhammad

[3] According to *Strong's Hebrew Lexicon* #H6290, the word **Paran** is the Hebrew word **pâ'rân** (pronounced "paw-rawn'"), from H6286; *ornamental; Paran*, a desert of Arabia: - Paran.

[4] *Desert of Paran:*
https://en.wikipedia.org/wiki/Desert_of_Paran

The Desert of Paran or Wilderness of Paran (also sometimes spelled Pharan or Faran; Hebrew מדבר פארן *Midbar Pa'ran*), is a location mentioned in the Hebrew Bible. It is one of the places where the Israelites spent part of their 40 years of wandering after the Exodus, was also a home to Ishmael and a place of refuge for David. In Arabic tradition, it has often been equated with an area of the Hejaz, around Mecca, linked to Ishmael and Abraham.

[5] *Hejaz:* https://en.wikipedia.org/wiki/Hejaz

Al-Hejaz, also Hijaz (Arabic: الحجاز *al-Ḥiǧāz*, literally "the barrier"), is a region in the west of present-day Saudi Arabia. It is bordered on the west by the Red Sea, on the north by Jordan, on the east by Najd, and on the south by Asir.[1] Its main city is Jeddah, but it is probably better known for the Islamic holy cities of Mecca and Medina. As the site of Islam's holy places, the Hejaz has significance in the Arab and Islamic historical and political landscape.

CHAPTER 27

[1]According to *Strong's Hebrew Lexicon* #H7533, the phrase **struggled together** is the Hebrew word *ratsats* (pronounced "*rä•tsats'*"), a primitive root; to crack in pieces, literally or figuratively:—break, bruise, crush, discourage, oppress, struggle together.

[2] According to *Strong's Hebrew Lexicon* #H1471, the usage of the word **nations** is the Hebrew word *gôy* (pronounced "go'ee"), which is apparently from the same root as H1465 (in the sense of *massing*); a foreign *nation*; hence a *Gentile*; also (figuratively) a *troop* of animals, or a *flight* of locusts. As used in KJV: Gentile, heathen, nation, or people. Therefore, the word **Gentile** is referring to heathen people or nations that practice or follow pagan rituals or false gods. In other words, they are not in covenant with *Yehôvâh*.

[3] According to *Strong's Hebrew Lexicon* #H3816, the word **people** or **peoples** is the Hebrew word *l'ôm* (pronounced "leh-ome'"), from an unused root meaning to *gather*; a *community:* - nation, people.

[4]According to *Strong's Hebrew Lexicon* #H6504, the word **separated** is the Hebrew word *pârad* (pronounced "paw-rad'"), a primitive root; to *break* through, that is, *spread* or

separate (oneself): - disperse, divide, be out of joint, part, scatter (abroad), separate (self), sever self, stretch, sunder.

[5]According to *Strong's Hebrew Lexicon* #H553, the word **stronger** is the Hebrew word *'âmats* (pronounced "aw-mats'"), a primitive root; to *be alert*, physically (on foot) or mentally (in courage): - confirm, be courageous (of good courage, steadfastly minded, strong, stronger), establish, fortify, harden, increase, prevail, strengthen (self), make strong (obstinate, speed).

[6]According to *Strong's Hebrew Lexicon* #H132, the word **red** is the Hebrew word *'admônîy* (pronounced "ad-mo-nee'"), from H119; *reddish* (of the hair or the complexion): - red, ruddy.

[7] According to *Strong's Hebrew Lexicon* #H8181, the word **hairy** is the Hebrew word *sê'âr* (pronounced "say-awr'"), from H8175 in the sense of *disheveling*; *hair* (as if tossed or bristling).

[8] According to *Strong's Hebrew Lexicon* #H155, the usage of the word **garment** is the Hebrew word **addereth** (pronounced "ad-deh'-reth"), which means mantle, garment, glory, goodly or robe.

[9] According to *Strong's Hebrew Lexicon* #H6215, the name **Esau** is the Hebrew name *'Ēsâv* (pronounced "ay-sawv'"), apparently a form of the passive participle of H6213 in the original sense of *handling*; *rough* (that is, sensibly *felt*)

506

"hairy"; *Esav,* a son of Isaac, including his posterity; Esau the eldest son of Isaac and Rebecca and twin brother of Jacob; sold the birthright for food when he was hungry and the divine blessing went to Jacob; progenitor of the Arab peoples.

(10) According to *Strong's Hebrew Lexicon* **#H3290**, the name *Jacob* is the Hebrew name **Ya'ăqŏb** (pronounced **yah-ak-obe'**), which means heel-catcher (i.e. supplanter); Jaakob, the Israelitish patriarch:–Jacob. Supplanter, deceiver, and conniver.

(11) According to *Strong's Hebrew Lexicon* **#H342**, the word *enmity* is the Hebrew word *'eybah* (pronounced **"ay-baw'"**), which means hostility, enmity, hatred.

(12) According to *Strong's Hebrew Lexicon* **#H7218**, the word *head* is the Hebrew word *ro'sh* (pronounced **"roshe"**), from an unused root apparently meaning to shake; the head (as most easily shaken), whether literally or figuratively (in many applications, of place, time, rank, etc.). KJV Usage: band, beginning, captain, chapiter, chief (-est place, man, things), company, end, X every [man], excellent, first, forefront, ([be-]) head, height, (on) high (-est part, [priest]), X lead, X poor, principal, ruler, sum, top.

(13) According to *Strong's Hebrew Lexicon* **#H6119**, the word *heel* is the Hebrew word `aqeb (pronounced **"aw-kabe'"**), from H6117; a *heel* (as *protuberant*); hence a *track*; figuratively the *rear* (of an army). (*lier in wait* is by mistake for H6120.):- heel, [horse-] hoof, last, lier in wait [by mistake for H6120], (foot-) step.

[14]According to *Strong's Hebrew Lexicon* #**H6117**, the word **heel** is from the root Hebrew word *'âqab* (pronounced **"aw-kab'"**), a primitive root; properly to *swell* out or up; used only as denominative from H6119, to *seize by the heel*; figuratively to circumvent (as if *tripping* up the heels); also to restrain (as if holding by the heel): - take by the heel, stay, supplant, X utterly.

CHAPTER 28

[1]According to *Strong's Hebrew Lexicon* #**H123**, the name **Edom** is the Hebrew word *'ĕdôm* (pronounced **"ed-ome'"**), from H122; *red* (see Gen 25:25); *Edom*, the elder twin-brother of Jacob; hence the region (Idumaea) occupied by him: - Edom, Edomites, Idumea.

[2]According to *Strong's Hebrew Lexicon* #**H959**, the word **despised** is the Hebrew word *bâzâh* (pronounced **"baw-zaw'"**), a primitive root; to *disesteem:* - despise, disdain, contemn (-ptible), + think to scorn, vile person.

[3]According to *Strong's Hebrew Lexicon* #**H8130**, the word **hated** is the Hebrew word *sânê'* (pronounced *"saw-nay'"*), a primitive root; to *hate* (personally): - enemy, foe, (be) hate (-ful, -r), odious, X utterly.

[4]According to *Strong's Greek Lexicon* #**G3404**, the word **hated** is the Greek word *miseō* (pronounced **"mis-eh'-o"**), from a primary word μῖσος misos (*hatred*); to *detest* (especially to *persecute*); by extension to *love less:* - hate (-

ful).

(5) **Source:** Wikipedia.org: *Teman:* The name Teman (Hebrew: תימן), was the name of an Edomite clan and the term is also traditionally applied to Yemenite Jews and is used as the Hebrew name of Yemen. There is other strong evidence that Teman could be identified as the site of the modern Ma'an. There is some information that says that the state which emerged in the south of the Arabian Peninsula in Yemen.

(6) **Source:** Wikipedia.org: *Dedan*

https://en.wikipedia.org/wiki/Dedan

The word *Dedan* (Hebrew: דדן *Dədān*) means *"low ground"* and is a city of Arabia, in modern times it is called Al-'Ula and is located in northern Saudi Arabia

(7) **Source***: Wikipedia.org: Bozrah*
https://en.wikipedia.org/wiki/Bozrah

Bozrah was the capital city of the Edomites, once they settled from their nomadic lifestyle. It is located in modern day Jordan along the King's Highway. *Bozrah* means "sheepfold" and was a pastoral city in Edom southeast of the Dead Sea.

CHAPTER 29

(1)According to *Strong's Greek Lexicon* #**G1556**, the word *avenge* is the Greek word *ekdikeō* (pronounced **"ek-dik-eh'-o"**), from G1558; to *vindicate, retaliate, punish:* - a (re-)

venge.

(2)According to *Strong's Greek Lexicon* #**G1558**, the word *avenge* is the Greek word *ekdikos* (pronounced **"ek'-dik-os"**), from G1537 and G1349; carrying *justice out*, that is, a *punisher:-* a (re-) venger.

(3)According to *Strong's Greek Lexicon* #**G1557**, the word *vengeance* is the Greek word *ekdikēsis* (pronounced **"ek-dik'-ay-sis"**), which is from G1556; *vindication, retribution:-* (a-, re-) venge (-ance), punishment.

(4)According to *Strong's Greek Lexicon* #**G4100**, the word *believe* is the Greek word *pisteuō* (pronounced **"pist-yoo'-o"**), which is from G4102; to *have faith* (in, upon, or with respect to, a person or thing), that is, **credit**, by implication to *entrust* (especially one's spiritual well-being to Christ): - believe (-r), commit (to trust), put in trust with.

(5)According to *Strong's Greek Lexicon* #**G1515**, the word *peace* is the Greek word *eirēnē* (pronounced **"i-rah'-nay"**), probably from a primary verb εἴρω eirō (to *join*); *peace* (literally or figuratively); by implication *prosperity:* - one, peace, quietness, rest, + set at one again.

(6)According to *Strong's Greek Lexicon* #**G38**, the word *holiness* is the Greek word *hagiasmos* which is (pronounced **"hag-ee-as-mos'"**), from G37; properly *purification*, that is, (the state) *purity*; concretely (by Hebraism) a *purifier:* - holiness, sanctification.

Donna M. Rogers

[7]According to *Strong's Greek Lexicon* #**G5485**, the word *grace* is the Greek word *charis* (pronounced "khar'-ece"), from G5463; *graciousness* (as *gratifying*), of manner or act (abstract or concrete; literal, figurative or spiritual; especially the divine influence upon the heart, and its reflection in the life; including *gratitude*): - acceptable, benefit, favour, gift, grace (-ious), joy liberality, pleasure, thank (-s, -worthy).

[8]According to *Strong's Greek Lexicon* #**G4088**, the word *bitterness* is the Greek word *pikria* (pronounced "pik-ree'-ah"), from G4089; *acridity* (especially *poison*), literally or figuratively: - bitterness.

[9]According to *Strong's Greek Lexicon* #**G3392**, the word *defiled* is the Greek word *miaino* (pronounced "me-ah'ee-no"), perhaps a primary verb; to *sully* or *taint*, that is, *contaminate* (ceremonially or morally): - defile.

[10]According to *Strong's Greek Lexicon* #**G4205**, the word *fornicator* is the Greek word *pornos* (pronounced "por'-nos"), from πέρνημι pernemi (to *sell*; akin to the base of G4097); a (male) *prostitute* (as *venal*), that is, (by analogy) a *debauchee* (*libertine*): - fornicator, whoremonger.

[11]According to *Strong's Greek Lexicon* #**G952**, the word *profane* is the Greek word *bebelos* (pronounced "beb'-ay-los"), from the base of G939 and βηλός belos (a *threshold*); *accessible* (as by *crossing the door way*), that is, (by implication of Jewish notions) *heathenish, wicked:* - profane (person).

511

(12) According to *Strong's Greek Lexicon* #**G593**, the word *rejected* is the Greek word **apodokimazo̅** (pronounced "ap-od-ok-ee-mad'-zo"), from G575 and G1381; to *disapprove*, that is, (by implication) to *repudiate:* - disallow, reject.

(13) According to *Strong's Greek Lexicon* #**G3341**, the word *repentance* is the Greek word **metanoia** (pronounced "met-an'-oy-ah"), from G3340; (subjectively) *compunction* (for guilt, including *reformation*); by implication, a *reversal* (of [another's] decision): - repentance.

CHAPTER 30

(1) According to *Strong's Hebrew Lexicon* #**H3290**, the name *Jacob* is the Hebrew name **Ya'aqob** (pronounced "yah-ak-obe'"), from H6117; *heel catcher* (that is, supplanter); *Jaakob*, the *Israelitish* patriarch: - Jacob.

(2) According to *Strong's Hebrew Lexicon* #**H3478**, the name *Israel* is the Hebrew name **Yisra'el** (pronounced "yis-raw-ale'"), and is from H8280 and H410; and means: *he will rule as God; Jisrael*, a symbolical name of Jacob; also (typically) of his posterity. KJV Usage: Israel. Also, according to *Brown-Driver-Briggs' Hebrew Definitions* it the name *Israel* means: "God prevails."

(3) According to *Strong's Hebrew Lexicon* #**H6439**, the name *Peniel* is the Hebrew name **P'nu'el** (pronounced "pen-oo-ale'"), from H6437 and H410; *face of God; Penuel* or *Peniel*,

a place East of Jordan; also (as Penuel) the name of two Israelites: - Peniel, Penuel.

CHAPTER 31

[1]According to *Strong's Hebrew Lexicon* #**H8165**, the name *Seir* is the Hebrew name *Séʿîyr* (pronounced "**say-eer**'"), which is formed like H8163; *rough*; *Seir*, a mountain of Idumaea and its aboriginal occupants, also one in Palestine: - Seir.

[2] *Mount Seir:* https://en.wikipedia.org/wiki/Mount_Seir

[3]According to *Strong's Hebrew Lexicon* #**H6144**, the name *Ar* is the Hebrew word *ʿÂr* which is (pronounced "**awr**"), the same as H5892; a *city*; *Ar*, a place in Moab: - Ar.

[4] *Ar:* https://en.wikipedia.org/wiki/Ar_(city)

Ar is mentioned in the Hebrew Bible several times as a city of ancient Moab (Numbers 21:15). While the exact location is unknown, it is likely to have been in the southern part of the Arnon Valley, which is the present day Wadi Mujib gorge in Jordan.[1] The city was one of Moab's most prominent, being listed by the prophet Isaiah in his denunciation of the Moabite nation (Isaiah 15:1). Matthew Poole suggested that "the city was seated in an island in the middle of the river."[2]The Bible speaks of Ar as being captured by the Amorite King Sihon (Numbers 21:28).Modern scholars believe that the word "Ar" likely meant "city."[3]

[5]According to *Strong's Hebrew Lexicon* #**H123**, the name **Edom** is the Hebrew word *'Edôm* (pronounced **"ed-ome'"**), from H122; *red* (see Gen 25:25); *Edom*, the elder twin-brother of Jacob; hence the region (Idumaea) occupied by him: - Edom, Edomites, Idumea.

[6] *The Historical Transjordan Territory of the Edomites in the Bible*

http://www.bible.ca/archeology/bible-archeology-Edomite-territory-mt-seir.htm

[7] *Where will the Remnant of Israel Gather during the Great Tribulation?*

http://www.tribulation.com/petra.htm.

[8] *Who Is Modern-Day Edom?* By Gary Stearman of Prophecy in the News

http://www.squidoo.com/who-is-modern-day-edom-

[9] *Hamas Charter, Unabridged (1988), Part 1*

http://middleeast.about.com/od/palestinepalestinians/a/m e080106b.htm

[10] *Hamas Charter, Unabridged (1988), Part 2*

http://middleeast.about.com/od/palestinepalestinians/a/m e080106c.htm

[11] *Vicar of Christ.* Wikipedia

https://en.wikipedia.org/wiki/Vicar_of_Christ

CHAPTER 32

[1] According to *Strong's Greek Lexicon* #**G571**, the word *unbelievers* is the Greek word ***apistos*** (pronounced "**ap'-is-tos**"), from G1 (as a negative particle) and G4103; (actively) *disbelieving*, that is, *without* Christian faith (specifically a *heathen*); (passively) *untrustworthy* (person), or *incredible* (thing): - that believeth not, faithless, incredible thing, infidel, unbeliever (-ing).

[2] According to *Strong's Greek Lexicon* #**G3352**, the word *fellowship* is the Greek word ***metoche*** (pronounced "**met-okh-ay'**"), from G3348; *participation*, that is, *intercourse; fellowship;* a close relation between partners, i.e. people sharing something held in common (used only in 2 Cor 6:14); joint-activity.

[3] According to *Strong's Greek Lexicon* #**G3348**, the word *fellowship* is from the root Greek word ***metecho*** (pronounced "**met-ekh'-o**"), from G3326 and G2192; to *share* or *participate*; by implication *belong* to, *eat* (or *drink*): - be partaker, pertain, take part, use.

[4] According to *Strong's Greek Lexicon* #**G1343**, the word *righteousness* is the Greek word ***dikaiosune*** pronounced ("**dik-ah-yos-oo'-nay**"), from G1342; *equity* (of character or act); specifically (Christian) *justification:* - righteousness.

515

[5]According to *Strong's Greek Lexicon* #**G458**, the word *lawlessness* is synonymous with the word *iniquity* as used in the KJV and is the Greek word *anomia* (pronounced **"an-om-ee'-ah"**), which means illegality, i.e. violation of law or (genitive base) wickedness derivation: from G459; KJV Usage: iniquity, X transgress(-ion of) the law, unrighteousness.

According to *Thayer's Greek*–English *Lexicon of the New Testament* means the following: 1) the condition of without law 1a) because ignorant of it 1b) because of violating it 2) contempt and violation of law resulting in iniquity or wickedness.

[6]According to *Strong's Greek Lexicon* #**G459**, the word *lawlessness* or *iniquity* is the Greek word *anomia* which comes from the Greek word *anomos* (pronounced **"an'-om-os"**), which is from G1 (as a negative particle) and G3551; *lawless*, that is, (negatively) *not subject to* (the Jewish) *law*, (by implication a *Gentile*), or (positively) *wicked:* - without law, lawless, transgressor, unlawful, wicked.

[7]According to *Strong's Greek Lexicon* #**G3551**, the word *lawlessness* or *iniquity* which is derived from the Greek word *anomos* is the root Greek word *nomos* (pronounced **"nom'-os"**), from a primary word νέμω nemō‾ (to *parcel* out, especially *food* or *grazing* to animals); *law* (through the idea of prescriptive *usage*), generally (*regulation*), specifically (of Moses [including the volume]; also of the Gospel), or figuratively (a *principle*): - law.

(8)According to *Strong's Greek Lexicon* #G2842, the word *communion* is the Greek word *koinōnia* (pronounced "koy-nohn-ee'-ah"), from G2844; *partnership*, that is, (literally) *participation*, or (social) *intercourse*, or (pecuniary) *benefaction:* - (to) communicate (-ation), communion, (contri-), distribution, fellowship.

(9)According to *Strong's Greek Lexicon* #G2844, the word *communion* is from the root Greek word *koinōnos* (pronounced "koy-no-nos'"), from G2839; a *sharer*, that is, *associate:* - companion, X fellowship, partaker, partner.

(10)According to *Strong's Greek Lexicon* #G4857, the word *accord* is the Greek word *sumphonēsis* (pronounced "soom-fo'-nay-sis"), from G4856; *accordance:* - concord.

(11)According to *Strong's Greek Lexicon* #G4856, the word *accord* is from the root Greek word *sumphōneō* (pronounced "soom-fo-neh'-o"), from G4859; to be *harmonious*, that is, (figuratively) to *accord* (*be suitable, concur*) or *stipulate* (by compact): - agree (together, with).

(12)According to *Strong's Greek Lexicon* #G5547, the word *Christ* is the Greek word *Christos* (pronounced "khris-tos'"), from G5548; *anointed*, that is, the *Messiah*, an epithet of Jesus: - Christ.

(13)According to *Strong's Greek Lexicon* #G5548, the word *Christ* is from the root Greek word *chriō* (pronounced "khree'-o"), probably akin to G5530 through the idea of *contact*; to *smear* or *rub* with oil, that is, (by implication) to *consecrate* to an office or religious service: - anoint.

(14)According to *Strong's Greek Lexicon* #G955, the word **Belial** is the Greek word **Belial** (pronounced "bel-ee'-al"), which is of Hebrew origin [H1100]; *worthlessness; Belial*, as an epithet of Satan: - Belial.

(15)According to *Strong's Hebrew Lexicon* #H1100, the word **Belial** is of Hebrew origin and is the Hebrew word *bᵉlîya'al* (pronounced "bel-e-yah'-al"), which is from H1097 and H3276; *without profit, worthlessness;* by extension *destruction, wickedness* (often in connection with H376, H802, H1121, etc.): - Belial, evil, naughty, ungodly (men), wicked.

(16)According to *Strong's Greek Lexicon* #G4103, the word **believer** is the Greek word **pistos** (pronounced "pis-tos'"), from G3982; objectively *trustworthy;* subjectively *trustful:* - believe (-ing, -r), faithful (-ly), sure, true.

(17)According to *Strong's Greek Lexicon* #G571, the word **unbeliever** is the Greek word **apistos** (pronounced "ap'-is-tos"), from G1 (as a negative particle) and G4103; (actively) *disbelieving,* that is, *without* Christian *faith* (specifically a *heathen*); (passively) *untrustworthy* (person), or *incredible* (thing): - that believeth not, faithless, incredible thing, infidel, unbeliever (-ing).

(18)According to *Strong's Greek Lexicon* #G4783, the word **agreement** is the Greek word **sugkatathesis** (pronounced "**soong-kat-ath'-es-is**"), from G4784; a *deposition* (of sentiment) in company *with*, that is, (figuratively) *accord* with: - agreement.

[19]According to *Strong's Greek Lexicon* #**G3485**, the word *temple* is the Greek word ***naos*** (pronounced "**nah-os'**"), from a primary word ναίω naio⁻ (to *dwell*); a *fane, shrine, temple*: - shrine, temple. Compare G2411.

[20] According to *Strong's Greek Lexicon* #**G2316**, the word *God* is the Greek word ***Theos*** (pronounced "**theh'-os**"), which is of uncertain affinity; a *deity*, especially (with G3588) *the* supreme *Divinity*; figuratively a *magistrate*; by Hebraism *very*: - X exceeding, God, god [-ly, -ward].

[21] According to *Strong's Greek Lexicon* #**G1497**, the word *idols* is the Greek word ***eidolon*** (pronounced "**i'-do-lon**"), from G1491; an *image* (that is, for worship); by implication a heathen *god*, or (plural) the *worship* of such: - idol.

[22] According to *Strong's Greek Lexicon* #**G873**, the word *separate* is the Greek word ***aphorizo⁻*** (pronounced "**af-or-id'-zo**"), from G575 and G3724; to *set off* by boundary, that is, (figuratively) *limit, exclude, appoint*, etc.: - divide, separate, sever.

[23] According to *Strong's Greek Lexicon* #**G169**, the word *unclean* is the Greek word ***akathartos*** (pronounced "**ak-ath'-ar-tos**"), from G1 (as a negative particle) and a presumed derivative of G2508 (meaning *cleansed*); *impure* (ceremonially, morally (*lewd*) or specifically (*demonic*)): -

foul, unclean.

(24) *Christian evangelist Lou Engle, Catholic leader Matteo Calisi kiss each other's foot in symbolic act of reconciliation*

http://www.christiantoday.com/article/christian.evangelist.lo u.engle.catholic.leader.matteo.calisi.kiss.each.others.foot.in.sy mbolic.act.of.reconciliation/83722.htm

(25) *Vatican makes history: Pope allows Islamic prayers, Koran readings*

http://www.washingtontimes.com/news/2014/jun/9/vatican -makes-history-pope-allows-islamic-prayers-/

(26) *Historic First: Islamic Prayers Held at the Vatican*

http://www1.cbn.com/cbnnews/world/2014/June/Historic-First-Islamic-Prayers-Held-at-the-Vatican

(27) *Historic First Ever Islamic Prayers At Vatican Signals Start Of One World Religion*

http://www.nowtheendbegins.com/historic-first-ever-islamic-prayers-vatican-signals-start-one-world-religion/

(28) *The One World Religion Cometh: Pope Francis Warmly Welcomes Top Islamic Cleric To The Vatican*

http://www.infowars.com/the-one-world-religion-cometh-pope-francis-warmly-welcomes-top-islamic-cleric-to-the-vatican/

(29) *Pope Francis To Followers: "Koran And Holy Bible Are The Same"*

http://www.jewsnews.co.il/2016/06/04/pope-francis-to-followers-koran-and-holy-bible-are-the-same-3.html

(30) *Sun and crescent moon manifested in the Roman Catholic Eucharist*

https://ivarfjeld.com/2013/07/13/sun-and-crescent-moon-manifested-in-the-roman-catholic-eucharist/

(31) *Pope Francis receives King of Bahrain*

http://www.news.va/.../pope-francis-receives-king-of-bahrain

(32) *Pope takes off shoes to enter Dome of the Rock*

https://news.yahoo.com/pope-takes-off-shoes-enter-dome...

(33) *Pope Francis Meets With Evangelical, Pentecostal Leaders in John 17 Spirit (Interview)*

http://www.christianpost.com/news/pope-francis-meets-with-evangelical-pentecostal-leaders-in-john-17-spirit-165196/#faLPMBRSSWMb0ih4.99

(34) *Mike Bickle Meets With Pope Francis to Discuss Jesus*

http://www.charismanews.com/world/57751-mike-bickle-meets-with-pope-francis-to-discuss-jesus

(35) *Pope Francis' prayer intentions for January 2016*

Who is Israel? Discovering our True Identity in Jesus Christ and Why it Matters! The Root

https://www.youtube.com/watch?v=-6FfTxwTX34

(36) *The Most Powerful Man In The World? "The Black Pope"?*

https://warningilluminati.wordpress.com/the-most-powerful-man-in-the-world-the-black-pope/

(37) **US Lutherans approve document recognizing agreement with Catholic Church**

http://religionnews.com/2016/08/15/u-s-lutherans-approve-document-recognizing-agreement-with-the-catholic-church/

(38) *Pope Francis calls for Israel to be divided in Christmas Day sermon*

http://www.nowtheendbegins.com/pope-francis-calls-for-israel-to-be-divided-in-christmas-day-sermon/

(39) *Historic Covenant Between Israel's Rabbis And The Pope of Rome*

https://www.youtube.com/watch?v=kq5e4zsgkUU

(40) Title: *Fervent Masonic Desire to Rebuild Solomon's Temple is the Driving Force Behind the Events of the Mid-East Today. Once Completed, End Times' Prophecy Will Be Fulfilled!*

http://www.cuttingedge.org/news/n1643.cfm

(41) *Is the Rothschild Temple being Prepared to be Built on the Temple Mount?*

http://destination-yisrael.biblesearchers.com/destination-yisrael/2011/12/is-the-rothschild-temple-being-prepared-to-be-built-on-the-temple-mount.html

(42) *Illuminati Dreams of Building Solomon's Temple*

http://www.illuminati-news.com/2006/1215a.htm

(43) *A Seat for the Pope at King David's Tomb*

http://www.israelnationalnews.com/Articles/Article.aspx/12
814

(44) *The Three World Wars according to Albert Pike*

http://www.threeworldwars.com/albert-pike2.htm

(45) *How the Vatican (Catholic Church) Created Islam - Part 1*

https://www.youtube.com/watch?v=WQZ8GrNmTlc

(46) *How the Vatican (Catholic Church) Created Islam - Part 2*
https://www.youtube.com/watch?v=5v4JSl73yI4

(47) *Walter J Veith Islam Catholic Connection 1*
https://www.youtube.com/watch?v=eRBhHgNc4js&list=PL2B
CE5588E472DBBB

(48) *The Islamic Connection to the Roman Catholic Church
(Part 1)*

https://www.youtube.com/watch?v=vOiiqSgoNxU

(49) *The Islamic Connection to the Roman Catholic Church (Part 2)*

https://www.youtube.com/watch?v=jaEAMpiVwss

(50) *The Islamic Connection to the Roman Catholic Church (Part 3)*

https://www.youtube.com/watch?v=uXUbASsZ5is

(51) *The Islamic Connection to the Roman Catholic Church (Part 4)*

https://www.youtube.com/watch?v=fx8E2C6DOzI

(52) *The Islamic Connection to the Roman Catholic Church (Part 5)*

https://www.youtube.com/watch?v=ERRAnj2Lwjc

(53) *The Islamic Connection to the Roman Catholic Church (Part 6)*

https://www.youtube.com/watch?v=Hyc2GBII78A

(54) *The Islamic Connection to the Roman Catholic Church (Part 7)*

https://www.youtube.com/watch?v=fZZKiSL5hJU

(55) *The Whore of Babylon [Baal versus The "Catholic" God]*

http://www.remnantofgod.org/whoreofbabylon.htm

(56) *Council of Religious Liberty Institute of the Holy Land*

http://www.crihl.org/.

(57) *Allah the Moon-God:*
http://www.billionbibles.org/sharia/allah-moon-god.html

(58) *Allah as Moon-God:*
http://en.wikipedia.org/wiki/Allah_as_Moon-god

(59) *"Allah"...The Moon God*

http://www.theprophecies.com/Allah%20Babylonian-ArabianMoonGod.html

(60) *YaQub—Yet Another Qur'an Browser.*

http://www.quranbrowser.com/cgi/bin/get.cgi?%20version=pickthall+yusufali+khan+shakir+sherali+khalifa+arberry+palmer+rodwell+sale+transliterated&%20layout=auto&%20searchstring=005:017

(61) *Quran:* http://quran.com/4/157-158

(62) *Jesus in Islam: Wikipedia*
http://en.wikipedia.org/wiki/Jesus_in_Islam

(63) *The Grand Design Exposed Sun Worship Of Baal*

http://www.granddesignexposed.com/sun/baal.html

(64) Mithra: The Pagan Christ
http://www.truthbeknown.com/mithra.htm

[65]Mithras in Modern Day Religion - Part 1

https://www.youtube.com/watch?v=s8yVeP82AMI&feature=share

[66]Mithras in Modern Day Religion - Part 2

https://www.youtube.com/watch?v=K2OsDbFOO7Y

[67] *Is the Pope and Israeli Rabbis Courting the Mahdi?* by Steven DeNoon with *Israeli News Live*

https://www.youtube.com/watch?v=OcHKjlMP68E

[68] **Kenneth Copeland calls for end of Protestant Reformation (2017)**

https://www.youtube.com/watch?v=iWJM-tP90Zo

[69] **Kenneth Copeland Recants And Returns To Catholicism!**

https://www.youtube.com/watch?v=2LNJ6Jb3DOc

[70] **I AM A PROTESTANT**

https://www.gofundme.com/i-am-a-protestant

[71] It's Not My Jesus vs. Your Jesus, But Our Jesus, Pope Says to Ecumenical Group https://zenit.org/articles/its-not-my-jesus-vs-your-jesus-but-our-jesus-pope-says-to-ecumenical-group/

CHAPTER 33

No References

CHAPTER 34

[1]According to *Strong's Hebrew Lexicon* #H1642, the name *Gerar* is the Hebrew name *G'râr* (pronounced "gher-awr'"), probably from H1641; a *rolling* country; *Gerar*, a Philistine city: - Gerar.

[2] **Gerar**: Wikipedia: https://en.wikipedia.org/wiki/Gerar

[3]According to *Easton's Bible Dictionary*, the biblical *valley of Gerar* (Genesis 26:17) was probably the modern **Wadi** el-Jerdr. Currently, it is believed to be the valley of Nahal Gerar.

[4]According to *Strong's Hebrew Lexicon* #H7621, the word *oath* is the Hebrew word *sh'bu'âh* (pronounced "sheb-oo-aw'"), which is a feminine passive participle of H7650; properly something *sworn*, that is, an *oath:* - curse, oath, X sworn.

[5]According to *Strong's Hebrew Lexicon* #H4931, the word *charge* is the Hebrew word *mishmereth* (pronounced "mish-meh'-reth"), Feminine of H4929; *watch*, that is, the act (*custody*) or (concretely) the *sentry*, the *post*; objectively *preservation*, or (concretely) *safe*; figuratively *observance*, that is, (abstractly) *duty*, or (objectively) a *usage* or *party:* - charge, keep, to be kept, office, ordinance, safeguard, ward, watch.

[6]According to *Strong's Hebrew Lexicon* #H4687, the word *commandments* is the Hebrew word *mitsvâh* (pronounced "mits-vaw'"), and is from H6680; a *command*, whether human

or divine (collectively the *Law*): - (which was) commanded (-ment), law, ordinance, precept.

[7]According to *Strong's Hebrew Lexicon* #H2708, the word *statutes* is the Hebrew word *chûqqâh* (pronounced "khook-kaw'"), and is the feminine of H2706, and meaning substantially the same: - appointed, custom, manner, ordinance, site, statute.

[8] According to *Strong's Hebrew Lexicon* #H8451, the word *laws* is the Hebrew word *tôrâh* (pronounced "to-raw'"), from H3384; a *precept* or *statute*, especially the *Decalogue* or *Pentateuch:* - law. In addition, *Brown-Driver-Briggs'* defines the word *law* as follows: the law, direction, instruction 1) instruction, direction (human or divine) 2) body of prophetic teaching 3) instruction in Messianic age 4) body of priestly direction or instruction 5) body of legal directives 6) law 7) law of the burnt offering 8) of special law, codes of law 9) custom, manner 10) the Deuteronomic or Mosaic law.

[9] *The Tribulation Judgments:*

http://www.angeloffaith777.com/chart-of-tribulation-period.html

CHAPTER 35

[1]According to *Strong's Hebrew Lexicon* #H6965, the word *establish* is the Hebrew word *qûm* (pronounced "koom"), a

primitive root; to *rise* (in various applications, literally, figuratively, intensively and causatively): - abide, accomplish, X be clearer, confirm, continue, decree, X be dim, endure, X enemy, enjoin, get up, make good, help, hold, (help to) lift up (again), make, X but newly, ordain, perform, pitch, raise (up), rear (up), remain, (a-) rise (up) (again, against), rouse up, set (up), (e-) stablish, (make to) stand (up), stir up, strengthen, succeed, (as-, make) sure (-ly), (be) up (-hold, -rising).

(2)According to *Strong's Greek Lexicon* #**G2137**, the word ***prosper*** or ***prospers*** is the Greek word **euodoō** (pronounced "yoo-od-o'-o"), from a compound of G2095 and G3598; to *help* on the *road*, that is, (passively) *succeed in reaching*; figuratively to *succeed* in business affairs: - (have a) prosper (-ous journey).

(3)According to *Strong's Hebrew Lexicon* #**H4687**, the word ***commandments*** is the Hebrew word ***mitsvâh*** (pronounced "mits-vaw'"), and is from H6680; a *command*, whether human or divine (collectively the *Law*): - (which was) commanded (-ment), law, ordinance, precept.

(4)According to *Strong's Hebrew Lexicon* #**H1952**, the word ***wealth*** is the Hebrew word ***hôn*** (pronounced **hone**), which is from the same as H1951 in the sense of H202; *wealth*; by implication *enough:* enough, + for nought, riches, substance, wealth.

(5)According to *Strong's Hebrew Lexicon* #**H6239**, the word *riches* is the Hebrew word *'ósher* (pronounced "o'-sher"), which is from H6238; *wealth:* X far [richer], riches.

(6)According to *Strong's Hebrew Lexicon* #H6238, the word *riches* is from the root Hebrew word *'âshar* (pronounced "aw-shar'"), a primitive root; properly to *accumulate*; chiefly (specifically) to *grow* (causatively *make*) *rich*: be (-come, en-, make, make self, wax) rich, make [H1 Kings H22 : H48 margin]. See H6240.

(7)According to *Strong's Hebrew Lexicon* #H1004, the word *house* is the Hebrew word **bayith** (pronounced "bah'-yith"), probably from H1129 abbreviated; a *house* (in the greatest variation of applications, especially *family*, etc.): court, daughter, door, + dungeon, family, + forth of, X great as would contain, hangings. home[born], [winter]house (-hold), inside(-ward), palace, place, + prison, + steward, + tablet, temple, web, + within (-out).

(8)According to *Strong's Greek Lexicon* #G3126, the word *mammon* is the Greek word **mammōnas** (pronounced "mam-mo-nas'"), of Chaldee origin (*confidence*, that is, figuratively *wealth*, personified); *mammonas*, that is, *avarice* (deified): mammon. The word *"avarice"* means the following: extreme greed for wealth or material gain; greed, greediness, materialism.

(9) *501c3: The Devil's Church*
http://www.creationliberty.com/articles/501c3.php

[10]According to *Strong's Hebrew Lexicon* #**H3782**, the word *feeble* is the Hebrew word *kâshal* (pronounced "**kaw-shal'**"), a primitive root; to *totter* or *waver* (through weakness of the legs, especially the ankle); by implication to *falter, stumble,* faint or fall: - bereave [from the margin], cast down, be decayed, (cause to) fail, (cause, make to) fall (down, -ing), feeble, be (the) ruin (-ed, of), (be) overthrown, (cause to) stumble, X utterly, be weak.

CHAPTER 36

[1]According to *Strong's Hebrew Lexicon* #**H2706**, the word *statute* or *statutes* is synonymous with the word *law* and is the Hebrew word *chôq* (pronounced "**khoke**"), from H2710; an *enactment*; hence an *appointment* (of time, space, quantity, labor or usage): appointed, bound, commandment, convenient, custom, decree (-d), due, law, measure, X necessary, ordinance (-nary), portion, set time, statute, task.

[2]According to *Strong's Hebrew Lexicon* #**H4941**, the word *ordinance* is the Hebrew word *mishpâṭ* (pronounced "**mish-pawt'**"), which is from H8199; properly a *verdict* (favorable or unfavorable) pronounced judicially, especially a *sentence* or formal decree (human or (particularly) divine *law*, individual or collectively), including the act, the place, the suit, the crime, and the penalty; abstractly *justice*, including a particular *right,* or *privilege* (statutory or customary), or even a *style:* - + adversary, ceremony, charge, X crime, custom, desert, determination, discretion, disposing, due, fashion, form, to be judged, judgment, just (-ice, -ly), (manner of) law

531

(-ful), manner, measure, (due) order, ordinance, right, sentence, usest, X worthy, + wrong.

[3]According to *Strong's Hebrew Lexicon* #H8085, the word *heed* or *hear* or *hearing* is the Hebrew word *shâma'* (pronounced "shaw-mah'"), a primitive root; to *hear* intelligently (often with implication of attention, obedience, etc.; causatively to *tell*, etc.): - X attentively, call (gather) together, X carefully, X certainly, consent, consider, be content, declare, X diligently, discern, give ear, (cause to, let, make to) hear (-ken, tell), X indeed, listen, make (a) noise, (be) obedient, obey, perceive, (make a) proclaim (-ation), publish, regard, report, shew (forth), (make a) sound, X surely, tell, understand, whosoever [heareth], witness.

[4]According to *Strong's Hebrew Lexicon* #H4687, the word *commandments* is the Hebrew word *mitsvâh* (pronounced "mits-vaw'"), from H6680; a *command*, whether human or divine (collectively the *law*): - (which was) commanded (-ment), law, ordinance, precept.

[5]According to *Strong's Hebrew Lexicon* #H430, the word *God* is the Hebrew word *'Elôhîym* (pronounced "el-o-heem'"), plural of H433; *gods* in the ordinary sense; but specifically used (in the plural thus, especially with the article) of the supreme God; occasionally applied by way of deference to *magistrates*; and sometimes as a superlative: - angels, X exceeding, God (gods) (-dess, -ly), X (very) great, judges, X mighty.

[6]According to *Strong's Greek Lexicon* **#G4991**, the word *salvation* is the Greek word *sōtēria* (pronounced "so-tay-ree'-ah"), a feminine of a derivative of G4990 as (properly abstract) noun; *rescue* or *safety* (physically or morally): - deliver, health, salvation, save, saving.

[7]According to *Strong's Greek Lexicon* **#G38**, the word *sanctification* is the Greek word *hagiasmos* (pronounced "hag-ee-as-mos'"), from G37; properly *purification*, that is, (the state) *purity;* concretely (by Hebraism) a *purifier:* - holiness, sanctification.

[8]According to *Strong's Greek Lexicon* **#G4102**, the word *belief* is the Greek word *pistis* (pronounced *"pis'-tis"*), from G3982; *persuasion*, that is, *credence;* moral *conviction* (of *religious* truth, or the truthfulness of God or a religious teacher), especially *reliance* upon Christ for salvation; abstractly *constancy* in such profession; by extension the system of religious (Gospel) *truth* itself: - assurance, belief, believe, faith, fidelity.

[9]According to *Strong's Greek Lexicon* **#G225**, the word *truth* is the Greek word *alētheia* (pronounced "al-ay'-thi-a"), from G227; *truth:* - true, X truly, truth, verity.

[10]According to *Strong's Hebrew Lexicon* **#H8451**, the word *law* is the Hebrew word *tôrâh* (pronounced *"to-raw'"*), from H3384; a *precept* or *statute*, especially the *Decalogue* or *Pentateuch:* - law. In addition, *Brown-Driver-Briggs'* defines the word *law* as follows: the law, direction, instruction 1)

instruction, direction (human or divine) 2) body of prophetic teaching 3) instruction in Messianic age 4) body of priestly direction or instruction 5) body of legal directives 6) law 7) law of the burnt offering 8) of special law, codes of law 9) custom, manner 10) the Deuteronomic or Mosaic law.

(11)According to *Strong's Greek Lexicon* #**G458**, the word **lawlessness** is the Greek word **anomia** (pronounced "an-om-ee'-ah"), which means illegality, that is, violation of law or (generally) *wickedness:* - iniquity, X transgress (-ion of) the law, unrighteousness.

(12)According to *Strong's Greek Lexicon* #**G364**, the word **remembrance** is the Greek word **anamnēsis** (pronounced "an-am'-nay-sis"), which is from G363; *recollection:* - remembrance (again).

(13)According to *Strong's Greek Lexicon* #**G363**, the word **remembrance** is from the root Greek word **anamimnēskō** (pronounced "an-am-im-nace'-ko"), which is from G303 and G3403; to *remind;* reflexively to *recollect:* - call to mind, (bring to, call to, put in), remember (-brance).

(14)According to *Strong's Greek Lexicon* #**G4221**, the word **cup** is the Greek word **potērion** (pronounced "pot-ay'-ree-on"), a neuter of a derivative of the alternate of G4095; a *drinking vessel;* by extension the contents thereof, that is, a *cupful* (*draught*); figuratively a *lot* or *fate:* - cup.

CONNECT WITH THE AUTHOR

I hope you have been greatly blessed and enlightened by this book so you may walk in a deeper relationship with our heavenly Father and our Lord and Savior, Jesus Christ.

If you have been blessed by reading this book, please tell those in your circle of influence about it. Also, you can assist me in getting the word out about this book by following me via Facebook at the link below and sharing my posts concerning this series with your family and friends.

https://www.facebook.com/donna.rogers.3760

You may also connect with me via Instagram under the username bella4jesus777.

In addition, if you purchased this book from Amazon, please consider blessing me with a favorable review under the Customer Review section.

I would love to hear from you. I may be contacted via my website by accessing the following link:

http://www.angeloffaith777.com/contact-me.html

Also, I have many more teachings which can be accessed via my website at the following link:

http://www.angeloffaith777.com/

Thank you in advance for your feedback and your help with sharing this critical message with your family and friends.

Who is Israel? Discovering our True Identity in Jesus Christ and Why it Matters! The Root

ABOUT THE AUTHOR

Donna Rogers is an ordained minister of the gospel and is the founder of Angel of Love and Light Ministries. Her website can be accessed at www.angeloffaith777.com.

Donna wrote her first book titled, *Shattered Dreams—Wake Up America Before It Is Too Late!* in 2004 when she started a Bible study out of her home for seven years. Three years later, on October 5, 2007, the Lord closed the door on her secular career as an international Critical Issues Manager and led her to begin her prophetic ministry.

Currently Donna serves as a servant of Jesus Christ in her role as the state of Florida coordinator for the Black Robe Regiment, the State of Florida Director for the Tea Party Command Center, and she has strategically partnered her ministry with many different ministries and grassroots organizations in the state of Florida and on a national level.

Donna was commissioned by Reinhard Bonnke, founder of Christ for All Nations and is a graduate of Reinhard Bonnke's School of Evangelism located in Orlando, Florida. She was ordained by Pastors Jerry and Anne Marie Mallory founders of Kingdom Life Builders Int'l Ministries.

Donna lives in Florida with her husband Jimmy and their children Kristen 31, Samantha 27, and Dylan age 17.

94956108R00299

Made in the USA
Lexington, KY
03 August 2018